CLASSICS IN THEORY

General Editors
**Brooke A. Holmes
Miriam Leonard
Tim Whitmarsh**

CLASSICS IN THEORY

Classics in Theory explores the new directions for classical scholarship opened up by critical theory. Inherently interdisciplinary, the series creates a forum for the exchange of ideas between classics, anthropology, modern literature, philosophy, psychoanalysis, politics, and other related fields. Invigorating and agenda-setting volumes analyze the cross-fertilizations between theory and classical scholarship and set out a vision for future work on the productive intersections between the ancient world and contemporary thought.

Homer's *Iliad* and the Problem of Force

Charles H. Stocking

Great Clarendon Street, Oxford, OX2 6DP,
United Kingdom

Oxford University Press is a department of the University of Oxford.
It furthers the University's objective of excellence in research, scholarship,
and education by publishing worldwide. Oxford is a registered trade mark of
Oxford University Press in the UK and in certain other countries

© Charles H. Stocking 2023

The moral rights of the author have been asserted

All rights reserved. No part of this publication may be reproduced, stored in
a retrieval system, or transmitted, in any form or by any means, without the
prior permission in writing of Oxford University Press, or as expressly permitted
by law, by licence or under terms agreed with the appropriate reprographics
rights organization. Enquiries concerning reproduction outside the scope of the
above should be sent to the Rights Department, Oxford University Press, at the
address above

You must not circulate this work in any other form
and you must impose this same condition on any acquirer

Published in the United States of America by Oxford University Press
198 Madison Avenue, New York, NY 10016, United States of America

British Library Cataloguing in Publication Data
Data available

Library of Congress Control Number: 2022948860

ISBN 978–0–19–286287–7

DOI: 10.1093/oso/9780192862877.001.0001

Links to third party websites are provided by Oxford in good faith and
for information only. Oxford disclaims any responsibility for the materials
contained in any third party website referenced in this work.

Acknowledgments

Special thanks are owed to a great number of people for their support in bringing this work to completion. I am especially grateful to the editors Miriam Leonard, Tim Whitmarsh, and Brooke Holmes for their constant support and for their efforts in general with the truly unique series Classics in Theory. I am also extremely grateful to the reviewers, who were challenging but ultimately made the book better. Chapter 4 was a direct result of their influence. Greatest thanks are owed to Cléo Carastro for inviting me to present the earliest stages of this work at the École des hautes études en sciences sociales in Paris over a series of lectures in the spring of 2019. It was in that lecture series that the book first took shape. The audience members of the EHESS and ANHIMA, including Manon Brouillet, Paulin Ismard, Vincent Azoulay, and Stella Geourgoudi, among others, provided excellent feedback and criticism. I am especially grateful to Pierre Judet de la Combe, Pietro Pucci, and Claude Calame, who were extremely generous with their time and expertise during my stay. And I received tremendous support from my colleagues at Western, Aara Suksi and Lawrence De Looze, who attended every one of my talks in Paris and continued to provide great feedback afterwards. Chapter 2 was presented at Cambridge University, and Renaud Gagné and Simon Goldhill offered excellent points of critique and valuable feedback. Sections of this book were also presented at my home institution, Western University, as well as at the University of Toronto, the University of Chicago, and for the Political Theory workshop at UCLA. The responses of friends and colleagues at each of these institutions made the manuscript better. A section of this book was presented in a panel for the Society of Classical Studies 2020 Annual Meeting titled "Foucault and Antiquity, beyond Sexuality." Thanks to the panel members, Marcus Folch, Miriam Leonard, Brooke Holmes, and Allen Miller, and to the audience of the SCS, who provided a lively and memorable discussion. I owe the deepest debt to Allen Miller in particular, who has long been a mentor and role model for thinking seriously about antiquity and its impact on the "history of the present." Thanks also to Richard Martin, Chris Faraone, Kendall Sharpe, and Jim Porter, who read and commented on sections of the book—all for the better. Thanks

vi Acknowledgments

also to Joseph Leivdal, who helped prepare and edit major sections of the appendix. Lastly, I would like to thank my family. My brother Damian Stocking not only taught me ancient Greek, but in many ways, this book is a continuation of his own dissertation on Homeric ontology. And above all, I am deeply grateful to my wife, Catherine Pratt. It was during the writing of this book that our daughter Stella was born, and she has been the most beautiful reminder there are forces in this world beyond our own will and agency.

Contents

Introduction: The Homeric Problem of Force, between Philology and Philosophy   **1**
Homer and the Philosophy of Force, between Language and the Subject   8
Homer and the Philology of Force, between the Human and Divine   14

1. "Stronger": Performative Speech and the Force of Achilles   **23**
The Homeric Scepter: Speech and the Source of Authority   28
A Performative Intervention: Nestor's Scale of Superiority in *Iliad* 1   33
Force, Speech, and the Genealogy of Achilles   53
The Force of Zeus and Its Performative Limits   65
Conclusion   72

2. *Kratos* before Democracy: Force, Politics, and Signification in the *Iliad*   **73**
Towards a Political Theology of Force in Homer and Hesiod   77
The Alterity of *Kratos*: Philological and Mythopoetic Interventions   85
Misinterpreting *Kratos*: Zeus' Deception of Agamemnon   93
Reinterpreting *Kratos*: Diomedes' Rebuke   100
Conclusion   109

3. Force and Discourse in the Funeral Games of Patroclus   **111**
The Problem of Force in the Funeral Games: Nestor's Advice to Antilochus   117
Foucault and the Funeral Games: Menelaus' Quarrel with Antilochus   125
Reversals in the "Regime of Truth": Eumelus and Ajax   142
Resolution through Discourse: Achilles' Interventions and the End of the *Agōn*   161
Conclusion   165

viii Contents

4. The "Force that Kills": Simone Weil and the Problem
   of Agency in the *Iliad*   **167**
   Simone Weil on Force and the Subject in Homer and History   169
   Subjects of Force in the *Iliad*   179
   Force, Fate, and Death: Sarpedon, Patroclus, and Hector   187
   Conclusion: Achilles' Awareness   204

   **Conclusion: Homeric Forces and Human Subjects
   Reconsidered**   **209**

   Appendix: Force in Early Greek Hexameter   225
   Kratos, Alkē, Biē, Menos, Sthenos, (W)is, Dynamis,
   Damazō/damnēmi

   References   251
   Index Locorum   271
   Index   273

Introduction

The Homeric Problem of Force, between Philology and Philosophy

The idea of "force" has taken on an all-pervasive significance in Homeric poetry ever since Simone Weil proclaimed it as such in her famous essay "L'*Iliade* ou le poème de la force."[1] According to Weil, force is uniform in character, a universal process with profound implications for human existence. Weil explains:

> Force is that which makes a thing of whoever submits to it. Exercised to the extreme, it makes the human being a thing quite literally, that is, a dead body. Someone was there and, the next moment, no one.
>
> **(Weil 2003: 45)**

Much of her essay goes on to describe the many ways in which the *Iliad* gives expression to this impersonal and *depersonalizing* process. For Weil, and for so many readers of the *Iliad* after her, Homeric poetry stands as a transhistorical monument to the singularity of force, which transforms the human subject into an object.[2]

---

[1] Weil's essay was first published in 1940 and 1941 in *Cahiers du Sud* under the pseudonym Émile Novis and republished under Weil's name in *Cahiers du Sud* in 1947. An English translation appeared in the journal *Politics* in 1945.

[2] Despite the great influence Weil's essay has exerted and its own merits as a literary work, there remain significant difficulties as far as the interpretation of Homeric poetry is concerned. On the heavily Christianizing influence in her essay, see Ferber 1981: 66; Summers 1981: 87–9; Fraisse 1989: 304–9; Benfey 2005: vii–xi, xv–xvi. For further treatment of her essay and its reception within Classical Studies, see Schein 1984: 82–3; Holoka 2002; Holoka 2003; Hammer and Kicey 2010; Holmes 2015: 29–30; Purves 2015: 75–8; Thalmann 2015; and Schein 2016: 149–70, who sees an anachronism in Weil's essay based primarily on the imposition of the "soul" and an assumption of the singular "human spirit" in her reading of Homer (Schein 2016: 154). See further Porter 2021: 212–14 on Weil in the context of modern disenchanted readings of Homer and the problem of war.

Homer's Iliad *and the Problem of Force*. Charles H. Stocking, Oxford University Press.
© Charles H. Stocking 2023. DOI: 10.1093/oso/9780192862877.003.0001

2 The Homeric Problem of Force

Soon after Simone Weil's essay was first published, however, the Classical scholar Bruno Snell published an equally influential and controversial work, *Die Entdeckung des Geistes*, in which Snell observed not one, but multiple forms of force in Homeric poetry.[3] He states:

> Mental and spiritual acts are due to the impact of external factors, and man is the open target of a great many forces which impinge on him and penetrate his very core. That is the reason why Homer has so much to say about forces, why, in fact, he has so many words for our term "force" [kraft]: *menos, sthenos, bie, kikus, is, kratos, alkē, dynamis*. The meaning of each of these words is precise, concrete, and full of implications; so far from serving as abstract symbols of force ... Homer's words refer to specific functions and particular provinces of experience.
>
> **(Snell, 1953: 20)**

Like Weil, Snell observed force in Homer as that which is external to the human and acts upon him or her. But unlike Weil, Snell gives more attention to linguistic expression in order to argue for multiple forms of force at work in Homeric poetry. At first glance, Snell's observation suggests a method based in a basic principle of "linguistic relativity" wherein culture affects thought and experience of the world by means of language.[4] Yet Snell employs a distinctly German version of linguistic relativity based on an evolutionary model of culture, wherein human thought and perception are believed to have moved from primitivism to enlightenment.[5] Snell's

---

[3] *Die Entdeckung des Geistes* includes a number of articles previously published dating back to 1929 and was published as a monograph in 1946. The English edition, under the title *The Discovery of the Mind*, appeared in 1953, translated by T. G. Rosenmeyer. The first chapter, "Homer's View of Man," appeared as the article "Die Sprache Homers als Ausdruk siener Gedankenwelt" in *Neue Jahrbuche für Antike und deutsche Bildung* in 1939 (Snell 1939a).

[4] On the history and ongoing controversy of the principle of linguistic relativity, see, among others, Gumperz and Levinson 1996; Niemeier and Dirven 2000; Pütz and Verspoor 2000; Reines and Prinz 2009; Leavitt 2011; Everett 2013.

[5] Snell's approach to language can be traced directly to the work of Wilhelm von Humboldt, whom he cites briefly as the basis for his approach in *Poetry and Society* (Snell 1961: 11). See further Snell 1939b, "Vom Übersetzen aus den alten Sprache." For Humboldt's more general influence on the study of antiquity, see Porter 2000: 186–91; Matthiessen 2003; Rebenich 2011. For further exposition of Humboldt's theory of linguistic relativity and its development in German thought, see R. L. Brown 1967; R. L. Miller 1968; Penn 1972; Trabant 2000; Mühlhäusler 2000. The reception of Snell, especially in North America, was largely associated with the Sapir-Whorf hypothesis of linguistic relativity (see for instance Pelliccia 1995: 17n.12). But the Humboldtian model presents a stark contrast with the development of linguistic relativity in North America, most popularly associated with Sapir-Whorf hypothesis. It should be further noted that neither Sapir nor Whorf presented their arguments on linguistic relativity as a single "hypothesis" as such. For the history of the

The Homeric Problem of Force **3**

observation on the plurality of forces parallels his other observations on the plurality of sight and cognition.[6] All such pluralities, in Snell's view, are symptomatic of a "primitive" form of "sense-consciousness" which is not yet capable of unifying, "self-conscious" thought.[7] The plurality of forces, in other words, plays a critical role in Snell's overall argument that "Homeric man" is incapable of understanding himself as a single, unified individual, neither in body nor in mind.[8]

Thus between Simone Weil and Bruno Snell, two highly influential and controversial figures, we are presented with a basic problem of interpretation that every reader of Homer must face: Is "force" in Homer to be understood in the singular or plural? Is it a universal and transhistorical process or one that is linguistically and culturally determined? As the arguments of Weil and Snell have already indicated, this seemingly simple question on the meaning of "force" in Homer is ultimately inseparable from the much larger problem of what it means to be a human subject, both for the ancient Greeks and for us.

Despite the large implications in this basic interpretive problem, the topic of force in Homer is often assumed and seldom analyzed directly by Classical scholars. The first to directly address the topic since Weil and Snell was the linguist Émile Benveniste. In his foundational work, *Le vocabulaire des institutions indo-européennes*, first published in 1969, Benveniste states the following under the heading of *kratos*:

The translation [of *kratos*] which is everywhere accepted as "force" is in our view unsatisfactory...That *kratos* cannot simply signify "force"

Sapir-Whorf hypothesis, see esp. Koerner 2000. For criticism of Snell's teleological model of language from a comparative perspective, see Burkert 2004, esp. p. 180.

[6] Snell 1953: 1–4, 8–15.

[7] As Snell himself asserts (Snell 1930: 157–8), his historical analysis of Greek literature as a history of the development of consciousness is heavily influenced by Hegel. See further N. Austin 1975: 81–5; MacCary 1982: 3–15; Gill 1996: 35–6; Lohse 1997: 1–2.

[8] Snell's argument thus parallels Hermann Fränkel's observation that Homeric man was a "Kraftfeld," a "field of force/energy" (Fränkel 1975: 80). For further critical discussion of Snell's view on the non-unified self and body, see Adkins 1970: 13–48; N. Austin 1975: 81–129; Renehan 1979; Williams 1993: 21–49; Pelliccia 1995: 17–27; Gill 1996: 1–40; Clarke 1999: 37–49; Bolens 2000: 19–59; Porter and Buchan 2004: 1–19; Burkert 2004; Holmes 2010: 1–40; Gavrylenko 2012; Purves 2015: 76–8; Holmes 2020. Most discussion of Snell has focused almost entirely on his observations regarding *psychē* and *sōma*, with no discussion to date on the issue "force." It should also be noted that Snell uses the same German word, "Kraft," for "force" throughout, whereas Rosenmeyer translates "Kraft" variously in English as "force" and "powers." For further discussion of distinctions in the many terms for "force" and "power"—Kraft, Macht, etc.—in German political thought and its relationship to the ancient world, see Meier 1972.

4 The Homeric Problem of Force

emerges from the fact that at least six other Homeric terms have this sense: *bia, is, iskhus, sthenos, alkē, dynamis*. This profusion creates many difficulties for translators. But the choice of equivalents can only be guided by exact definitions, that is, an exact idea of the *differences* between these seven ways of designating "force."

(Benveniste 2016: 362, italics in original)[9]

On one level, Benveniste's linguistic approach to *kratos* parallels Snell's observation on the plurality of forces in Homer. Both acknowledge the fact of multiple terms as a significant indication that each term presents a different meaning and aspect to the idea of force. Yet Benveniste differs from Snell in his ultimate objectives and methodological presuppositions. Snell, working out of the German philosophical tradition, is concerned with the development of the autonomous and self-conscious individual, whereas Benveniste, following in the French sociological tradition, is more interested in how language contributes to the construction of political ideologies and social institutions.[10] For Snell, force in Homer is a starting point for explaining the modern human subject in isolation *qua* individual. For Benveniste, it is an endpoint for analyzing the human subject in relation to early Greek society and its prehistory. Furthermore, Benveniste's approach is understandably more linguistic, based on a principle known as the "semantic set" or "lexical field," wherein synonyms retain differences in meaning by virtue of the fact that they are grouped together under a single broad category.[11] Hence, Benveniste does not use the fact of a plurality of terms for force as a symptom of "primitive thought" in the same

---

[9] The English translation is from the Elizabeth Palmer translation, which was republished in 2016, but I have made slight modifications in order to more accurately reflect the French. To be precise, Palmer's translation is symptomatic of Benveniste's own point on the problem of synonyms for "force" since Palmer used various terms—"strength," "force," "power"— when Benveniste uses only one in French, namely "force." See the previous note for similar problems with translations of "Kraft" in Snell.

[10] The more abstract nature of Benveniste's enterprise is made evident in the preface to *Le vocabulaire*, when he explains that his project "is of a wholly different nature" compared to other attempts at studying Indo-European culture, which typically involve compiling lists of common expressions in Indo-European languages in order to uncover aspects of a common culture (Benveniste 2016: xxii). In studying what Benveniste terms "institutions" he takes up the study of institutions proper, such as government, law, etc., as well as what he considers more abstract institutions, ways of life, and social relationships. Benveniste's method also begins with the vocabulary within specific, individual languages and so many of his observations may remain valid for individual cultures, even if one does not subscribe to the more general assumptions regarding the status of a common Indo-European culture.

[11] For a summary of the theory and history of the lexical field theory in semantics, see Geeraerts 2010: 47–69.

The Homeric Problem of Force **5**

manner as Snell. Rather, his approach implies that such plurality is in fact a regular feature of *all* language use, while the plurality of "forces" in Homer is more specifically indicative of complex social and political thought in Greek prehistory.

Benveniste serves as an important starting point for revisiting the question of force in Homer from a more philological perspective. And yet Benveniste himself did not actually offer a comprehensive account of the seven different terms for force he outlines, having dealt in detail only with *kratos*. Since Benveniste's work, several scholars have treated terms for force in Homer on a case-by-case basis. Gregory Nagy's *Best of the Achaeans* remains the most extensive discussion thus far on various terms for force in Homer, with a primary focus on their oral-poetic implications.[12] In *Immortal Armor*, Derek Collins offers an in-depth study of *alkē* in Homer, and Michael Clarke offers various expositions of terms for embodiment, especially *menos*.[13] Gregory Nagy and Egbert Bakker also discuss in detail the semantics and etymological significance of *menos* in Homer.[14] Furthermore, one might expect that the entries in the *Lexikon des frühgriechischen Epos*, originally directed by Snell, would serve as an occasion to distinguish between these different Homeric force terms. Yet the entries for each of the force terms in the lexicon are never treated as the semantic set originally proposed by Snell.[15] While each of these studies has made vital contributions, thus far no work has taken up a comprehensive view of Homeric force.

This book, *Homer's Iliad and the Problem of Force*, therefore offers the first full-scale treatment of the topic of force in Homer, with a view to the distinct interactions between philology and philosophy. In terms of philology, this work confirms that each word for force does indeed present a fairly distinct sphere of usage.[16] In particular, one will find that each term implies a different mode of force, defined by different relationships between self and other, where the category of "other" includes humans, gods, ancestors, animals, and other nonhuman meta-persons. Furthermore, as we shall see, these relations are primarily conceptualized as objects of exchange in a more general embodied economy shared between the human and nonhuman. As such, from a more philosophic perspective, the

---

[12] See esp. Nagy 1979: 88–93, 317–45.   [13] Collins 1998; Clarke 1999: 110–11.
[14] Nagy 1974: 266–9; Bakker 2008; Bakker 2013.
[15] For a history of the *LfgrE* and Snell's involvement, see esp. Schmidt 2012.
[16] The relationship of the Iliadic language of force compared with the role of force in the *Odyssey* will be addressed in the conclusion of the book. Details on the specifics for each term and its relationship to other terms are presented in the appendix.

6 The Homeric Problem of Force

philology of force has significant implications for Homeric subjectivity. Rather than treat force strictly as a negation of the self, in Weil's sense, or as an indication of the deficiency of awareness of the self in Snell's view, the study of force presented here serves as a further occasion for rethinking the Homeric self beyond the unitary subject.

When analyzed in light of the topic of force, the Homeric subject appears to be founded on a double layer of contingency. On the one hand, there are several ways in which the concept of force is shown to be a defining feature of the Homeric warrior's subjective identity.[17] On the other hand, no form of force is understood to be an attribute of the person as individual. Instead, different types of force in Homer are presented as coming from outside the person, primarily given from the gods. Thus, the various terms for force in Homer serve as points of relation that operate from both inside and outside of the human subject. If we take this internal/external relationality of Homeric force at face value then the vocabulary of force presents an entirely different kind of subjectivity, compared with the models of Weil, Snell, and others. That is to say, Homeric subjectivity is founded on a principle of *interactive interdependence* rather than *independent autonomy*. What Homeric subjectivity presents is an alternative to the ideology of the individual. In Homer, the forces that come to define oneself do not emanate strictly from one's own will, intentions, or actions, but from gods and other nonhuman agents. And because the gods themselves are also in conflict, there is no single god, not even Zeus, who controls the operation of all forces for all humans at any given time.

As we shall see in the course of this book, the topic of force in its various Homeric forms becomes a means of expressing the very limits of human agency and identity in the *Iliad*. In this regard, the inherent contingency and multiplicity of Homeric forces renders the very topic of force a problem of interpretation not just for modern scholars but also for characters *within* the poem itself. Weil, Snell, and Benveniste each had their own agenda in their discussion of Homeric force, and none was particularly interested in how the different types of Homeric force contributed to the overall narrative of the *Iliad*. But if we approach the Homeric vocabulary of force with regard to its poetic contexts, a distinct thematic pattern emerges. First and foremost, the majority of terms for force occur in

---

[17] The clearest example of the close connection between force and identity occurs in phrases such as *biē* + name of warrior in the genitive, such as *biē Heraklēos* "force of Heracles," as a means of naming the warrior, on which see Nagy 1979: 317–19; D. Stocking 2007: 63–4; and further discussion in Chapter 3 of this book.

The Homeric Problem of Force   7

speech rather than narrative. Such contexts introduce a striking and problematic feature of Homeric force—the very terms in the *Iliad* meant to designate different modes of embodied physicality and presence are often presented at one level removed from any type of purely material expression. One might assume that we would see force "in action," but the enactment of what modern readers would consider "force" in Homer is seldom described as such in the poem.[18] Instead, readers have access to the notion of force only indirectly, by way of the characters' own interpretations. Even when the enactment of force appears in its most final and physical form, in the act of killing, the verbal expressions of "force" are invoked primarily by the speakers who praise and blame such acts. In this regard, the conceptualization of different types of force in Homer appears to play a more important role in the self-fashioning of speakers' subjective identity through speech rather than in the objective action of the poem per se. Second, we can add to this fact an even more surprising trend concerning the problematic of force in the *Iliad*. On almost every occasion in which a speaker makes an appeal to a certain relation of force, that very claim is *contradicted* almost immediately by other speakers or by the narrative events of the poem. One is able to observe this contradiction in the claims to force expressed by nearly all characters, including Achilles. The narrative of the *Iliad* itself reflects different levels at which this contradiction plays out. The contradiction appears in the faulty assessment of the significance of Achilles' force at the outset of the poem by both Agamemnon and Nestor (Chapter 1). A similar contradiction occurs in reference to the false significance attributed to Agamemnon's political force in the first half of the poem by Odysseus and others (Chapter 2). It further applies to the general assessment of each of the characters in their agonistic ability as an expression of social hierarchy or *aretē* in the funeral games of Patroclus (Chapter 3). And finally, it applies even to the false attributions of human agency in the act of killing itself in the *Iliad* (Chapter 4). Whenever a certain mode of force is invoked in the *Iliad*, one is thus able to observe a double action. On the one hand, nearly every utterance pertaining to force in the *Iliad* is used in the service of self-identification or in the

---

[18] To be sure, this feature may be a function of the fact that speech constitutes 45 percent of the verses in the *Iliad* (on which see Griffin 1986). For the broader significance of speech presentation in the *Iliad*, see esp. Griffin 1986; Martin 1989; Beck 2012; Knudsen 2014. Nevertheless, because the topic of "force" is so much about physicality, and the *Iliad* itself is so replete with violence, one would still expect a more even distribution between speech and narrative for such terms for force.

8 The Homeric Problem of Force

characterization of others. On the other hand, every assertion of force in the *Iliad* presents the possibility of undoing those very identities.

Homer and the Philosophy of Force, between Language and the Subject

When taken together, the terms for force in Homer all point to a more general view on force and human subjectivity distinct from modern assumptions. As Bruno Snell observed early on:

> We believe that a man advances from an earlier situation by an act of his own will, through his own power. If Homer, on the other hand, wants to explain the source of an increase in strength, he has no course but to say that the responsibility lies with a god.
>
> **(Snell 1953: 20)**

And Snell further explains that Homeric forces are viewed as a "fitting donation from the gods." (Snell 1953: 21). Simone Weil had also observed this fact but dismissed the Homeric perspective on the gods as a way to explain away the more general irrationality of force and war in which all humans participate (Weil 1955: 67). Through a careful study of the Homeric vocabulary of force, however, one can observe that not all forms of force in Homer are conceptualized as "donations from the gods" in the manner asserted by Snell. Two specific terms, *(w)is* and *dynamis*, are *not* described as a gift from the gods.[19] Thus, careful attention to the philology of force reveals that the Homeric view is in fact more complicated than Weil or Snell had believed. That humans can enact force of their own accord separate from the gods is feasible according to Homeric vocabulary, but that feasibility is largely understood only as a *negative* possibility. For the noun *dynamis* and the verb *dynamai*, which give expression to human potential, are predominantly expressed in the negative in the *Iliad*.[20] In other words, the different relations of force do more than present a picture of force distinct from the modern notion of the self-determined

---

[19] These exceptions are described later in this introduction and more completely in the appendix.

[20] It occurs in the negative forty-three times out of fifty-two total occurrences in the *Iliad*. See full citations in the appendix.

Homer and the Philosophy of Force 9

individual. Rather, those terms in the *Iliad* actively problematize the status of humans by giving expression to the limits of agency as such.[21]

This problematization of human subjectivity and agency in the *Iliad* is further underscored by the fact that most terms for force are invoked in speech rather than narrative. That is to say, the problem of force and the human subject in the *Iliad* is inseparable from the problem of what it means to be a *speaking* subject. Because speech turns out to be so critical for framing the very analysis of force and the Homeric subject, it is useful to return to the "linguistic turn" and to the problem of the relationship between language and the subject first inaugurated by the intellectual movement broadly known as "structuralism."[22] In recent years, scholars such as Miriam Leonard and Paul Allen Miller have called attention to the important role antiquity played for theorizing the subject from different perspectives within the structuralist tradition, especially in reference to Classical Greek genres of tragedy and philosophy.[23] For the most part, the close connection between antiquity and structuralism is acknowledged to have developed out of a sustained engagement with these Classical genres. Yet Homeric and Hesiodic poetry have also played a significant role in structuralist thought.[24] In fact, Homer's *Iliad* has factored directly into the works of Pierre Bourdieu, Jacques Derrida, and Michel Foucault in important but largely unacknowledged ways. Thus, in *Language and Symbolic Power*, Pierre Bourdieu uses the case of the Homeric scepter in order to argue that the "illocutionary force" of speech acts does not come from speaking but from the objective conditions of power in which the speaker participates. In *Rogues* (2005), one of Derrida's last major publications,

---

[21] This problematization of force therefore parallels Porter's more general observation on war in the *Iliad*: "It would, in any event, be a mistake to claim that either poem celebrates war. On the contrary, they problematize war, the *Iliad* above all, since war is its theme" (Porter 2021: 201).

[22] Under the category of structuralism, I include those thinkers classified in North America as "poststructuralists," including Bourdieu, Derrida, and Foucault discussed below. On the categorization of twentieth-century French thinkers and their reception in the anglophone world, see Cusset 2008. Equally useful is the monograph by Angermüller 2015 appropriately titled *Why There Is No Poststructuralism in France*. A full discussion of the history of language and the subject in structuralism is beyond the scope of this book, but key aspects of that history will be addressed in separate chapters. For an overview and defense of structuralism's central focus on subjectivity, see esp. Balibar 2003. For criticism of the use of linguistics as a model in structuralist discourse, see Pavel 2001.

[23] See Miller 1998; Leonard 2000; Leonard 2005; Miller 2007; Leonard 2010a; Miller 2010; Miller 2015a; Miller 2015b.

[24] On the influence that Hesiodic poetry played in structuralism, see Stocking 2017b; Stocking 2020.

10   The Homeric Problem of Force

Derrida quotes the "one king" speech of Odysseus from *Iliad* Book 2 in order to offer an account of political force, which in turn serves as the basis for his deconstruction of democracy. And finally, in a more recently published lecture series, *Wrong-Doing, Truth Telling* (2014), Michel Foucault offers an extensive analysis of the funeral games of Patroclus in order to explore how individuals are tied to hierarchical relations of "force" and "truth" which are exerted over them by others and by their own speech. For each of these figures, the topic of force in Homeric poetry plays a critical role in articulating the larger problem of language and the human subject in society. As I shall argue in the course of this book, these lesser-known engagements with Homer presented in the works of Bourdieu, Derrida, and Foucault will in fact prove useful for more fully appreciating the distinct types of force and their roles in the *Iliad*.

Of course, one could well argue that there is little need to invoke such thinkers for the sake of interpreting Homeric poetry because structuralism and its aftermath are now considered *passé*. But I believe there are at least three reasons why one should avoid such a dismissal. The first reason is supplied by Jacques Derrida himself. As early as 1967, when structuralism was still on the rise, Derrida anticipated its future fall and offered the following response in his essay "Force and Signification":

> If it recedes one day, leaving behind its works and signs on the shores of our civilization, the structuralist invasion might become a question for the historian of ideas, or perhaps even an object. But the historian would be deceived if he came to this pass: by the very act of considering the structuralist invasion as an object he would forget its meaning and would forget that what is at stake, first of all, is an adventure of vision, a conversion of the way of putting questions to any object posed before us, to historical objects—his own—in particular.
>
> **(Derrida 1978: 1)**

According to Derrida, to treat the intellectual movement of structuralism solely as a historical object is to dismiss the object of structuralism itself, namely the very process of signification. As Derrida goes on to state: "It is certain that the question of the sign is itself more or less, or in any event something other than a sign of the times."[25] In other words, to suggest that structuralism is *passé* is to suggest that the problem of meaning itself is

---

[25] Derrida 1978: 2.

passé. The problem of meaning and how it is produced, however, can never be irrelevant or unfashionable.

The second reason we should not dismiss these "structuralist" discussions of Homer out of hand is because Bourdieu, Derrida, and Foucault all present a deep engagement with the linguistic problem of force in the study of antiquity. Although ancient Greece is a well-acknowledged *topos* of French thought, none of the thinkers discussed here ever presented a particular proclivity towards Homeric poetry. In fact, their discussions of Homer are relegated almost entirely to the works mentioned above.[26] Why then do all three figures discuss Homer specifically in light of the topic of force? On a general level, their engagements with Homeric force are certainly indebted to the popularity of Simone Weil's essay. But at a more detailed level, the discussions of Homer by Bourdieu, Derrida, and Foucault all seem to be directly indebted to the work of two highly influential Indo-Europeanists, Émile Benveniste and George Dumézil. Bourdieu's discussion of the Homeric scepter and his more general discussion of the function of persuasion is a direct result of Benveniste's study of sovereignty and obedience from his work on Indo-European language and society. Likewise, Derrida's discussion of *kratos* and politics in *Rogues* as well as in his last major seminar, *The Beast and the Sovereign*, also relies heavily on Benveniste's etymologies from his Indo-European dictionary. And finally, Michel Foucault cites George Dumézil on a number of occasions as a major source for his inquiry into the relationship between power and truth, beginning with Homer and Hesiod. Hence, the structuralist problem of force, language, and the subject appears to be largely founded on the linguistic prehistory of ancient Greece itself.

Such an intimate interaction between continental philosophy and Classical philology would indeed seem strange to anglophone audiences, especially in North America. As Allen Miller has commented:

---

[26] Bourdieu is perhaps less well known for a sustained engagement with antiquity in his publications, and yet Bourdieu regularly attended the seminars of Jean Bollack (personal communication from Pierre Judet de la Combe).

Derrida's use of the Classical past is almost entirely relegated to philosophy and tragedy. Foucault seems to present a more wide-ranging engagement with ancient Greek and Latin texts. In addition to *Wrong-Doing, Truth-Telling*, Foucault discusses Homer and the funeral games of Patroclus in his inaugural lecture series at the Collège de France, delivered in 1970–1, *Lectures on the Will to Know* (Foucault 2013), and in a lecture in Brazil delivered in 1973, "Truth and Juridical Forms" (Foucault 2000). In part, such engagement with Archaic Greek poetry is no doubt a result of the influence of the so-called "Paris School" of French Classical scholars, which included Jean-Pierre Vernant, Marcel Detienne, Pierre Vidal-Naquet, and Nicole Loraux, among others, on which see Loraux, Nagy, and Slatkin 2001 and Stocking 2020.

12 The Homeric Problem of Force

The kind of profound classical culture that makes a figure like the great comparative Indo-Europeanist scholar George Dumézil easily cited and appreciated by figures as diverse as Foucault, Derrida, and Kristeva is simply not available to most Anglophone scholars. The notion of Jonathan Culler, Richard Rorty, or Hillis Miller having the same easy familiarity with the works of such American Indo-Europeanists as Calvert Watkins or Jaan Puhvel is all but inconceivable. Consequently, an entire idiom of thought, which these French thinkers simply assume, often remains opaque even to their most ardent enthusiasts.

(Miller 2007: 4)

By taking up the problem of the meaning of force, which is common to Indo-Europeanists, Classical scholars, and continental philosophers, this book may therefore help gain access to that particular "idiom of thought" on force and the subject within structuralist discourse, the "roots" of which have hitherto gone unappreciated.

Lastly, it should be noted that taking up structuralist thinkers' use of Homer on force is not the same as a structuralist reading of Homeric force. Indeed, one of the greatest problems in the reception of structuralist thought more generally is the confusion between theory and method.[27] Such confusion stems in large part from the popularity of Claude Lévi-Strauss's appropriation of linguistic structuralism in order to develop what he considered to be a universal method of analysis.[28] One should certainly be wary of any universalizing will-to-system that would reduce to a single mathematical formula a vast array of different materials, from Oedipus to the Zuni emergence myth.[29] Indeed, if there is any unity to structuralist thought in postwar France, it might be best summarized by Foucault, when he was asked to define himself as a "poststructuralist." Foucault denied the category of "poststructuralism" and responded as follows:

---

[27] See esp. Miller 2003.   [28] See esp. Lévi-Strauss 1963: 206–31.

[29] In *Structural Anthropology*, Lévi-Strauss does indeed apply the following mathematical formula to explain his technique of myth analysis: $F_x(a): F_y(b) \simeq F_x(b):F_{a-1}(Y)$ (Lévi-Strauss 1963: 228). Lévi-Strauss's methods proposed in *Structural Anthropology* were controversial from the outset. An entire conference, Entretiens sur les notions de genèse et structure, was quickly organized in Cerisy-la-Salle France in 1959, soon after publication of *Structural Anthropology*. The major purpose of the conference was to question the type of synchronic and universal methods proposed by Lévi-Strauss. For the significance of the Genesis and Structure conference in the history of structuralist thought, see Dosse 1997a: 175–80; Stocking 2017b: 387–93. For the great debates around Lévi-Strauss's structural method, especially as it was applied to the Oedipus myth, see Leonard 2005: 38–68.

Behind what was known as structuralism, there was a certain problem—
broadly speaking, that of the subject and the recasting of the subject.
[Yet I] do not see what kind of problem is common to those referred to
the people we call "postmodern" or "poststructuralist."

(Foucault 1998: 448)

As we have seen from the earlier arguments of Weil, Snell, and Benveniste, the question of Homeric force centers precisely on the problem of the subject, and it is for this reason as well that Bourdieu, Derrida, and Foucault also take up the question of force in Homeric poetry. As will be made clear in the following chapters, the work of each is in many respects an extension of the projects initiated by Weil, Snell, and Benveniste.[30] Because Bourdieu, Derrida, and Foucault take up different approaches to the problem of Homeric force, each treatment opens up new avenues of inquiry into the study of Homeric poetry proper. Pierre Bourdieu offers an occasion for us to reconsider the relationship between force and the speaking subject in Homer. Jacques Derrida allows us to investigate more deeply the relationship between force and the political subject in the *Iliad*. And Michel Foucault invites us to rethink the relationship between force and truth in the Homeric *agōn* within the broader context of the relational human subject. Each of these thinkers' engagement with Homeric force thus offer the opportunity to investigate and ultimately deconstruct the very idea of the human subject as a self-contained, autonomous individual within the realms of speech, politics, and competition more generally.

This book therefore presents readings of Homeric poetry on force *in dialogue* with these structuralist thinkers in order to address the much larger problem of subjectivity in the Homeric poems. As I make clear, however, the treatments of Homer by Bourdieu, Derrida, and Foucault should by no means be adopted wholesale. Thus, each approach requires what I term "philological interventions" in their more philosophical treatments. Such interventions come about largely through a detailed study of the force terms in context using oral-poetic methods for analyzing Homeric poetry. When coming to terms with the meaning of each term related to "force," basic methodology in lexical semantics requires that one

---

[30] On Weil's influence on Derrida, see Bennington 1999: 325–36. Snell's influence may be more indirect, and perhaps a function of the influence of Jean-Pierre Vernant, who viewed his own work in part as a continuation of Snell's project (on which see Vernant 1991: 159 and the essays of both Detienne and Vernant in Meyerson 1973). Benveniste, on the other hand, is quoted extensively in the works of all three figures, as explained below.

14 The Homeric Problem of Force

take into account all occurrences of such terms. In Homer, however, those occurrences themselves are often found within formulaic contexts. Hence the semantics of lexical items in Homer are inseparable from more pragmatic questions regarding issues of formula and theme.[31] And even though the origins of oral-formulaic analysis, beginning with Milman Parry, seemed to work against the ability of Homeric poetry to express unique modes of meaning, the most recent advances suggest that formulas provide the opportunity to generate even more meaning and nuance than would otherwise be possible.[32] A more rigorous, oral-poetic approach to Homeric force will therefore supplement and improve upon the arguments proposed by Bourdieu, Derrida, and Foucault. And it thereby serves as a further occasion to revisit the early arguments of Weil and Snell.

Homer and the Philology of Force, between the Human and Divine

In order to fully explore the problem of force and the subject in Iliadic narrative, it is important to first detail the different terms and semantic roles of force, which were briefly mentioned but never fully developed by Snell and Benveniste. Each of the terms, their uses, and contexts are presented in full in the appendix and those results are summarized here.[33]

---

[31] The unique requirements of Homeric lexical semantics are clearly established by Leonard Muellner in his important work on the verb *euchomai* (Muellner 1976, esp. 12–13). Such method has been further exemplified and expanded upon by Richard Martin on the distinction between *muthos* and *epos*, where Martin explains, "We must rewrite the dictionaries, by looking afresh at the exact contexts, associations, and disjunctions in which these words play a part. When we do pay attention to context, synonymity recedes" (Martin 1989: 14). Further exemplary models of oral poetic approaches to Homeric vocabulary include Wilson 2002 on *poinē* and *apoina*, as well as Walsh 2005 on *cholos* and *kotos*. This book's treatment of Homeric force may therefore be considered yet one more effort to "rewrite the dictionary" of Homeric language.

[32] For a concise summary of debates on the Homeric formula in the twentieth century beginning with Milman Parry, see Russo 1997. Most recently, Egbert Bakker has offered a programmatic solution to the problem of meaning and the Homeric formula through a model which he terms "the scale of interformularity" (Bakker 2013: 157–69). There appears to be a high degree of "interformularity" when it comes to the language of force in Homer, and so Bakker's model and its implications will be discussed in greater detail with regard to specific formulas in each chapter.

[33] From Snell's original list, kikus has been omitted because it only appears once in the *Odyssey* (11.393). From Benveniste's list, *ischus* has been omitted because it appears in Hesiod but does not appear in the Homeric epics.

Kratos

According to both Snell and Benveniste, the central and most significant term for force in Homer is *kratos*, which conveys a basic meaning of "superiority."[34] As Benveniste noted, the term always implies a contest, where *kratos* is presented as the factor which ultimately accounts for the result of the contest. In this respect, the contrary of *kratos* may be *achos* or "grief" within the epic tradition.[35] Furthermore, *kratos* as superiority seems to operate as a central, organizing principle for other forms of force and may function as the basis for other comparative terms designating superior force.[36] Furthermore, it is predominantly described as something given by the gods.[37] It is Zeus who most often gives *kratos* because, as Zeus himself asserts, he has the most *kratos* of all the gods (*Iliad* 8.17). But because *kratos* is given and not understood as a permanent attribute of any single figure, human or divine, one should not confuse the notion of "superiority" with "sovereignty." Instead, as I argue in Chapter 2, *kratos* encapsulates a notion of "agonistic alterity," where the force of *kratos* requires supremacy over *others* and also must come from an *other*. Indeed, when *kratos* is invoked as a gift from the gods, most contexts ultimately emphasize the divine contingency of events turning out in a way contrary to human expectation.

Alkē

Another external notion of force is *alkē*, which may be understood as a type of "fighting force" specific to the contexts of defense and attack in battle.[38] What makes *alkē* unique compared to other terms for force is its conceptualization as a type of outer layer which the warrior wears, reflected in its use with verbs such as "putting on" (*duō*) and "clothed in" (*epiennumi*).[39] According to Derek Collins, it may therefore function as a type of "immortal armor" that further reflects a unique form of divine

---

[34] Snell 1953: 21. Benveniste 2016: 365; s.v. Nordheider's entry under *kratos, kartos* in *LfgrE*, pp. 1527–30.
[35] Nagy 1979: 85–90.   [36] Benveniste 2016: 364; 367–71.
[37] See appendix under *kratos*, II–IV.
[38] Snell 1953: 21; Benveniste 2016: 363; Collins 1998; s.v. *alkē* in *LfgrE*.
[39] See appendix under *alkē*, II and III.

16 The Homeric Problem of Force

possession.[40] At the same time, I would note that *alkē* is not entirely external to the human subject since it can be roused and suppressed specifically through mental processes of remembering and forgetting respectively.[41] Thus, *alkē* reflects the ways in which internally conceptualized human operations of thought interact with external factors established by the gods.

Menos

The externalized notions of *kratos* and *alkē*, however, may be contrasted with *menos*, which is better understood as a type of "life force" which animates the limbs, is associated with the living person (*zōos*), drives a human to action, and leaves the body upon death together with the *psychē*. It is especially related to embodied action.[42] Unlike other terms, however, the force of *menos* may also be "breathed" into the warrior by a god, further underscoring its relationship to human vitality.[43] But like *alkē*, it too has a mental component, reflected in its etymological root **men-*.[44] And yet, even though *menos* is more directly a feature of the internal aspects of the human body in Homer, nevertheless it too can be supplemented and increased by the intervention of the gods. *Menos* is given to one hero over another in order to explain the *aristeia* of a particular person in battle, as with Athena's aid of Diomedes in *Iliad* Book 5 (*Iliad* 5.1–2, 125), the divine favor and intervention of the gods as the Trojans and Greeks battle (especially as it applies to Hector and Aeneas) (*Iliad* 15.59–60, 262; *Iliad* 20.79–80), and also when two humans compete who are favored by two different divinities, as seen in the chariot race of the funeral games of Patroclus (*Iliad* 23.390, 399–400).[45] In sum, when *menos* is given to a human and enters their physical body, it is a reflection of the political intrigue among the gods and their contrasting desires in the Trojan war. Lastly, the operation of *menos* as a vital force in acts of war reflects an inherently tragic view of the Homeric warrior's undertaking and the involvement of the gods.[46] Thus, at the outset of the *Iliad*, Athena appears

---

[40] See Collins 1998: 15–45.

[41] See appendix under *alkē*, IV, V, VI. On the relationship between notions of "force" and memory as a specifically epic phenomenon, see Nagy 1974: 266–9; Collins 1998: 111–12; Bakker 2008; Bakker 2013: 143–50.

[42] See Clarke 1999: 112–13.   [43] See Appendix under *menos*, VII.

[44] Nagy 1974: 266–8; Collins 1998: 111–12; Bakker 2008: 67–73; Chantraine 2009: 703; Beekes 2010: 930–1.

[45] For further examples, see the appendix.

[46] *Menos* therefore may contribute to the problematization of the warrior mentality that may be implicit in the *Iliad*, on which see Graziosi and Haubold 2003.

Homer and the Philosophy of Force **17**

to stop the *menos* of Achilles when he is about to kill Agamemnon (*Iliad* 1.207). And yet that cessation of *menos*, to save the life of Agamemnon, will in turn precipitate the death of countless Greeks, including Patroclus and Achilles himself. Similarly, in the case of Hector, Zeus supplies Hector with additional *menos* in battle (*Iliad* 15.232) as well as *kratos* (*Iliad* 17.206–7) in part as recompense for the fact that Hector will eventually die at the hands of Achilles.[47] And Andromache herself comments on the tragic irony of Hector's *menos*, when she tells Hector, "Your own *menos* will cause your demise" (φθίσει σε τὸ σὸν μένος) (*Iliad* 6.407). That is to say, it is Hector's own "life force," his *menos*, supplemented by Zeus, which will cause Hector's own life to decay (*phthinein*).[48]

Sthenos

The term *sthenos* seems to imply a more general quality of force or "strength" that is neither event-specific as with *kratos* and *alkē*, nor is it strictly internal as with *menos*. This general quality is conveyed by the fact that *sthenos* is often paired with other terms for force, and can also be seen in the formula σθένος οὐκ ἀλαπαδνόν, "his/her/their force is not weak/small," indicating there are degrees of *sthenos* a person may display.[49] *Sthenos* is also described as being placed in humans by gods, but only on three occasions.[50] As I argue in Chapter 1, both *menos* and *sthenos* may also convey a sense of strength from a perspective that combines "nature" and "culture."[51] *Menos*, typically associated with the vital force of human embodiment, can be associated with one's ancestors, but it can also apply to environmental elements, predominantly fire, and occasionally applies to animals. *Sthenos* also often applies to environmental forces, specifically Orion, Ocean, and rivers, and it may also apply to animals who "exult in their strength."[52] Most importantly, as I argue in Chapter 1, *sthenos* plays a key role when Achilles attempts to make distinctions in force relations between himself and Asteropaeus through a comparison of kinship and genealogy, his claimed from Zeus, Asteropaeus' from a river (*Iliad*

---

[47] On the problematic nature of this recompense from Zeus, see Wilson 2002: 163; Pucci 2018: 68–71.
[48] See Chapter 4 for further discussion of the tragic aspects of *menos* in the *Iliad*.
[49] See appendix under *sthenos*, II.
[50] By Eris at *Iliad* 11.11, by Poseidon at *Iliad* 14.151, by Athena at *Iliad* 21.304.
[51] It may therefore be referred to as "natureculture," on which see Haraway 2003 and Holmes 2015.
[52] See appendix under *sthenos*, III.

18 The Homeric Problem of Force

21.184–91). The ways in which genealogy itself crosses the human-nonhuman threshold in terms of force relations thus reflects how the concept of force entangles the human subject with the environment. At the same time, environmental features, whether rivers, winds, fire, or Ocean, are also divine beings and so the fluid interchange between humans and the nonhuman environment is also an interchange between the human and divine.

Biē

In contrast to these four other terms, *biē* may be understood to convey physical, violent action.[53] And as I suggest in Chapter 3, it is this term which is most strongly associated with human subjectivity since the "naming formula," *biē* + name of a warrior in the genitive or adjectival form, functions as a periphrasis for the person in question, most often applied to Heracles.[54] To be sure, the naming formula also occurs with other terms for force, specifically *menos*, *sthenos*, and *(w)is*, yet those occurrences are far less frequent and can be contextually explained in ways beyond *metri causa*.[55] The naming formula with *menos* in the *Iliad* occurs in contexts related to a warrior's life force and it occurs strictly with Alcinous in the *Odyssey*.[56] In particular, the naming formula shows how *biē* is critical to the subjective identity of ancient Greek warriors and Heracles, above all others.[57] Furthermore, as Gregory Nagy has noted, the *biē* naming formula occurs often with heroes whose names are built with the epic theme of reputation or *kleos*.[58] Thus, as Nagy explains, "The heroic resource of *biē* then has a distinctly positive aspect as a key to the hero's *kleos*."[59] Such an association is further underscored by the other formulaic uses of *biē* as it

---

[53] Chantraine 2009: 174; Beekes 2010: 312. s.v. *biē* in *LfgrE*.

[54] Snell 1953: 19–20; Schmitt 1967: 109–11; Nagy 1979: 318–19; Chantraine 2009: 174.

[55] See appendix for further discussion.

[56] See appendix under *menos*, XXVII. Indeed, the naming formula applied to Alcinous creates a *figura etymologica*, since the root of *menos* relates to mental capacity, *men-, while Alcinous' name captures the double sense of force (*alkē*) and mind (*noos*). See appendix for citations.

[57] See appendix under *biē*, I. See further D. Stocking 2007: 63: "'Force' and 'power' are treated as the real 'subjects' of those actions and passions which we would normally ascribe to the 'whole person.' It is 'force' that speaks, falls, hears, feels, and so forth. And in a way, this is precisely the point. The 'person' in Homer is clearly interchangeable with the idea of 'force' and 'might,' and the genitive in these phrases denotes not possession, but predication."

[58] See Nagy 1979: 318–19. The *biē* naming formula occurs specifically with Eteokles (*Iliad* 4.386), Iphicles (*Odyssey* 11.290, 296), and Patroclus (*Iliad* 17.187, 22.323).

[59] Nagy 1979: 319. Nagy goes on to demonstrate the negative aspects also associated with *biē* in Homeric epic.

applies to a warrior who is "confident in his force," *peith-* + *biēphi*, and it is also a primary means by which one warrior is determined to be better, *pherteros*, than another.[60] At the same time, although the naming formula might provide a type of grammatical key to Homeric identity, it also presents a complication since it is not by the hero's agency alone that a warrior determines *kleos* and epic identity. Even though *biē* may constitute the identity of a hero, it should also be noted that *biē*, like other forms of force, is also explicitly given by the gods.[61] Herein lies the dilemma of Homeric subjectivity. A Homeric warrior's identity is determined largely through the enactment of violent force, while even the enactment of violent force itself is not strictly a function of the autonomous will and agency of that warrior.

(W)is

Unlike these first five terms, however, there are two terms for force which are never described as objects given by the gods. The first is *(w)is*, which occurs predominantly with the instrumental formulas *iphi machesthai* "to fight with force" and *iphi anassein* "to rule with force." Those usages therefore parallel the use of the verb *kratein* in so far as Homeric force expresses some ambivalence with regard to distinctions between the physical and political realms of action.[62] It applies once to non-anthropomorphic wind in the *Iliad* and several times in the *Odyssey*. Although this term for strength has a different etymology from *is, inos* referring to tendons in the body, there may be some general association between the two in the Homeric epics.[63] Overall, *(w)is* does convey a sense of innate bodily force that may be contrasted with the other types involved with divine intervention.

Dynamis

The last term Benveniste and Snell suggest connotes "force" is the noun *dynamis* and related verb *dynamai*. *Dynamis* in early Greek hexameter clearly conveys a sense of physical potential. This potential, however, is

---

[60] See items III, VI under *biē* in the appendix.

[61] See, for instance, *Iliad* 7.205, when men pray to give *biē* and *kudos* to both Hector and Ajax, or *Iliad* 17.569, when Athena places *biē* in the shoulders and knees of Menelaus after he prays to her.

[62] See the appendix for further discussion.

[63] See Chantraine 2009: 469; Beekes 2010: 599.

20 The Homeric Problem of Force

never described as something that is given by the gods, but it is relative to specific agents, and it is also understood to be inherently limited. The relative and limited nature of *dynamis* as potential is reflected in formulas such as ὅση δύναμίς γε πάρεστι, "however much power/potential is present [for me]," i.e. "as much as I am able."[64] This inherently limited perspective on potential becomes especially clear if we take a macroscopic view of the lexical occurrences of *dynamis*. Of the fifty-two occurrences of the noun *dynamis* and the verb *dynamai* in the *Iliad*, it is used in the negative forty-three times. In Homer, Hesiod, and the Hymns, the negative of terms related to *dynamis* are used a total of eighty times in the negative out of 114 total occurrences, and only twenty-four times in a purely positive context, primarily in relationship to the gods. Thus, in early Greek epic, and especially in the *Iliad*, human potential is an overwhelmingly negative concept.

Damazō/Damnēmi

Lastly, there is one term which I include in the semantic set of force terms not mentioned by Snell or Benveniste, namely the verb *damazō* and its cognates.[65] This verb takes on a basic meaning of "subjugation" that occurs within a semantic sphere that covers both male and female, human and nonhuman.[66] In particular, the verb takes on three distinct objects and its meaning changes slightly with each. With animals as the object, the verb means to "tame." With women, it means to subjugate in marriage or also to "enslave." The use of this verbal root thus speaks to the problematic sexual politics of Archaic Greece that often equates women and animals.[67] And finally, when men are the object of this verb, the notion of "subjugation" takes on its most final form as the act of killing. Thus, the verb presents three levels at which force is enacted relative to different objects. Furthermore, the deployment of this verb, especially in the act of killing, speaks directly to the problem of human-divine relations in the enactment

---

[64] *Iliad* 8.294, 13.787.
[65] On the relationship of the Homeric verbal forms *damazō* and *damnēmi* from the root *demh$_2$-, see Beekes 2010: 301; Chantraine 2009: 251; Chantraine 1948: 301.
[66] It should be noted, however, that the English verb "dominate," from Latin *dominus*, is actually derived from the IE root *domh$_2$-o-*, different from the root *demh$_2$*, on which see Benveniste 2016: 239–50. Nevertheless, our English term "dominate" does capture the range of meanings for the root *demh$_2$* in Homeric Greek.
[67] See further discussion in Chapter 4.

Homer and the Philosophy of Force 21

of force. For the verb appears predominantly in the passive form, with humans as the subject-object of force. And when the verb does take on an active form, it is most often a god rather than a human who is the active, nominative subject of the verb, and any human agency is expressed primarily in the instrumental form. Thus, for instance, Zeus famously asks, "Or will I kill [Sarpedon] at the hands of the son of Menoetius" (ἦ ἤδη ὑπὸ χερσὶ Μενοιτιάδαο δαμάσσω) (*Iliad* 16.433–8). Similarly, in his threat to Hector, Achilles announces, "But Athena will kill you with my spear" (ἄφαρ δέ σε Παλλὰς Ἀθήνη/ἔγχει ἐμῷ δαμάᾳ) (*Iliad* 22. 270–1). Of all the terms for force, therefore, it is the verb *damazō* and related forms that give expression to Simone Weil's argument for the subject-object status of humans created by the enactment of force. At the same time, as I shall argue in Chapter 4, this particular verb for the enactment of force departs from Weil's argument. For it also fully captures the unique co-agency between human and divine in Homeric poetry, which Weil failed to properly acknowledge.

Ultimately, therefore, a detailed study of the types of Homeric force and their roles in the Iliadic narrative allows us to rethink the notion of Homeric subjectivity *beyond the individual*. Indeed, in recent years, there has developed a rich body of "post-Snell" literature dedicated to rethinking Homeric subjectivity.[68] This book's treatment of the vocabulary of force may be seen as an extension of that endeavor. Relying on recent posthumanist work and its anthropological precedents, this book concludes by recasting the Homeric subject as an intersubjective *dividual*.[69] What the vocabulary of force reveals is a notion of the Homeric self that is never self-contained, but defined instead by a human-divine symbiosis. Such a model of symbiotic subjectivity, however, does far more than reduce the Homeric self to yet another static anthropological category. As I aim to show throughout each of the individual chapters, that very interdependence between human and divine remains a point of contention and

---

[68] For criticism of Snell as well as similar arguments made by Adkins 1970, see Gill 1996. For the anachronistic categories of "mind" and "body" as it pertains to native Homeric vocabulary, see Clarke 1999. For further reanalysis of Homeric embodiment and subjectivity, see esp. Holmes 2010; Holmes 2015; Holmes 2017. And for a rethinking of Snell in light of the Homeric body in movement, see Purves 2019. Indeed, there is a way in which the post-Snell treatment of the Homeric subject is fully in accord with a more general posthumanist approach to Classics. As Bianchi, Brill, and Holmes explain in the introduction to *Antiquities beyond Humanism*, "Classical thinking displaces and complicates the modern notion of subjectivity and finds movement and life inherently at work in both organic and inorganic phenomena" (Bianchi, Brill, Holmes 2019: 3).

[69] On this concept see Haraway 2016 as well as Dumont 1980; Dumont 1986; Dumont 1994; and Strathern 1988.

22 The Homeric Problem of Force

frustration for human agents themselves throughout the poem. As we shall see, such frustration is made most apparent with the poem's main protagonist, Achilles—from Athena's prevention of Achilles' murder of Agamemnon in *Iliad* 1 to Achilles' vain attempts at mutilating the corpse of Hector in *Iliad* 24.

1

"Stronger"

Performative Speech and the Force of Achilles

Simone Weil famously asserted that "the true hero, the true subject, the center of the *Iliad* is force."[1] Yet it could quite easily be argued that the entire narrative of the *Iliad* is set in motion not through the enactment of force, but through its denial and deferral. In *Iliad* 1, after the conflict between Agamemnon and Achilles has begun, Achilles contemplates whether he should cut the conversation short through the use of his sword (*Iliad* 1.188–92). In Weil's terms, he considers whether or not to transform Agamemnon into a thing, a dead body. At this critical juncture, the goddess Athena intervenes in a unique epiphanic moment.[2] The significance of Athena's physical presence has been hotly debated regarding the psychology of the Homeric self.[3] It is Athena's words to Achilles, however, which are perhaps more important.[4] When Achilles faces the goddess and asks why she has appeared to him, she states her intentions clearly: "I have come to stop your *menos*, should you obey" (ἦλθον ἐγὼ παύσουσα τὸ σὸν μένος, αἴ κε πίθηαι) (*Iliad* 1.207).

[1] Weil 2003: 45. Here I part slightly from Holoka, who translates the French "sujet" as "subject matter." By retaining the more simple translation of "subject," one captures the double meaning of French "sujet" as both "subject as topic" and "subject as person." See Chapter Four for further discussion on Weil and subjectivity.

[2] On epiphanies more generally in early Greek hexameter, see Richardson 1974: 207–8; Sowa 1984: 236–72; J. F. García 2002; Turkeltaub 2007. As Pucci 1998: 71–3 notes, Athena's epiphany in this episode is doubly unique, first because it is a rare occasion when the goddess appears undisguised to a Homeric warrior, and second, her "appearance" is initially not seen by Achilles because she is behind him and physically grabs him.

[3] Athena's appearance has long been viewed as an extension of Achilles' own personal psychology, on which see Nilsson 1924: 363–90; Dodds 1951: 2–18; Otto 1954: 183–4; Whitman 1958: 231; Kirk 1985: 73. Those who contest the psychologizing view include, among others, Schrade 1952: 149; Lloyd-Jones 1971: 9–10; Tsagarakis 1980: 57–80; Hooker 1990: 25–32; Janko 1992: 3; Redfield 1994: 77; Heiden 1997: 224; Pucci 1998: 77; Pulleyn 2000: 176–7; Turkeltaub 2007: 61.

[4] As Pelliccia 1995: 267 notes, Achilles' own impulses are "suppressed through the intervention of an agency whose instrument is *logos*." Pucci 1998: 76 also places emphasis on her divine voice and Turkeltaub 2007: 60–3 describes this moment as an "aural epiphany" of the goddess.

Homer's Iliad *and the Problem of Force.* Charles H. Stocking, Oxford University Press.
© Charles H. Stocking 2023. DOI: 10.1093/oso/9780192862877.003.0002

24 Performative Speech and the Force of Achilles

In her opening statement to Achilles, Athena invokes a unique form of Homeric force. In general terms, *menos* is conceptualized as a substance that is contained within the body, it is roused to action, it is uniquely associated with the living body, and is said to leave the body upon death.[5] In short, *menos* may be understood, above all other terms, as a type of "life force." In Athena's statement, we further see how this particular type of force is understood as a property specific to Achilles' own person, indicated by the possessive adjective (*Iliad* 1.207: *to son menos*).[6] Her use of the possessive in reference to Achilles is all the more striking since *menos* is often treated as an object "given by the gods," especially by Athena herself.[7] Yet here, Athena sets her own actions in opposition to the force of Achilles.[8] That *menos* belongs specifically to Achilles at this point in the narrative may be explained by virtue of its etymology. Derived from the Proto Indo-European root **men-*, *menos* may be cognate with the very first word of the *Iliad* describing the anger of Achilles: *mēnis*.[9] And as Pietro Pucci has noted, it is in fact Athena's appearance to Achilles that sets the main narrative theme of the *Iliad* in motion: "As he slowly draws his sword, Athena arrives and without elaborate explanations exhorts him to replace it in its scabbard. The story of *mēnis* has begun."[10] One must add to this formulation that the story of *mēnis* begins only at the precise moment when the *menos* of Achilles has come to a halt.

Yet Athena does not request a complete abandonment of Achilles' force. Rather, she suggests that it be redirected through speech against Agamemnon. She further promises that the use of reproach will result in

---

[5] *Menos* contained in the body, see, for instance, *Iliad* 5.125, 5.513, as that which is roused for action, *Iliad* 5.563, 15.500, 15.594, 16.529; as associated with breath, *Iliad* 6.182, 15.60, 15.262, 17.454, 20.110; associated with the living body, *zōion*, see 5.516; as that which leaves with the *psuchē* upon death, see *Iliad* 8.123. For a more complete list of citations and further discussion, see the appendix.

[6] *Iliad* 1.207 *to son menos* in vulg./ *teon menos* in Eust. and codices e. On the possessive use of *menos*, see further Holmes 2010: 69. Other uses of possessive with *menos*, see *Iliad* 5.472, 6.407, 8.450, 13.287, 22.459.

[7] As an object given by the gods, see *Iliad* 15.493, 15.594, 16.529. Given by Athena specifically, see *Iliad* 5.2, 5.125, 10.366, 10.482. Athena also plays a key role in giving *menos* to Telemachus in the *Odyssey*, at *Odyssey* 1.89, on which see Nagy 1974: 266–9; Collins 1998: 111–12; Bakker 2008; Bakker 2013: 143–50.

[8] Thus, Athena's own words may be yet one more reason to view Athena as a being separate from Achilles rather than as a psychological projection.

[9] On **men-* as the etymological root of Grk. *mēnis* see Schwyzer 1931: 213–17 (later detracted in Schwyzer 1968, I: 260); Watkins 1977; Nagy 1979: 73n.2; Muellner 1996: 177–94. For an alternative etymology, see Buck 1949: 1134; Considine 1985; Chantraine 2009: 696–7; and Beekes 2010: 946, all of whom consider the etymology unknown, although Beekes acknowledges an obvious semantic connection between *menos* and *mēnis* in Greek.

[10] Pucci 1998: 71.

Performative Speech and the Force of Achilles   25

three times more gifts for Achilles on account of Agamemnon's own act of *hubris*. She states:

ἀλλ' ἄγε λῆγ' ἔριδος, μηδὲ ξίφος ἕλκεο χειρί
ἀλλ' ἤτοι ἔπεσιν μὲν ὀνείδισον ὡς ἔσεταί περ
ὧδε γὰρ ἐξερέω, τὸ δὲ καὶ τετελεσμένον ἔσται
καί ποτέ τοι τρὶς τόσσα παρέσσεται ἀγλαὰ δῶρα
ὕβριος εἵνεκα τῆσδε· σὺ δ' ἴσχεο, πείθεο δ' ἡμῖν.

Iliad 1.210–14

Come, leave off from strife and do not seize your sword with your hand but reproach him with words [telling] how it will be.
For I will say this, and it will be accomplished
at some point for you there will be three times as many glorious gifts on account of this hubris. But you hold back and obey me.

According to Athena's own logic, it is speech itself which may function as a replacement for the execution of physical force. And it is this very different mode of attack through speech that is purported to add to the recognition of Achilles' own status and superiority. Hence, the story of the anger of Achilles begins not only when Achilles' own force is suspended, but also when it is supplemented with speech.

This divine intervention on the part of Athena, which prevents a premature end to the Iliadic narrative, speaks to a more general correlation between physical force and speech, which runs throughout the poem. Indeed, the ideal Homeric warrior is often defined as a "speaker of words and doer of deeds." As Richard Martin (1989: 27) explains: "We must remember that the heroic ideal of speaking and fighting virtuosity is always being propounded in the poem. 'Word and Deed' become a merismus, expressing an ideal totality by reference to the extremes which shape it." Throughout the *Iliad*, certain modes of speech, especially words of reproach, are understood as the verbal equivalent to physical fighting.[11] In this regard, Athena's request is consistent with the traditional modes of heroic speech in the *Iliad*. At the same time, however, there remains a certain discomfort with Athena's directive and Achilles' decision. If the correlation between force and speech were complete and absolute, then Achilles would have successfully brought to an end his quarrel with Agamemnon through his

---

[11] On which see Martin 1989, esp. 111–18; Ford 1992: 64–67; Hesk 2006; Parks 2014.

26 Performative Speech and the Force of Achilles

words, just as easily as he could have killed him. Yet this does not happen. Indeed, Achilles' use of speech rather than actions does not end the quarrel but prolongs it and ultimately leads to a fundamental misrecognition of the significance of Achilles' own force. And even though Achilles will eventually receive even more than what Athena promises, it comes at the cost of many Greek lives, including the life of Achilles' companion Patroclus, and eventually Achilles' own.[12] Far from offering a solution to Achilles' dilemma, Athena's intervention actually calls attention to the many ways in which the relationship between force and speech remains problematic, especially for the figure of Achilles. In light of the narrative events of the poem, Athena's epiphany compels us to consider whether speech is indeed an effective supplement to physical force for Achilles and other characters within the poem.

Of course, the relationship between force and speech is not only relevant to the *Iliad*, but it has been a major topic of modern inquiry ever since J. L. Austin's *How to Do Things with Words*. In that work, Austin sought to account for a particular category of speech, defined as "performatives," which do not have a referential function, but the act of speaking itself is equivalent to the doing of an action. Austin's theory of performatives has in turn been fruitfully applied to Homeric poetry by Richard Martin in his seminal work *The Language of Heroes*. In particular, Martin demonstrated that certain modes of Homeric speech, including boasts, threats, and commands, all indicated by the term *muthos*, functioned in a manner equivalent to Austin's notion of the performative.[13] The Homeric *muthoi* such as threats, boasts, and commands are modes of speech that do far more than convey information. They are acts in themselseves, intended to produce an effect, and that effect itself is dependent on the ability and authority of the speaker to enact that effect on his or her given addressee. In the context of speech act theory, the action conveyed by Homeric *muthoi* would be referred to as its "illocutionary force," where this unspoken "force" of the speech act is meant to contrast with the more typical role of speech to simply convey "meaning."[14]

But how, we might ask, does the Homeric *muthos* and its "illocutionary force" as a speech act relate to the physical force of the speakers within the

---

[12] On Athena's promise and Achilles' compensation, see Wilson 2002: 60. On the ultimate cost of Achilles' compliance with Athena's request, see Pucci 1998: 77.

[13] See Martin 1989: 22–7 on *muthos* (vs. *epos*) and Martin 1989: 43–88 on the genres of heroic speech.

[14] See Austin 1962: 100–7. For examples of illocutionary force in Homeric *muthoi*, see Martin 1989: 52, 187, 191.

poem? As I shall argue in this chapter, the correlation between Homeric performatives and physical force is not as straightforward as Athena originally suggests to Achilles in the opening of the *Iliad*. Indeed, one specific verbal strategy used within Homeric *muthoi* is to invoke the very language of physical force *within* those very performatives, which are meant to supplement acts of force. That is to say, force is not only an inherent feature of performative speech, but overt mention of the speaker's physical "force" also functions as a self-justifying strategy of performative speech throughout the *Iliad*. As far as Homeric poetry is concerned, the "illocutionary force" of speech depends largely on the very elocution of force as such.

In order to fully explore how pronouncements of force function as a performative strategy in the *Iliad*, I focus in particular on the use of comparative terms for physical force, where one speaker claims to be "stronger" than another. Analysis of the use of comparatives allows us to appreciate how the relative asymmetries between speakers in the *Iliad* do not exist in absolute, objective terms. Instead, those asymmetries are tied to the moment of speech itself. In this respect, I give special attention to the figure of Achilles. Indeed, Achilles, above all other warriors, is generally acknowledged to be the character with superlative force and status as "best of the Achaeans."[15] And yet, as I argue in this chapter, from the moment when Athena suppresses his force at the outset of the poem, he himself experiences constant misassessments of his own superiority, and his force is often framed in negative comparative terms. Such misassessment of Achilles by various characters, I suggest, is largely dependent on a misunderstanding of the cosmic significance of Achilles' own genealogy. This chapter will therefore give special attention to the performance of force as it relates to kinship and genealogy.

Through close reading of key speeches concerning Achilles and his genealogy, specifically the speeches of Nestor (*Iliad* 1.247–84), Apollo (*Iliad* 20.104–9), Aeneas (*Iliad* 20.200–9), Poseidon (*Iliad* 20.332–4), and Achilles himself (*Iliad* 21.184–91), we may see how the force inherited by way of genealogy is often invoked as though it were a function of external, objectively determined conditions. But upon closer examination, the larger narrative context of these speeches reveals that the supposedly inherited force determined by genealogy is itself forged through performative speech. That is to say, performative speech does not simply supplement force in

---

[15] See esp. Nagy 1979: 26–41.

28 Performative Speech and the Force of Achilles

the *Iliad*. Rather, Homeric characters actively attempt to construct the very relations of physical force upon which their speech acts rely. But what is most intriguing is that the poem itself often reveals these relations of physical force conveyed in speech to be false constructs. For the narrative of the poem calls into question or directly contradicts the assertions of force made by and for characters, even Achilles himself.

The Homeric Scepter: Speech and the Source of Authority

The very status and functional value of performative speech as a replacement for force seems to be called into question already in *Iliad* 1, very soon after Athena had advised Achilles to replace the act of violence with violent words. At the climax of Achilles' quarrel with Agamemnon, Achilles attempts to put an end to the exchange of threats by swearing a great oath on a scepter, promising that the Greeks will regret not giving Achilles his due share of honor (*Iliad* 1.234–45). In Achilles' oath, he first describes it as an object transformed from the vegetal world, as "that which will never again grow leaves and roots" (τὸ μὲν οὔ ποτε φύλλα καὶ ὄζους/ φύσει) (*Iliad* 1.234–5).[16] He then proceeds to describe its current social function: "Now the sons of Achaeans hold it in their hands, as conveyors of justice, who speak forth rights of judgement on behalf of Zeus" (νῦν αὖτέ μιν υἶες Ἀχαιῶν/ ἐν παλάμῃς φορέουσι δικασπόλοι, οἵ τε θέμιστας/ πρὸς Διὸς εἰρύαται·) (*Iliad* 1.237–9).

Emile Benveniste described the function of the scepter in Homer as follows:

> In Homer, the *skēptron* is the attribute of the king, of heralds, messengers, judges, and all persons who, whether of their own nature or because of a particular occasion, are invested with authority.
>
> **(Benveniste 2016: 325)**

Benveniste further notes that the etymology of the scepter is based on the verb *skēpto*, "to lean on," which, according to Benveniste, implies that the scepter was most likely first understood as a walking stick. From there

---

[16] On the unique vegetal description, esp. as it pertains to Achilles' own act of speech, see esp. Nagy 1979: 179–80; Griffin 1980: 9–12; Mondi 1980: 211; Schein 1984: 96; Kirk 1985: 77–8; Easterling 1989: 112–14; Pulleyn 2000: 193; Sfyroeras 2009; Stein 2016.

Speech and the Source of Authority   29

Benveniste posits that the walking stick must have been originally associated with messengers and then later took on the specialized association with kingship.[17] Benveniste continues his line of reasoning on the history of the scepter as follows:

> From the fact that it is necessary to the bringer of a message the *skēptron* becomes a symbol of his function and a mystic sign of his credentials. Henceforward it is an attribute of the person who brings a message, a sacred personage whose mission it is to transmit the message of authority. This is why the *skēptron* starts with Zeus from whom, by a succession of holders, it descends to Agamemnon. Zeus gives it a kind of credential to those whom he designates to speak in his name.
>
> **(Benveniste 2016: 327)**

According to Benveniste, the scepter was first associated with official forms of heraldic speech. But in the course of history, the scepter developed additional levels of involvement with authority, where speech itself became associated with the authority of the king, and that royal authority in turn was understood to be legitimated by the authority of Zeus, as Achilles himself asserts.[18]

But immediately after describing its relationship to authority and speech, Achilles throws the scepter to the ground (*Iliad* 1.245). At first, one might see this gesture as a simple and petulant expression of Achilles' anger. Yet the petulance of the act is perhaps more properly expressed in the parallel gesture of Telemachus' first public speech in the *Odyssey*, where, after throwing the scepter to the ground, Telemachus bursts into tears (*Odyssey* 2.80-1).[19] Alternatively, one could interpret Achilles' act in

---

[17] For skepticism on Benveniste's account of the scepter's prehistory, see Unruh 2011: 289n.26.

[18] There remains a long history of debate on the prehistory of the scepter as well as the number in circulation in the *Iliad*, and whether scepters belonged to heralds or kings. See, among others, Combellack 1948; Gernet 1968: 240; Mondi 1980; Griffin 1980: 9–12; Kirk 1985: 128–9; Easterling 1989; van Wees 1992: 276–80; Ruzé 1997: 48–52; Bouvier 2002: 273–5; Unruh 2011. Unruh is especially critical of earlier approaches, but it should be noted that his conclusion parallels precisely that of Benveniste. Just as Benveniste ultimately stressed the function of the scepter to "transmit the message of authority" (Benveniste 2016: 327), so Unruh concludes that the scepter "symbolizes one's right to express such authoritative speech" (Unruh 2011: 290). In this regard Kelly 2011: 761 summarizes the problem best when he states, "Procedural precision is less important to the poet than the *skēptron*'s connotation of authority."

[19] As Barker 2009: 101–2 notes, the exact parallel in physical gesture highlights a stark difference in emotional strength between Telemachus and Achilles, suggesting that Achilles' gesture is not simply an empty emotional expression.

30 Performative Speech and the Force of Achilles

symbolic terms based on Achilles' own vegetal description—Achilles has cast back to earth that which has grown from the earth, and this may parallel Achilles' own desire to return to his native Phthia, a place whose vegetal connotations are implied by the name.[20] Lastly, one could also interpret the gesture in relationship to the social function of the scepter itself. If the scepter has an authorizing function as a "talking stick," which is passed from one speaker to another, then Achilles' gesture is indicative of his more general effort to have the final say in the exchange. Rather than pass the scepter either to Agamemnon or another speaker, he throws it to the ground, thereby symbolizing his effort to effectively end any further speech exchange.

Of course, Achilles does not have the final say despite his efforts, and the scepter continues to play a symbolic role with regard to speech and authority yet again in *Iliad* Book 2. It is in *Iliad* Book 2, after Achilles himself has challenged Agamemnon's own authority, where we find the narrative description of the genealogy of Agamemnon's scepter:

ἔστη σκῆπτρον ἔχων τὸ μὲν Ἥφαιστος κάμε τεύχων.
Ἥφαιστος μὲν δῶκε Διὶ Κρονίωνι ἄνακτι,
αὐτὰρ ἄρα Ζεὺς δῶκε διακτόρῳ ἀργεϊφόντῃ·
Ἑρμείας δὲ ἄναξ δῶκεν Πέλοπι πληξίππῳ,
αὐτὰρ ὃ αὖτε Πέλοψ δῶκ' Ἀτρέϊ ποιμένι λαῶν,   (105)
Ἀτρεὺς δὲ θνῄσκων ἔλιπεν πολύαρνι Θυέστῃ,
αὐτὰρ ὃ αὖτε Θυέστ' Ἀγαμέμνονι λεῖπε φορῆναι,
πολλῇσιν νήσοισι καὶ Ἄργεϊ παντὶ ἀνάσσειν.

Iliad **2.101–8**

[Agamemnon] stood with the scepter,
which Hephaestus made ready and fashioned.
And Hephaestus gave it to lord Zeus, son of Cronus,
But Zeus gave it to Hermes Diaktoros, slayer of Argos.
And lord Hermes gave it to horse-striking Pelops,
But Pelops gave it in turn to Atreus, shepherd of the people.
But Atreus, after he died, left it to Thyestes, rich in flocks.
But Thyestes in turn left it to Agamemnon to carry,
and to rule over many islands and all of Argos.

---

[20] Sfyroeras 2009: 56 thus describes the gesture in metapoetic terms: "By hurling the scepter to the ground, Achilles signals his temporary rejection of that *kleos*-giving process as it applies to himself."

Speech and the Source of Authority **31**

This very genealogy of the scepter indicates an exterior basis for determining one's status and authority—that one's authority comes from an object, which in turn comes from outside the human realm itself. The genealogy of Agamemnon's scepter, at least, indicates that the authority of speech must be granted from another, inherited rather than self-imposed or self-asserted.

The Homeric scepter, as a source for authoritative speech, was in fact invoked by the sociologist Pierre Bourdieu in order to criticize J. L. Austin's own theory of performative speech. In an essay titled "Authorized Language: The Social Conditions for the Effectiveness of Ritual Discourse," Bourdieu finds fault with Austin's attempt to explain and locate illocutionary force within language itself.[21] To be sure, Austin does acknowledge that performatives depend on external conditions. As Austin states, "There must exist an accepted conventional procedure having a certain conventional effect, the procedure to include the uttering of certain words by certain persons in certain circumstances."[22] Yet, according to Bourdieu, Austin gives too much attention to the performatives themselves and does not go far enough in accounting for the conditions of those performatives. Bourdieu suggests that performatives "seem to possess *in themselves* the source of a power which in reality resides in the institutional conditions of their production and reception."[23] In order to explain that the source of authority for speech comes from external conditions of authority, Bourdieu calls to mind the Homeric scepter as follows:

> By trying to understand the power of linguistic manifestations linguistically, by looking in language for the principle underlying the logic and effectiveness of the language of institution, one forgets that authority comes to language from outside, a fact concretely exemplified by the *skēptron* that, in Homer, is passed to the orator who is about to speak. Language at most *represents* this authority, manifests and symbolizes it.
>
> **(Bourdieu 1991: 109)**

So, according to Bourdieu, the authority of performative speech must have a source that is external to the speaker. Such a view on externalized authority seems to be confirmed by the *Iliad*'s description of the scepter, which is not only the external source of authority for the speaker, but that external authority ultimately rests outside the human realm itself, that is, with Zeus.

---

[21] Bourdieu 1991: 107–16. [22] Austin 1962: 26.
[23] Bourdieu 1991: 111.

32 Performative Speech and the Force of Achilles

At the same time, it must be pointed out that the description of the genealogy of Agamemnon's scepter in *Iliad* 2 is not without complications. These complications are coextensive with problems in Agamemnon's own genealogical history and ultimately seem to undermine the very source of Agamemnon's authority. First, we should note the act of "giving" is repeated four times in the description of the transfer of the scepter—from Hephaestus to Zeus, from Zeus to Hermes, from Hermes to Pelops, and from Pelops to Atreus (*Iliad* 2.101–5). And then the verb of transfer dramatically shifts. As the text states, "When Atreus died, he *left* it to Thyestes" (*Iliad* 2.106) and Thyestes in turn "left it" to Agamemnon (*Iliad* 2.107). We move from the active verb of "giving" to the more passive sense of "leaving" precisely at two moments of interfamilial conflict in the genealogy of Agamemnon. Aristarchus comments that the poet did not know the tragic story of the house of Atreus, but G. S. Kirk and Brügger et al. suggest the myth was probably known, as seen in the *Odyssey*, and that the verbs for "leaving" the scepter indicate a glossing over or active suppression of that particular myth.[24] As the bT scholia comment on these lines, "the poet says 'gave' as a sign of friendship, but 'leaving' as a sign of necessity" (τὸ μὲν γὰρ δῶκε φιλίας τεκμήριόν φησι, τὸ δὲ καταλιπεῖν ἀνάγκης). In this regard, the genealogy of the scepter betrays a point of difference between the perspective of the narrator and that of the speakers within the *Iliad*, who make use of the scepter. Speakers such as Odysseus (*Iliad* 2.200) and Diomedes (*Iliad* 9.37) will state that Zeus "gave" the scepter to Agamemnon, but the narrator offers a slightly more complex picture.[25] Zeus did not actively "give" it to Agamemnon. Rather, it was "left" to him in the wake of family tragedy. In other words, the scepter itself, a material manifestation of royal authority, calls into question the validity of such authority by its very history. Yes, the genealogy of the scepter creates a material connection between Zeus and the one in possession of the scepter, but that connection is by no means rectilinear and without complications. Instead, the very history of the scepter contains within it the possibility of

---

[24] Kirk 1985: 127; Brügger et al. 2010: 39. Wilamowitz, however, viewed these lines as an indication that the tragic myth of the house of Atreus was not known, and they served as the basis for one of his critiques in his review of Nietzsche's *Birth of Tragedy*: "And the family curse of the Atridae, etc.—all this should be Homeric, even pre-Homeric! What a disgrace, Mr. N, to alma mater Pforta! It must appear as if you were never given Iliad B 101 or the corresponding passage in Lessing's *Laokoon* to read" (Wilamowitz-Moellendorf 2000: 9).

[25] The ideology of royal authority implicit in the speeches of Odysseus and Diomedes is discussed at length in Chapter 2.

Nestor's Scale of Superiority in *Iliad* 1   **33**

the undoing of the authority it is meant to represent.[26] Thus, on the one hand, the genealogy of the scepter of Agamemnon confirms Bourdieu's view that the source of authoritative speech is external to speech, and even external to the speaker. On the other hand, the very external conditions of such authority are what also allows for that authority to be questioned.

In *Iliad* 1, it is the very external conditions of speaking authority, located not just in the scepter but with Zeus himself, which allow Achilles to challenge Agamemnon. For both Achilles and Agamemnon turn to Zeus as the source for their authority. And yet, when Achilles casts the scepter to the ground, it would seem that he is not only challenging Agamemnon, but he is challenging the very conditions that authorize any and all forms of performative speech. In his gesture, it would seem, Achilles is attempting to put an end to performative speech as such. In modern parlance, it would seem that Achilles is "dropping the mic."

A Performative Intervention: Nestor's Scale of Superiority in *Iliad* 1

After Athena's command to Achilles to continue his quarrel with Agamemnon, and after Achilles attempts to end the quarrel with his oath and symbolic gesture of casting the scepter to the ground, Nestor, oldest and most loquacious of the Greeks at Troy, intervenes with a performative in the form of a command directed at both warriors (*Iliad* 1.247–84).[27] Given the scepter's close association with authoritative speech, Nestor's command may be seen not only as an effort to prevent the dissolution of the Greek army, but also as an effort to reaffirm the force of authoritative speech more generally.[28] He does this, I argue, by creating a "scale of superiority" in which he locates his own status as a speaking subject in relationship to the asymmetries in force between Agamemnon and Achilles. Ultimately, however, Nestor's scale of superiority fails in its

---

[26] Parallel to the ironic history of Agamemnon's scepter, therefore, is Achilles' discussion of the history of the scepter as a vegetal object in *Iliad* 1. As Pavlos Sfyroeras explains, "The very image that Achilles employs to stress his oath turns out to undermine it: the description of the scepter looks forward to the moment when Achilles returns to battle and precipitates his death, in effect negating his oath" (Sfyroeras 2009: 56).

[27] On the parallel between Nestor's intervention in the quarrel and that of Athena, see Barker 2009: 47–8. On commands as performatives, see Austin 1962: 28, 73. On commands as performatives in Homer, see Martin 1989: 83–110.

[28] On Nestor's speaking ability and his more general role as counselor and mediator, see Schofield 1986: 8–13, 22–30; Martin 1989: 101–9; Dickson 1995: 101–55; Roisman 2005.

34 Performative Speech and the Force of Achilles

objective, and, I suggest, that failure may be viewed as a function of Nestor's own misassessment of Achilles. Thus, Nestor's speech in *Iliad* 1 may be taken as the first of many in which physical force is problematically and ineffectively invoked as a type of strategy within the context of performative speech.

In order to intervene in the quarrel, Nestor first places himself verbally in between Achilles and Agamemnon through a series of comparative relationships. Nestor's speech act is a command, whose purpose is to get both quarreling warriors to "obey" him, and he uses his own superior status in age as a first mode of justification for the command.[29] Nestor states: "But obey. You are both younger than me" (ἀλλὰ πίθεσθ᾽· ἄμφω δὲ νεωτέρω ἐστὸν ἐμεῖο·) (*Iliad* 1.259). Émile Benveniste has noted that the middle form of the verb *peithō*, historically prior to the active, is ultimately derived from the root *bheid-*, related to "trust" and "faith," such that the middle form means to put one's own "faith" in another.[30] Benveniste suggests that the person who commands obedience and faith has a type of mystic or magical power about them. One might very well consider Nestor's age as a type of mystical basis for obedience.[31]

Yet it is not merely age in and of itself that justifies the need for faith and obedience. Rather, it is because Nestor's age also entails an association with men of superior force from a seemingly mythical past. For his age associates him with the Lapiths, a group of men famous for fighting the Centaurs (*Iliad* 1.260–5). Nestor describes the Lapiths as follows:

κάρτιστοι δὴ κεῖνοι ἐπιχθονίων τράφεν ἀνδρῶν·
κάρτιστοι μὲν ἔσαν καὶ **καρτίστοις** ἐμάχοντο
φηρσὶν ὀρεσκῴοισι καὶ ἐκπάγλως ἀπόλεσσαν.

Iliad 1.266-8

Of the men upon the earth, these were reared with the most *kratos*. They possessed the most *kratos* and they fought against those with the most *kratos*, mountain dwelling beasts, and they destroyed them entirely.

Here Nestor describes the Lapiths in distinctly superlative terms through one of the most significant terms for force, *kratos*. Indeed, it was the term

---

[29] As Minchin 2007: 204 notes, Nestor's authority is further conveyed through his use of imperatives in the speech.
[30] Benveniste 2016: 85; Chantraine 2009: 869.
[31] On Nestor's own constant emphasis on age, see Minchin 2005.

Nestor's Scale of Superiority in *Iliad* 1 35

kratos itself which inspired Benveniste to insist that each of the words designating "force" had separate and distinct meanings and spheres of usage.[32] According to Benveniste, *kratos* has an especially marked meaning as "force." In Homer and Hesiod, at least, it designates "the superiority of a man, whether he manifests his force over those of his own camp or the enemy."[33] Hence, there is a degree of relationality already built into the term's semantic content because it always implies contest.[34] It is striking, then, that Nestor would present the term *kratos* in the superlative adjectival form, *kartistoi*, repeated three times in total. At first glance, the use of the superlative and its repetition might seem semantically and syntactically redundant, used simply to create emphasis. Why else would one place a term meaning "superior" in the superlative?

Given the comparative context with which Nestor begins his speech, I suggest his use of the superlative form of *kratos* is not just for emphasis. Rather, his speech as a whole presents us with a diachronic "scale of superiority." The Lapiths, described in the superlative as *kartistoi*, may in fact be contrasted with both Agamemnon and Achilles, whom Nestor describes in comparative terms relative to each other when he states, just a few lines later:

εἰ δὲ σὺ καρτερός ἐσσι θεὰ δέ σε γείνατο μήτηρ,
ἀλλ' ὅ γε φέρτερός ἐστιν ἐπεὶ πλεόνεσσιν ἀνάσσει.
Iliad 1.280–1

Perhaps you are *karteros*, but a goddess as mother bore you,
but he is *pherteros*, since he rules over more men.

If *kratos* is always already relational, as Benveniste suggests, then Nestor's own characterization of Achilles and Agamemnon highlights this fact through the use of the comparative. On the surface, it would appear that Nestor is attempting to mark a qualitative difference in the two warriors through the use of two comparative forms, *karteros* and *pherteros*.[35] It should

---

[32] Benveniste 2016: 362.

[33] Benveniste 2016: 365. This is also consistent with Snell's very brief account that "kratos is supremacy, the superior force" (Snell 1953: 21). And the same sense is presented in Chantraine ad loc.

[34] Further details of *kratos* will be discussed when relevant in both this chapter and in Chapter 2. For a more complete discussion, see the appendix.

[35] Indeed, this is how many translators of the *Iliad* have taken these lines. See, for instance, the translation of Lattimore 1951 ad loc.: "Although you are the stronger man, and the mother who bore you was immortal, yet is this man greater who is lord over more than you rule" and similar renderings in Verity 2011 and Powell 2014.

36 Performative Speech and the Force of Achilles

be noted, however, that from a grammatical perspective such a reading is somewhat inaccurate. As the scholiast Herodian noted, based on accentuation, *karteros* (καρτερός) is *not* a comparative, but simply the positive adjectival form of *kratos*.[36] Furthermore, Pierre Chantraine has argued that the comparative adjective *pherteros* is derived from the formulaic phrase *pherein kratos*, "to carry away *kratos*."[37] Thus, we have two different modes of the grammatical expression of superiority between the two warriors, one marked with the positive, the other with the comparative proper. Walter Leaf had made the following comment on the proximity and phonetic pairing of *karteros* and *pherteros*: "The similarity of the terminations has its effect, though they are of course different in origin and meaning as well as accent."[38] Of course, Leaf's comment does not help us come down one way or the other on interpreting the passage. If the similarity has its effect, the question remains—on whom does it have this effect? Does it have its effect on Nestor's addressees? Or does it have its effect on the notional audience of the poem? And if it does have its effect, we cannot help but ask, is the effect *intended* and, if so, by whom?

I suggest that there is in fact a double effect of the semantic and phonetic pairing of *karteros* and *pherteros* for his adressees, and this is a function of Nestor's particular rhetorical strategy in establishing his own performative power.[39] On the one hand, it is true that, semantically, there would be no difference between the positive adjective designating "superiority" and the comparative form. Hence, the similarity in form makes it such that Nestor seems to be striking a balance between the two warriors, where each warrior is superior to the other in a qualitatively different way—they appear "equal in their inequality." And yet, when we consider the positive adjectival form *karteros* and the comparative *pherteros* in relation to Nestor's description of the Lapiths, what we are presented with is a complete grammaticalized hierarchy of *kratos*.

---

[36] Segal 1971a: 91 notes the inequality implied by the two terms, as does Muellner 1996: 108–10.

[37] Chantraine 2009: 1146. On the formation of *pherteros* and its Indo-European inheritance, see further García Ramón (2010), who traces the synonymy between the IE roots *$h_1$ne k-* and *b^her-*. In terms of the semantics of comparative and superlative forms derived from *b^her-*, García Ramón sees the possibility of an intransitive sense such as "profitable" as well as a transitive sense, with implied objects such as *kratos* or other "good things" including *kleos* (García Ramón 2010: 84–6).

[38] Leaf 1900: 24.

[39] Indeed, Eustathius cited this speech as a case of Nestor acting as the *Homērikos rhētōr* par excellence, since he "seems to praise, when praising himself" (ἐπαινῶν ἑαυτὸν δοκεῖ ἐπαινεῖν) (Eustathius 1.591.17). For further discussion of Nestor's speaking ability in reference to later categories of "rhetoric," see Knudsen 2014: 48–50.

Achilles is "superior"—*karteros* in the positive, Agamemnon is "more superior"—*pherteros* in the comparative, and the Lapiths are "most superior"—*kartistoi* in the superlative.

Nestor's grammatical scale of superiority reflects a view of the past as superior to the present, a perspective common throughout antiquity. Thus, for instance, in the foot race of the funeral games for Patroclus, Antilochus, the son of Nestor, accounts for the results of the race based on an inverse relationship with age, where the oldest finishes first, and he himself, the youngest, finishes last.[40] The philosopher Jean-Luc Nancy has defined this general view of the past as superior to the present as "restrospective consciousness of lost community." He explains:

> At every moment in its history, the Occident has given itself over to the nostalgia for a more archaic community that has disappeared, and to deploring a loss of familiarity, fraternity and conviviality.
>
> **(Nancy 1991: 10)**

With Nestor's invocation of the Lapiths in the first book of the *Iliad*, which in turn is one of our earliest sources of Greek literature, we have perhaps our earliest account in the Greek tradition of this nostalgia for a more archaic community.[41] Indeed, although nostalgia itself may be a modern term, the concept of *nostos* or "return," upon which it is based, is not.[42] Nor is it insignificant that Nestor would be the first figure to lament the loss of a prior community. At an etymological level, Nestor's own name signifies the desire for a return, a *nostos*—not a return home per se, but a return to the past.[43] Indeed, the invocation of the past is characteristic of nearly every speech Nestor performs in the *Iliad*.[44]

---

[40] *Iliad* 23.785–96, on which see Purves 2011: 535–6. On the theme of generational decline, especially as it applies more generally to Archaic Greek thought, see Clay 2003: 82–5; Calame 2009: 71–85; Currie 2012.

[41] Nancy himself sees the first instance of this retrospective consciousness in the figure of Odysseus. He states: "Our history begins with the departure of Ulysses and with the onset of rivalry, dissension, and conspiracy in his palace. Around Penelope, who reweaves the fabric of intimacy without ever managing to complete it, pretenders set up the warring and political scene of society—pure exteriority" (Nancy 1991: 10). More recently, Barbara Cassin (2016) offers a more in depth analysis of Odysseus and the *Odyssey* in relationship to the modern notion of nostalgia.

[42] On the history of the concept of nostalgia in the modern era and its relationship to the Hellenic tradition, see Guthenke 2008; Cassin 2016.

[43] On Nestor and *nostos*, see Chantraine 2009: 717; Frame 1978; Bonifazi 2008.

[44] On the role of the past in Nestor's speech performances, see Martin 1989: 80–1; Minchin 2005.

38 Performative Speech and the Force of Achilles

Consistent with Nancy's own explanation of retrospective consciousness, Nestor invokes the lost community of Lapiths at the moment when the community of Greek warriors at Troy is on the verge of dissolution. In this respect, Nestor delivers his diachronic scale of superiority in order to prevent that very dissolution. By creating his hierarchical scale, it would seem that Nestor is keenly aware of the true cause of the conflict between Achilles and Agamemnon. This conflict is not simply over who gets what war prize. Rather, the true source of conflict is that eternally recurring question of the *Iliad*: "Who is best?" Is it Achilles or Agamemnon?[45] Surprisingly, in response to that question, Nestor's first speech seems to answer entirely in the negative. Neither Achilles nor Agamemnon is best. Rather, the absolute standard of superiority is reserved for a generation of men who no longer exist. By reserving superlative status for a lost generation, Nestor thus attempts to end the current and continually recurring conflict over status that plagues the Greek army.

At the same time, however, the scale of superiority also has a more immediate function relative to his performative command, namely, to establish Nestor's own superior status. To be sure, Nestor does not claim to be physically or politically stronger than either Achilles or Agamemnon. Indeed, he often laments the loss of his former prowess.[46] Yet in establishing the Lapiths as an absolute standard, he ultimately offers himself as a type of representative of the Lapiths' own past greatness. Indeed, he brings up the community of Lapiths in order to isolate his own superiority separate and distinct from the current community. Immediately after describing the feats of the Lapiths, he states:

καὶ μαχόμην κατ' ἔμ' αὐτὸν ἐγώ· κείνοισι δ' ἂν οὔ τις
τῶν οἳ νῦν βροτοί εἰσιν ἐπιχθόνιοι μαχέοιτο·
καὶ μέν μευ βουλέων ξύνιεν πείθοντό τε μύθῳ·

Iliad 1.271–3

And I fought on my own. And no one
of those mortals on the earth now could fight with them.
And they listened to my counsel and obeyed my *muthos*.

---

[45] See Nagy 1979: 26. See van Wees 1992: 69–77; Scodel 2008: 127–40 on the interpretation of this question of status in relationship to Irving Goffman's *Interaction Ritual* and the issues of "deference" and "face." See Judet de la Combe 2012 for an interpretation of the crisis of the *Iliad* in metapoetic terms specific to the genre of epic.

[46] A recurring formula of Nestor is "would that my force were fixed" *βίη δέ μοι ἔμπεδος εἴη* (*Iliad* 4.314, 7.157, 11.670, 23.629). For the significance of this formula in relationship to Nestor, see Chapter 3.

Nestor's Scale of Superiority in *Iliad* 1   39

In his self-description, Nestor aligns himself with the ideal Homeric warrior as both fighter and speaker. Yet the claim itself is somewhat perplexing. On the one hand, he has brought up the Lapiths in order to establish his superiority by association. As he explained when he introduced the Lapiths: "I once kept company with men better than you" (ἤδη γάρ ποτ᾽ ἐγὼ καὶ ἀρείοσιν ἠέ περ ὑμῖν/ ἀνδράσιν ὡμίλησα) (*Iliad* 1.260–1). Yet, after describing the Lapiths and their fight with "mountain-dwelling beasts" (*Iliad* 1.268), i.e., the Centaurs, he claims "I myself fought on my own" (καὶ μαχόμην κατ᾽ ἔμ᾽ αὐτὸν ἐγώ) (*Iliad* 1.271). The preposition *kata* plus a reflexive pronoun usually has a distributive meaning such that κατ᾽ ἔμ᾽ αὐτὸν means "by myself."[47] Yet, clearly, Nestor was not entirely alone, since he states that the Lapiths took his advice, and so he presumably fought alongside them.[48] What, then, is the function of Nestor's declaration of his singularity?

On one level, Nestor's insistence on his singular status could reflect the back story of Nestor's own family history. In *Iliad* 11, Nestor describes how Heracles attacked Pylos and killed all of Neleus' sons, except for Nestor.[49] Hence, fighting by himself could mean without his brothers. Yet, the number of Nestor's brothers is by no means consistent in the Greek epic tradition, nor are their names, except for one particular brother, Periklumenos. Based on his association with this one other brother, and the potential Indo-European etymology of Nestor's own name, Douglas Frame has suggested that Nestor's singularity in Greek epic is a function of the active suppression of Nestor's association with the Indo-European twin myth.[50]

I would add that there is also a more immediate pragmatic motivation for Nestor's singularity in his opening speech of *Iliad* 1. As we have already mentioned, the entire purpose of Nestor's performative speech is to get both Achilles and Agamemnon to obey, to get them to place their faith and trust in himself. By calling direct attention to himself and his own pronouncement, Nestor's strategy is consistent with Émile Benveniste's own theory of performative speech.

In an essay titled "Analytic Philosophy and Language," originally published in 1963, Benveniste offered his own critique of J. L. Austin's theory of performatives, suggesting an alternative, which he termed

---

[47] See *LSJ* B.II and compare *Iliad* 2.336: κ. σφέας μαχέονται "they fought separately."
[48] There is an inherent ambiguity in the κείνοισι of *Iliad* 1.271 as the dative following μαχέοιτο. It could be a dative of accompaniment so that the the κείνοισι refers to the Lapiths and is the same as the subject of the verbs ξύνιεν and and πείθοντό in the next sentence. However, the T scholia gloss κείνοισι specifically as the "Centaurs." Both readings seem plausible.
[49] *Iliad* 11.692–3.   [50] See Frame 2009: 9–94.

40 Performative Speech and the Force of Achilles

énonciation.[51] In particular, Benveniste, like Bourdieu after him, criticized Austin for focusing too much on the verbal aspects of performatives. Thus, Benveniste explains:

> A performative utterance that is not an act does not exist. It has existence only as an act of authority. Now, acts of authority are first and always utterances made by those to whom the right to utter them belongs. This condition of validity, related to the person making the utterance and to the circumstances of the utterance, must always be considered met when one deals with the performative. The criterion is here and not in the choice of verbs. Any verb of speaking, even the most common of all, the verb *say*, is capable of forming a performative utterance if the formula, *I say that*..., uttered under the appropriate conditions, creates a new situation. That is the rule of the game.
>
> **(Benveniste 1971: 236)**

Here we find a near exact parallel with Bourdieu's later criticism of Austin. In anticipation of Bourdieu, Benveniste focuses on the notion of "authority," which exists outside of the verbal performance itself such that the very authority of the speaker can transform any verb of speech into a speech act. As a result, Benveniste notes that a second requirement of the performative utterance is its uniqueness as an event: "It is an event because it creates the event."[52] And lastly, again in a way that anticipates Bourdieu, Benveniste explains that the utterance of a performative is uniquely *reflexive* in so far as it calls direct attention to the speaker of the performative. Benveniste thus criticizes Austin for equating imperatives and performatives:

> An utterance is performative in that it *denominates* the act performed because Ego pronounces a formula containing a verb in the first person of the present: "*I declare* the meeting adjourned"; "*I swear* to

---

[51] In that essay, Benveniste makes a point to note that he independently developed his approach to what Austin termed "performatives" (Benveniste 1971: 234). Benveniste's theory comes in bits and pieces throughout his works, but is summarized in a later essay "L'appareil formel de l'énonciation" (Benveniste 1970). For discussion of the development of Benveniste's theory within its intellectual and historical context, see Dessons 2006; Dufaye and Gournay 2013; Angermuller 2014. For the application of Benveniste's theory of *énonciation* to Archaic Greek poetry, see esp. Calame 1995: 3–57.

[52] Benveniste 1971: 236. Consequently, this notion of the utterance constituting an event is the basis for his later definition of the utterance as an "individual act of use" as described in "L'appareil formel de l'énonciation."

Nestor's Scale of Superiority in *Iliad* 1   **41**

tell the truth." Hence a performative utterance must name the spoken performance as well as its performer. There is nothing like this in the imperative.

(Benveniste 1971: 236)[53]

Benveniste's comments on the "ego" of performative speech reflect observations he made in his earlier essay "Subjectivity in Language," first published in 1958, where he explains:

> It is in and through language that man constitutes himself as a *subject*, because language alone establishes the concept of "ego" in reality, in *its* reality which is that of the being… "Ego" is he who *says* "*egō*." That is where we see the foundation of "subjectivity," which is determined by the linguistic status of "person."
>
> **(Benveniste 1971: 224)**

This constitution of the self as a speaking subject, however, does not occur in isolation, according to Benveniste, but specifically through the dialectic that is established between the speaking subject and his or her addressee:

> It is in a dialectic reality that will incorporate the two terms [I/you] and define them by mutual relationship that the linguistic basis of subjectivity is discovered.
>
> **(Benveniste 1971: 225)**

Lastly, Benveniste singles out the performative utterance as a unique case where the formation of subjectivity is uniquely strong. Thus, when Benveniste describes performative events such as "I swear" and "I promise," he comments that "the utterance is identified with the act itself. But this condition is not given in the meaning of the verb, it is the 'subjectivity' of discourse which makes it possible."[54]

Thus, it would seem that Nestor's own rhetorical strategy in *Iliad* 1 is consistent with Benveniste's theory of the speech act as *énonciation*. On the one hand Nestor's performative may be classified simply as a command. Yet, we can follow Benveniste in understanding this command is

---

[53] Cf. Austin 1962: 60, who focuses on the implicit operation of the first person in performatives rather than in its pronouncement.

[54] Benveniste 1971: 229.

42 Performative Speech and the Force of Achilles

more than a simple imperative because it is actively calling attention to the authority of Nestor as the speaking subject in the command. As Benveniste states, "Ego is he who *says* 'ego'."[55] Not only does Nestor proclaim *egō* in his speech to Achilles and Agamemnon, but he adds a double level of reflexivity to that proclamation of *egō*. First, he makes use of the middle voice of the verb for "fighting," μαχόμην (*Iliad* 1.271). In one of his more celebrated essays, "Active and Middle Voice in the Verb," cited often by continental philosophers, Benveniste observed that the middle voice in Indo-European languages is used strictly for those activities that presuppose and require a subject.[56] And if the pronouncement of *egō* and the use of the middle voice did not provide enough emphasis on Nestor's own subjectivity, he includes the self-reflexive prepositional phrase: κατ᾽ ἔμ᾽ αὐτόν. The phrase μαχόμην/ κατ᾽ ἔμ᾽ αὐτόν/ ἐγώ (*Iliad* 1.271) thus establishes Nestor's status as subject three times over.

According to Benveniste, the pronouncement of "ego" in a performative speech is normally anchored in the present moment of speech. Yet Nestor's own self-reflexive pronouncement of "ego" is in reference to his past self. After his pronouncement of a past "ego," he then goes on to state that his past self is beyond comparison with the present generation (see *Iliad* 1.272). In this way, his egoic boast simultaneously establishes his status as a speaking subject and aligns that subject with the ultimate superiority of the Lapiths located in a distant past. And at the same time, his boast of a superior past self also excludes him from the present conflict over status in which Achilles and Agamemnon are involved. As such, Nestor establishes himself simultaneously at the highest level on the scale of superiority at the same time that he exists outside of the scale. It is that position both inside and outside the scale which serves to justify his call for obedience from both parties. Nestor's nostalgia for the past, in other words, is part of a complex performative strategy used to establish his own absolute authority, external to the conditions of the present quarrel.

Nestor's authority is well acknowledged by both Achilles and Agamemnon. Yet despite this fact, Nestor's speech ultimately fails.[57] Neither Achilles nor Agamemnon obeys his *muthos*. And so we must ask why does his speech fail and what does this failure tell us about speech and force relations in

---

[55] Benveniste 1971: 224.   [56] Benveniste 1971: 145–52.

[57] See Roisman 2005: 18; Barker 2009: 48: "Nestor's intervention has shown the desirability of mediation; but the fact that it fails defers providing any answer to the community's woes."

Nestor's Scale of Superiority in *Iliad* 1   43

the *Iliad* more generally? Typically, the failure of performative speech is attributed to a lack of acknowledged authority on the part of the speaker, or it may be the result of the deployment of a performative in the wrong context.[58] Yet neither of these reasons applies to the speech of Nestor.[59] Rather, Nestor's speech fails, I suggest, because the logic, which informs his scale of superiority, is based on a fundamental misassessment of Achilles' own force and its larger significance.[60] Through a formulaic analysis of Nestor's comparison of Achilles and Agamemnon, we will see that Nestor's attempt to make a division between the two warriors is based on gender politics among the gods. Nestor's reasoning, however, fails to account for the political significance of Achilles' own divine genealogy.

In his instructions to Achilles, Nestor first advises against quarreling with a king, based on the divine favor given from Zeus. He states:

μήτε σὺ Πηλείδη 'θελ' ἐριζέμεναι βασιλῆϊ
ἀντιβίην, ἐπεὶ οὔ ποθ' ὁμοίης ἔμμορε τιμῆς
σκηπτοῦχος βασιλεύς, ᾧ τε Ζεὺς κῦδος ἔδωκεν.

Iliad **1.277-9**

You, son of Peleus, do not wish to contend with a king,
force against force, since the scepter-bearing king
to whom Zeus has given *kudos*, has never had an equal share of *timē*.

From a formulaic perspective, the phrase "to contend with a king" has an extremely limited usage. It occurs only two other times in the *Iliad*, specifically in reference to Thersites. It is used by the narrator in describing Thersites:

ὃς ἔπεα φρεσὶν ᾗσιν ἄκοσμά τε πολλά τε ᾔδη
μάψ, ἀτὰρ οὐ κατὰ κόσμον, ἐριζέμεναι βασιλεῦσιν,
ἀλλ' ὅ τι οἱ εἴσαιτο γελοίϊον Ἀργείοισιν
ἔμμεναι· αἴσχιστος δὲ ἀνὴρ ὑπὸ Ἴλιον ἦλθε·

Iliad **2.213-16**

---

[58] See J. L. Austin 1962: 12–24; Benveniste 1971: 233–6; Bourdieu 1991: 73–5.

[59] Segal 1971a: 93 notes that Nestor has the necessary authority to speak and does indeed seem to intervene at the right time: "To intervene between two angry, violent, and powerful kings is no task to be assumed lightly; and Nestor, aged, respected, calm and reasonable is the inevitable choice, probably the only possible choice."

[60] As Cedric Whitman explains: "Nestor has stated the case precisely as Achilles will not allow it" (Whitman 1958: 157).

44 Performative Speech and the Force of Achilles

[Thersites]
who knew many unmeasured words in his mind
and how to contend with kings in vain, beyond due portion,
but [he said] whatever he thought to be amusing to the Argives
and he came to Troy as the worst of men.

And the command Nestor gives to Achilles is repeated nearly verbatim by Odysseus in his chastisement of Thersites as well:

ἴσχεο, μηδ' ἔθελ' οἶος ἐριζέμεναι βασιλεῦσιν·
οὐ γὰρ ἐγὼ σέο φημὶ χερειότερον βροτὸν ἄλλον

Iliad **2.247–8**

Hold off, and do not wish alone to contend with kings.
For I say that no other mortal is worse than you.

Given the limited scope of the formula, the occurrences of "to contend with kings" present a high degree of what Egbert Bakker terms "inter-formularity." According to Bakker, the less frequently a formula occurs within the Homeric corpus, the more likely it is that the occasions of a particular formula will consciously refer to each other.[61] Such seems to be the case with these two episodes. Scholars have long acknowledged that Thersites functions as a type of "shadow Achilles" in contesting the authority of Agamemnon. It has been debated whether Thersites is a leader or simply a member of the *dēmos* in the *Iliad*.[62] Regardless of one's take, however, it is clear that the basis for the command "do not wish to contend with king(s)" is determined based at least on *relative* inequality in social status. The formula simply implies that Agamemnon outranks the one engaged in contest with him, whether it be Achilles or Thersites.

That Agamemnon is thought to outrank Achilles is made clear by Nestor's reference to Agamemnon as the "scepter-bearing king" (σκηπτοῦχος βασιλεύς), who is given *kudos* from Zeus (*Iliad* 1.279). Although the phrase "scepter-bearing king" is a common formula,[63] Nestor's reference to Agamemnon as such may be viewed in direct response to Achilles' casting down of the herald's scepter just prior to Nestor's intervention

---

[61] Bakker 2013: 157–69.
[62] On debates concerning Thersites' status in the Achaean camp, see Rose 1988; Thalmann 1988; Lincoln 1994: 14–36; Schmidt 2002; Marks 2005: 1–6; Elmer 2013: 93–100.
[63] In the plural: *Iliad* 2.86, 8.41; *Odyssey* 4.64. In the singular, *Iliad* 1.279; *Odyssey* 2.231, 5.9.

Nestor's Scale of Superiority in *Iliad* 1   45

(*Iliad* 1.245–6). Where Achilles uses the scepter as a symbol of authoritative speech in a more general and juridical capacity (*Iliad* 1.238–9), Nestor describes the scepter as a unique privilege from Zeus specific for the *basileus*.[64] Indeed, the debate between Achilles and Agamemnon actually centers on whom Zeus will ultimately favor. In response to Achilles' first volley of insults, Agamemnon states:

φεῦγε μάλ' εἴ τοι θυμὸς ἐπέσσυται, οὐδέ σ' ἔγωγε
λίσσομαι εἵνεκ' ἐμεῖο μένειν· πάρ' ἔμοιγε καὶ ἄλλοι
οἵ κέ με τιμήσουσι, μάλιστα δὲ μητίετα Ζεύς.
ἔχθιστος δέ μοί ἐσσι διοτρεφέων βασιλήων·

Iliad 1.173–6

Flee then, if your *thumos* urges you. I do not entreat
you to remain on my account. For there are others by my side
who will honor me, especially Zeus, endowed with *mētis*.
But to me you are the most hated of divinely reared kings.

Contained within Agamemnon's initial dismissal of Achilles is the central problem of divine politics for the *Iliad* as a whole.

On the one hand, Agamemnon claims that Zeus will honor him specifically, but at the same time he acknowledges that Achilles too is a divinely reared *basileus*. In other words, all "kings" are thought to be divine to a certain extent.[65] Yet somehow Agamemnon is thought to occupy the position of "king of kings." Agamemnon's sentiment is reiterated by Odysseus in his speech to the kings in *Iliad* 2, when he states:

θυμὸς δὲ μέγας ἐστὶ διοτρεφέων βασιλήων,
τιμὴ δ' ἐκ Διός ἐστι, φιλεῖ δέ ἑ μητίετα Ζεύς.

Iliad 2.196–7

---

[64] On the scepter and connections to the relationship of the *basileus* to the divine, see Mondi 1980. For debates on the number of scepters in circulation, see van Wees 1992: 276–80; Bouvier 2002: 273–5; Unruh 2011.

[65] See Benveniste 2016: 320–7; Carlier 1984: 187–94. Of course, from a social perspective the representation of the *basileus* in Homer does not necessarily represent a "king" in the sense of sovereign monarch but most likely has more resemblance to the notion of a "chief" from Iron Age Greece, on which see Carlier 1984: 137–230; Donlan 1985; van Wees 1992: 31–6; Hall 2014: 127–34. Nevertheless, the complex and problematic nature of the transmission of Homeric poetry makes it such that the poems cannot be said to reflect a single historical time period.

46 Performative Speech and the Force of Achilles

Great is the *thumos* of divinely reared kings,
timē is from Zeus, and Zeus endowed with *mētis* loves him.

In a majority of manuscripts, and according to most scholiasts, except for Zenodotus, *Iliad* 2.196 presents "divinely reared king" in the singular in order to agree with the pronoun of *Iliad* 2.197 in reference to Agamemnon. Otherwise, it is difficult to explain how and why Agamemnon has a privileged position with Zeus, if all kings are "divinely reared."[66]

It is in view of Nestor's insistence on Agamemnon's own divine political favor that we should analyze Nestor's assessment of both Achilles and Agamemnon, when Nestor states:

εἰ δὲ σὺ καρτερός ἐσσι θεὰ δέ σε γείνατο μήτηρ,
ἀλλ' ὅ γε φέρτερός ἐστιν ἐπεὶ πλεόνεσσιν ἀνάσσει.

Iliad **1.280-1**

Perhaps you are superior, but a divine goddess as mother bore you.
But he is more superior, since he rules over more men.

As discussed at the outset of this chapter, if we take these two lines on their own, without reference to the larger speech context, then Nestor seems to create a distinction between Achilles' physical force, which has a divine source, and Agamemnon's political power, which is based in the human realm. Yet the seemingly structural opposition between Achilles and Agamemnon as a difference between the physical and political, the divine and human, does not hold if we consider the statement in relationship to Nestor's reasoning just prior to these lines, since he claims that Agamemnon's privileged position also comes from Zeus. Hence, Nestor is comparing Agamemnon's divine political power with Achilles' divine birth, rendering the former superior to the latter.

The contrast Nestor makes between divine political power and divine birth is made evident if we analyze *Iliad* 1.280 in formulaic terms. As several scholars have noted, *Iliad* 1.280 is a near exact repetition of Agamemnon's own acknowledgement of Achilles' force, when he states: "If you do have *kratos*, a god I suppose gave it to you," εἰ μάλα καρτερός ἐσσι, θεός που σοὶ

---

[66] It is precisely this problem of plurality that Odysseus further addresses in his speech to the *dēmos*, which he delivers after the speech to the kings at *Iliad* 2.200–6. Odysseus' speech to the *dēmos* is the major topic of discussion in Chapter 2.

Nestor's Scale of Superiority in *Iliad* 1   **47**

τό γ' ἔδωκεν· (*Iliad* 1.178).[67] Agamemnon's statement is consistent with yet another feature of the general cultural semantics of *kratos*, namely, that *kratos* is often conceptualized as an object given by the gods, especially by Zeus.[68] Yet in Agamemnon's statement, he supplies only a generic god, *theos*, as the source of Achilles' *kratos*. Agamemnon presumably does not name Zeus in particular because he wishes to shore up his own position of authority based on Zeus' favor. Nestor then repeats Agamemnon's acknowledgement, but with a slight variation. He replaces the generic masculine god, *theos*, with an as of yet unnamed goddess, and he replaces the act of "giving" with the act of "giving birth":

εἰ μάλα καρτερός ἐσσι, **θεός** που σοί τό γ' **ἔδωκεν·**

(*Iliad* 1.178)

εἰ δὲ σὺ καρτερός ἐσσι **θεὰ** δέ σε **γείνατο μήτηρ**

(*Iliad* 1.280)

The formula *ei* + *karteros* + verb "to be" occurs nowhere else in early Greek hexameter, and so we should consider Nestor's repetition to be very high on Bakker's scale of interformularity. That is to say, within the fictional space of the *Iliad*, Nestor was present to hear Agamemnon's words against Achilles, and so we should treat his repetition at *Iliad* 1.280 as a highly marked repetition. Nestor's acknowledgement of Achilles' superiority offers more specificity than Agamemnon with regard to its source, but it nevertheless retains the concessive quality in Agamemnon's original statement.[69] It certainly presents Achilles' force in a more positive light than Agamemnon had. Nevertheless, Nestor's comment on Achilles at *Iliad* 1.280 is still framed by two claims concerning Agamemnon's own political power:

σκηπτοῦχος βασιλεύς, ᾧ τε **Ζεὺς** κῦδος **ἔδωκεν**

(*Iliad* 1.279)

---

[67] See, among others, Leaf 1900 ad. loc; Segal 1971a: 98; van der Mije 1987: 240; Muellner 1996: 108–10; Pulleyn 2000: 200; Latacz et al. 2009: 84.

[68] Benveniste 2016: 365–6. *Kratos* as an object given: *Iliad* 1.509, 11.192, 11.207, 11.319, 11.753, 12.214, 13.743, 15.216, 16.524, 17.206, 17.613, 20.121; *Odyssey* 21.280. *Kratos* is predominantly an object given by Zeus precisely because Zeus is defined as the one with the most *kratos*, seen in the formula *kratos esti megiston*: *Iliad* 2.118, 9.25, 9.39, 13.484, 24.293, 24.311; *Odyssey* 5.4.

[69] *Pace* Segal 1971a: 99, who considers the mention of a goddess to serve the purpose of lending greater power to Achilles. See further van der Mije 1987, on the attribution of divine aid in speech as a mode of belittling other characters.

48 Performative Speech and the Force of Achilles

εἰ δὲ σὺ **καρτερός** ἐσσι **θεὰ** δέ σε **γείνατο μήτηρ**

(*Iliad* 1.280)

ἀλλ' ὅ γε **φέρτερός** ἐστιν ἐπεὶ πλεόνεσσιν ἀνάσσει.

(*Iliad* 1.281)

Despite the positive rendition of Achilles' force, the larger context of Nestor's account seems to denigrate that force by reiterating the political nature of Agamemnon's power, both from Zeus and from the warriors over whom he rules.[70] Essentially, what we have in Nestor's speech is a comparison between a male-oriented political economy shared between Zeus and the king in contrast with Achilles' genealogical power determined by his mother.

Concerning Nestor's speech, Charles Segal has claimed that "By his very commitment to the established order of things Nestor is bound to be ineffectual in affirming the justice of Achilles' position."[71] Based on our discussion of performatives, it could be said that Nestor does not merely commit to "the order of things," so much as he engages in the process of actively constructing that very order through his speech. This "order of things" is presented in Nestor's speech as a series of structural oppositions: political versus physical power, male deity (Zeus) versus female deity (*thea*), gift-giving (*dōke*) vs. birth (*geinato*). Scholars have commented well on the balanced syntactic style of Nestor's speech.[72] That balance is further reflected in structural oppositions created at the semantic level. And yet the seemingly balanced nature of these structural oppositions actually serves to reinforce hierarchy. Given the positive and comparative terms used by Nestor, *karteros* vs. *pherteros*, as it is framed within his "scale of superiority," Achilles' divine lineage, an otherwise positive feature of his identity, puts him on the wrong side of the structural paradigm, one which, according to Nestor, renders Agamemnon "stronger" than Achilles.[73]

---

[70] See also Wilson 2002: 63: "In as much as he seems to give each man his due *timē*, Nestor appears to be an impartial arbiter. But Nestor speaks from the perspective of the same model of leadership and distribution of goods as Agamemnon does." Both Kirk 1985: 81 and Latacz et al. 2009: 109–10 also see Nestor favoring Agamemnon in his assessment.

[71] Segal 1971a: 97.

[72] Lohmann 1970: 224; Martin 1989: 101–3; Toohey 1994: 154–8; Minchin 2007: 29–33.

[73] As such, Nestor simply provides an alternative form of reasoning that reiterates the relationship that Agamemnon establishes between himself and Achilles at *Iliad* 1.185–6, when he states, "In order that you may well know by how much I am stronger than you" (ὄφρ' ἐῢ εἰδῇς/ ὅσσον φέρτερός εἰμι σέθεν). See Taplin 1990: 65; Pulleyn 2000: 200.

Nestor's Scale of Superiority in *Iliad* 1   **49**

Thus, despite Nestor's own efforts to create peace through divisions and distinctions in force relations, his performative command ultimately fails, and it does so, I suggest, precisely because Nestor fails to appreciate the cosmic and political significance of Achilles' own unique genealogy.

In order to understand the cosmic implications in Achilles' genealogy, Laura Slatkin's foundational work, *The Power of Thetis*, points us to the myth of Thetis in *Isthmian* 8, where Pindar recounts that both Poseidon and Zeus were in conflict over the divine sea nymph until Themis gave a prophecy:

εἶπε δ' εὔβουλος ἐν μέσοισι Θέμις,	(31)
εἴνεκεν πεπρωμένον ἦν, φέρτερον πατέρος	
ἄνακτα γόνον τεκεῖν	
ποντίαν θεόν, ὃς κεραυ-	
νοῦ τε κρέσσον ἄλλο βέλος	(34)
διώξει χερὶ τριόδον-	(35)
τός τ' ἀμαιμακέτου, Ζηνὶ μισγομέναν	(35)
ἢ Διὸς παρ' ἀδελφεοῖσιν.	

Pindar, *Isthmian* 8.31–5

Themis of good counsel said in their midst that it was fated that the queen goddess would bear a ruler son, stronger than his father, who would wield another weapon in his hand greater than the thunderbolt or the irresistible trident, if she lay with Zeus or with the brothers of Zeus.

Pindar here uses a unique adjective in the Pindaric corpus to describe the status of the future child born from Achilles' mother Thetis: "stronger" *phrteros* (*Isthmian* 8.32). In Pindar, the term only occurs two other times (*Olympian* 1.7, *Pythian* 1.35), and so Pindar's use of the comparative here may invoke specifically Homeric associations. Indeed, all of *Isthmian* 8 seems to be focused broadly on the issue of force, since the poem was written in honor of Kleandros, the Aeginetan victor in the Pankration, and the ode begins by stating that Kleandros "found *kratos*" κράτος ἐξεῦρε (*Isthmian* 8.4–5). In *Isthmian* 8, then, we have a general discussion of *kratos*, coupled with a rare usage of the comparative *phrteros* in reference to Achilles. As such, *Isthmian* 8 helps us to better appreciate what is at stake in the comparative and superlative adjectives used by Nestor in *Iliad* 1. As Pindar states, the child born to Thetis will be *phrteros* compared with his

50 Performative Speech and the Force of Achilles

father. Pindar thus provides a mythic logic, one tied to the specific language of force, which helps us to understand the basis for Nestor's own characterization of Achilles. The implication in Nestor's claim is that because Achilles was born from Thetis to Peleus rather than to Zeus, Achilles may be "stronger," *pherteros*, than his father, but in the broader realm of mortal politics, he cannot be *pherteros* compared to Agamemnon.

Indeed, in the *Iliad*, Agamemnon's own response to Nestor's speech provides good evidence for what is at stake in Nestor's scale of superiority. Agamemnon suggests that Nestor has spoken "in good order" (*kata moiran*), but he then shifts his attention to Achilles and states:

ἀλλ᾽ ὅδ᾽ ἀνὴρ ἐθέλει περὶ πάντων ἔμμεναι ἄλλων,
πάντων μὲν κρατέειν ἐθέλει, πάντεσσι δ᾽ ἀνάσσειν,
πᾶσι δὲ σημαίνειν ἅ τιν᾽ οὐ πείσεσθαι ὀΐω·

Iliad 1.287-9

But this man wishes to be above all others
And he wishes to be superior over all, and to rule over all,
And to command all, but I think no one will obey.

Agamemnon's repetition of "all," *pantōn...pantōn...pantessi...pasi*, reverberates with Nestor's own anaphora in the repetition of *kratistoi* in reference to the Lapiths and Centaurs (*Iliad* 1.266-8). Furthermore, where Nestor states that Agamemnon "rules over more" (*Iliad* 1.281: πλεόνεσσιν ἀνάσσει), Agamemnon states that Achilles desires "to rule over all" (*Iliad* 1. 288: πάντεσσι δ᾽ ἀνάσσειν). Thus, in response to Nestor, Agamemnon suggests that Achilles desires to transcend the scale of superiority as a whole.[74] Such desire may be fueled in some sense by the missed opportunity in the conditions of his birth. Were Achilles born to Zeus rather than Peleus, Agamemnon would not be *pherteros*, and it would have been Achilles who possessed *kratos* in the superlative.[75]

Nevertheless, despite Nestor's own misassessment of Achilles, we find that Nestor does indeed eventually recognize his mistake, specifically in *Iliad* Book 9. As with *Iliad* 1, the beginning of *Iliad* 9 presents yet another

---

[74] Both Nagy 1979: 174-210 and Pucci 1998: 199-214 see such a desire expressed through the desire for *kleos*.

[75] Or as Slatkin 1991: 49 states, "The *Iliad*'s vision is of an exacting mortal aspect that exerts its leveling effect on the immortal affiliations and expectations of the hero."

Nestor's Scale of Superiority in *Iliad* 1   51

crisis of authority in the form of Diomedes' challenge to Agamemnon.[76] As in *Iliad* 1, so in *Iliad* 9, Nestor intervenes at that moment of crisis and offers a critique of Diomedes in order to maintain Agamemnon's authority.[77] Yet, immediately after Nestor's public praise of Agamemnon, in a private meeting, Nestor offers a severe criticism of Agamemnon, one which also belies Nestor's own mistaken assessment of Achilles. Nestor begins his critique by first reiterating the power of Agamemnon:

Ἀτρεΐδη κύδιστε ἄναξ ἀνδρῶν Ἀγάμεμνον
ἐν σοὶ μὲν λήξω, σέο δ' ἄρξομαι, οὕνεκα πολλῶν
λαῶν ἔσσι ἄναξ καί τοι Ζεὺς ἐγγυάλιξε
σκῆπτρόν τ' ἠδὲ θέμιστας, ἵνά σφισι βουλεύῃσθα.

Iliad 9.96–9

Son of Atreus, most glorious lord of men, Agamemnon
I will end with you and begin with you, since you are the lord
of the people and Zeus placed in your hands
the scepter and *themistes* in order that you might counsel for them.

As in *Iliad* 1, Nestor insists that the foundation of Agamemnon's power is the scepter as the material symbol of authority.[78] Nestor also introduces his critique by first establishing his own power as the speaking subject:

αὐτὰρ ἐγὼν ἐρέω ὥς μοι δοκεῖ εἶναι ἄριστα.
οὐ γάρ τις νόον ἄλλος ἀμείνονα τοῦδε νοήσει
οἷον ἐγὼ νοέω ἠμὲν πάλαι ἠδ' ἔτι καὶ νῦν

Iliad 9.103–5

But I will tell you how it seems best to me.
For no one else will make a better observation than what
I observe both before and still now...

Nestor's strategy of critique here is also similar to his speech in *Iliad* 1, in so far as his pronouncement of the "ego" is framed in incomparable terms.

---

[76] Diomedes' challenge is discussed at length in Chapter 2.
[77] On Nestor's critique, see Christensen 2009.
[78] The formula itself is also the same used by Odysseus at *Iliad* 2.206. *Themis* or the abstract plural *themistes* is also understood, in part, as a prerogative of the kings, as described by Benveniste 2016: 385–90.

52 Performative Speech and the Force of Achilles

The speaking "ego" is contrasted with "no one" *ou tis* (cf. *Iliad* 1.271, *Iliad* 9.104). This time, however, his assertion of his own power as "ego" leads to a proverbial "I told you so," i.e., that he should never have taken Briseis, the *geras* of Achilles. He states:

μάλα γάρ τοι ἔγωγε
πόλλ᾽ ἀπεμυθεόμην· σὺ δὲ σῷ μεγαλήτορι θυμῷ
εἶξας ἄνδρα φέριστον, ὃν ἀθάνατοί περ ἔτισαν,
ἠτίμησας, ἑλὼν γὰρ ἔχεις γέρας·

Iliad 9.108-11

For indeed I commanded many things. But you, having yielded to your great-hearted *thumos*, you dishonored the most superior of men, whom the gods honored, for you have his *geras*, having seized it.

In his retelling of the advice given in *Iliad* 1, we see a distinct shift in his actual assessment of Achilles. In *Iliad* 1, he had described Achilles simply as *karteros*, in contrast with Agamemnon who was described with the comparative *pherteros*. Agamemnon's superior status in *Iliad* 1, according to Nestor, was based on the divine favor of Zeus in the form of *timē*. Here in *Iliad* 9, however, Nestor contrasts Agamemnon's actions and those of the gods based precisely on the issue of *timē*: where the gods honored Achilles, Agamemnon dishonored him (*Iliad* 9.110-11: ἔτισαν/ ἠτίμησας). Thus, in *Iliad* 9, we see that Nestor has in fact changed his mind with regard to the scale of superiority he had constructed in *Iliad* 1. It has become evident to Nestor that Achilles should not be labeled merely with the positive adjective, *karteros*, nor even with the comparative *pherteros*. Rather, Nestor finally acknowledges the superlative status of Achilles as *pheristos*.[79]

Where Bourdieu had suggested that speech acts depend on objective social conditions of authority, Nestor's opening speech in *Iliad* 1 shows how speakers must often actively construct those very conditions of authority in the process of delivering their performatives. Nestor's claims regarding the asymmetries of force between Achilles and Agamemnon regarding who is "stronger" would appear to be objective. But in order to establish that appearance of objectivity, Nestor must first establish his own

---

[79] As noted by Muellner 1996: 110n.41. Similarly, as Nagy 1979: 27n.2 notes, Achilles is also one of the only heroes addressed with the alternative superlative form, *phertatos*. On the formation of the superlative *pheristos* and *phertatos* and their Indo-European inheritance, see García Ramón 2010.

authority through speech. In giving his command to obey, Nestor offers a scale of superiority which serves to re-emphasize his own status as a speaking subject vis-à-vis his audience, while that scale also serves to create a hierarchy of force relations that will prevent the Achaean camp from completely dissolving. Yet the narrative of the poem and Nestor's own words in *Iliad* 9 reveal that those conditions to which Nestor refers are by no means objective. In his effort to establish the proper relationship between himself, Achilles, and Agamemnon, Nestor himself misses the mark in the larger workings of cosmic politics. In *Iliad* 1, Nestor implicitly downgraded the role that Achilles' genealogy plays in the broader political economy of power and force shared between mortals and immortals. In his initial assessment of Achilles, Nestor failed to acknowledge the "power of Thetis."

Force, Speech, and the Genealogy of Achilles

Nestor's failure to properly acknowledge the force of Achilles, and, by extension, the power of Thetis, introduces us to a second problem concerning performative speech: What role does speech play in the relationship between force and genealogy? One might assume that a warrior's genealogy is an uncontestable and "natural" fact, such that the physical force one inherits from one's kin is equally "natural" and not subject to construction by way of speech performance. That is to say, perhaps it is a warrior's genealogy that provides those "objective conditions" for the authority of speech. Recent research in anthropology, however, has shown that even birth and genealogy should not be interpreted in terms of "nature" as opposed to "culture."[80] In his recent work, *What Kinship Is and Is Not*, Marshall Sahlins has explained that "any relationship constituted in terms of procreation, filiation, or descent can also be made postnatally or performatively by culturally appropriate action."[81] In other words, genealogical kinship, like all other forms of relationality, is itself a function of socio-cultural performance. As such, speech acts themselves, such as boasts, commands, and threats, may be considered one of the primary occasions to perform kinship and genealogy. Indeed, Nestor is not the only figure to both construct and downgrade the force and significance of Achilles' genealogy through speech. For even the gods themselves contest

---

[80] See esp. Descola 2013. [81] Sahlins 2013: 2.

54 Performative Speech and the Force of Achilles

the force of Achilles' genealogy, while Achilles himself also reconstitutes his own genealogy within the context of performative speech.

The status and significance of Achilles' genealogy and its construction through speech is most dramatically foregrounded in the confrontation between Achilles and Aeneas, two heroes born from divine mothers.[82] Much of the encounter between the two heroes deals with the subject of genealogy in direct relationship to the effectiveness, or lack thereof, regarding "fighting words."[83] In disguise as Lykaon, son of Priam, the god Apollo goads Aeneas to face Achilles, citing Aeneas' own previous boasts as a call to action (*Iliad* 20.83–95).[84] And in order to inspire confidence in Aeneas, Apollo invokes Aeneas' own genealogy. The disguised god commands:

ἥρως ἀλλ᾽ ἄγε καὶ σὺ θεοῖς αἰειγενέτῃσιν
εὔχεο· καὶ δὲ σέ φασι Διὸς κούρης Ἀφροδίτης
ἐκγεγάμεν, κεῖνος δὲ χερείονος ἐκ θεοῦ ἐστίν·
ἣ μὲν γὰρ Διός ἐσθ᾽, ἣ δ᾽ ἐξ ἁλίοιο γέροντος.
ἀλλ᾽ ἰθὺς φέρε χαλκὸν ἀτειρέα, μηδέ σε πάμπαν
λευγαλέοις ἐπέεσσιν ἀποτρεπέτω καὶ ἀρειῇ.

Iliad 20.104–9

Hero, come and pray to the ever-living gods.
Indeed, they say that you are born from Aphrodite
daughter of Zeus, but that man is from a lesser goddess.
The one (Aphrodite) is from Zeus, while the other (Thetis) is
from the old man of the sea.
But carry the tireless bronze straight, and do not let
him in any way turn you with destructive words and threats.

---

[82] This encounter itself has many resonances with the encounter between Achilles and Memnon, recounted in the *Aithiopis*, on which see Edwards 1991: 315–17. For interaction between the Homeric poems and the Epic cycle see further Burgess 2001.

[83] On the role of genealogy in this particular boast, see Muellner 1976: 74–8; Martin 1989: 85–7; Ford 1992: 64–7. On the potentially metapoetic significance of the exchange, see Nagy 1979: 270–5; Elmer 2013: 167–9. Mackie 1996: 71–4 sees the genealogy as a type of delay tactic: "His ability to continue to talk testifies to his tenacity in maintaining poetic discourse and thereby fending off fighting." Donlan 2007: 39 takes the episode as a strong indication that *genos* in Homer is "not so much a group as a cultural concept."

[84] Apollo's exhortations to Aeneas have been interpreted as a foreground to the issues of divine intervention and withdrawal of divine aid in the last five books of the *Iliad*, on which see Adkins 1975; Alden 2000: 176–8. Hesk 2006: 7–11, on the other hand, sees Apollo's intervention as a type of metacommentary on the performance of boasts more generally, since Apollo comments on Aeneas' previous boasts (*Iliad* 20.83–5).

Force, Speech, and the Genealogy of Achilles 55

Where Nestor's scale of superiority in *Iliad* 1 only implied Achilles' lesser status based on his genealogy, Apollo's states the argument outright, this time framed in negative comparative terms (*Iliad* 20.106). In Nestor's scale, however, the comparison contrasted Achilles' divine matrilineal genealogy with Agamemnon's political genealogy, signified by the scepter. But lest we think that Apollo is somehow less gender-biased, it should be noted that Apollo does not define the superiority of one goddess mother over the other in terms of their own attributes. The comparison of the two goddesses is ultimately based on the patrilineal descent of the two goddesses. Aphrodite's superiority is based on her kinship with Zeus (*Iliad* 20.107). Thus, in the case of both Nestor's scale of superiority and Apollo's own comparison, Zeus is meant to be the deciding factor.

Aeneas himself follows through on the advice given by the disguised Apollo, and when he confronts Achilles, he is sure to first address the issue of their respective genealogies. Aeneas states:

> Πηλεΐδη μὴ δὴ ἐπέεσσί με νηπύτιον ὥς
> ἔλπεο δειδίξεσθαι, ἐπεὶ σάφα οἶδα καὶ αὐτὸς
> ἠμὲν κερτομίας ἠδ' αἴσυλα μυθήσασθαι.
> ἴδμεν δ' ἀλλήλων γενεήν, ἴδμεν δὲ τοκῆας
> πρόκλυτ' ἀκούοντες ἔπεα θνητῶν ἀνθρώπων·
> ὄψει δ' οὔτ' ἄρ πω σὺ ἐμοὺς ἴδες οὔτ' ἄρ' ἐγὼ σούς.
> φασὶ σὲ μὲν Πηλῆος ἀμύμονος ἔκγονον εἶναι,
> μητρὸς δ' ἐκ Θέτιδος καλλιπλοκάμου ἁλοσύδνης·
> αὐτὰρ ἐγὼν υἱὸς μεγαλήτορος Ἀγχίσαο
> εὔχομαι ἐκγεγάμεν, μήτηρ δέ μοί ἐστ' Ἀφροδίτη·

Iliad 20.200–9

Son of Peleus, do not wish to frighten me with words
as if I were a child, since I myself know well
how to make insults and harsh words.
And we know each other's genealogies, and we know our parents
having heard the famed words of mortal men.
But you have never seen my parents with your eyes, nor I yours.
They say that you are the offspring of blameless Peleus, and
[you were born] from your mother Thetis, seaborn, of lovely hair;
but I boast to have been born the son of great-hearted Anchises
and my mother is Aphrodite.

56 Performative Speech and the Force of Achilles

In Aeneas' speech, we first see that genealogical knowledge is indeed a function of cultural performance. Aeneas explains that each know the other's lineage by way of heroic song rather than through sight (*Iliad* 20.204–5).[85] And although Aeneas does not reiterate the genealogical inequality of the two warriors in terms as stark as Apollo had described, Aeneas' speech implies genealogical superiority.[86] Aeneas accounts for Achilles' genealogy in terms of a generic "they say," φασί (*Iliad* 20.206), which contrasts with Aeneas' own proclamation of his ancestry in the form of the performative "boast," signaled through the first-person verb εὔχομαι (*Iliad* 20.209).[87] In a manner similar to Apollo's own speaking strategies, Aeneas also shifts from matriline to patriline. For even though the overall message in Aeneas' speech is that actions are better than words, Aeneas nevertheless recites his entire patrilineal genealogy, beginning first with Zeus: "Zeus the cloud gatherer first sired Dardanos" (Δάρδανον αὖ πρῶτον τέκετο νεφεληγερέτα Ζεύς) (*Iliad* 20.215).[88] And Aeneas' own performative strategy is made clear by the time he gets to the end of his genealogy, when he states:

ταύτης τοι γενεῆς τε καὶ αἵματος εὔχομαι εἶναι.
Ζεὺς δ᾽ ἀρετὴν ἄνδρεσσιν ὀφέλλει τε μινύθει τε
ὅππως κεν ἐθέλῃσιν· ὃ γὰρ κάρτιστος ἁπάντων.

Iliad **20.241–3**

I boast to be from this generation and blood.
And Zeus increases and diminishes the excellence of men,
however he wishes. For he has the most *kratos* of all.

Thus, Aeneas' recitation of his genealogy begins and ends with Zeus. His speech reiterates the belief discussed in Chapter 1 that it is Zeus who distributes *kratos* to mortal men.[89] In terms of comparative genealogical force relations, Aeneas' speech is consistent therefore with Apollo's speech and with Nestor's speech in *Iliad* 1. All three figures turn to Zeus, who

---

[85] See Ford 1992:65: "Even for these god-sprung heroes, genealogies are a matter of *kleos*."

[86] Hesk interprets the connection between Apollo's exhortation and Aeneas' counter-boast as a point of failure on the part of Aeneas because "We, the audience, know that Aeneas has received divine help with his performance" (Hesk 2006: 18).

[87] See Muellner 1976: 77–8, who also takes into account Benveniste's observations on the significance of the first-person pronouncement.

[88] On the associations of the verb *tiktein* with male-oriented conceptions of birth, see Leitao 2012: 281–4.

[89] See further Benveniste 2016: 365.

Force, Speech, and the Genealogy of Achilles 57

functions, in some sense, as the "gold standard" in the economy of force and performative power.

Of course, the supposed physical superiority that is meant to be derived from genealogy does not quite work out the way Aeneas had presumed. During their battle, it becomes clear that Achilles will overpower Aeneas.[90] And for this reason, Poseidon intervenes, making the following comment about the Trojan warrior's fate:

ὢ πόποι ἦ μοι ἄχος μεγαλήτορος Αἰνείαο,
ὃς τάχα Πηλεΐωνι δαμεὶς Ἄϊδος δὲ κάτεισι
πειθόμενος μύθοισιν Ἀπόλλωνος ἑκάτοιο
νήπιος, οὐδέ τί οἱ χραισμήσει λυγρὸν ὄλεθρον.

Iliad 20.293–6

Oh, I have grief for great-hearted Aeneas,
who will soon go down to the house of Hades
overpowered by the son of Peleus,
having trusted the words of Apollo the far shooter,
fool, nor will he ward off the destructive day for him.

Poseidon's response to the potential death of Aeneas is curious on two counts. First, Poseidon is a pro-Greek god, who intervenes on behalf of a Trojan. His intervention is inspired by his own fear of Zeus lest the patriline of Dardanos be destroyed.[91] And so, in this respect, Aeneas' boast does prove to be true, despite the fact that Aeneas was going to be beaten in combat.[92] But perhaps even more interesting is Poseidon's comment on Apollo's own intervention, where he states that Aeneas foolishly "placed his trust in the words of Apollo" (*Iliad* 20.295). In what respect, we might

[90] The term used to describe how Aeneas will be overpowered by Achilles, *dam-*, is significant and will be discussed at length in Chapter 4.

[91] Nagy 1979: 268 views Poseidon's aid in metapoetic terms as an indication that Aeneas is "beyond the scope of the Trojan War tradition in general." There is a long scholarly tradition, including, among others, Janko 1982: 158; Janko 1991: 13; Edwards 1991: 301; West 2001: 7; West 2003b: 15, and most recently Faulkner 2008, which maintains that the prophecy stated by Poseidon concerning the children of Dardanus (*Iliad* 20.302–8), a prophecy also mentioned in the *Homeric Hymn to Aphrodite* 196–7, indicates the existence of a powerful Aeneadae family in the Troad. For arguments concerning a lack of evidence for the Aeneadae see Nagy 1979: 269; van der Ben 1980; Clay 1989: 153. For a summary of the role of Poseidon's prophecy in post-Homeric literature, see Casali 2010.

[92] Achilles himself takes note of this fact when he exclaims, "Aeneas was indeed dear to the immortal gods" ἦ ῥα καὶ Αἰνείας φίλος ἀθανάτοισι θεοῖσιν (*Iliad* 20.346). And so Nagy 1979: 269 concludes, "The divine intervention of Poseidon is a clear sign even to Achilles that Aeneas had not 'boasted in vain' about his heroic identity (μὰψ αὔτως εὐχετάασθαι *Iliad* 20.348)."

58 Performative Speech and the Force of Achilles

ask, should Aeneas not have trusted Apollo? Poseidon cites the fact that Apollo did not come to his aid, and the scholia ad loc. further comment that his mother Aphrodite did not come to his aid this time either. But in terms of the content of Apollo's actual speech to Aeneas, Poseidon's claim also casts doubt on the unequal genealogical relations Apollo attempted to create between Achilles and Aeneas. Upon rescuing Aeneas, Poseidon asks him:

Αἰνεία, τίς σ' ὧδε θεῶν ἀτέοντα κελεύει
ἀντία Πηλεΐωνος ὑπερθύμοιο μάχεσθαι,
ὃς σεῦ ἅμα κρείσσων καὶ φίλτερος ἀθανάτοισιν;

Iliad 20.332-4

Aeneas, who of the gods orders you in your folly
to fight against the great-spirited son of Peleus,
who is both stronger than you and more dear to the immortals?

Of course, Poseidon's question is rhetorical and simply highlights that Poseidon's own assessment of the two warriors is quite different from that of Apollo. Where Apollo had implied that Achilles was inferior because of his genealogy (*Iliad* 20.106), Poseidon insists that Achilles is superior (*Iliad* 20.332–4). In this regard, the use of the comparatives in the speeches of Apollo and Poseidon in *Iliad* 20 take the inherent *relativity* of power relations one step further than *Iliad* 1. In the case of Nestor's initial scale of superiority, one might attribute Nestor's own misassessment of Achilles and the significance of his genealogy to the fundamental limitations of mortal knowledge. Yet in *Iliad* 20, we find contradiction even among the gods themselves concerning the hierarchy of mortal power relations. Thus, the designation "stronger" is not determined by genealogy per se, but the very use of genealogy and such comparative adjectives such as "stronger" and "weaker" should be seen as rhetorical "power moves" in and of themselves. That is to say, the use of such comparative force terms should be viewed as critical strategies for performative speech. At the same time, however, as we see with Achilles and Poseidon, those particular relations constructed through speech can just as well be overturned by the actions of others or by counter speech acts.

Why then, we might ask, is Achilles himself continually undervalued in the *Iliad* by both mortals and immortals? If we follow Slatkin on the "power of Thetis," then we might surmise that the undervaluing of

Achilles is a function of the unique quality of Thetis' particular power. As Slatkin explains:

> The central element in the structure of Thetis's mythology...is the covertness of her power; it is a secret weapon, a concealed promise, a hidden agenda requiring discovery, revelation. It is precisely this covert, latent aspect of Thetis's potential in cosmic relations to which the *Iliad* draws attention as well, both exploiting and reinforcing it *as allusion.*
>
> **(Slatkin 1991: 83)**

The allusive power of Thetis is conveyed through the fact that her power is one of birth. And it is precisely because of the nature of that power that she has had to suffer—by being married off to the mortal Peleus and giving birth to a mortal son. Hence, the source of her power is also the source of her suffering. Yet it is her latent, unrealized power, and the suffering that comes from it, which in turn give her a privileged status with Zeus himself. In this regard, the power of Thetis and its impact on Achilles will always be misassessed because it can never be openly pronounced or performed.

The fact that the power of Thetis cannot be so easily performed is made most evident in a unique boast of Achilles after he has slain the warrior Asteropaeus in *Iliad* 21. Like other warriors in the *Iliad*, Achilles too makes use of comparative adjectives coupled with genealogical justification to bolster his power and status.[93] He states:

κεῖσ' οὕτως· χαλεπόν τοι ἐρισθενέος Κρονίωνος
παισὶν ἐριζέμεναι ποταμοῖό περ ἐκγεγαῶτι.   (185)
φῆσθα σὺ μὲν ποταμοῦ γένος ἔμμεναι εὐρὺ ῥέοντος,
αὐτὰρ ἐγὼ γενεὴν μεγάλου Διὸς εὔχομαι εἶναι.
τίκτέ μ' ἀνὴρ πολλοῖσιν ἀνάσσων Μυρμιδόνεσσι
Πηλεὺς Αἰακίδης· ὃ δ' ἄρ' Αἰακὸς ἐκ Διὸς ἦεν.
τὼ κρείσσων μὲν Ζεὺς ποταμῶν ἁλιμυρηέντων,   (190)
κρείσσων αὖτε Διὸς γενεὴ ποταμοῖο τέτυκται.
καὶ γὰρ σοὶ ποταμός γε πάρα μέγας, εἰ δύναταί τι
χραισμεῖν· ἀλλ' οὐκ ἔστι Διὶ Κρονίωνι μάχεσθαι,
τῷ οὐδὲ κρείων Ἀχελώϊος ἰσοφαρίζει,

---

[93] Of course, in this case, he has already demonstrated his superiority and gives his boast addressed to Asteropaeus after he has already slain him. See Donlan 2007: 38.

60 Performative Speech and the Force of Achilles

οὐδὲ βαθυρρείταο μέγα σθένος Ὠκεανοῖο,   (195)
ἐξ οὗ περ πάντες ποταμοὶ καὶ πᾶσα θάλασσα
καὶ πᾶσαι κρῆναι καὶ φρείατα μακρὰ νάουσιν·
ἀλλὰ καὶ ὃς δείδοικε Διὸς μεγάλοιο κεραυνὸν
δεινήν τε βροντήν, ὅτ' ἀπ' οὐρανόθεν σμαραγήσῃ.

Iliad **21.184–91**

Lie thus, for it is indeed difficult for you to contend
with the children of the excessively strong son of Cronus,
even if you have been born from a river.
For you say that you are from the race of a wide flowing river,
but I boast that my genealogy is from great Zeus.
For Peleus, son of Aeacus, a man ruling over many Myrmidons,
sired me. And Aeacus was born from Zeus.
Just as Zeus is stronger than rivers flowing to the sea,
so the generation from Zeus has been made stronger than that of
the rivers.
For there is a great river beside you, if it is able to help some.
But it is not possible to fight with Zeus the son of Cronus,
not even the very powerful Acheloeus equal him, nor the strength of
deep-eddying Ocean,
from which all rivers and the entire sea, and all springs and great
wells flow,
but even he is afraid of the lightning of great Zeus
and the terrible thunder, when it crashes from the sky.

In the very first lines of this speech, Achilles contrasts Asteropaeus' river genealogy, traced to the river Axios, with his own. It is surprising that here Achilles would not pronounce his own status as the son of the goddess Thetis. In his slaying of Lykaon, just prior to his encounter with Asteropaeus, Achilles pronounced his "beauty and greatness" as a function of both parents, Peleus and Thetis.[94] In his encounter with Asteropaeus, however, he chooses to perform his patriline alone, which he ties back to Zeus through two prior generations.[95] On the one hand, by leaving out

---

[94] *Iliad* 21.108–10. See further Coray and Krieter-Spiro 2021: 112–13 on Achilles' strategies for genealogical boasting. Part of Achilles' own logic in boasting of his divine lineage to Lykaon is that even he, Achilles, son of an immortal must die, and so too will Lykaon.

[95] As Schein 1984: 122n.8 has noted, the poet of *Iliad* 21 seems to reconfirm this genealogy by the constant reference to Achilles as Aeakides.

Force, Speech, and the Genealogy of Achilles   61

Thetis, Achilles may be matching patriline for patriline with Asteropaeus, since Asteropaeus had pronounced his own patriline from Axios before they engaged in battle (*Iliad* 21.152–60). At the same time, however, Achilles is fairly explicit that it is his patrilineal connection to Zeus that allowed him to overpower Asteropaeus (*Iliad* 21.190–1). Can we take Achilles' own genealogical explanation at face value? Is Achilles' superiority based solely on his Zeus-born patriline? Such a claim can only be partially true, since his birth from Thetis is what has allowed him not only to equal but also to surpass his own patriline, to be "stronger than the father."[96] In this regard, Achilles' failure to mention Thetis in his own genealogical boast is telling. Despite Thetis' power and influence, Achilles instead makes use of the same genealogical strategy that Aeneas used against him—he invokes Zeus as the ultimate standard.

From a narrative perspective, Achilles' belittlement of Asteropaeus' river genealogy serves to anticipate Achilles' own battle with the river Scamander in *Iliad* 21. Given the unique situation in which Scamander mobilizes himself against Achilles, not in human form but *qua* river, one might be inclined to interpret Achilles' battle with Scamander in broad structuralist terms, as a matter of "culture vs. nature."[97] Recently, however, Brooke Holmes has offered an analysis of the Scamander episode in terms that move beyond the culture vs. nature paradigm.[98] Instead, Holmes invokes a notion of "natureculture," developed by Donna Haraway.[99] According to Holmes, "Haraway's neologism … does not situate itself in an orthogonal relation to a discourse of 'nature and culture' but, rather, attends to the thick skein of manifold differences between human and non-human—in short, to relationality as dynamic and specific."[100] Indeed, it is precisely the dynamic, physical force of Scamander, combined with its motivation

---

[96] See Slatkin 1991: 70–2.

[97] On this quintessential structuralist opposition, see the works of Lévi-Strauss, esp. Lévi-Strauss 1969. On its application to Homeric poetry, see Redfield 1994 (originally published 1975), although it should be noted that Redfield complicates the opposition rather than reducing episodes in the *Iliad* to such terms, and Redfield himself states, "I do not declare myself a structuralist. The distinction between nature and culture is not the property of any school; it is already present in Aristotle's remark that 'of things, some are by nature and some are by other causes' " (Redfield 1994: xii).

[98] Indeed, "nature" or *phusis* does not come about as a category of analysis in Greek thought until later, on which see Naddaf 2005. In addition, as Phillipe Descola 2013 has argued, the modern analytic category of "nature" in opposition to culture can itself be seen as a product of intellectual trends from the nineteenth century, and may not be so useful for other cultures and time periods.

[99] Haraway 2003. Haraway's term, however, was developed within the context of "companion species."

[100] Holmes 2015: 33.

62 Performative Speech and the Force of Achilles

for intervention in the battle, which gives the best representation of the "natureculture" paradigm at work. On the one hand, Holmes notes, Scamander's significance in the episode is informed by the sheer physical force of water and wind that is capable of overtaking everything in its path. On the other hand, the river Scamander demonstrates a "will-to-protect" that results from the kourotrophic function of the river as a protective agent, who has played a key role in coming of age rituals for young Trojans.[101] Thus, Scamander represents both "nature and culture" or "nature and nurture" simultaneously.

The concept of "natureculture," I suggest, could be applied not just to the river Scamander, but to the role of genealogy more generally, especially in the *Iliad*. Indeed, as we have seen already, genealogy and kinship can be understood at a general level as a function of performance, and this is why Sahlins has proclaimed that kinship is not "nature" but "culture." At the same time, when performative kinship includes relations with nonhuman life, then kinship genealogies may be better described as a function of "natureculture."[102] In fact, the Archaic Greek language of force presents us with at least two terms that capture perfectly the concept of "natureculture" inherent in genealogy, namely *menos* and *sthenos*.

Thus far, we have already been introduced to the possibility of separate semantic spheres for force through the usages of *menos* and *kratos*. *Kratos* is broadly understood as a form of "superiority" used in the context of competition and is external to the subject. By contrast, as explained earlier, *menos* is understood in fairly physical terms as a person's "life force," internal to the human subject. At the same time, *menos* may also apply to "natural" elements, especially fire.[103] Lastly, as a "life force" etymologically born out of the root related to memory, **men-*, *menos* is also explicitly associated with the force of one's ancestors. Thus, Athena places "paternal *menos*" (μένος πατρώϊον) (*Iliad* 5.125) in Diomedes while he fights, and she also places *menos* in Telemachus in the *Odyssey* in order that he might remember his father (*Odyssey* 1.88–90).[104]

---

[101] Holmes 2015: 42–6. On the kourotrophic function of rivers more generally see Burkert 1985: 196–7.

[102] Sahlins himself is well aware of the ways in which performative kinship cuts across the nature-culture divide, and his many examples of performative kinship do include cultures who establish kin relations with nonhuman life. See Sahlins 2013: 30. In addition, Haraway's concept of "natureculture" is equally concerned with kinship. As she states, "In old fashioned terms, the Companion Species Manifesto is a kinship claim" (Haraway 2003: 9). Haraway follows through with this claim in her subsequent work *Staying with the Trouble: Making Kin in the Chthuluscene* (2016).

[103] *Iliad* 6.182, 16.621, 17.565, 22.96, 23.177, 23.190–1, 23.237–9.

[104] See Nagy 1974: 266–9; Collins 1998: 111–12; Bakker 2008: 69–70; Bakker 2013: 147.

Force, Speech, and the Genealogy of Achilles   63

The term *sthenos* occupies a similar range of contexts as *menos*, dealing with the physical body, "natural forces," and genealogy, but it also remains distinct. First and foremost, *sthenos* seems to refer to a type of general "strength" associated with bodily action.[105] In this respect, *sthenos* can often be paired with other types of force, including *kratos*.[106] And like other forms of force, *sthenos* can be placed into the body by gods.[107] The embodied force of *sthenos*, however, extends beyond the human-god threshold. Several times, a warrior's power is compared with the *sthenos* of animals.[108] And lastly, the term *sthenos* can also refer to the force of non-human, non-animal entities including rivers and the Ocean.[109] Thus, on the one hand, if one were inclined to refer to the strength of *sthenos* as "embodied," it could only be true if bodily strength also included not just anthropomorphic and zoomorphic bodies, but also other material "bodies," such as that of water. On the other hand, one might be inclined to refer to this type of strength referenced by *sthenos* as "natural." Yet we see that the "natural" strength of *sthenos* is not just "naturally occurring" or a "natural attribute" of the body but can be placed there by gods. Like *menos*, this "natural" and "embodied" form of force found in *sthenos* is just as much a part of the larger political economy of power that is shared between mortals and immortals. Thus, both *sthenos* and *menos* give expression, albeit in different ways, to the force of "natureculture" because they are both embodied, one internal to the body, the other in action, and because both include nonhuman forces, and lastly, because both are also part of an economy shared between humans and gods.

But it is in Achilles' speech over the corpse of Asteropaeus that we see most clearly the genealogical implications involved with the "natureculture" of *sthenos*. Indeed, Achilles' speech is in fact framed by the concept of *sthenos*. First, when Achilles compares the power of the "children of the

---

[105] *Iliad* 15.358: the narrator compares the path created by Apollo over the ditches of the Achaean camp to the length of a spear throw when a man "tries his strength" (σθένεος πειρώμενος). *Iliad* 20.361: Achilles refers to his own efforts against the Trojans through the use of his "hands, feet, and strength" (χερσίν τε ποσίν τε/ καὶ σθένει). *Iliad* 23.827, in reference to the pig iron, which "formerly the great strength of Eëtion used to throw" (ὃν πρὶν μὲν ῥίπτασκε μέγα σθένος Ἠετίωνος·). And lastly, the term is also used in the *Odyssey*, when the Phaeacian youth Laomedon refers to the athletic build of Odysseus in terms of body parts, *Odyssey* 8.136.

[106] *kratos* and *sthenos* paired: *Iliad* 8.32, 8.463, 15.108, 17.322, 17.329; *alkē* and *sthenos* paired: *Iliad* 17.212, 17.499.

[107] See *Iliad* 2.451, 11.11, 14.151, 17.212, 17.499, 21.304. These usages of *sthenos* are described in terms of interiority.

[108] See *Iliad* 5.139, 5.783, 7.257, 8.337, 12.42, 17.22, 17.135. Other terms for force, esp. *alkē* and *biē*, also apply to animals, on which see the entries in the appendix.

[109] For example, at *Iliad* 17.751, 18.607, 21.195.

64 Performative Speech and the Force of Achilles

son of Cronus" with Asteropaeus' *genos* from a river, he refers to Zeus as *eristhenos*, i.e. having much *sthenos* (*Iliad* 21.184). That Zeus possesses not only the most *kratos* but also *sthenos* is made evident in his threats against the Olympians in *Iliad* 8.[110] And then Achilles concludes his speech by saying that Zeus is not only greater than the rivers, but even greater than the Ocean, the source of all bodies of water. Here Achilles specifically invokes the notion of *sthenos* a second time (*Iliad* 21.195). Thus, the speech offers an implicit comparison between the *sthenos* of Zeus, an Olympian god, and the *sthenos* of the Ocean. This comparison is framed in terms of unequal relations of force when he asserts: "Just as Zeus is stronger than rivers flowing to the sea/ so the generation from Zeus has been made stronger than that of the rivers" (*Iliad* 21.190–1). As with his conflict with the river Scamander, one might be inclined to interpret Achilles' claim in terms of the nature-culture divide, where the anthropomorphic, Olympian Zeus has a quality of physical force superior to "natural" forces. Yet in the comparison, Achilles makes use of Zeus' own power in the "natural" world, namely, through lightning and thunderbolts. Zeus, in other words, as the sky god, is just as much a part of the "natural" world as the Ocean and the rivers.[111] Thus, here too Achilles' speech anticipates his conflict with Scamander as a conflict between the forces of fire and water.[112]

Lastly, when we compare Achilles' speech with the broader narrative context of *Iliad* 21, we see that the "natureculture" of genealogy nevertheless remains inherently contingent and performative. Achilles may have proved physically superior to Asteropaeus, and his boast confirms this fact. But it is important to note that his genealogical reasoning does not apply *tout court*. In the first place, there is an inherent contradiction in his claim that the children of Zeus are stronger than the children of rivers (*Iliad* 21.191). His claim implies a typological divide between Olympian genealogies and "nature" genealogies. And yet we are told at the outset of *Iliad* 21 that the river Scamander, also known as Xanthus, is in fact a child of Zeus as well (*Iliad* 21.1–2). The bT scholia are especially concerned with the contradiction between Achilles' claim that the Ocean is "that from which all rivers exist" (*Iliad* 21.196) and Scamander's genealogy from Zeus. The scholia resolve the conflict by explaining that Zeus is the father

---

[110] See *Iliad* 8.32 with Athena speaking and *Iliad* 8.463 with Hera speaking. This episode is discussed in greater detail in Chapter 2.

[111] Redfield 1994: 250n.15: "The combat between Achilles and Asteropaeus is represented as a combat between two natural spheres."

[112] Coray and Krieter-Spiro 2021: 113; Whitman 1958: 139–43.

The Force of Zeus and Its Performative Limits   **65**

of Scamander, but Ocean is the "chorus leader" or director of its flow (ῥεύματος χορηγός).[113] Yet, despite the scholia's genealogical reasoning, the discrepancy remains. As Holmes explains, "Achilles' oversight drives home his heedless violation of the divine river's honor."[114] Indeed, as the narrative shows, Achilles himself would have succumbed to the force of the river were it not for the intervention of Hephaestus, a fact that Achilles himself also acknowledges (cf. *Iliad* 21.274–83).[115] Once more, then, through an analysis of the deployment of comparatives, we see how a character's effort to construct a specific force relation in speech is in fact contradicted by the narrative events and broader context of that speech. Such contradiction occurs even when that speech is based on the seemingly "natural" category of genealogy, and even when that speech is delivered by the divinely favored Achilles.

The Force of Zeus and Its Performative Limits

Thus far, the effort of various characters in the *Iliad* to determine who precisely is "stronger" has seemed entirely contingent on speech performance. Nevertheless, there has remained one constant in each of these speeches: the figure of Zeus. Indeed, Nestor, Aeneas, Apollo, Poseidon, and even Achilles himself have appealed to Zeus as an absolute standard of superiority. Just as Bourdieu had used the example of the Homeric scepter as a demonstration that the authority of performative speech must come from an external source, so Zeus, who is the reason for the authority of the Homeric scepter, stands as the extreme case of the external source of force for various speakers throughout the *Iliad*. But despite this basic agreement among characters in the *Iliad*, Zeus' own force remains relational and contingent throughout the poem. Such contingent relationality is best observed in the threat Zeus delivers to Poseidon by way of Iris in *Iliad* 15, after Poseidon has intervened in the Trojan war contrary to Zeus' command. A formulaic analysis of the language of Zeus' command and Poseidon's

---

[113] According to the Hesiodic tradition, however, Scamander/Xanthus is said to be born from Tethys and Ocean (see *Theogony* 337–45).

[114] Holmes 2015: 43.

[115] Achilles' potential death from Scamander thus reflects the death without burial that Achilles has imposed on his own victims in *Iliad* 21. For the significance of these deaths in *Iliad* 21 in relation to the theme of the "mutilation of the corpse" see Segal 1971b: 30–2; Redfield 1994: 168–9. For further discussion of the significance of mutilation as an inversion of "beautiful death" see Vernant 1991: 50–74.

66 Performative Speech and the Force of Achilles

reaction to that command reveals a type of limit case for the ways in which force in the *Iliad* is always under negotiation, even among the immortals.

At the beginning of *Iliad* 15, the self-proclaimed pre-eminence of Zeus is re-emphasized, when all the gods, even Hera, conform to the command first uttered by Zeus in *Iliad* 8.[116] After the other gods have capitulated to Zeus, Poseidon, however, remains on the battlefield, and here is where Zeus once again delivers a speech professing his superiority. The speech, however, is given to Iris to deliver, and in this way, as the scholia explain, a direct confrontation between the two sons of Cronus is avoided. Zeus' order to Iris, and his indirect command to Poseidon, is as follows:

βάσκ᾽ ἴθι Ἶρι ταχεῖα, Ποσειδάωνι ἄνακτι
πάντα τάδ᾽ ἀγγεῖλαι, μὴ δὲ ψευδάγγελος εἶναι.
παυσάμενόν μιν ἄνωχθι μάχης ἠδὲ πτολέμοιο
ἔρχεσθαι μετὰ φῦλα θεῶν ἢ εἰς ἅλα δῖαν.
εἰ δέ μοι οὐκ ἐπέεσσ᾽ ἐπιπείσεται, ἀλλ᾽ ἀλογήσει,
φραζέσθω δὴ ἔπειτα κατὰ φρένα καὶ κατὰ θυμὸν
μή μ᾽ οὐδὲ κρατερός περ ἐὼν ἐπιόντα ταλάσσῃ
μεῖναι, ἐπεί εὖ φημὶ βίῃ πολὺ φέρτερος εἶναι
καὶ γενεῇ πρότερος· τοῦ δ᾽ οὐκ ὄθεται φίλον ἦτορ
ἶσον ἐμοὶ φάσθαι, τόν τε στυγέουσι καὶ ἄλλοι.

Iliad **15.158–67**

Go then Iris, quickly and announce all the following
to lord Poseidon, and do not give a false message.
Order him, after stopping from battle and war,
to go among the tribes of the gods or into the divine sea.
And if he does not obey my words, but pays no regard,
let him ponder in his mind and *thumos*
that he not endure to stand against me when I come at him
though he has *kratos*, since I say that I am stronger by far in *biē*
and older in age. Yet in his heart he does not hesitate
to say he is equal to me, before whom others shudder.

As several scholars have noted, Zeus' speech shares several formulaic parallels, which are common only with the conflict between Achilles and

---

[116] See esp. Hera's speech: *Iliad* 15.104–9.

The Force of Zeus and Its Performative Limits   67

Agamemnon.[117] In this regard, we might consider the two conflicts, Agamemnon vs. Achilles and Zeus vs. Poseidon, in interformulaic terms. The two conflicts, Achilles vs. Agamemnon and Poseidon vs. Zeus, both center on the issue of unequal relations of force. Indeed, within Zeus' speech, we see that Zeus actually anticipates Poseidon's noncompliance and even provides a reason for that noncompliance: because Poseidon dares "to say he is equal to me" (ἶσον ἐμοὶ φάσθαι) (*Iliad* 15.183–7). Other than Iris' repetition of Zeus' words (*Iliad* 15.187), the only other occurrence of this formula is in Agamemnon's quarrel with Achilles, when Agamemnon states:

... ἐγὼ δέ κ' ἄγω Βρισηΐδα καλλιπάρηον
αὐτὸς ἰὼν κλισίην δὲ τὸ σὸν γέρας ὄφρ' ἐῢ εἰδῇς
ὅσσον φέρτερός εἰμι σέθεν, στυγέῃ δὲ καὶ ἄλλος
ἶσον ἐμοὶ φάσθαι καὶ ὁμοιωθήμεναι ἄντην.

Iliad 1.184–6

And I would lead away fair-cheeked Briseis, your *geras*,
going to your tent myself in order that you may know well
how much I am stronger than you, and any other will shudder
to say he is equal to me and to compare himself face to face.

Not only do both Zeus and Agamemnon argue against any claims for equality, but both also make a claim to being "stronger," *pherteros* (*Iliad* 1.185, 15.165).[118] At the same time, I would note, Zeus' own comparison of himself and Poseidon also invokes the "scale of superiority" used by Nestor, first discussed at the beginning of this chapter. Just as Nestor had framed the difference between Achilles and Agamemnon as a difference between *karteros* and *pherteros*, so Zeus makes the same distinction between himself and Poseidon:

μή μ' οὐδὲ κρατερός περ ἐὼν ἐπιόντα ταλάσσῃ
μεῖναι, ἐπεί εὑ φημὶ βίῃ πολὺ φέρτερος εἶναι

Iliad 15.164–5

---

[117] Reinhardt 1961: 285–6; Janko 1991: 245; Lowenstam 1993: 73–7; Muellner 1996: 29–30, 109–11; Yasumura 2011: 66–70.

[118] One may further note a transfer of the formulaic expression "another fears/shudders" στυγ- + ἄλλος/ἄλλος (*Iliad* 1.185/15.167), although that is a more common formula occurring five times in total in the *Iliad* (1.186, 7.112, 8.515, 15.167, 15.183), but it is still a relatively limited usage of that formula.

68 Performative Speech and the Force of Achilles

Let him not endure to stand against me when I come at him,
strong though he be, for I claim to be stronger by far in force.

Compare with:

εἰ δὲ σὺ <u>καρτερός</u> ἐσσι θεὰ δέ σε γείνατο μήτηρ,
ἀλλ' ὅ γε <u>φέρτερός</u> ἐστιν ἐπεὶ πλεόνεσσιν ἀνάσσει.

Iliad 1.280–1

Perhaps you have *kratos*, but a goddess mother bore you.
But he is stronger since he rules over more men.

In Nestor's attempt at reconciliation, Nestor created an opposition between the two warriors based on the difference between the physical, embodied force of Achilles and the political power of Agamemnon (which involves control over multiple bodies). In Zeus' rendition of this comparison, however, we do not see such a distinction nor is it for the sake of reconciliation. Rather, Zeus claims to be superior precisely in terms of "force," *biē*. Indeed, where Benveniste noted that *kratos* did not mean "force" per se, it is in fact the concept of *biē* that connotes the quintessential notion of "force" as physical violence.[119] At the same time, however, upon closer examination of Poseidon's response, it becomes clear that Poseidon actually robs Zeus of the force relation he aims to construct, despite Poseidon's eventual obedience.

When Iris delivers Zeus' command to Poseidon, we find a near verbatim repetition of Zeus' words, except for one telling difference. Iris simply explains that Zeus threatens to come down and meet Poseidon and she does not repeat the negative command, which involves the concessive participial phrase describing Poseidon, "although he has *kratos*" (κρατερός περ ἐών) (*Iliad* 15.164). But Iris does repeat Zeus' own claim to be "stronger by far in physical force" (βίῃ πολὺ φέρτερος εἶναι) (cf. *Iliad* 15.164–5; 15.179–81). The same concessive participial phrase, "although he has *kratos*," however, is in fact restated, only it is restated by Poseidon in response to Zeus, explaining that he will not comply:

καὶ κρατερός περ ἐὼν μενέτω τριτάτῃ ἐνὶ μοίρῃ.
χερσὶ δὲ μή τί με πάγχυ κακὸν ὣς δειδισσέσθω·

Iliad 15.195–6

---

[119] The concept of *biē* will be discussed at length in Chapter 3.

The Force of Zeus and Its Performative Limits   69

And although he has *kratos*, let him remain in his third portion,
and let him not make me afraid with his hands as though I were base.

The transfer of the referent for the concessive participial phrase, "although he has *kratos*," from Poseidon to Zeus has an important effect: it functionally denies Zeus' initial force claim. Just as Zeus acknowledged that Poseidon has *kratos*, Poseidon does the same, and in doing so, he denies that Zeus is *pherteros* (*Iliad* 15.165). In fact, Poseidon's entire response is framed by concessive participle phrases in reference to Zeus. Where he concludes his speech with "although he has kratos" (κρατερός περ ἐὼν) (*Iliad* 15.195), he begins his speech describing Zeus with the statement, "oh, good though he be, he has spoken insolently" (ὦ πόποι ἦ ῥ' ἀγαθός περ ἐὼν ὑπέροπλον ἔειπεν) (*Iliad* 15.185). The formula "good though he be" (ἀγαθός περ ἐὼν) has a limited scope in the *Iliad*, and the limited scope makes the sequence of usages itself significant. The first time the formula occurs is when Agamemnon warns Achilles not to try and deceive him "good though he be" (*Iliad* 1.131). The phrase is then repeated by Nestor in *Iliad* 1 in reference to Agamemnon (*Iliad* 1.275). And finally, it is used once more of Achilles in *Iliad* 19, when Odysseus argues against Achilles about going directly into the fight without eating (*Iliad* 19.155). The phrase is thus used primarily of Achilles, and it is used generally in conflicts over status aimed at limiting Achilles' own power. Taken together, then, Poseidon's double use of concessive participial phrases, "good though he be" (ἀγαθός περ ἐὼν) (*Iliad* 15.185) and "though he has *kratos*" (κρατερός περ ἐὼν) (*Iliad* 15.195), does double duty in attempting to limit the power of Zeus.

. In his response, Poseidon effectively transfers the issue of authority from physical force or *biē*, as described by Zeus, to issues of status or *timē*. In his defense, Poseidon specifically offers an account of the equal division of *timē* between himself, Hades, and Zeus:

τρεῖς γάρ τ' ἐκ Κρόνου εἰμὲν ἀδελφεοὶ οὓς τέκετο Ῥέα,
Ζεὺς καὶ ἐγώ, τρίτατος δ' Ἀΐδης ἐνέροισιν ἀνάσσων.
τριχθὰ δὲ πάντα δέδασται, ἕκαστος δ' ἔμμορε τιμῆς·

Iliad 15.187–9

For we three from Cronus are brothers, whom Rhea bore,
Zeus and I, and Hades as the third, ruling over those below.
And all has been divided in three, and each received his portion of *timē*.

70   Performative Speech and the Force of Achilles

Here Poseidon gives an account of the division of the cosmos, quite distinct from that presented in the Hesiodic *Theogony*, where Zeus himself was chosen as the one in charge of the distribution of *timai* among the Olympian gods (*Theog.* 885).[120] As Christopher Faraone has noted, this discrepancy reflects "oligarchic" versus "monarchic" views of cosmic organization:

> Hesiod famously suppresses the myth that Zeus, Poseidon, and Hades divided the world among themselves, with each ruling over his own province. This alternate story presents, in a way, an oligarchic or balkanized vision of divine politics: there is no omnipotent monarch, but rather the universe is shared by three powerful brothers who reign as independent princes. The central theme of the Hesiodic *Theogony*, on the other hand, is one of monarchic succession (son following father) to a single hereditary throne and then the permanent monarchy of Zeus as guarantor of divine and universal order.
>
> **(Faraone 2012: 45–6)**

The point here is that origin myths may change to fit poetic context just as much as genealogies of individual characters can change to fit performative speech contexts. And so, in addition to monarchic vs. oligarchic, we could also call the difference between the two traditions "patriarchal" vs. "fraternal."[121] What is especially striking is that Poseidon's insistence on the oligarchic or fraternal cosmogony highlights the same tension *within* the *Iliad* as that which exists between the Iliadic and Theogonic traditions. For Poseidon cites the fraternal division in response to Zeus' own gestures toward monarchic or patriarchal power among the gods. This is precisely why Poseidon concludes his response by asserting that such commands are more suited for Zeus' own children (*Iliad* 15.198–9).[122]

---

[120]   See further Janko 1992: 247, who suggests, based on parallels in Apollodorus (1.2.1) and the Orphica (frag. 56), that this particular account is based on an earlier version of the Titanomachy. For accounts of this division as it pertains to Near Eastern myth, see Burkert 1992: 90–1; West 1997: 109–10; Rollinger 2015: 19–21; Lardinois 2018: 909–15.

[121]   On the patriarchal ideology of the *Theogony*, see Arthur [Katz] 1982; Zeitlin 1996; Clay 2003: 27–8; Stocking 2017a: 55–89.

[122]   Graziosi and Haubold 2005: 71 dub Poseidon's challenge "the most serious in the whole of the *Iliad*." And as Pucci 2018: 197 states, "With this statement, the *Iliad* has Poseidon give a neat formulation of the motif that Zeus has no more legitimate, superior power over the world and human destinies than do his brothers and sisters. He denies him his supremacy on Olympus and his role as god of fate."

The Force of Zeus and Its Performative Limits   71

By representing the conflict with Zeus as a quarrel over *timē*, we are presented with a variation of the conflict over *timē* between Achilles and Agamemnon. The difference between Achilles and Agamemnon's quarrel versus that between Poseidon and Zeus is highlighted by a very precise formulaic intertext. When Poseidon explains that Zeus, Poseidon, and Hades are on equal terms, he states "each received his portion of *timē*" (ἕκαστος δ' ἔμμορε τιμῆς) (*Iliad* 15.189). The formula ἔμμορε τιμῆς occurs nowhere else in the *Iliad*, except in Nestor's speech from *Iliad* 1. Thus, the formula is extremely high on Bakker's scale of interformularity and it is instructive to read the two episodes in reference to each other. The limited distribution of this formula highlights the difference in usage and context. In Nestor's speech, the formula was used to argue that Agamemnon in fact had greater *timē* because of this superior position of kingship. Thus, Nestor chided Achilles for contending with Agamemnon:

μήτε σὺ Πηλείδη 'θελ' ἐριζέμεναι βασιλῆϊ
ἀντιβίην, ἐπεὶ οὔ ποθ' ὁμοίης ἔμμορε τιμῆς
σκηπτοῦχος βασιλεύς, ᾧ τε Ζεὺς κῦδος ἔδωκεν.

Iliad 1.277–9

You, son of Peleus, do not wish to contend with a king
force against force, since the scepter-bearing king,
to whom Zeus has given kudos, never received the same portion of *timē*.

Nestor makes use of the formula ἔμμορε τιμῆς precisely for the sake of promoting a "monarchic" ideology of sovereignty shared between mortal and immortal king, the same monarchic ideology that Odysseus also promotes in *Iliad* 2. In Nestor's speech, the point is precisely that Achilles and Agamemnon do not have the same equal status in *timē*. Poseidon's use of the phrase ἔμμορε τιμῆς, however, is for the exact opposite purpose—in order to demonstrate a nonhierarchical distribution of *timē*. Although mortals are in a constant effort to construct hierarchies based on a divine hierarchy, Poseidon's oligarchic or fraternal model of the cosmic division of honors presents us with a single instance of a uniquely nonhierarchical model of divine relationality.[123]

---

[123] The uniqueness in Poseidon's claim is reflected in the fact that his use of the *homotimos* "of the same honor," to describe himself in relation to Zeus, is a hapax in Homer (*Iliad* 15.186).

Conclusion

Overall, then, what we find is that even though performative speech, as an act in itself, is meant to function as a type of supplement to physical force, speakers nevertheless seek to actively construct those unequal force relations within their speeches in order to lend greater authority and effectiveness to their speech acts, whether those speeches are commands, threats, or boasts. And in this regard, these relations of force are consistent with Bourdieu's own insistence that performative speech must rely on external material conditions as the source for authoritative speech. All the figures who employ comparative force terms point beyond themselves as the basis for more general claims to authority and superiority. Yet, when we expand our analysis beyond the speeches themselves and include the narrative contexts and outcomes of those speeches, we see that events within the poem often run contrary to the hierarchies of force presented within speech by individual characters. Although Nestor had insisted that Achilles was *karteros* and Agamemnon *pherteros* in *Iliad* 1, he corrects himself in *Iliad* 9 and insists that Achilles is *pheristos*. And even though the genealogy of Achilles might be viewed as a reason for him being undervalued both by Nestor and by Apollo, still Achilles himself constructs the force of his own genealogy in *Iliad* 21, not based on Thetis, who is the true source of his superiority, but instead based on Zeus as well. Hence, the externality of force relations, upon which Bourdieu insists, is appealed to not only by way of the scepter, but ultimately through Zeus. And yet, in Poseidon's response to Zeus' own performance of force through comparative terms (*karteros* vs. *pherteros*) in *Iliad* 15, we see that Zeus himself is not necessarily the absolute standard he professes to be. The comparative relationship is explicitly denied by Poseidon in favor of a principle of genuine equality. Poseidon's response thus offers us a rare glimpse into the ways in which performative speech not only constructs relations of force but can also rob another of the social foundations that would allow for the enactment of force. By tracing the use of comparative terms for force in the speeches of both humans and gods, we find that the only constant is the very contingency and instability of those force relations, which are continually modified and remodified through speech. Or, to frame it another way, the *Iliad* not only demonstrates "how to do things with words" but also how to undo them.

2

Kratos before Democracy

Force, Politics, and Signification in the *Iliad*

In the beginning of Book 2 of the *Iliad*, in the so-called Diapeira or "Testing" episode, after Nestor's own failed attempt to create peace between Achilles and Agamemnon, Odysseus, at the behest of Athena, attempts once more to prevent the dissolution of the Greek army.[1] He does so by taking up the scepter of Agamemnon and delivering two types of speeches, whose purpose is to reconfirm the central authority of Agamemnon. One type of speech is delivered to the kings (*Iliad* 2.190–7) and another to the *dēmos* (*Iliad* 2.200–6). It is in his speech to the *dēmos* that one finds one of the most politically controversial statements in all of early Greek poetry. Odysseus addresses the members of the *dēmos* of the Achaean camp and proclaims:

οὐ μέν πως πάντες βασιλεύσομεν ἐνθάδ' Ἀχαιοί·
οὐκ ἀγαθὸν πολυκοιρανίη· εἷς κοίρανος ἔστω,
εἷς βασιλεύς ᾧ δῶκε Κρόνου πάϊς ἀγκυλομήτεω
σκῆπτρόν τ' ἠδὲ θέμιστας, ἵνά σφισι βουλεύῃσι

Iliad **2.203–6**

Not all of us Achaeans will rule as king here.
Rule by many lords is not good. Let there be one lord,
one king, to whom the son of crooked-counseling Cronus has given
the scepter and judgments in order that he might provide council for them.

---

[1] For a thorough review of the scholarship on the Diapeira and an analysis of Agamemnon's test in light of speech act theory, see Christensen 2015. On Odysseus' motives for wishing to prevent Greek flight, see Cook 2003. The complex sequence of events inaugurated by Zeus at the beginning of *Iliad* 2, which leads to this second possible breakup of the army, will be discussed later in the chapter.

Homer's Iliad *and the Problem of Force*. Charles H. Stocking, Oxford University Press.
© Charles H. Stocking 2023. DOI: 10.1093/oso/9780192862877.003.0003

74 Force, Politics, and Signification in the *Iliad*

In response to these lines, the bT scholia offer the following short comment: οὐκ ἔσται δημοκρατία—"It will not be a democracy."[2] On one level, this statement from the scholia is both uninformative and anachronistic.[3] And yet the anachronistic nature of the comment from the scholia also perfectly captures the diachronic reception of these lines. For the speech of Odysseus to the *dēmos* has been quoted extensively throughout antiquity and modernity as a distinctly antidemocratic claim for monarchic sovereignty.[4]

Surprisingly, despite the problematic popularity of the "one king" speech throughout history, it has received little direct attention from Classical scholars, aside from passing reference.[5] Indeed, far more attention has been given to the actions of Odysseus in *Iliad* 2 than to his words. For immediately following the speech of Odysseus to the *dēmos* comes the infamous Thersites episode, in which Odysseus brutally beats the supposed "worst of the Greeks" with approval and laughter from the Achaean camp.[6] The Thersites episode has garnered great attention in part because it seems to demonstrate a fundamental disjunction between ancient and modern attitudes towards the use of force and violence.[7]

---

[2] Aristarchus proposed moving lines 203–5 to the speech addressed to kings, following line 192, on which see Kirk 1985: 135. Schironi 2017 is in favor of Aristarchus' transposition. However, concerning the proclamation of "one king," contrary to Aristarchus, the bT scholia further state εἰ δὲ τοῖς μείζοσι ταῦτα ἔλεγεν, ἐξῆπτε τὴν στάσιν, "If he said this to the better men (i.e. the kings), he would have incited stasis."

[3] Indeed, the *dēmos* of the Achaean camp is certainly not the same as the *dēmos* of Classical democracy. On the semantics of the term *dēmos* in Homer see Casewitz 1992; on *dēmos* as distinct from the *laos*, see Wyatt 1994–5: 169; Haubold 2000: 58n.60, 114n.316. On the anachronism of the scholia, particularly with regard to the projection of later political structures onto the *Iliad*, see Taplin 1992: 42.

[4] In antiquity, see Xen. Mem. 1.2.56; Arist. *Metaph.* 1076a4, Arist. *Pol.* 1292a13; Thphr. *Char.* 26.2; D.H. *Rh.* 9.8; D. Chr. 1.11, 3.46; Aristid. Or. 11 (Eis eteona). In modernity, the speech of Odysseus has been a favorite in the Royalist use of Homer (on which see Machacek 2002), and it has often been quoted extensively in political-philosophical arguments, from Thomas Hobbes (on which, see J. Wolfe 2015: 375–413) to Martin Heidegger (on which see M. Müller 1990: 183).

[5] The speech is often briefly cited in reference to discussion of communal and political organization represented in the *Iliad*. See Redfield 1994: 92; Raaflaub 1993: 50n.32 (with references) for this speech as an instance of *primus inter pares*; McGlew 1993: 54 cites the speech as an indication that kingship is necessary but fragile; Hammer 2002: 88 makes a brief comment considering the speech to be ironic; Cartledge 2009: 35 comments that the speech is "conservative, if not reactionary" and points to its overall political importance in early Greek political thought. Cairns 2017: 388–9 cites Odysseus' statement about *polukoiraniē*, "many-princes," as the starting point for a general discussion of the problematization of leadership in the *Iliad* as a whole.

[6] *Iliad* 2.211–77. On public laughter as a mode of shaming in Homeric poetry, see C. Brown 1989.

[7] For debates on the Thersites episode, esp. regarding the relationship between physical and verbal abuse, see, among others, Lavigne 2017: 137–41; Elmer 2013: 93–100; Steiner

Force, Politics, and Signification in the *Iliad*   **75**

If we interpret the actions of Odysseus and his use of violent force against Thersites in light of his speech to the *dēmos*, a fairly coherent image of political power begins to emerge. In the first place, we find a correlation of comparatives. Odysseus commands the *dēmos* stating "listen to others who are stronger than you" (ἄλλων μῦθον ἄκουε/ οἳ σέο φέρτεροί εἰσι) (*Iliad* 2.200–1), and he likewise chastises Therisites, "I say that there is no other mortal worse than you" (οὐ γὰρ ἐγὼ σέο φημὶ χερειότερον βροτὸν ἄλλον/ ἔμμεναι) (*Iliad* 2.248–9). Odysseus' own claim that the kings are "stronger" compared to the *dēmos* thus parallels Nestor's own claim that Agamemnon should be respected by Achilles because Agamemnon is also "stronger" (*Iliad* 1.281).[8] At the same time, Odysseus uses the scepter of Agamemnon, the symbol of royal authority, to physically drive the *dēmos* back to the assembly, and he uses that same scepter to beat Thersites.[9] Thus, the words and actions of Odysseus seem to coincide.[10] His speech to the *dēmos* and his beating of Thersites present a distinct political principle, which we might refer to as "rule of the stronger"—a principle which Friedrich Nietzsche succinctly articulated for the Greeks as follows: "Force gives the first right, and there is no right, which at bottom is not arrogance, usurpation, an act of violence."[11]

But is this notion of "rule of the stronger" the true driving principle of the *Iliad* and of early Greek culture more generally? When we consider the words and actions of Odysseus in light of the larger narrative trajectory of the *Iliad*, such a principle becomes problematic. Were we to apply the political logic of violent force to the *Iliad* as a whole, then Achilles would have easily cut down Agamemnon with his sword during their initial quarrel, just as Odysseus used his scepter to silence Thersites, and the *Iliad* as we have it would not have taken place. Thus, when we compare the words of Odysseus in *Iliad* 2 with the poem's larger narrative context, we are faced with a major interpretive problem concerning the ideological

---

2009: 92; Rosen 2007: 81–91; Marks 2005; Schmidt 2002; Lincoln 1994: 14–36; Thalmann 1988; Rose 1988; Nagy 1979: 253–64; Ebert 1969.

[8] See discussion in Chapter 1.

[9] Whitman 1958: 161 thus describes it as the "scepter of kingly violence." Likewise, Unruh 2011 suggests that its use as a tool of violence in *Iliad* 2 is indicative of its more general function, symbolizing the basilees' "right to discipline anyone who dared to usurp or challenge their control of authoritative μῦθος" (Unruh 2011: 293).

[10] See, for instance, Schofield 1986: 9, where the Thersites episode presents a general principle in which fighting and counsel are "not opposed but interdependent." Odysseus, in general, is thought to be a character that is able to overcome any possible division between word and deed, on which see A. Parry 1981: 24 and see Martin 1989: 63–4, 120–4 for further stylistic details in Odysseus' speech and performance habits.

[11] From his essay "The Greek State," Nietzsche 2005: 50.

76 Force, Politics, and Signification in the *Iliad*

import of the *Iliad* as whole: What is the relationship between physical force and political power?

This question concerning the relationship between force and politics is relevant not only to the *Iliad*, but it has in fact been central to the entire history of modern political thought.[12] Most recently, in his last major publication, *Rogues*, Jacques Derrida specifically used the "one king" speech of Odysseus from *Iliad* 2 in order to account for this more general problematic. In particular, Derrida argued that the speech of Odysseus represents what he termed "ipsocentrism," a self-referential correspondence between physical force and political power. Within the *Iliad*, and in early Greek culture more generally, Derrida suggests, this ipsocentric form of force is explained and justified through divine corollary with the *kratos* of Zeus. Ultimately, Derrida argued for the notion of *kratos* as ipsocentric in order to contrast that notion with the institution of democracy, which, for Derrida, is a political manifestation of his philosophy of *différance*. Thus, according to Derrida, the speech of Odysseus to the *dēmos* in *Iliad* 2 holds the key to a broader understanding of *kratos* before democracy.

Derrida's arguments on Homer in *Rogues* offers an important starting point for analyzing the problematic relationship between force and politics in the *Iliad* as a whole. Indeed, Derrida's analysis of the "one king" speech is especially useful because it demonstrates how issues of politics in early Greek poetry and culture are inseparable from larger cosmic concerns regarding mortal-immortal relations. Yet, as I shall argue, we do not necessarily need to posit a future "democracy," as Derrida does, in order to deconstruct the notion of ipsocentric force represented by the speech of Odysseus. Rather, I argue, such a unified notion of force and power is already deconstructed in the *Iliad* itself. This deconstruction occurs, I argue, because the relationship between physical force and political power represented in the *Iliad* and other early Greek poetry is mediated through an embodied economy enacted by Zeus and the other gods.[13] Because most types of force are perceived to be given by the gods, relations of force among both mortals and immortals remain in a constant state of contestation, contingency, and uncertainty. As this chapter will demonstrate, such an undermining of ipsocentric force is most readily observed in the

---

[12] For a concise survey of the role of force and violence in the history of modern political thought from Homer to Hobbes and beyond, see, for instance, Baracchi 2011.

[13] By "embodied economy" I refer to the way in which human activity and physical attributes are thought to be achieved by way of acts of reciprocity with the gods. For the idea of an embodied economy shared between mortals and immortals in Archaic Greek thought, see Holmes 2010: 77–8.

general cultural semantics of *kratos*, in its mythological implications for the rule of Zeus, and in the uniquely discursive role that *kratos* plays between *Iliad* Book 2 and *Iliad* Book 9.

Towards a Political Theology of Force in Homer and Hesiod

Derrida's engagement with Classical antiquity has been well acknowledged.[14] For the most part, however, discussion of Derrida and antiquity has focused primarily on tragedy and philosophy. Yet in his last major publication while still alive, *Rogues* (*Voyous*), Derrida took up a direct analysis of Homeric poetry, as well as Hesiod, for the first time.[15] In order to fully appreciate how and why Derrida makes use of Homer and Hesiod in *Rogues* and how his reading may help us with the general problematic of force and politics in the *Iliad*, it is first necessary to briefly discuss Derrida's engagement with structuralist analysis and his concept of *différance*.

Where many have argued against structuralism based on extra-linguistic aspects of cultural and historical analysis, as seen for instance in Bourdieu's notion of "practice theory," Derrida argued that the critique of structuralism was already a fundamental feature of structuralist discourse based on its own linguistic foundations. For Derrida, the Saussurian emphasis on the *arbitrary* relationship between signifier and signified and the theory of linguistic structuralism that it entailed presented a profound moment in the history of philosophy. In one of his most foundational essays, "Structure, Sign, and Play in the Discourse of the Human Sciences," Derrida explains:

---

[14] See esp. Miller 1998; Leonard 2000; Leonard 2005; Miller 2007, Leonard 2010a; Leonard 2010b; Leonard 2010c; Miller 2010; Miller 2015a.

[15] Derrida's discussion of Homer and Hesiod appears in the first half of the work in an essay titled "Reason of the Strongest," which was delivered at a conference in honor of Derrida at Cerisy-la-salle in 2002. And it was at a conference at Cerisy-la-salle in 1959 titled "Genesis and Structure" where Derrida delivered one of his first major lectures, " 'Genesis and Structure' and Phenomenology." Consequently, it was at this same conference in 1959 that Jean-Pierre Vernant delivered a paper titled "Genesis and Structure in the Hesiodic Myth of Races," which later served as a foundational essay in the structuralist movement broadly construed. Indeed, that conference at Cerisy marked the beginning of a long history of debates on the political ramifications of structuralist thought. For Derrida to discuss Homer and Hesiod in his last lecture at Cerisy only solidifies the ever-present role that early Greek poetry has played in modern, and especially French, philosophical discourse. On the significance of the 1959 Cerisy conference in the dialogue between ancients and moderns, see Stocking 2017b.

78 Force, Politics, and Signification in the *Iliad*

> This moment was that in which language invaded the universal problematic; that in which, in the absence of a center or origin, everything became discourse—provided we can agree on this word—that is to say, when everything became a system where the central signified, the original or transcendental signified, is never absolutely present outside a system of differences. The absence of the transcendental signified extends the domain and the interplay of signification *ad infinitum*.
>
> **(Derrida 1972: 249)**

This "signification *ad infinitum*" is eventually defined by Derrida through the neologism *différance*—a process of endless deferral of meaning through the difference that is generated between signifier and signified.[16] At the same time, however, Derrida shows that it is also impossible to conceptualize this process of *différance* without a basic presupposition regarding the "transcendental signified." In particular, Derrida demonstrates how the critique of the notion of a transcendental signified cannot be applied to the very signifier "sign." "For the signification 'sign' has always been comprehended and determined, in its sense, as sign of, signifier referring to a signified, signifier different from its signified."[17] Thus, on the one hand, semiotics makes it such that meaning is always undergoing a process of *différance*, but for *différance* to take effect, one must necessarily have in place a presupposition regarding the very opposite of that process, where sign is reduced to and the same as thought. This is the paradox of deconstruction. "The paradox is that the metaphysical reduction of the sign [i.e., reducing sign to thought] needed the opposition it was reducing [i.e., between sign and thought]. The opposition is part of the system, along with the reduction."[18] Thus every positing of meaning must both assert and undermine that meaning, every structure already contains within it the possibility of its own deconstruction.

Many have suggested that Derrida's initial work in deconstruction was in some sense apolitical, and that the "political turn" in his philosophy came only later.[19] Miriam Leonard, however, has clearly shown how Derrida's philosophy of deconstruction was engaged in politics from the outset, specifically through his use of antiquity.[20] In *Rogues*, this political

---

[16] See Derrida 1981a: 21–30; Derrida 1982: 3–27.   [17] Derrida 1972: 250.

[18] Derrida 1972: 251.

[19] See, among others, Descombes 1980; Ferry and Renaut 1985; Mitchell and Davidson 2007.

[20] See esp. Leonard 2000; Leonard 2005: 9–12, 135–47, 189–215; Leonard 2010c: 135–8.

Towards a Political Theology of Force   **79**

engagement through antiquity becomes explicit. Indeed, it is in *Rogues* that Derrida insists, "The thinking of the political has always been a thinking of *différance* and the thinking of *différance* always a thinking of the political."[21] Above all other political forms, Derrida suggests that democracy is most representative of deconstruction. He thus claims: "Democracy is what it is only in the *différance* by which it defers itself and differs from itself."[22] According to Derrida, the *différance* of democracy comes about as a function of joining and juxtaposing its two constituent signifiers, *kratos* and *demos*. For Derrida, *kratos* represents a principle of unified power or sovereignty, which must be deferred and distributed between self and others, i.e., through the *dēmos*. That is to say, it is the very signifiers that constitute "democracy" that facilitate the process of *différance*, and these signifiers themselves are historically anchored in antiquity. Thus, Derrida takes up the "one king" speech of Odysseus in order to first establish the principle of sovereign power, which he considers to be always already at work in democracy.

Derrida arrives at the "one king" speech of Odysseus by way of Aristotle's quotation of that speech at the end of Book 12 of the *Metaphysics*, when Odysseus proclaims, "Rule by many lords is not good; let there be one lord, one king" (Aristotle, *Metaphysics* 1076a; Homer, *Iliad* 2.204). In this regard, Derrida's use of antiquity is already engaged in the process of deferral. As he explains: "The end of book 12 (Lambda) thus seems written under, or underwritten by, the sovereign authority of Homer, of his words and his verdict, precisely where Homer himself cites a word of sovereign authority."[23] Unlike Aristotle, however, Derrida provides the speech of Odysseus in full. For Derrida, what is most significant about the "one king" speech are its theological implications. Derrida places the greatest emphasis on the conclusion of the speech, a line coming after the one quoted by Aristotle, where Odysseus proclaims: "One king, to whom the son of crooked-counseling Cronus has given the scepter and judgments" (εἷς βασιλεύς, ᾧ δῶκε Κρόνου πάϊς ἀγκυλομήτεω/ σκῆπτρόν τ᾽ ἠδὲ θέμιστας) (*Iliad* 2.205–6). In citing this line, Derrida gives special attention to the unique manner in which Zeus is described, through the patronymic epithet "son of crooked-counseling Cronus." He states,

> Zeus is first of all a son, male child and descendant who, by means of a ruse (*mētis*) but also with the help of his mother, manages to escape

---

[21] Derrida 2005: 39.   [22] Derrida 2005: 38.   [23] Derrida 2005: 17.

80   Force, Politics, and Signification in the *Iliad*

time. He thus wins out over his father, Cronos, who himself had won out over, whom he himself emasculated, his own father, Ouranos.

(Derrida 2005: 17) [24]

In the first place, Derrida is here clearly influenced by the seminal work of Detienne and Vernant, *Cunning Intelligence in Greek Culture and Society*, along with Vernant's account of the myth of the succession of Zeus.[25] Of course, following Milman Parry's original formulations on oral poetics, one might object that a noun-epithet phrase for Zeus such as "son of crooked-counseling Cronus" would not necessarily have any semantic weight.[26] Since the work of Parry, however, Gregory Nagy, Egbert Bakker, and others have shown that such noun-epithet formulas do indeed have semantic value, and Jonathan Burgess has further argued through a principle of "mythic intertextuality" that certain formulas can refer to larger mythic narratives without necessarily referring to particular works.[27] Here, then, I would suggest that Derrida is right and that we do have a mythic reference in that epithet, "son of crooked-counseling Cronus," invoking the myth of Zeus' succession.[28]

In order to elucidate on this mythic reference, Derrida brings to attention the famous "children of Styx episode" from the Hesiodic *Theogony* as a quintessential account of Zeus' kingship, where the poet states that *Nikē* and *Zēlos*, Victory and Envy, along with *Kratos* and *Biē* "sit forever beside deep-thundering Zeus" (*Theogony* 383–8). As Marcel Detienne remarks in *Cunning Intelligence* on that Hesiodic episode:

---

[24] The English "wins out over" is translated from the French "à raison de," thus supplying a play on the notion of the "reason of the strongest"—*la raison du plus fort*—which is the running theme of the first half of *Rogues*.

[25] Detienne and Vernant 1978. Derrida contributed an essay in the volume *Poikilia*, dedicated to Jean-Pierre Vernant, and they presented in several of the same conferences, especially the "Genesis and Structure" conference of 1959, on which see Stocking 2017b as well as the famous conference at Johns Hopkins, "The Structuralist Controversy" in 1966. For further discussion of Derrida's relationship to French Classicists such as Vernant see Leonard 2000; Leonard 2005: 205–15; Leonard 2010b: 11–12; Miller 2010: 326–7.

[26] See Parry 1971: 118–72.

[27] See Nagy 1990b: 18–35; Bakker 2005: 22–37; Burgess 2009: 56–71; Burgess 2012.

[28] Indeed, the succession myth seems to be invoked through a similar epithet, $\mu\eta\tau\acute{\iota}\epsilon\tau\alpha$ $Z\epsilon\acute{\upsilon}s$ (*Iliad* 2.197), which Odysseus uses in a speech to the kings, given just prior to the speech to the *dēmos*. In addition, it is Odysseus' own capacity for *mētis* that is emphasized when Athena visits Odysseus and commands him to gather the troops (see *Iliad* 2.173). To be sure, the cosmogonic division of honors or *timai* is not the same in the *Iliad* (*Iliad* 15.185–99) and in the myth of succession as represented in Hesiod's *Theogony*, on which see Faraone 2012. Nevertheless, the fact of this difference in the division of *timai* does not preclude a basic parallel in narrative patterns and common mythological discourse regarding how Zeus came to power between the two poems, on which see Muellner 1996: 56–93; Stocking 2017a.

Kratos and Biē, Domination and Brute Force, flank the throne of Zeus as servants forever following at his heels. But they only do so in as much as the power of the Olympian god is more than mere strength and is unaffected by the vicissitudes of time.

(Detienne and Vernant 1978: 13)

It is precisely the permanence of Zeus' power and the issue of "time" that Derrida likewise stresses when he states, "It is by winning out over time, by putting an end to the infinite order of time, so to speak, that [Zeus] asserts his sovereignty."[29] Here Derrida is in agreement with most Classical scholars who view Zeus' kingship as a result of a sequence of violent successions, which come to an end with Zeus only because he is able to take permanent control of those means of force.[30]

Indeed, not only in Hesiod, but in the *Iliad* as well, we see Zeus himself assert his privileged political position among the gods by appeal to his supremacy in physical force and violence. For instance, at the beginning of *Iliad* 8, Zeus utters a threat against any Olympian god who thinks to intervene in the Trojan war. He first states that that any god who disobeys "will go to Olympos, being struck in an unseemly way" (πληγεὶς οὐ κατὰ κόσμον ἐλεύσεται Οὔλυμπον δέ·) (*Iliad* 8.12). Regarding such a threat, we should first note that the phrase *kata kosmon* is a formula in early Greek hexameter designating "propriety" as it relates to word and action.[31] One usage of the formula that is especially relevant comes from *Iliad* 2, where Odysseus characterizes the speech of Thersites against Agamemnon as *ou kata kosmon* (*Iliad* 2.214).[32] Because Thersites' speech goes against the social order, Odysseus would therefore appear justified in physically beating Thersites.[33]

---

[29] Derrida 2005: 17. Such a statement further reflects Derrida's claim in "Violence and Metaphysics" that "time is violence" (Derrida 1978: 166). Derrida further collapses the idea of Cronus with Chronus (time), as also presented in his work *Glas* (Derrida 1986: 232). But, as Simon Goldhill commented to me at a presentation of this chapter at Cambridge in May 2018, Zeus may not be putting an end to time in the way Derrida describes but inaugurating time, as seen with the birth of the seasons in the *Theogony* (*Theog.* 901–6).

[30] On Zeus' succession as a control of the means of force, see further Detienne and Vernant 1978; Muellner 1996; Clay 2003; Scully 2015, among others.

[31] See Diller 1956; Kerschensteiner 1962; Martin 1989: Ford 1992: 121–5; Elmer 2010: 290–2. It is primarily used in the negative, *ou kata kosmon*, as it is in Book 8, but there is also the phonetically parallel positive version of the formula, *eu kata kosmon*. *ou kata kosmon*: *Iliad* 2.214, 5.759, 8.12, 17.205, *Odyssey* 3.138, 8.179, 14.363, 20.181, *Hymn to Hermes* 255; *eu kata kosmon*: *Iliad* 10.472, 11.48, 12.85, 24.622, *Hymn to Hermes* 479.

[32] See Kelly 2007: 78 with further discussion of the more traditional usage of this phrase.

[33] See, among others, Reinhardt 1961: 112–15; Gschnitzer 1976; Griffin 1980: 9–12; Schmidt 2002; Scodel 2002: 204–9; Thalmann 1988: 21–6 views the violence against Thersites as not necessarily justified, but still necessary, as a "scapegoat." Elmer 2013: 97, on the other

82 Force, Politics, and Signification in the *Iliad*

By contrast, Zeus himself asserts that he will physically beat any god *ou kata kosmon* who is disobedient. In Zeus' threat, therefore, we see that the disobedient god is not punished for violating the social and "cosmic" order, that is the order that is *kata kosmon*. Rather, Zeus asserts that his own physical force is so great that he is actually able to transcend the limits of what is "proper" in the enforcement of his will.

Immediately after this initial threat, Zeus levels a second threat in *Iliad* 8, in which he suggests that he will throw any disobedient Olympian god down into Tartarus, thus treating the Olympians in the same fashion as he did the Titans (*Iliad* 8.13–16).[34] Zeus then makes a boast to accompany these two threats: "Then you will recognize by how much I of all the gods am the one who possesses the most *kratos*" (γνώσετ᾽ ἔπειθ᾽ ὅσον εἰμὶ θεῶν κάρτιστος ἁπάντων) (*Iliad* 8.17). And as if these two threats and the boast were not enough, he makes a further threat that he could bind all the gods together and hang them from a golden cord (*Iliad* 8.18–26).[35] With this threat, he then concludes with one final boast that extends his power to both the mortal and the immortal realms: "So much am I superior to gods and humans" (τόσσον ἐγὼ περί τ᾽ εἰμὶ θεῶν περί τ᾽ εἴμ᾽ ἀνθρώπων) (*Iliad* 8.27). Given Zeus' own claims to *kratos* and superiority, Derrida's suggestion that the speech of Odysseus to the *dēmos* contains within it an implicit reference to a political theology of power and force seems justified, not only in terms of the myth of sovereignty in the Hesiodic *Theogony* but also according to the representation of Zeus himself in the *Iliad*.[36]

Derrida defines this political theology of force associated with Zeus as "ipsocentric." Derrida's notion of "ipocentism" is derived from the work of Émile Benveniste. It is most fully articulated in the publication of Derrida's last lecture series at the École des hautes études en sciences sociales from 2001 to 2003 titled "The Beast and the Sovereign."[37] In that lecture series, Derrida took up Benveniste's account of the Indo-European root **poti-* related to English "power" and French "pouvoir."[38] For Benveniste,

---

hand, interprets the violence as necessary in order to allow for proper protocols of speech to be enacted, both consensus and dissent.

[34] On the threat of throwing one into Tartarus as recollection of Zeus' treatment of the Titans in general, as seen also in Apollo's threat against Hermes in the *Homeric Hymn to Hermes* 256, see Harrell 1991: 308–9.

[35] On which see Yasumura 2011: 40.

[36] For further discussion of Zeus' claim to absolute force in this episode, see Pucci 2018: 153–8.

[37] This lecture series has much overlap with *Rogues* with regard to themes and topics, especially concerning the "reason of the strongest" and sovereignty, on which see Hobson 2012.

[38] See Benveniste 2016: 61–5.

Towards a Political Theology of Force   83

this particular root presents a difficulty in its semantic range. On the one hand, it can refer to the sense of "master," as seen in Sanskrit *pátiḥ* or Greek *pósis*, "husband" and Greek *despótēs*, "master of the house." In Latin, it also relates to the verb "to be able" *possum, potui, posse* derived from **potere*, which may also have the sense of "be master." For Benveniste, however, the problem arises from a second sense of the root **poti-*. In Lithuanian the adjective *pats*, derived from **poti-*, can have the meaning "master" in the substantive, but it also has a reflexive sense as an adjective, "himself." And a similar phenomenon for the root can be observed in Hittite, which has no form corresponding to **poti-* but does have an enclitic particle, *pet* (*-pit*), which means "precisely (him)self." Lastly, this enclitic form corresponds to a parallel form in Latin related to the root **poti*, namely the Latin *-pse* of *ipse* also designating a reflexive sense of "self." In order to explain the semantic range of this root, Benveniste argued for a particular sociohistorical development:

> For an adjective meaning 'himself' to develop into the meaning 'master' there is one necessary condition: there must be a circle of persons subordinated to a central personage who assume the personality and complete identity of the group to such an extent that he is its summation: in his own person he is its incarnation.
>
> **(Benveniste 2016: 64)**

For Derrida, this root, which signifies "power," "master," and "self," had extreme politico-philosophical significance. In *The Beast and the Sovereign*, Derrida suggested that the historical/etymological significance of **poti-* offered a perennial account of political power more generally: "The concept of sovereignty will always imply the possibility of this positionality, this thesis, this self-thesis, this auto-position of him who posits or posits himself as *ipse*, the (self)-same, oneself."[39]

In *Rogues*, Derrida suggests that the entire myth of succession is defined precisely by a contest in force that involves the "self-thesis" of different male figures as sovereign rulers: Uranus, Cronus, and Zeus. Thus Derrida explains, "The attribute 'ipsocentric' intersects and links with a dash all others (those of the phallus, of the father, of the husband, son, or brother)."[40] The ipsocentric force of Zeus may therefore be understood as a result of male-male, interfamilial violence which is capped with Zeus' ultimate

---

[39] Derrida 2009: 102.   [40] Derrida 2005: 17.

84 Force, Politics, and Signification in the *Iliad*

self-thesis and claim to ultimate sovereignty.[41] Although the principle of ipsocentrism is derived from the Proto-Indo-European root *poti-*, Derrida sees the same principle at work with regard to the *kratos* of Zeus.[42]

Ultimately, Derrida develops this ipsocentric notion of sovereign force as *kratos* in order to account for the *différance* of democracy. Democracy is *différance* according to Derrida first because it relies on the same notion of sovereignty, *kratos*, as found in the Greek myth of divine sovereignty.[43] But at the same time, the notion of sovereignty depends on a basic assertion of oneness and indivisibility that is impossible with democracy because the very notion of democratic sovereignty requires that power be distributed and deferred between self and others. Ultimately, therefore, the role of sovereignty in the *Iliad* and the Hesiodic myth of succession serve to articulate a basic political analogy based on Derrida's philosophy of deconstruction:

Sign: Signification:: Kratos: Democracy

Just as the notion of a transcendental "sign" is required for the *différance* at work in "signification," so an ipsocentric notion of *kratos* is required for the *différance* of "democracy."[44]

According to Derrida, the "one king" speech of Odysseus is thus politically significant, not simply because it contrasts with democracy but also because the political theogony of Zeus has deep affiliations with a modern political theology:

> This political theogony or theology gets revived or taken over...by a so-called modern political theology of monarchic sovereignty and even by the unavowed political theology—itself just as phallocentric, phallo-paterno-filio-fraterno-ipsocentric—of the sovereignty of the people, that is of democratic sovereignty.
>
> **(Derrida 2005: 17)**

Where the bT scholia simply contrast the "one king" speech with the institution of democracy, Derrida suggests that it is this very notion of divine,

---

[41] Consequently, one might observe such a "self-thesis" in his boast of ultimate force in *Iliad* 8.
[42] Derrida 2005: 17.   [43] See Derrida 2005: 22–3.
[44] On the necessity of the transcendental sign, see Derrida's essay "Structure, Sign, and Play in the Sciences of Man": "For the signification 'sign' has always been comprehended and determined, in its sense, as sign-of, signifier referring to a signified, signifier different from its signified" (Derrida 1972: 250).

Philological and Mythopoetic Interventions **85**

ipsocentric sovereign power, as uttered by Odysseus in *Iliad* 2, upon which will depend all future democracies, both ancient and modern.[45]

The Alterity of *Kratos*: Philological and Mythopoetic Interventions

Derrida's analysis of the "one king" speech is important, not just for the sake of deconstructing democracy, but also because it offers a vital first step in coming to terms with the general problematic of force and politics in the *Iliad*. As we have said, it is easy enough to assume a direct correlation between force and politics in a time before democracy, especially among the warrior elites represented in Homer. Derrida's notion of ipsocentric force, as a type of self-centeredness and self-thesis, does indeed seem to accurately reflect the immediate efforts of Odysseus. At the beginning of the second book of the *Iliad*, the Greek army is on the verge of dissolution as a function of the quarrel between Agamemnon and Achilles. Thus, Odysseus' own speech may be viewed as an effort to reunite force and politics under the singular authority of Agamemnon based on his presumed connection with Zeus.[46] In this regard, it would appear that Odysseus' effort to make Agamemnon the central authority of the Greek army at Troy is to enable Agamemnon himself to participate in the ipsocentrism inaugurated by Zeus. And yet, such a reading, following Derrida, offers only a *first* step, because it does *not* accurately reflect a more general political theology of force for the *Iliad* as a whole. Rather, I argue, the ipspocentric vision of force represented by the words and actions of Odysseus is undermined and contradicted both by Hesiod and in the course of the *Iliad* itself.

First and foremost, the notion of ipsocentric force is already contraindicated by the very cultural semantics of *kratos*. In this respect, Derrida's philosophical treatment of ipsocentrism requires philological intervention. In particular, we should note that Derrida creates a semantic slide between the "ipseity" of "power," derived from the root **poti-*, and what he considers to be the "force" of *kratos*. Derrida states:

---

[45] For Derrida, because democracy exists as a mode of *différance*, it can never exist in actuality, but only as a "democracy to come/democracy of the future"—démocratie à venir (avenir), on which see Derrida 2005: 80–4.

[46] On the unifying function of *Iliad* 2, esp. from a metapoetic perspective, see Elmer 2013: 86–104.

86   Force, Politics, and Signification in the *Iliad*

Ipsocentric could even be replaced by ipsocratic, were that not a pleonasm, for the idea of force (*kratos*), of power, and of mastery, is analytically included in the concept of ipseity.

(Derrida 2005: 17)

If we follow Benveniste rather than Derrida, however, then we will see that *kratos* has its own etymology and semantic range quite distinct from the notion of ipseity implied by the root *poti-*. Indeed, Benveniste asserts, "The translation [of *kratos*] which is accepted everywhere as 'force, power' is in our view unsatisfactory."[47] Instead, Benveniste notes, there are at least six other terms for "force" in Homer, and he suggests that the choice to use one term over another is guided "by exact definitions, that is an exact idea of the *differences* between these seven ways of designating 'force'."[48] Thus, Derrida is perhaps guilty of doing precisely what Benveniste argues against, namely, glossing over different terms for "force" through appeal to a single concept.[49] In collapsing the concepts of "superiority" and "force," Derrida may be following Detienne and Vernant, who propose a notion of "force" as an unmarked category in opposition to *mētis*.[50] Or it may be a function of Simone Weil's influence.[51]

Benveniste, however, is adamant that *kratos* does not simply designate "force." To reiterate once more, according to Benveniste, the term *kratos* specifically designates "the superiority of a man, whether he manifests his force over those of his own camp or the enemy."[52] The "superiority" of *kratos*, in other words, almost always implies an *agōn*, it is "set in contest"— *mise en jeu*, where *kratos* designates physical superiority, political superiority, or both.[53] As such, from a social perspective, *kratos* is not ipsocentric, but requires the presence of an *other*, against whom one may be victorious. In addition, Benveniste points out that *kratos* is also represented as an object specifically given to mortals by Zeus. For instance,

---

[47] Benveniste 2016: 362.

[48] Benveniste 2016: 362, emphasis in the original. The English translation of Benveniste here uses the term "strength," but the original French has the term "force," which I have retained for clarity and consistency with Benveniste's own language and argument.

[49] Derrida does not in fact make reference to Benveniste's work on *kratos*, but only his etymology of *poti-*, which is most likely a result of Derrida's earlier work "The Politics of Friendship," wherein he cites Benveniste's entry on hospitality, which addresses that etymology. See Derrida 1997: 87–98.

[50] Detienne and Vernant 1978: 13.

[51] For the influence of Weil on Derrida, see Bennington 1993: 325–36, and for new reassessments of Weil's treatment of the *Iliad*, see Purves 2015; Holmes 2015; Schein 2016.

[52] Benveniste 2016: 365.   [53] Benveniste 2016: 365.

Philological and Mythopoetic Interventions   87

in the *Iliad*, Thetis demands that Zeus "place *kratos* among the Trojans until the Achaeans repay my son" (τόφρα δ' ἐπὶ Τρώεσσι τίθει κράτος ὄφρ' ἂν Ἀχαιοί/ υἱὸν ἐμὸν τίσωσιν) (*Iliad* 1.509–10). Indeed, from a formulaic perspective, most occurrences refer to *kratos* as an object given by the gods.[54] We are therefore presented with yet a second way in which *kratos* demonstrates a non-ipsocentric notion of force, since the source of force is not the self, but the gods.[55] Hence, in socioreligious terms, *kratos* may be viewed as a type of force that is ultimately external to the mortal subject, rather than strictly constitutive of it. Thus, *kratos* should not be defined as ipsocentric. Rather, *kratos* itself seems to more accurately reflect the actions of difference and deferral at work in the concept of *différance*. For the significance and value of *kratos* as force is first determined by difference from others, that is, difference from those with whom one contends. And second, nearly all forms of *kratos* are not native or inherent features of the human subject, but always from outside. The value and extent of one's *kratos* as a mortal depends on *deferral* to others, namely the gods.

The attributes of difference and deferral specific to *kratos* can be observed at a mythopoetic level in both Hesiod and Homer. Derrida specifically invoked *Kratos* and *Biē*, the children of Styx in the *Theogony*, as a demonstration of Zeus' ipsocentric sovereignty.[56] Yet it is that very episode, I suggest, where we find strong evidence for a *non*-ipsocentric notion of force. The episode is presented in Hesiod as follows:

Στὺξ δ' ἔτεκ' Ὠκεανοῦ θυγάτηρ Πάλλαντι μιγεῖσα
Ζῆλον καὶ Νίκην καλλίσφυρον ἐν μεγάροισι
καὶ Κράτος ἠδὲ Βίην ἀριδείκετα γείνατο τέκνα.
τῶν οὐκ ἔστ' ἀπάνευθε Διὸς δόμος, οὐδέ τις ἕδρη,
οὐδ' ὁδός, ὅππῃ μὴ κείνοις θεὸς ἡγεμονεύει,
ἀλλ' αἰεὶ πὰρ Ζηνὶ βαρυκτύπῳ ἑδριόωνται.

Hesiod, *Theogony* 383–8

---

[54] *Kratos* as an object given: *Iliad* 1.509, 11.192, 11.207, 11.319, 11.753, 12.214, 13.743, 15.216, 16.524, 17.206, 17.613, 20.121, *Odyssey* 21.280. *Kratos* is predominantly an object given by Zeus precisely because Zeus is defined as the one with the most *kratos*, seen in the formula *kratos esti megiston*: *Iliad* 2.118, 9.25, 9.39, 13.484, 24.293, 24.311, *Odyssey* 5.4. For further references, see the appendix.

[55] *Kratos* may therefore be included as one of the concepts that are primary objects of exchange in an embodied economy shared with the gods. For further discussion of a shared embodied economy, see Holmes 2010: 77–8.

[56] Derrida 2005: 17.

88   Force, Politics, and Signification in the *Iliad*

Styx, the daughter of ocean, mixed with Pallas,
and bore *Zēlos*, beautiful ankled *Nikē* in her halls,
and *Kratos* and *Biē*, glorious children.
There is no house for them apart from Zeus', nor any seat,
nor road, upon which Zeus does not lead them.
But always they sit beside deep-thundering Zeus.

First, we should note that the children of Styx are distinctly agonistic personifications.[57] In Hesiod, there is only one other instance where the concepts *Nikē*, *Kratos*, and *Biē* are invoked (although *Zēlos* is absent), namely, in reference to a mortal *agōn* in the "hymn to" of the *Theogony*:

ἐσθλὴ δ' αὖθ' ὁπότ' ἄνδρες ἀεθλεύωσ' ἐν ἀγῶνι·
ἔνθα θεὰ καὶ τοῖς παραγίνεται ἠδ' ὀνίνησι·
νικήσας δὲ **βίῃ** καὶ **κάρτει**, καλὸν ἄεθλον
ῥεῖα φέρει χαίρων τε, τοκεῦσι δὲ κῦδος ὀπάζει.

Hesiod, *Theogony* 435–8

She is a good goddess, whenever men compete for prizes in the *agōn*.
There the goddess is present and benefits them,
when one has won by force and superiority, a beautiful prize
he easily carries away, and gives *kudos* to his parents.

Not only is the Hecate episode the only other occurrence that provides the collocation of "victory, force, and superiority" in Hesiod, but the grouping appears only one other time in all of early Greek hexameter poetry.[58] Given the limited scope of these co-occurrences, the two passages may be

---

[57] Hermann Fränkel cites the children of Styx episode as evidence for early abstract thinking through personifications (Fränkel 1975: 99–101). Both Solmsen and West view the children of Styx as a function of the narrative program of the *Theogony* (Solmsen 1949: 32–4; West 1966: 272). Regarding the religious and cultural significance of Hesiodic personifications more generally, Detienne and Vernant explain, "What are known as Hesiod's 'abstractions' are something quite other than concepts disguised as gods through the device of poetic metaphor. They are true religious 'powers,' which preside over clearly defined types of activity and which operate within specific sectors of reality" (Detienne and Vernant 1978: 57). In terms of the appearance of these personifications in later periods, *Kratos* and *Biē* appear most famously in the *Prometheus Bound*. For the relationship between the myth of sovereignty in Hesiod and the *Prometheus Bound*, esp. with regard to these two figures, see Solmsen 1949: 132–8; Detienne and Vernant 1978: 60–1; Griffith 1983: 79–100. In addition, there are several other minor representations specifically of *Biē/Bia* in the Classical era, on which see Simon 1986 and Bloch 1997.

[58] *Iliad* 21.501, when Hermes refuses to fight with Leto and explains that she will boast that she was victorious in force and superiority, εὔχεσθαι ἐμὲ νικῆσαι κρατερῆφι βίηφιν.

Philological and Mythopoetic Interventions **89**

fruitfully analyzed in terms of each other.[59] Indeed, both episodes present structural parallels in so far as Zeus must incorporate female powers in order to ensure his future rule.[60] At the same time, the specific verbal parallels also reveal how force associated with the mortal *agōn* is transposed onto the divine story of cosmogonic conflict. According to Clay, Hecate's prime function in the *Theogony* is mediation: it is only *by the will* of the gods (*hekēti*) achieved through Hecate that mortals can accomplish their ends.[61] Likewise, it will be through the will of Styx, in allowing her children to become a part of Zeus' "winning team," so to speak, that Zeus' own future success is secured.[62] Thus, superiority in the *agōn*, whether for a mortal or even for Zeus himself, is located outside of the agency of the subject who participates in the *agōn*.[63]

Not only does the children of Styx episode allude to a distinctly agonistic context for the alterity of *kratos*, but it makes it especially clear from a broader religious perspective. Following Benveniste, *Kratos* and *Biē* must exist as two distinct principles—*kratos* indicating "superiority" and *biē* representing physical violent "force."[64] That is to say, *Kratos* and *Biē* do not exist simply as a type of hendiadys, but as separate entities, even from Zeus himself. To be sure, Hesiod insists that *Kratos and Biē* sit forever beside Zeus, but such a declaration only underscores the identity and status of these two figures as separate from him. That is to say, the children of Styx come to represent social relations that are precisely the *opposite* of ipsocentrism and what Benveniste described for the social context associated with the root **poti-*. For Benveniste suggested that the root **poti-* indicated a sociohistorical context in which a group was defined in terms of a single "central personage." In Hesiod, Zeus, as the "central personage," does not define the children of Styx, who stand as two different

---

[59] The terms do not occupy the same metrical positions, but the limited scope of co-occurrence seems to justify analyzing these episodes according to Bakker's scale of intertextuality in Greek hexameter poetry, on which see Bakker 2013: 157–69.

[60] See Clay 2003: 22–4.

[61] See Clay 2003: 137. There are numerous formulas related to the "will of the gods" *hekēti theōn*, and the "will of Zeus" *hekēti Dios* (*Works and Days* 3–4; *Theogony* 529; *Iliad* 12.8, 15.720; *Odyssey* 1.79, 3.28, 4.504, 6.240, 12.290, 20.42, 24.444; *Hymn to Aphrodite* 147).

[62] On the proleptic nature of the children of Styx episode, see Clay 2003: 22.

[63] This basic principle of the *agōn* is more fully explored in Chapter 3.

[64] Unlike *kratos*, which can be defined as an object external to the individual subject, *biē* is often associated specifically with the subject, hence we have phrases such as *biē Herakleiē* as an expression that stands in place of the name and person of Heracles, on which see Nagy 1979: 318–19. See Chapter 3 for a more complete discussion of *biē* within the network of Homeric power terms.

90 Force, Politics, and Signification in the *Iliad*

personifications of force. Indeed, the very fact that *Nikē*, *Kratos*, *Biē*, and *Zēlos* are part of a genealogy separate from Zeus indicates as much.

As separate divine beings, these children of Styx, which will ultimately come to define Zeus' winning ways, must first be won over to Zeus' side. And this is precisely what Zeus accomplishes, not through violence but through a political strategy of alliance. Indeed, like a true politician, Zeus makes a campaign for his future rule based on promises. In explaining why the children of Styx never leave Zeus' side, the poet of the *Theogony* states:

ὡς γὰρ ἐβούλευσε Στὺξ ἄφθιτος Ὠκεανίνη
ἤματι τῷ, ὅτε πάντας Ὀλύμπιος ἀστεροπητὴς
ἀθανάτους ἐκάλεσσε θεοὺς ἐς μακρὸν Ὄλυμπον,
εἶπε δ', ὃς ἂν μετὰ εἷο θεῶν Τιτῆσι μάχοιτο,
μή τιν' ἀπορραίσειν γεράων, τιμὴν δὲ ἕκαστον
ἐξέμεν ἣν τὸ πάρος γε μετ' ἀθανάτοισι θεοῖσι.

Hesiod, *Theogony* 389–94

Thus undecaying Styx, daughter of Ocean, planned it
on that day when the Olympian god of lightning
called all the immortals to great Olympos,
and he said that whoever of the gods would fight with him against
the Titans,
they would not be deprived of privileges, and that each would have the
honor (*timē*) which they previously held among the immortal gods.

Styx and her children, we are told, are the first to take Zeus up on his offer of future honors. Consequently, Zeus uses the very same strategy to acquire the Hundred Handers, those figures who stand as the supreme manifestation of overly masculine physical force.[65] Thus, the very means by which Zeus acquires *kratos* and the other children of Styx present us with a type of *mise en abyme* for relations of power established through reciprocity. As we have noted, in Homeric poetry, *kratos* for mortals is specifically given by the gods. But the *Theogony* takes the god-given nature of *kratos* one step further. That is to say, *kratos* is god-given, even for the gods themselves.

---

[65] See *Theogony* 639–63. On the thematic role of the Hundred Handers in the *Theogony* as a manifestation of force, see Detienne and Vernant 1978: 68–125. On the textual debates concerning the presence of the Hundred Handers and the Cyclopes early in the *Theogony* (139–53), see Vergados 2013.

Philological and Mythopoetic Interventions **91**

The children of Styx episode, therefore, cannot be used to demonstrate the ipsocentric force of Zeus, as Derrida suggests. Rather, the Zeus of the *Theogony* seems to acquire his own *kratos* through *différance*, that is, by *differing* from his violent male predecessors, Uranus and Cronus, and by *deferring* to other divinities through the offer of honors and *timē*.[66] In addition, where Derrida viewed ipsocentric power as phallocentric, the *Theogony* presents Zeus acquiring his force primarily through the help of female divinities. It is really the agency of Styx that allows for Zeus to acquire her children, and the role of Styx also parallels the incorporation of Hecate. And lastly, after the Titanomachy, it is Gaia who urges on the other Olympians to promote Zeus as king (*Theogony* 883–5). Thus, in the end, Zeus acquires his position as sovereign king not through an act of "self-thesis" or "autoposition," not through an act of male ipsocentric violence, but through the agency of *others*.[67]

The same principle of alterity and agonism at work regarding the *kratos* of Zeus in Hesiod may also apply equally to the *Iliad*. Indeed, nearly every assertion of force by Zeus reveals a dependency on the other gods, while that force is also challenged by the other gods. As an example, we might consider Zeus' strongest proclamation of superiority in *Iliad* 8. After his boast and threat against the Olympians, Athena objects, and Zeus immediately backs down, demonstrating a potential discrepancy between Zeus' own words and actions. He states,

θάρσει Τριτογένεια φίλον τέκος· οὔ νύ τι θυμῷ
πρόφρονι μυθέομαι, ἐθέλω δέ τοι ἤπιος εἶναι.

Iliad **8.39–40**

Take courage, Tritogeneia, my dear child. Not with an anxious *thumos* do I speak, but I wish to be gentle to you.

As Richard Martin has shown, the concept of *muthos* in Homer most often refers to performatives, those parts of language where speaking is equivalent to doing.[68] Yet here, Zeus seems to undermine the immediate effectiveness

---

[66] For the concept of *timē* as "deference" in early Greek poetry, see van Wees 1992: 69–71 as well as Scodel 2008, who sees *timē* as a matter of interaction between "deference" and "face."

[67] The nonviolent aspect of Zeus' political reign, based on alterity rather than ipseity, is fully articulated by Stephen Scully: "It is worth noting that *no component* of Zeus' power in the *Theogony* is innate. It *all* comes from others, male and female, whom Zeus has either included into his rule or liberated from oppression" (Scully 2015: 35, italics in original).

[68] Martin 1989: 1–42. See Chapter 1 for further discussion of speech acts and their relationship to the role of force in the *Iliad*.

92 Force, Politics, and Signification in the *Iliad*

of his own performative threat. These lines of reconciliation to Athena were questioned for their authenticity in antiquity, precisely because the statement runs contrary to the threatening speech Zeus had just uttered.[69] And yet, this is not the first time in the *Iliad* where Zeus does not act on his own words. On three different occasions, when Zeus contemplates an action that favors the Trojans, he is rebuked, either by Hera or Athena, with the same concluding formula: "Do it, but the rest of us gods do not at all give approval" (ἔρδ᾽· ἀτὰρ οὔ τοι πάντες ἐπαινέομεν θεοὶ ἄλλοι).[70] In all of these occasions, Zeus does not follow through on the course of action he contemplates.[71] David Elmer identifies this phenomenon of communal approval by the term *epainos*. In describing the immortal application of *epainos*, Elmer explains:

> The practice of politics is not a solely human activity in the *Iliad*. The gods, too, are subject to the political imperatives of collective decision making. No less than their human protégés, they must make accommodations and negotiate conflicting preferences in pursuit of a common basis for group action.
>
> (Elmer 2013: 146)

Elmer further demonstrates that Zeus, despite his superior capacity for force, is still constantly subjected to the constraints of communal consent. Communal approval is even acknowledged in Zeus' proclamation of his superior power in his *muthos* of *Iliad* 8, when he states, "Consent, in order that I may accomplish this task" (αἰνεῖτ᾽, ὄφρα τάχιστα τελευτήσω τάδε ἔργα) (*Iliad* 8.9).[72] Thus, even though Zeus' superiority would seem like a form of "self-thesis," it still nevertheless depends on the presence and approval of *others*. That presence of the *other* is found even in his boast to superiority, when he proclaims: "<u>You will recognize</u> by how much I have the most *kratos* of all the gods" (γνώσετ᾽ ἔπειθ᾽ ὅσον εἰμὶ θεῶν κάρτιστος ἁπάντων)

---

[69] The line was athetized by Aristarchus. Kelly 2007: 91 views the introduction of Zeus' speech, "he spoke, smiling at her" (*Iliad* 8.38) as an indication of deception and misrepresentation. Elmer 2013: 162 sees Zeus' change of tone as a means for the advancement of the plot of the *Iliad*. See further Pucci 2018: 159, who comments, "These lines trigger critical embarrassment from antiquity to our days. By Athena's request and by Zeus' unlikely concession— the critics argue—the text enfeebles the strong image it depicted of Zeus' hegemony and absolute power."

[70] *Iliad* 4.29, 16.443, 22.181.

[71] The difference of course is that these other occasions are not *muthoi* per se.

[72] Concerning this particular line, Elmer claims, "The appeal to *ainos* provides thin cover for a policy that requires a temporary suspension of the rules" (Elmer 2013: 160). Yet I would emphasize the fact that Zeus must make appeal to communal consent nonetheless.

Zeus' Deception of Agamemnon   **93**

(*Iliad* 8.17). Metrical arguments aside, Zeus could have simply made a simple claim to physical superiority. But instead, his boast follows the logic of honor culture more generally, where the superiority of *kratos* does not just depend on dominance *of* others, but also requires the communal consensus *by* others.[73] In this regard, the same logic of *kratos* in Hesiod, which allows for Zeus to secure his rule, is also at work in the maintenance of that rule in the *Iliad*.[74]

Misinterpreting *Kratos*: Zeus' Deception of Agamemnon

Not only can we observe a principle of alterity and *différance* at work in the general cultural semantics of *kratos* and its mythopoetic associations, but we may also observe the deconstruction of Agamemnon's own political force within the *Iliad* when we compare the words and actions of Odysseus with the narrative context of *Iliad* 2. Regarding the role of Odysseus in *Iliad* 2, scholars tend to focus on his success in reconsolidating the authority of Agamemnon and reuniting the Greek army.[75] Most recently, David Elmer has interpreted this unification in metapoetic terms, given that the unification of the army leads eventually to the Catalogue of Ships. Hence the events of *Iliad* 2 constitute "so many reiterated manifestations of the community's will to reconstitute itself after nearly falling apart." And he further states, "The Catalogue occupies a privileged position as the

[73] Similarly, Martin 1989: 55 views the need for approval in Zeus' boast as a function of oral poetic culture: "The critical need for the approval of Zeus' Olympian audience, the 'praise' alluded to at 8.9, shows most clearly how an oral culture's notions of performance structure the distribution of power. In effect, only an acceptable 'performance' of a proposal can enable the speaker to accomplish his will; only a counter performance, the actual voicing of 'praise,' certifies the audience's consent." See also Kelly 2007: 45: "The 'how far/ I am' comparison tends to emphasize authority in contexts where the acknowledgement of that quality is paramount."

[74] Again, despite differences in detail concerning the cosmogonic narratives of the *Theogony* and that implied in the *Iliad*, there nevertheless remain thematic parallels. See note 28 above.

[75] See Gschnitzer 1976; Carlier 1984: 201–3; McGlew 1989; Easterling 1989; Schmidt 2002. The one notable exception is Hammer, who sees irony in the fact that Agamemnon's own authority is asserted through the agency of Odysseus: "In upholding Agamemnon's authority as the one king, Odysseus is actually the only one at this point acting as a king" (Hammer 2002: 88). Scodel, on the other hand, sees Odysseus' intervention on behalf of Agamemnon as a means of saving "face," especially with regard to the abuse of Thersites: "Agamemnon does not have to lower himself by trading abuse with a social inferior...Thersites' humiliation is a distraction from Agamemnon's or even a substitute for it" (Scodel 2008: 66). Whether positive or ironic, Odysseus' intervention on behalf of Agamemnon underscores the fact that Agamemnon's own power is not established by a "self-thesis" in Derridean terms.

94 Force, Politics, and Signification in the *Iliad*

last and most conspicuous of these statements of unity."[76] It is certainly true from the focalized perspective of the Greek warriors that unity under Agamemnon has been achieved, and it is equally true that such unification has metapoetic significance, since it is that unification which allows for the plot of the *Iliad* to move forward. What I would like to note, however, is that this newly forged unity in *Iliad* 2 rests on a false assumption on the part of Agamemnon, Odysseus, and the rest of the Greek army. For that unity assumes an intimate connection between Agamemnon's political rule and the *kratos* of Zeus, a connection which is supposed to result in the immediate success of the Greeks in battle. Yet the very narrative context of *Iliad* 2 undermines that close connection between god and king. For the entire series of events in *Iliad* 2 is inaugurated by the "destructive dream" *oulos oneiros* (*Iliad* 2.6) sent by Zeus—a dream intended to convince Agamemnon of the very opposite of Zeus' own intentions.[77] Thus, while the mortal community of Greek warriors acts under the assumption of total cohesion, that very cohesion belies a stark separation between mortal and immortal.

The difference between mortal perception and divine power appears most strongly in a unique moment of ritual practice, during Agamemnon's sacrifice after reunification of the Greek army. As Richard Seaford has noted, sacrifices in the *Iliad* tend to cluster in episodes either before or after battle, and for Seaford, the purpose of such sacrifice is to create a sense of community, *koinōnia*.[78] Furthermore, it has been shown that most sacrifices in the *Iliad* serve to increase the power and prestige of Agamemnon specifically as leader of the Greek army.[79] In *Iliad* 2, Agamemnon himself offers a sacrifice with his inner circle separate from the Achaean camp, which may very well serve the ostensible purpose of creating community and reconfirming the power of Agamemnon. But the actual outcome of that sacrifice is far different. In the course of the sacrifice, Agamemnon offers the following prayer:

Ζεῦ κύδιστε μέγιστε κελαινεφὲς αἰθέρι ναίων
μὴ πρὶν ἐπ᾽ ἠέλιον δῦναι καὶ ἐπὶ κνέφας ἐλθεῖν
πρίν με κατὰ πρηνὲς βαλέειν Πριάμοιο μέλαθρον

---

[76] Elmer 2013: 103.

[77] On the deceptive capacity of this dream see Nelson 1996/1997: 190. Although most scholars view the events of *Iliad* 2 in positive terms, Thalmann 1988 and Taplin 1992: 92–3 emphasize how that dream might negatively reflect on the authority of Agamemnon. Christensen 2015: 77 nicely extrapolates from the Diapaira episode a basic interpretive stance on the poem as a whole: "The *diapeira* stands *pars pro toto* for the epic itself and warns us not to take the narrator or the poem at its word."

[78] Seaford 1994: 42–4.   [79] Hitch 2009: 142.

Zeus' Deception of Agamemnon   95

αἰθαλόεν, πρῆσαι δὲ πυρὸς δηΐοιο θύρετρα,
Ἑκτόρεον δὲ χιτῶνα περὶ στήθεσσι δαΐξαι
χαλκῷ ῥωγαλέον· πολέες δ᾽ ἀμφ᾽ αὐτὸν ἑταῖροι
πρηνέες ἐν κονίῃσιν ὀδὰξ λαζοίατο γαῖαν.

Iliad 2.412–18

Oh greatest Zeus, with the most *kudos*, dark clouded, dwelling in the sky,
may the sun not go down and the darkness not come
until I have thrown down the house of Priam
ablaze, and burned the doors with destructive fire,
and cleaved Hector's tunic around the chest,
torn with the bronze blade. And may many of his companions
around him gnaw the earth with their teeth face down in the dirt.

Here we see Agamemnon pray not just for conquest, but for total annihilation of Troy, Priam, and Hector.[80] Following Agamemnon's prayer, the narrator makes the following comment concerning the success of the sacrifice:

Ὣς ἔφατ᾽, οὐδ᾽ ἄρα πώ οἱ ἐπεκραίαινε Κρονίων,
ἀλλ᾽ ὅ γε δέκτο μὲν ἱρά, πόνον δ᾽ ἀμέγαρτον ὄφελλεν.

Iliad 2.419–20

Thus he spoke, but Zeus did not accomplish [his prayer] for him,
but he accepted the sacrifices and increased the unenviable toil.

This semi-failed sacrifice presents us with an extremely important moment in religious politics. For it presents a distinct break in reciprocal relations between humans and gods, between a mortal and divine king.

Rejected prayers and failed sacrifices are not entirely uncommon in the Homeric epics.[81] Yet, Agamemnon's sacrifice in *Iliad* 2 is the only instance

---

[80] As Haft 1990: 39–45 notes, the destruction of Troy is mentioned more in *Iliad* 2 than any other book. Haft further suggests that Odysseus' prominent role in *Iliad* 2 is proleptic of the fact that he is responsible for the sack of Troy, more so than Agamemnon.

[81] On the general structure of Homeric prayers and the gods' responses, see Morrison 1991; Lateiner 1997. For an extensive overview of rejected sacrifices and their manifold causes in Greek and Roman antiquity, see Naiden 2013: 131–82. For negative reactions to prayer and sacrifice by the gods in Homer, see *Iliad* 3.297–302: rejection of the results of the duel between Paris and Menelaus; *Iliad* 6.297–311: Athena's rejection of Trojan prayer; *Iliad* 12.162–74: prayer of Trojan Asios; *Iliad* 16.249–56: Achilles' two-part prayer for Patroclus half accepted and half rejected by Zeus. In each of these cases in the *Iliad* the narrator

96   Force, Politics, and Signification in the *Iliad*

where a god accepts the sacrifice and rejects the prayer.[82] As such, the episode has made both ancient and modern commentators uncomfortable. In the first place, Aristarchus (by way of Didymus in the Venetus A manuscript) suggests that the phrase "he accepted the sacrifices" (δέκτο μὲν ἱρά) (*Iliad* 2.420) means that Zeus must have sent a favorable omen indicating so. At the same time, Kirk, Brügger et al., and others suggest that the πώ in *Iliad* 2.419 has a temporal rather than emphatic function here, such that Zeus "did not *yet* accomplish his prayer for him."[83] Yet Agamemnon's own prayer has a very specific temporal constraint, namely, that he should sack the city of Priam and kill Hector *within a single day*. This is something that Zeus does not allow. And the narrator of the poem further points out that Agamemnon's own folly is based on the temporal aspects of his desire. Immediately after the destructive dream came to Agamemnon, the narrator explained:

φῆ γὰρ ὅ γ' αἱρήσειν Πριάμου πόλιν ἤματι κείνῳ
νήπιος, οὐδὲ τὰ ἤδη ἅ ῥα Ζεὺς μήδετο ἔργα·

Iliad 2.37–8

For he thought that he would sack the city of Priam on that very day, fool, nor did he know the events Zeus was planning.

Thus, rather than assume that Zeus is merely enacting a form of delayed reciprocity, it seems more likely that Zeus is in fact rejecting the prayer, thereby re-emphasizing the fact of Zeus' deception of Agamemnon.[84]

Furthermore, from a more general anthropological and religious perspective, Zeus' taking of the sacrifice and rejection of the prayer would appear to mark a major violation in standard ritual procedures. For Greek

---

describes the rejection but gives no indication of mortal knowledge of that rejection. For failed sacrifices where participants are aware of the failure, see esp. *Odyssey* 9.548–55: Odysseus narrating the sacrifice of the ram stolen from the Cyclops cave; *Odyssey* 12.353–96: cattle of the Sun, where Odysseus describes the negative portents. As Naiden notes, there are various reasons for the different types of rejection of sacrifice and prayer.

[82] As noted by Kirk 1985: 160. The closest parallel is *Iliad* 16.249–56, where Zeus rejects half the prayer.

[83] Kirk 1985: 160; Brügger et al. 2010: 126. Also following this interpretation is Morrison 1991: 151 as well as Lateiner 1997: 260. One should note, however, that in Homer the particle πώ may also have a strictly emphatic function, on which see *LfgrE* ad loc.

[84] For further discussion on timing and delayed reciprocity in the *Iliad*, see Widzisz 2012. Indeed, as Widzisz notes, it is in fact Agamemnon's failure to appreciate the timing of reciprocity, and his demand for *immediate* compensation for the loss of Chryseis, which brings about the entire series of tragic events beginning in Book 1 (Widzisz 2012: 157–61).

Zeus' Deception of Agamemnon   97

prayer and sacrifice is generally considered to follow a general principle of reciprocity, most famously articulated by Marcel Mauss in *Essai sur le don*.[85] In that seminal work, Mauss outlined three obligations of gift exchange: the obligation to give, to receive, and to reciprocate.[86] Indeed, up to this point in the narrative of the *Iliad*, there have been various occasions in which the obligatory principles of reciprocity have followed course. Thus, Apollo sent a plague to the Achaean camp in response to Chryses' prayer: "May the Danaans pay the price for my tears with your arrows" (τίσειαν Δαναοὶ ἐμὰ δάκρυα σοῖσι βέλεσσιν) (*Iliad* 1.42).[87] In addition, Zeus also granted Thetis' request to honor Achilles out of obligation to Thetis for her prior actions in aiding Zeus (*Iliad* 1.503–27).[88] And yet, in Agamemnon's sacrifice, the narrator presents what at first glance seems to be a clear violation of Mauss's third obligation, the obligation to reciprocate.[89] That violation of reciprocity with Agamemnon is of course a direct result of Zeus' own competing obligation to Thetis and, by extension, Achilles.[90]

This ritual episode in *Iliad* 2 also introduces us to a larger problem, which both philosophers and anthropologists have long dealt with, namely, how can reciprocity be obligatory in the context of unequal relations of force?[91] In Archaic Greek poetry, at least, the obligatory aspects of reciprocal exchange seem to operate in a strictly unidirectional manner. That is, humans are obligated to gods, but not vice versa. Thus, for instance, in the *Hymn to Demeter*, in a point of ritual irony, a mortal maiden explains the reasons for hardship to Demeter, who is disguised as a mortal:

---

[85] Mauss did not directly address Greek practice in that essay, but for applications and modifications of his model to ancient Greek contexts, see the essays in Gill, Postlethwaite, and Seaford 1998 as well as Satlow 2013.

[86] These obligations are most clearly defined in relation to the social institution known as the "potlatch" but Mauss clearly means for such obligations to be abstracted to other contexts of reciprocal exchange. See Mauss 1970: 37–41.

[87] Chryses' prayer also follows the model of obligatory exchange by first invoking prior services rendered for Apollo, which takes a literary form of prayer, which Robert Parker refers to as the "*ei pote*" or "If ever" prayer (Parker 1998: 106–107).

[88] Thetis' supplication of Zeus follows the same "*ei pote*" model used by Chryses. For the mythic background and perhaps deeper obligations that Zeus may owe to Thetis as a result of her unique status and power, see Slatkin 1991.

[89] As Leaf 1900 ad loc. comments: "That Zeus should accept the one and deny the other shews that he is deliberately deceiving Agamemnon."

[90] For the plot of the *Iliad* as a causal chain of reciprocities, see Cook 2016, although Cook does not directly discuss this particular ritual episode.

[91] See for instance, Plato's *Euthyphro* (12e–15b) and Parker 1998: 121. For modern concerns with issues of Mauss' notion of "obligation" in his account of reciprocity, see most recently Frank 2016; Pommier 2010, among others.

98 Force, Politics, and Signification in the *Iliad*

Μαῖα θεῶν μὲν δῶρα καὶ ἀχνύμενοί περ ἀνάγκῃ
τέτλαμεν ἄνθρωποι· δὴ γὰρ πολὺ φέρτεροί εἰσιν.

Homeric Hymn to Demeter 146–7

Mother, although vexed by necessity,
we humans *endure* the gifts of the gods, for they are far stronger.

Thus, because the gods are stronger, *pherteroi*, humans have an *obligation* to receive. Through an extension of this same logic, because the gods are stronger, we can infer that humans do not have control over what the gods reciprocate. Indeed, Zeus' response to Agamemnon's prayer in *Iliad* 2 does not result, strictly speaking, in a complete denial of reciprocity. Instead, it presents us with an instance of *negative* reciprocity.[92] Zeus does not grant Agamemnon's prayer, but the text clearly states that Zeus does offer something in return, namely "unenviable toil" (πόνον δ' ἀμέγαρτον) (*Iliad* 2.420).[93]

In addition, the verb employed by the narrator to describe the non-fulfilment of Agamemnon's prayer, οὐδ'…ἐπεκραίαινε (*Iliad* 2.419), further underscores a dramatic disjunction in reciprocal ties between mortal and immortal king. According to Benveniste, the verb *krainō* designates "the sanctioning with authority the accomplishment of a human project and so according it existence."[94] Benveniste further notes that this sanctioning occurs within Homer first and foremost by divine authority.[95] Thus, concerning Zeus' rejection of Agamemnon's prayer, Benveniste explains:

> Only the god has the capability of *krainein*, which indicates not the actual execution but (1) the acceptance by the god of the wish formulated by the man and (2) the divine authorization accorded to the wish to reach accomplishment.
>
> **(Benveniste 2016: 330)**

Yet this divine sanctioning of authority, at least within Homer, is also understood to transfer to the king's authority. Thus, in *Iliad* 9, Nestor

---

[92] Marshall Sahlins describes negative reciprocity as "the attempt to get something for nothing with impunity" and "ranges through various degrees of cunning, guile, stealth, and violence" (Sahlins 1972: 195).

[93] Martin 2015: 159 also notes how the comment of the narrator also creates a contrast with the sacrifice of the soldiers (*Iliad* 2.400–1): "With grim irony, Agamemnon's overconfident prayer for conquest contrasts with the words of anonymous soldiers who wish merely to survive."

[94] Benveniste 2016: 335.

[95] See for instance the prayer/supplication formula "accomplish my desire" (τόδε μοι κρήηνον/ κρηῆνατ' ἐέλδωρ) (*Iliad* 1.41, 1.504; *Odyssey* 3.418, 17.242).

Zeus' Deception of Agamemnon 99

too seeks to shore up the authority of Agamemnon and addresses him as follows:

λαῶν ἐσσι ἄναξ καί τοι Ζεὺς ἐγγυάλιξε
σκῆπτρόν τ' ἠδὲ θέμιστας, ἵνά σφισι βουλεύῃσθα.
τώ σε χρὴ περὶ μὲν φάσθαι ἔπος ἠδ' ἐπακοῦσαι,
κρηῆναι δὲ καὶ ἄλλῳ, ὅτ' ἄν τινα θυμὸς ἀνώγῃ
εἰπεῖν εἰς ἀγαθόν· σέο δ' ἕξεται ὅττί κεν ἄρχῃ.

Iliad 9.98–102

You are lord of the people, and Zeus granted to you
the scepter and *themistes*, in order that you may counsel for them.
Thus, it is necessary that you speak and listen,
and to sanction speech on behalf of others, whenever the *thumos*
compels one to speak for a good purpose. It will be for you however
you rule.

We should first note that *Iliad* 9.99 presents a near exact parallel with *Iliad* 2.206, where the authority of Agamemnon is determined by his divine favor, symbolized by the scepter.[96] In this second effort to emphasize the divine favor of Agamemnon, Nestor gives special attention to Agamemnon's own ability to listen to others and sanction their requests (κρηῆναι δὲ καὶ ἄλλῳ).[97] Just as Zeus is able to sanction mortal requests, so Agamemnon, in turn, because of his divine favor, is meant to be able to do the same. In summarizing the significance of *krainō* Benveniste states:

The Greek *krainō* is used of the divinity who sanctions (by a nod, *krainō* being derivative of *kara* 'head') and, by imitation of the divine authority, also the king who gives executive sanction to a project or a proposal but without carrying it out himself. *Krainō* thus appears as the specific

---

[96] *Iliad* 2.206 is found only in a quotation in Dio Chrysostom 1.11 and not in the manuscript tradition. West 1998 therefore does not provide the line in main body of his text because it is a "plus line." But to have Odysseus' speech end "To whom the son of crooked-counseling Cronus" without specifying an object makes for an awkward reading. Furthermore, one could argue for the importance and presence of *Iliad* 2.206 precisely because it is Agamemnon's scepter that Odysseus holds in his hand, and the very genealogy of the scepter is also provided at *Iliad* 2.101–8. On the scepter as a link between divine and mortal king, see Mondi 1980; on *themis* having the same function, see Benveniste 2016: 388. For further discussion of the scepter and its significance, see Chapter 1.

[97] Hainsworth 1993: 71 suggests that *epos* may be the object of the verb at 9.101, or the entire temporal clause may also be the object.

100 Force, Politics, and Signification in the *Iliad*

expression for the act of authority—divine in origin and subsequently also royal and even susceptible of other extensions in given contexts—which allows a word to be realized in action.

(Benveniste 2016: 329)

Where Odysseus refers to the scepter as a material symbol of the connection between Agamemnon and Zeus, it is the act of *krainein* that creates a praxis-based connection between mortal and immortal king. Thus, for Zeus to refuse to sanction Agamemnon's prayer in *Iliad* 2 with the phrase οὐδ…ἐπεκραίαινε presents a distinct moment of rupture in mortal-immortal relations, which undermines the very foundations of Agamemnon's royal authority. Immediately after Odysseus has insisted upon the authority and ipsocentric force of Agamemnon based on his connections with Zeus, the intentions and actions of Zeus contradict that very claim.

Reinterpreting *Kratos*: Diomedes' Rebuke

The undermining of Agamemnon's authority, which is only implicit in *Iliad* 2, is brought to the fore in *Iliad* 9, where we can observe the *différance* of *kratos* in full force. At the beginning of *Iliad* 9, a disheartened Agamemnon comes to realize that his prayer for the immediate annihilation of Troy will not be answered, and so he delivers a speech to the leaders of the Greek army calling for flight (*Iliad* 9.17–28). This speech presents a near exact repetition of the speech Agamemnon delivered to the entire Greek army at the beginning of *Iliad* 2, where Agamemnon had called for flight in order to test the Greek army (*Iliad* 2.111–18, 139–41). Because of the repetition, the bT scholia considered this second speech to be yet another attempt at testing the Greek army. Yet this could hardly be the case, since we have no other indication of such a test, compared with the explanation given in *Iliad* 2 (cf. *Iliad* 2.73). In addition, the narrator specifically comments on the pain and tears of Agamemnon as he delivers this second call for flight, a pain which was not mentioned in the first speech (*Iliad* 9.14–16). Hainsworth, however, has further commented on these lines, suggesting caution in analyzing the repetition:

It does not follow that a passage cannot recall a previous context, only that such a recall may be read into the text at some risk of

Diomedes' Rebuke   **101**

over-interpretation and should rest on thematic correspondence rather than verbal repetitions.

(**Hainsworth 1993: 61**)[98]

Yet, as Bakker has shown in his method of "interformularity," there is in fact a way to gauge whether verbal repetition itself may in fact recall other previous contexts, namely through the frequency of those repetitions.[99] Although the speech does contain some more general formulas, there are several key formulaic elements that are exclusive to the speeches of *Iliad* 2 and *Iliad* 9. The relative infrequency of the verbal parallels, in other words, allows us to read the two speeches in direct relation to each other. What we find is that the points of high interformulaic repetition underscore the break between Zeus and Agamemnon as a function of Zeus' own *kratos*. In the opening of both speeches, Agamemnon explains, Zeus "promised and agreed" that Agamemnon would sack the city of Troy (ὑπέσχετο καὶ κατένευσε) (*Iliad* 2.112; *Iliad* 9.19).[100] Such a promise speaks to the assumption of obligation between mortal and immortal king, which Zeus clearly violated in Agamemnon's sacrifice from *Iliad* 2. At the same time, Agamemnon points to a discrepancy between Zeus' act of signification with his nod and the overall effect of his actions. Agamemnon then goes on to state that "now he has planned an evil deception" (νῦν δὲ κακὴν ἀπάτην βουλεύσατο) (*Iliad* 2.114, *Iliad* 9.21). The formula "planned an evil deception" occurs nowhere else in the *Iliad*, and points directly to the play of signification and deception inaugurated by Zeus in *Iliad* 2. For Zeus first sent the destructive dream to Agamemnon, which reported the opposite of Zeus' own intentions. Then Agamemnon himself delivered his test speech to the Achaean army, in which his own words did not match what he believed to be true. When Agamemnon first stated that "Zeus planned an evil deception," he thought it was a false statement, when in reality it was true. Zeus had in fact deceived Agamemnon. And finally, in *Iliad* 9,

---

[98] Griffin 1995: 77 is less cautious than Hainsworth: "It is just a repetition—the singer felt no need to try to improve on these lines."

[99] Bakker 2013: 157–69.

[100] This formula is on the high end of the scale of interformularity. Aside from the occurrences in *Iliad* 2 and *Iliad* 9, there is only one other instance of the formula "promised and agreed"—when Hector rebukes Poulydamas for suggesting retreat after the eagle and snake portent of Zeus. Hector denies the significance of the omen specifically because Zeus has "promised and agreed" to Hector's own victory in battle (*Iliad* 12.235–6). As with Agamemnon's uses of the formula, the invocation of the "promise" of Zeus by Hector will ultimately end in a break of that promise. Thus the formula itself underscores the limited knowledge of mortals regarding the actions of the gods.

102 Force, Politics, and Signification in the *Iliad*

Agamemnon repeats that phrase, "Zeus planned an evil deception." But unlike the first time he uttered these words, this second pronouncement accurately reflects the intentions of Zeus—Agamemnon's initial lie has proved to be true. And yet the final truth of Agamemnon's statement is a function of Agamemnon realizing the non-correspondence between what Zeus himself promises and what he accomplishes.

Finally, in the speeches of Agamemnon in *Iliad* 2 and *Iliad* 9, Agamemnon justifies the break between Zeus and Agamemnon by appeal to Zeus' absolute superiority or *kratos*. In both episodes, Agamemnon proclaims: "for his *kratos* is the greatest" ($\tau o \hat{v} \gamma \grave{a} \rho \kappa \rho \acute{a} \tau o \varsigma \acute{\epsilon} \sigma \tau \grave{\iota} \mu \acute{\epsilon} \gamma \iota \sigma \tau o \nu$) (*Iliad* 2.118; *Iliad* 9.25). In this final claim, Agamemnon himself supplies the logic for how and why Zeus violated the reciprocity between himself and Agamemnon in *Iliad* 2. Agamemnon's logic parallels that provided in the *Hymn to Demeter*, when the mortal maiden explained that it is because the gods are "stronger," *pherteroi*, that humans must accept the gifts of the gods. Similarly, according to Agamemnon, it is because of the superlative *kratos* of Zeus that Zeus does not need to follow through on his promises with mortals, not even with Agamemnon. Thus, the formulaic repetition in the two episodes highlights the *différance* at work in the force of Zeus. First, the formulaic repetition highlights a difference in meaning between Agamemnon's first speech and the second, where that difference is a function of acknowledging the *kratos* of Zeus. At the same time, the very semantic content of these formulas indicates a difference between what Zeus signifies to mortals and what he accomplishes. The effect is a constant deferral and demonstrates the inability of mortals to properly and accurately make pronouncements on the intentions of Zeus and his *kratos*.

Consequently, the chain of signification and deception from *Iliad* 2 to *Iliad* 9 allows us to rethink the significance of the epithet of Zeus, "son of crooked-counseling Cronus," used by Odysseus to reconstitute the authority of Agamemnon (*Iliad* 2.205). On the one hand, Derrida may be correct that the epithet invokes the myth of succession, which tells how Zeus became sole divine ruler, thereby providing a divine analogy for Agamemnon as the "one king." On the other hand, the epithet may in fact have a second level of signification, unintended by Odysseus. For it invokes Zeus' own capacity for deception or *mētis*, a capacity which Zeus makes use of against Agamemnon in *Iliad* 2. Indeed, that same irony is present when Odysseus concludes his speech to the kings, delivered first, with the pronouncement: "*Timē* is from Zeus, and Zeus endowed with *mētis* loves him [Agamemnon]" ($\tau \iota \mu \grave{\eta} \delta$ $\acute{\epsilon} \kappa \Delta \iota \acute{o} \varsigma \acute{\epsilon} \sigma \tau \iota, \varphi \iota \lambda \epsilon \hat{\iota} \delta \acute{\epsilon} \acute{\epsilon} \mu \eta \tau \acute{\iota} \epsilon \tau a Z \epsilon \acute{v} \varsigma$) (*Iliad* 2.197). As in the second speech to the *dēmos*, the supposedly intimate filiation between Agamemnon

Diomedes' Rebuke **103**

and Zeus is directly contradicted by Zeus' own acts of deception. In this regard, Odysseus' two speeches to the kings and *dēmos* respectively, which are meant to shore up the authority of Agamemnon, already contain within them the undoing of that authority through Zeus. Lastly, the effect of *différance*, which is expressed through formulaic repetition in Agamemnon's two speeches concerning the *kratos* of Zeus, is further emphasized by the figure of Diomedes in his response to Agamemnon's second call for flight (*Iliad* 9.32–49). Scholars have often viewed Diomedes as a type of "second Achilles," and so his challenge of Agamemnon in *Iliad* 9 might invoke Achilles' own contest with Agamemnon in *Iliad* 1.[101] Diomedes, however, also has his own unique status and character as a heroic warrior. As Richard Martin observes, "Diomedes, in the *Iliad*, becomes the model of the young Greek male initiated into forceful speaking, a learning of *muthoi*" (Martin 1989: 23). His speech against Agamemnon can therefore be seen as an important first step in that initiation. At the same time, Diomedes' speech also marks an important moment in the social process of deliberation and dissent more generally. Originally, Benveniste had suggested that the concept of *themis* was a prerogative of the king.[102] Diomedes, however, takes up the theme of *themis* in order to challenge Agamemnon: "Son of Atreus, I will be the first to fight with you in your thoughtlessness, as is allowed in the assembly" (Ἀτρεΐδη σοὶ πρῶτα μαχήσομαι ἀφραδέοντι,/ ἧ θέμις ἐστὶν ἄναξ ἀγορῆ·) (*Iliad* 9.32-3). On the one hand, these lines may reflect the more generic function of the assembly.[103] Yet this episode is in fact the first occasion of dissent against Agamemnon in the assembly that does not result in negative consequences.[104] As several scholars have noted, Diomedes' effort at

---

[101] Christensen 2009: 140 emphasizes the threat Diomedes' speech poses to Agamemnon. Barker 2009: 61-2 notes that Diomedes makes it so that his own effort at verbal dispute with Agamemnon does not end in the same way as the quarrel in *Iliad* 1. On Diomedes as a second Achilles, see Schofield 1999: 29; Griffin 1980: 74-5; Andersen 1977; Lohmann 1970: 217-21; Reinhardt 1961: 79.

[102] Thus, Benveniste states, "*Themis* is the prerogative of the *basileus*; it is of heavenly origin, and the plural *themistes* stands for the sum total of these ordinances, which is a code inspired by the gods" (Benveniste 2016: 388). It is for this reason that the *themistes* are often paired with the scepter in Homeric formulas, as seen in the phrase used by Odysseus as well as Nestor (*Iliad* 2.206, 9.99). See also *Iliad* 9.156 and *Iliad* 9.298.

[103] See Foley 1991: 175.

[104] As noted by Barker 2009: 62-3. According to Griffin 1986: 38, the formula "It is themis" is only used by speakers and so serves as an occasion for the enactment of speech. Similarly, Hammer 2002: 127 sees the invocation of *themis* as critical to public claim. The negative consequences of dissent are made clear in Book 1, since the seer Calchas was clearly afraid to criticize Agamemnon, and all of the Greek warriors saw the negative consequences of Achilles' challenge in *Iliad* 1. The Greek warriors also observed the negative consequences of dissent in *Iliad* 2 with Thersites.

104 Force, Politics, and Signification in the *Iliad*

dissent, however, is not entirely successful, and this is most easily gauged by Nestor's critique of his speech (*Iliad* 9.53–64).[105]

For present purposes, however, we may leave aside the shortcomings of Diomedes' speech and instead focus on the content of what Diomedes actually claims in his challenge to Agamemnon. Despite the fact that scholars have understood the challenge of Diomedes as thematically central to the issues of authority and political force in the *Iliad*, almost no attention has been given to the precise argument and language used by Diomedes. To be sure, from a structural perspective, it is clear that Diomedes' challenge parallels that of Achilles in *Iliad* 1. From a formulaic perspective, however, Diomedes' challenge of Agamemnon actually shares very precise interformulaic connections with Odysseus' support of Agamemnon in his speech to the *dēmos* in *Iliad* 2.[106]

Diomedes begins his rebuke of Agamemnon by justifying his speech act based on the precedent that Agamemnon had criticized Diomedes first. He states, "You said that I was unwarlike and without strength" (φὰς ἔμεν ἀπτόλεμον καὶ ἀνάλκιδα·) (*Iliad* 9.35). Here Diomedes is referring to Agamemnon's rebuke of Diomedes in the *epipolesis*, the rousing of the troops in *Iliad* 4. The precise criticism uttered by Agamemnon in *Iliad* 4 was that Tydeus bore a son who is "worse in battle, better in the assembly" (χέρεια μάχῃ, ἀγορῇ δέ τ' ἀμείνω) (*Iliad* 4.400). Surprisingly, at that time, Diomedes did not get angry and seemed to approve of the rebuke.[107] But the rebuke itself, "worse in battle, better in the assembly," from Book 4 is not quite the same as the statement "unwarlike and without strength" in Book 9. Indeed, the latter phrase was in fact used by Odysseus in his chastisement of the *dēmos* (*Iliad* 2.201).[108] In fact, although both separate terms *aptolemos* and *analkis* occur quite often throughout the *Iliad*, they

---

[105] On Nestor's critique of Diomedes, see Martin 1989: 24–6; Christensen 2009; Elmer 2013: 118–19.

[106] See Martin 1989: 120–30 for more general stylistic parallels in the speech habits of Diomedes and Odysseus.

[107] Martin offers the following explanation for Diomedes' response in *Iliad* 4: "The apparent gesture of support for the chief, by reference to the way the game is played, reinforces the agonistic intention of Diomedes' silence. By directing his reply to Sthenelos and then getting him to consent to a *muthos* of command (412), he acknowledges that he knows the ambiguous import of his silence in the duel. Then, singling out Agamemnon for responsibility in the success of the war, Diomedes has also posed the unspeakable possibility of defeat (417–18). This effectively silences the abuser" (Martin 1989: 71–2). On the ambiguous value of Tydeus as a paradigm for Diomedes, one which must be emulated and surpassed, see Christensen and Barker 2011 and O'Maley 2018.

[108] Martin 1989: 24 also notes the parallel, but as a sign of Diomedes' relative inexperience in speaking.

Diomedes' Rebuke 105

appear together nowhere else except in these two episodes. Thus the repetition is high on the scale of interformulularity.[109] In *Iliad* 2, Odysseus uses that phrase "unwarlike and without strength" to demonstrate how it is that the kings are "stronger" than the *dēmos*, thereby further arguing for a correspondence between physical force and political power such that Agamemnon is meant to be the supreme manifestation of that correspondence. Within the speech of Diomedes, however, this particular phrase would seem to have a metonymic function, in so far as the phrase does not refer to Odysseus' rebuke of the *dēmos* per se, but rather to the broader theme of a general correspondence between force and political power.

In the course of his speech, Diomedes then takes up the topic of *kratos* in order to argue for a distinct division between force and political authority. He states,

σοὶ δὲ διάνδιχα δῶκε Κρόνου πάϊς ἀγκυλομήτεω·
σκήπτρῳ μέν τοι δῶκε τετιμῆσθαι περὶ πάντων,
ἀλκὴν δ᾽ οὔ τοι δῶκεν, ὅ τε κράτος ἐστὶ μέγιστον.

Iliad 9.37–9

The son of crooked-counseling Cronus gave to you only half.
With the scepter he granted to you that you be honored above all others.
But he did not give you *alkē*, which is the greatest form of *kratos*.

Within these lines, we have yet a second interformulaic connection with the speech of Odysseus in *Iliad* 2. Although the epithet "son of crooked-counseling Cronus" is fairly regular, the larger phrase, "the son of crooked-counseling Cronus gave ..." (δῶκε Κρόνου πάϊς ἀγκυλομήτεω), occurs only here at *Iliad* 9.37 and in Odysseus' speech to the *dēmos* at *Iliad* 2.205. These two specific instances of interformularity allow us to read the speeches of Diomedes and Odysseus in direct relationship to each other. But the parallel usage of these formulas is for precisely opposite ends.

---

[109] In his commentary on *Iliad* 9, Hainsworth suggests that phrase is a generic formula occurring five times. He does not provide citations. But his count of the number of formulas must include two formulas, since he equates *aptolemos kai analkis* with *kakos kai analkis*, where both formulas together total five occurrences. By lumping together the two formulas, and failing to account for the contexts of these formulas, Hainsworth misrepresents the status of the phrase *aptolemos kai analkis*. The formula is by no means as generic as Hainsworth suggests.

106 Force, Politics, and Signification in the *Iliad*

Where Odysseus aimed to promote a total correspondence theory of force, one in which physical force was coextensive with political power, Diomedes makes use of the language of Odysseus in order to argue for a major *disjunction* between force and political power. Thus, Diomedes claims that what Zeus gave was only "half" or split in two—*diandicha* (*Iliad* 9.37). Typically, the term *diandicha* is used in situations where a hero contemplates one of two options, reflecting what Christopher Gill refers to as "the divided self."[110] Here Diomedes is not referring so much to the divided self of Agamemnon but suggests rather that Agamemnon is only half of the complete picture of an ideal warrior-ruler. Diomedes accedes that yes, Agamemnon has the symbol of authoritative power that is the scepter, but he further states that Agamemnon did not receive another, equally important gift from Zeus, namely *alkē* (*Iliad* 9.39).

In his work *Immortal Armour*, Derek Collins offers an in-depth analysis of the term *alkē* in Homer. *Alkē* is one of the distinct terms for "force" discussed by Benveniste and generally refers to strength in battle, often used in contexts of exhortation.[111] Thus, a common formula for *alkē* is the following: "be men, dear friends, remember your brave *alkē*" (ἀνέρες ἔστε φίλοι, μνήσασθε δὲ θούριδος ἀλκῆς).[112] Regarding this formula and similar uses, Collins calls attention to the unique mental component of *alkē*, where this strength in battle is activated through memory.[113] Consequently, *alkē* is also an object that is forgotten, taking the verb *lanthanō*, but only in moments of adversity or death, and it is also frequently used with the noun *menos*, which itself is derived from the Indo-European root for "memory."[114] At the same time, *alkē* is not just activated through mental procedures, but it is also understood to be an object given by Zeus. For instance, in *Iliad* Book 8, Nestor chides Diomedes and encourages him to flee from battle with the following words:

Τυδεΐδη ἄγε δ᾽ αὖτε φόβον δ᾽ ἔχε μώνυχας ἵππους.
ἦ οὐ γιγνώσκεις ὅ τοι ἐκ Διὸς οὐχ ἕπετ᾽ ἀλκή;
νῦν μὲν γὰρ τούτῳ Κρονίδης Ζεὺς κῦδος ὀπάζει
σήμερον· ὕστερον αὖτε καὶ ἡμῖν, αἴ κ᾽ ἐθέλῃσι,

---

[110] *Iliad* 1.89, 8.167, 13.455. See Gill 1996: 41–60, 175–239.
[111] Benveniste 2016: 362–4.
[112] *Iliad* 6.112, 8.174, 11.287, 15.487, 15.734, 16.270, 17.185.
[113] Collins 1998: 99–104.
[114] Collins 1998: 104–14. On *menos* and its relationship to IE *mne-h₁-, see Nagy 1974: 266–9; Bakker 2008; Bakker 2013: 143–50.

δώσει· ἀνὴρ δέ κεν οὔ τι Διὸς νόον εἰρύσσαιτο
οὐδὲ μάλ' ἴφθιμος, ἐπεὶ ἦ πολὺ φέρτερός ἐστι.

Iliad 8.139–44

Son of Tydeus, come, put your single-hoofed horses to flight.
Do you not recognize that the *alkē* from Zeus is not following you?
For now, Zeus the son of Cronus sends *kudos* to that man today.
Later he will give it to us, if he wishes.
For a man could not guard against the intentions of Zeus,
no matter how strong he is, since Zeus is much stronger.

Here, with *alkē*, we seem to have yet another example of an economy of force shared between mortals and immortals, where Zeus' own superiority is what allows him to give that physical capacity for battle to whomever he intends.[115] Thus, *alkē* is different from *kratos* in so far as it is activated through human agency by way of memory. But at the same time, like other types of force such as *kratos* and *menos*, *alkē* is distinctly external to the human subject, given by Zeus. It is this exteriority of *alkē*, as an object given by Zeus, which serves as the basis for Diomedes' rebuke of Agamemnon in *Iliad* 9.

Ultimately, in making this claim for a critical divide between force and politics, Diomedes appeals to the concept of *kratos*, stating that *alkē* "is the greatest form of *kratos*" (ὅ τε κράτος ἐστὶ μέγιστον) (*Iliad* 9.39). In his discussion of *kratos*, Benveniste himself used this very line from Diomedes' speech in order to suggest that the different terms for force in Homer each had a separate and distinct meaning. Otherwise, the phrase "*alkē*, which is the greatest *kratos*" would be a meaningless pleonasm. And this is why Benveniste further suggests that *kratos* stands for superiority more generally. Benveniste thus states, "There are therefore, according to circumstances, different conditions of *kratos*, some pertaining to age and physical condition, and others to qualities such as *alkē*."[116] According to Benveniste, therefore, Diomedes' claim that *alkē* is the greatest form of *kratos* adds a degree of distinction to the general conceptualization of force, arguing that in the many different ways one can be superior, *alkē* is the best.

---

[115] See discussion in Collins 1998: 47–77. The granting of fighting force is thus parallel here with the giving of *kudos*. As Kelly 2007: 170 notes, the use of the verb *opazien* (*Iliad* 8.141) is usually confined to Zeus describing moments of favor. For further discussion of that speech within the context of *Iliad* 8, see Cook 2009.

[116] Benveniste 2016: 364.

108 Force, Politics, and Signification in the *Iliad*

While Benveniste's general account of the relationship between *kratos* and *alkē* in Diomedes' speech seems correct, his strictly lexical semantic approach fails to capture an additional poetic and pragmatic point of significance in the speech. As we have already noted, the phrase *kratos esti megiston* was understood since antiquity as the "Zeus formula." And most importantly, it was that very phrase which Agamemnon used to explain why Zeus had not kept his initial promise to Agamemnon both at *Iliad* 2.118 and at *Iliad* 9.25. Thus, what Benveniste failed to notice is the meaningful repetition of the formula *kratos esti megiston*, uttered by Agamemnon twice before Diomedes' use of the formula in his own rebuke against Agamemnon. Given the close proximity of the repetition of this phrase in *Iliad* 9, first spoken by Agamemnon and then directly repeated by Diomedes, I suggest we take Diomedes' use of the phrase as a direct response to Agamemnon. That is to say, Diomedes is using Agamemnon's own words against him. It is as though Diomedes were saying, "Yes, Agamemnon, I agree with you that Zeus has the greatest *kratos*, and yes he did give you the scepter, but he did not give you *alkē*, and it is *alkē* which is in fact the greatest gift from Zeus."[117]

The speeches of Agamemnon and Diomedes in *Iliad* 9 thus present a unique instance in which language concerning the power of Agamemnon creates a distinct mirroring effect of *différance*. The formulaic repetitions point to an overall significance to *kratos* quite different from what those formulas signify, and that meaning is only brought about in the play between those repetitions and their specific sequencing in the narrative. First, Agamemnon's near exact repetition of his testing speech reveals a message the opposite of his original intentions from *Iliad* 2. It reveals the breakdown in reciprocal relations of force between the mortal and immortal king, precisely because of the superior *kratos* of Zeus. And Diomedes' speech in turn makes use of the language of Odysseus' speech to the *dēmos* in *Iliad* 2 for a purpose contrary to Odysseus' original intentions. Thus, in place of a unified, ipsocentric model of force, where physical force and political power coincide in the "one king," as Odysseus had argued, Diomedes argues that power is dyadic, divided in two (*diandicha*). And through Diomedes' repetition of the "Zeus formula" used twice by Agamemnon, Diomedes further undermines the theological foundations of Agamemnon's political power. It is in the formulaic repetitions

---

[117] Collins 1998: 71 also makes a similar suggestion in general terms, but does not note the full significance of formulaic repetition in Diomedes' speech.

pertaining to *kratos* and political power that we are able to observe the active deconstruction of Agamemnon's authority.

Conclusion

Derrida's reading of the speech of Odysseus to the *dēmos* in *Rogues* is important both for what it positively contributes and for its philological infelicities. First, Derrida's reading helps us to appreciate how force and politics are forged together in the *Iliad* through theological reasoning on the part of characters within the poem. To invoke Zeus, as Derrida points out, is to seek the origin of force and authority beyond the realm of human agency, *au-delà*, and thus to assume a type of transcendental source for political force. Just as Nestor had attempted to shore up the authority and prestige of Agamemnon by appeal to Zeus in *Iliad* Book 1, so Odysseus does the same in *Iliad* Book 2. Where Nestor failed, it would seem that Odysseus was indeed successful. Yet one of Derrida's fundamental mistakes is to assume that the theological reasoning proposed by Odysseus would apply *tout court* both to the *Iliad* and to western culture as a whole.[118] The narrative context of Odysseus' speech suggests otherwise. Both the destructive dream and the semi-rejected sacrifice of Agamemnon in *Iliad* Book 2 run contrary to the efforts of Odysseus and underscore the deep divide that exists between limited human knowledge and divine action. Hence, the poem calls into question the very political theology of force and divine kingship represented by characters within the poem.

Second, Derrida's misreading of *kratos* as an "ipsocentric" principle also helps us to appreciate the ways in which force, in its many forms, stands for the very opposite of that principle of ipsocentrism. Indeed, from the perspective of both Hesiodic myth and Homeric poetics, it is a mistake to assume that the force of *kratos* is a function of a "self-thesis" or "auto-position" either on the part of Zeus or any other character. Rather, as I have argued, *kratos* manifests a principle of *alterity* in a twofold capacity, both as a form of superiority in contest over an *other* and also as an object given by the gods, coming from an *other*. In this regard, Homeric *kratos*

---

[118] As Derrida states, "This political theogony or theology gets revived or taken over (despite claims to the contrary by such experts as Bodin and Hobbes, whom I cannot treat here) by a so-called modern political theology of monarchic sovereignty and even by the unavowed political theology—itself just as phallocentric, phallo-paterno-filio-fraterno-ipsocentric-of the sovereignty of the people, that is, of democratic sovereignty" (Derrida 2005: 17).

110   Force, Politics, and Signification in the *Iliad*

may be viewed as part of a larger embodied economy shared between mortals and immortals. Indeed, such a principle of alterity applies even to the figure of Zeus.[119] It is the operation of this economy that further undermines the singularity of the "self," *ipse*, implicit both philosophically and philologically in the very concept of "ipsocentrism."

Ultimately, for Derrida, "force" must have an ipsocentric quality, because it is that very transcendence upon which acts of signification must rely and to which they must stand in opposition.[120] Yet the poetics of *kratos* in the *Iliad* demonstrate that force in Homer can never take on such an ipsocentric and self-justifying quality because its source and significance are subject to constant debate through speech. This is made most evident in the close formulaic interconnections between *Iliad* 2 and *Iliad* 9, which point to differences in meaning and result in a constant deferral of force and authority. Thus, if various characters within the *Iliad* assert a close convergence between force and political power based on divine analogy with the *kratos* of Zeus, the poem seems to constantly call that convergence into question through the unique interactions of formula, speech, and narrative. Indeed, we might assert that the very invocation of force in its many forms in the *Iliad* "extends the domain and interplay of signification ad infinitum."[121]

---

[119] For Zeus' dependence on others in the *Theogony*, see, for instance, Scully 2015: 35; for Zeus' dependence on the consent others in the *Iliad*, see Elmer 2013: 146–73.

[120] This transcendental role attributed to the concept of "force" in Derrida is made clear in his essay "Force and Signification," on which see Derrida 1978: 1–36.

[121] Derrida 1972: 249. Indeed, even though the analysis of *kratos* in this chapter ends with Diomedes' critique of Agamemnon, it could continue with Nestor's own critique of Diomedes, which begins "Son of Tydeus, you above others have *kratos* in war" Τυδεΐδη περὶ μὲν πολέμῳ ἔνι καρτερός ἐσσι (*Iliad* 9.53). Nestor's statement responds to Diomedes' own language of *kratos* and reflects the association between Diomedes and *kratos* from a formulaic perspective, since the adjectival form *krateros*, in the nominative, refers to Diomedes twenty times out of thirty-three total instances in the *Iliad* (on which see the appendix). At the same time, Nestor's statement also resonates with his own earlier description of Achilles as *karteros* (*Iliad* 1.280), thereby extending the process of difference and deferral even further with regard to Iliadic *kratos*.

3
Force and Discourse in the Funeral Games of Patroclus

Among the broad range of different terms for force discussed thus far, what remains constant is the fact that every utterance pertaining to force, every use of a force term within the *Iliad*, brings with it a distinctly *discursive* and *agonistic* context. Despite the claims by various characters, no notion of force exists in absolute terms. No claim to authority through force in the *Iliad* goes unchallenged. Such challenges are often presented at two levels—by other characters and/or through the dramatic narrative action of the poem.

But what role, we might ask, does the language of force play in the *agōn* proper within Homeric poetry? Does the discursivity of force remain when dealing with truly physical contests? Are there conceptualizations of force, as the pure embodiment of action, which might move us beyond the deconstructive processes we have observed so far? And would such a non-discursive demonstration of force somehow be more determinative of social ranking compared with the various other claims to force and status uttered through speech? In short, does the very physicality of the *agōn* provide a way of determining a form of force that exists beyond language?

The athletic *agōn* has long been understood as a quintessentially Greek phenomenon ever since the work of Friedrich Nietzsche and Jacob Burckhardt.[1] At the same time, Homeric poetry itself offers us our earliest and most in depth description of athletic competition in Greek history. Yet the relationship between Homeric poetry and more general conceptions of the Greek *agōn* are far from straightforward. According to Burckhardt, athletic competition rose to prominence in the Archaic period, which he dubbed the "Agonal Age," wherein "the whole of life was dedicated to this activity, and only then the victors became great celebrities."[2] Burckhardt

---

[1] On the idea of the *agōn* in Nietzsche and Burckhardt, see, among others, Gossman 2000; Ruehl 2003; Tuncel 2013; Acampora 2013.
[2] Burckhardt 1998: 165.

Homer's Iliad *and the Problem of Force*. Charles H. Stocking, Oxford University Press.
© Charles H. Stocking 2023. DOI: 10.1093/oso/9780192862877.003.0004

112 Force and Discourse in the Funeral Games

believed that the Archaic period was the time of the *agōn* because that was a time of "aristocracies," where competition could occur among a small group of relative coequals.[3] Because of his emphasis on the Archaic period, Burckhardt gave little attention to Homeric poetry, which he relegated to the time of "heroic kingship," and he further suggests, "The *agōn* in [Homer's] poems is never more than an innocent first step compared with its later developments."[4] Nietzsche, on the other hand, saw far less innocence in the contests of Homeric poetry.[5] Rather, he considered that the rivalry found in Homer was characteristic of nearly all phases of Greek history and culture. That is to say, the representation of rivalry in Homer offered a form of sublimation for natural violence, a *tigerartigen Vernichtungslust*—"a tigerish lust to annihilate," which was typical of the "pre-Homeric" world.[6]

While the specific arguments of Nietzsche and Burckhardt have rightly been challenged as far as Greek history and culture are concerned, scholars still continue to concur with their assessment of the high value placed upon the *agōn* in early Greek culture. Yet how and why the *agōn* came about and rose to such prominence remains difficult to determine.[7] While spectacle sport was certainly a feature of Bronze Age Greece, most scholars today agree that Greek agonistic competition was largely a function of the somewhat fluid social and political dynamics of the Iron Age and early Archaic periods of Greek history. Thus for instance, in analyzing the material remains and early pre-Panhellenic history of sites such as Olympia, Catherine Morgan has suggested that "it is easy to see how meetings at a sanctuary like Olympia, outside the territory controlled by participant chiefs, may have provided opportunities for the conspicuous consumption of wealth, and perhaps also athletic display, necessary to maintain an

---

[3] For the debates regarding the problematic concept of "aristocracy" in Archaic Greece and its role in the history of scholarship, see van Wees and Fisher 2015.

[4] Burckhardt 1998: 165.

[5] There seems to have been a mutual influence between Burckhardt and Nietzsche on the broader significance of the *agōn*. Although it has typically been understood that Burckhardt influenced Nietzsche, Oswyn Murray corrects this view in the introduction to the English edition of Burckhardt's lecture series *The Greeks and Greek Civilization*, Burckhardt 1998: xxv–xxxi. For possible influences on Nietzsche's thinking concerning the *agōn* other than Burckhardt, see further Acampora 2013: 211n.7.

[6] From *Homer's Contest* (Nietzsche 2005: 81). On the idea of the "pre-Homeric" in Nietzsche, see Porter 2000: 246–7; Porter 2004: 19–22; Porter 2021: 208–11.

[7] On the cultural and historical semantics of *agōn*, see Scanlon 1983. On the historiography of the *agōn*, see Wacker 2006; Ulf 2008; Weiler 2010; Ulf 2011. On the idea of the athletic *agōn* and its extension to the realm of politics in Homer and the Classical period, see Barker 2009.

Force and Discourse in the Funeral Games   113

individual's status, and thus his prestige, relative to his peers."[8] Similarly, from a sociological perspective, Paul Christesen has characterized the practice of athletic competition in the Iron Age and early Archaic periods as both a reflection and a function of semi-meritocratic status competition among elites.[9] Regarding the earliest historical phases of Greek athletic competition, Christesen reasons as follows:

> Anyone who hoped to enjoy high social status and political influence had to demonstrate that he possessed the sort of physical prowess necessary to defend the community on the battlefield, and the best warrior in town could expect to enjoy the most *timē*... Athletic contests were ideal substitutes for the battlefield because they provided a venue in which men could compete on equal terms in activities that made their relative levels of physical prowess clear while performing in front of the assembled community.
>
> **(Christesen 2012: 153)**

In this respect, the high value placed on the *agōn* during the Iron Age and early Archaic periods may be the result of an underlying assumption among elites that physical force did indeed correlate with social and political standing.

Of course, as I have argued thus far, it is precisely the correlation between physical force and political power that is problematized throughout the *Iliad*, beginning with the conflict between Agamemnon and Achilles in *Iliad* 1. Nearly all scholars agree, however, that the funerary *agōn* for Patroclus in *Iliad* 23 presents a distinct resolution to the very crisis of authority and status with which the *Iliad* began.[10] First and foremost, such a resolution seems to be achieved by virtue of the fact that Achilles organizes the event and removes himself from the competition. As discussed in Chapter 1, it was the constant misassessment of Achilles' own ability and status that brought about and perpetuated the crisis of *Iliad* 1. In *Iliad* 23, however, Achilles' refusal to participate is a gesture that makes

---

[8] Morgan 1990: 93.

[9] See Christesen 2012: 105–6, 166–8 for further discussion of meritocracy in ancient and modern contexts.

[10] On the generally positive nature of the funeral games of Patroclus, see Willis 1941; Willcock 1973; Clay 1983: 176–80; Dunkle 1981; Dunkle 1987; Taplin 1992: 251–60; Richardson 1993: 165–6; Scott 1997; Hammer 2002: 134–43; Kitchell 1998; Beck 2005; Clay 2007; Barker 2009: 86–8; Elmer 2013: 187–97; Kyle 2015: 56–62; B. K. M. Brown 2016. Exceptions, which emphasize the ambiguity of the funeral games of Patroclus, are Allan and Cairns 2011; Buchan 2012: 99–113; Kelly 2017; Scanlon 2018.

114 Force and Discourse in the Funeral Games

his own true worth and ability clear at the same time that it gives other warrior-athletes a "fighting chance." Thus Achilles declares:

εἰ μὲν νῦν ἐπὶ ἄλλῳ ἀεθλεύοιμεν Ἀχαιοὶ
ἦ τ᾽ ἂν ἐγὼ τὰ πρῶτα λαβὼν κλισίην δὲ φεροίμην.

Iliad **23.274–5**

If we Achaeans were competing for prizes on behalf of another man, I, having taken up the first prizes, would carry them to my tent.

As Nietzsche explains regarding the general logic of the Greek *agōn*: "One removes the over-towering individual, thereby now again the contest of forces awakens."[11] Furthermore, Achilles' nonparticipation as presider over the games allows him to take charge in the distribution of the prizes.[12] This very fact creates an implicit contrast with Agamemnon.[13] Indeed, it is not just the fact of Achilles' control over prizes that marks a difference, but it is also the sheer number of prizes or *athla* and the nature of their distribution that presents a second basis for explicit contrast with the general crisis of status in the *Iliad*. As several scholars have noted, there is in fact an equal number of prizes and participants for nearly every event in the funeral games of *Iliad* 23.[14] What this means is that no warrior will go without, thus avoiding the very "zero sum" situation that brought about the initial conflict between Agamemnon and Achilles.[15] In addition, at a cultural-semantic level, *athla* are functionally distinct from war prizes such as *gera*, even though the very objects designated by these terms may

---

[11] Nietzsche 2005: 89. Nietzsche's comment is intended to explain the logic of ostracism, but it works just as well to explain Achilles' own non-participation in the funeral games.

[12] One might assume that such a role would be standard practice for the next of kin, or inheritor, who would hold the funeral contest in honor of the deceased. For discussion and speculation on the psychological reasons for death ritual as an occasion for athletic contest, see, among others, Meuli 1968; Nagy 1990a: 120–2; Seaford 1994: 120–3. For connections between the funerary *agōn* and wealth distribution, see Redfield 1994: 204–10; B. K. M. Brown 2016: 194–7.

[13] See esp. Wilson 2002: 123–6.

[14] The one exception is the weighted throw, for which the only prize is the iron itself. On the prizes in the games, see esp. Papakonstantinou 2002: 60: "The award of multiple prizes mediates a compromise between ascribed and achieved elite status."

[15] As Redfield 1994: 209 states: "These games are an arena in which honor can be won, but they are also a stage upon which honor is recognized. The competition is not zero sum, and attention is paid to status as much as to the outcome of the events." Although Agamemnon presents the deprivation of his own prize in in *Iliad* 1 in terms of a "zero sum" game, "zero sum" is not necessarily the only mode of enacting honor culture, on which see Scodel 2008: 16–20.

Force and Discourse in the Funeral Games **115**

be the same. To be sure, *athla* most likely developed historically from the practices of gift exchange and reciprocity among elites.[16] But unlike war prizes, which, as the *Iliad* demonstrates, can be arbitrarily given and taken away by those in command, athletic prizes entail a certain level of prescriptive certainty: such public prizes are meant to be taken by the victor without deliberation, in accordance with the seemingly objective results of each contest.[17] In this regard, the funeral games of *Iliad* 23 should offer an opportunity to streamline the process of determining social value or *timē* for the community of warrior-athletes.[18] The third and final reason that the funeral games seem to resolve crises over status comes from Achilles' own handling of potential conflicts that result from complications in the individual events.[19] It is indeed Achilles' peaceful distribution of both public prizes and personal goods that marks the strongest contrast with the earlier conflicts of the *Iliad* and makes the overall conclusion of the funeral games for Patroclus a seemingly happy event.

Yet even though the contests do conclude peacefully, this does not mean that the funeral games of Patroclus should be taken as a prescriptive model for the Greek *agōn* more generally. Indeed, upon closer examination, the individual events of the funeral games are riddled with internal conflicts, arguments, and unexpected outcomes. It is hardly a paradigm for how athletic contests should proceed. Such complications indicate that the games of *Iliad* 23 represent far more than Burckhardt's notion of an "innocent first step" in agonal history. It was in fact those very problematic aspects of the funeral games that attracted the attention of the historian and philosopher Michel Foucault.[20] For Foucault, the funeral games of

---

[16] Kyle 1996: 108–11; Papakonstantinou 2002: 52–60; Elmer 2013: 190–1. That relationship may also be triangulated through religious dedication, on which see Morgan 1990: 30–47. In the case of the funeral games for Patroclus, Scodel 2008: 38 notes that each prize was essentially war booty.

[17] See Gernet 1955, esp. 16–17. For the historical and cultural semantic connection between contest and prize represented by the semantic grouping *aethlos/aethlon*, see Scanlon 1983. As Scanlon notes, "The splendor of the contest is determined by its prizes, which not only glorify the victor with preeminent status, but also give fair fame to the hero or person to whom the games are dedicated" (Scanlon 1983: 159). For further elaboration on the difference between war prizes and *athla*, see B. K. M. Brown 2016: 203–11.

[18] As Scodel 2008: 37 notes, face-threat is controlled during the funeral games of Patroclus. See further B. K. M. Brown 2016: 211.

[19] Achilles' various interventions will be discussed in detail below. For potential mismanagement in the games on the part of Achilles see Kelly 2017, also discussed below.

[20] Foucault discusses the funeral games on three separate occasions: in his inaugural lecture series at the Collège de France, delivered in 1970–1, *Lectures on the Will to Know* (2013), in a lecture in Brazil delivered in 1973, "Truth and Juridical Forms," and in his most recently published lecture series from Louvain, *Wrong-Doing, Truth-Telling* (2014), delivered in 1981.

116 Force and Discourse in the Funeral Games

Patroclus represent a complex event—"a vast interplay of the relations of force, manifestations of truth, and the settlement of litigation."[21] Relying on the work of Classical scholars from Glotz and Gernet to Vernant and Detienne, Foucault argued that the Homeric representation of the *agōn* was coextensive with the beginnings of juridical practice in Greece, and that ultimately, the Greek *agōn* served as a cultural site of contest over what Foucault terms "regimes of truth."[22] Thus, Foucault understood the funeral games to mark the beginning stages in a much broader "history of truth" that spans from antiquity to the present. This is a history in which one may observe a transformation in the very concept of truth from the performative to the rational, from the intersubjective to the objective.

Foucault's arguments concerning the funeral games of Patroclus, I believe, will prove extremely valuable for coming to terms with the more general problematic of force in Homer's *Iliad*. To be sure, Foucault's use of Homeric poetry for the sake of historical analysis presents its own difficulties, which will be addressed below.[23] Nevertheless, Foucault's observations, especially from the recently published lecture series *Wrong-Doing, Truth-Telling*, do offer a new avenue of inquiry for questioning the predominance of "force" in the Homeric poems as an uncomplicated and unitary phenomenon.

In this chapter, therefore, I begin by first setting out a basic problem concerning the role of force in the funeral games, as demonstrated in the chariot race, the first event of the contest. I then take up Foucault's analysis in order to further explore how the language of force in the games interacts with issues of status and rank. As discussed above, it is generally assumed that the *agōn* in early Greek history served as an embodied mode for determining and demonstrating social hierarchies, where physical force is meant to correlate with social and political power. Yet Foucault's reading of the chariot race in particular shows how physical contests and their results may not only construct such hierarchies or "regimes of truth," but they can just as easily undermine them. Building on Foucault's observations, I further demonstrate that the results of the other individual

---

[21] Foucault 2014: 31.

[22] Although the phrase was used throughout many of his works, the notion of "regime of truth" was best summarized in an interview as follows: "The types of discourse it harbors and causes to function as true; the mechanisms and instances which enable one to distinguish true from false statements, the way in which each is sanctioned; the techniques and procedures which are valorized for obtaining truth; the status of those who are charged with saying what counts as true" (Foucault 1977: 13).

[23] For a critique of Foucault's treatment of the funeral games in "Truth and Juridical Forms," see Leonard 2005: 75–9. The most thorough discussion of the funeral games by Foucault is provided in *Wrong-Doing, Truth-Telling*, which was unfortunately not available to Leonard at the time of her publication.

Nestor's Advice to Antilochus   **117**

events in the funerary *agōn* not only run contrary to the expected outcomes and presupposed hierarchies within *Iliad* 23, but the results actually contradict the authoritative hierarchy of force and status pronounced by the muse-inspired narrator (*Iliad* 2.760–70). In this regard, we can observe in the Homeric *agōn* of the *Iliad* an inherent contingency in the performativity of force that extends well beyond the contest proper. Far from being a manifestation of the athlete-warriors' purely physical abilities, the *agōn* of *Iliad* 23 demonstrates that it is nearly impossible to disentangle force from discourse.

The Problem of Force in the Funeral Games: Nestor's Advice to Antilochus

The question of force is brought to the fore in the very first event of the funeral games, the chariot race.[24] Achilles sets out the prizes in the middle of the gathering and they are listed in order by the narrator, and then individual warriors volunteer to take part in the contest: Eumelus, Diomedes, Menelaus, Antilochus, and Meriones (*Iliad* 23.287–305, 351). The description of each warrior gives special attention to the horses and provides some indication of the status of the warriors based on their involvement in the war. Diomedes' horses are Trojan and formerly belonged to the warrior Aeneas. The horses of Menelaus include Menelaus' own horse and the mare belonging to Agamemnon, which was a gift from Echepolus in order that the latter might avoid participation in the war. Antilochus' horses, we are told, are Pylian, but no story is attached to them. And in a single line, Meriones is mentioned, but no comment on the horses is made. In some sense, the very listing of the warriors and the number of lines dedicated to describing their horses anticipates the relative significance of each figure in the race as the contest unfolds. Even though there is no mention of the precise genealogy of Antilochus' horses, nevertheless, more lines are dedicated to Antilochus than the other warriors in the list, but only indirectly, by way of a speech delivered by Nestor to his son (*Iliad* 23.306–48). Nestor's speech is embedded in the listing of the warriors, indicated by the awkward mention of Meriones in a single

---

[24] For alternative sequence of events in the literary tradition, see Willis 1941. In the *Iliad*, Achilles frames the chariot race as a form of honor for the death of Patroclus, who tended to the immortal horses of Achilles, on which see *Iliad* 23.280–6. For potentially alternative versions of the chariot race for the funeral of Patroclus, as it pertains to vase painting (Sophilos dinos, François vase), see Burgess 2001: 81–2.

118 Force and Discourse in the Funeral Games

line after Nestor's speech (*Iliad* 23.351). As such, Nestor's speech serves as a type of supplement for the missing genealogy of Antilochus' own horses, and it is that speech that introduces the problem of force for the funeral games as a whole. For Nestor proposes an opposition between physical force and intelligence as the two means by which the race can be run and prizes won. That is to say, according to Nestor, victory may be determined almost entirely by two different modes of human agency. Yet, the race itself demonstrates that the results go far beyond the neat structural paradigm found in Nestor's advice to his son.

Nestor begins his piece of fatherly advice to Antilochus by contrasting Antilochus' skill in horsemanship with the slowness of the horses themselves (*Iliad* 23.309–10). Nestor then presents the concept of *mētis* as a solution to the discrepancy:

τῶν δ᾽ ἵπποι μὲν ἔασιν ἀφάρτεροι, οὐδὲ μὲν αὐτοὶ
πλείονα ἴσασιν σέθεν αὐτοῦ μητίσασθαι.
ἀλλ᾽ ἄγε δὴ σὺ φίλος μῆτιν ἐμβάλλεο θυμῷ
παντοίην, ἵνα μή σε παρεκπροφύγῃσιν ἄεθλα.
μήτι τοι δρυτόμος μέγ᾽ ἀμείνων ἠὲ βίηφι·   (315)
μήτι δ᾽ αὖτε κυβερνήτης ἐνὶ οἴνοπι πόντῳ
νῆα θοὴν ἰθύνει ἐρεχθομένην ἀνέμοισι·
μήτι δ᾽ ἡνίοχος περιγίγνεται ἡνιόχοιο.

Iliad **23.311–18**

Their horses are swifter, but they themselves
do not know more than you how to use *mētis*.
But come, dear boy, place *mētis* of all sorts in your *thumos*.
By *mētis*, the woodcutter is much better than by *biē*.
By *mētis*, the helmsman drives straight his swift ship
On the wine-dark sea, although buffeted by the winds.
And by *mētis*, chariot driver surpasses chariot driver.

In their foundational work *Cunning Intelligence in Greek Culture and Society*, Detienne and Vernant suggest that *mētis* defies any simple definition, although it may be glossed as a type of "wily intelligence."[25] In *Iliad* 23,

---

[25] "There is no doubt that *mētis* is a type of intelligence and thought, a way of knowing; it implies a complex but very coherent body of mental attitudes and intellectual behavior, which combine flair, wisdom, forethought, subtlety of mind, deception, resourcefulness, vigilance, opportunism, various skills, and experience acquired over the years" (Detienne and Vernant 1978: 3).

Nestor presents a rhetorical repetition of *mētis*, which is structured around a series of oppositions culminating with the event at hand, the chariot race. In each of the three examples provided, we have a human agent engaged in a particular task—woodcutting, steering a ship, and steering a chariot. In each case, it would appear that the human agent is opposed to nonhuman elements—the tree, the sea, and horses. There is also a subtle shift in Nestor's threefold repetition, where the first two instances show a type of struggle between the human and nonhuman elements, and that same struggle is then expanded into a distinctly agonistic context in the last utterance, where the chariot driver is not explicitly described in opposition to the nonhuman element, i.e. his horses, but in opposition to another chariot driver (*Iliad* 23.318). Such a statement could be viewed as yet another example of the type of competition mentioned in the Hesiodic *Works and Days*, where "potter contends with potter" (*Works and Days* 25). Thus, in Nestor's speech we move from the realm of struggle and contest in a natural environment to the cultural context of contest proper, the *agōn*—from woodcutters and helmsman against nonhuman forces to chariot driver against chariot driver.

Within this series of oppositions, from "human vs. nonhuman" to "human vs. human," Nestor also presents the concept of *mētis* in opposition to *biē* (*Iliad* 23.315). Thus far, we have already encountered many different terms referring to types of force, but *biē* is perhaps the most common for designating the physicality of force. Indeed, it is this very speech on *mētis* and its opposition to *biē* that Marcel Detienne used for discussing the "first principle" of *mētis* in more general terms in *Cunning Intelligence*. As Detienne explains:

> It shows the opposition between using one's strength and depending on *mētis*. In every confrontation or competitive situation—whether the adversary be a man, an animal, or a natural force—success can be won by two means, either thanks to superiority in "power" in the particular sphere in which the contest is taking place, with the stronger gaining the victory; or by the use of methods of a different order whose effect is, precisely, to reverse the natural outcome of the encounter and to allow victory to fall to the party whose defeat appeared inevitable.
>
> **(Detienne and Vernant 1978: 13)**

It is generally agreed that the opposition Detienne describes between physical force and intelligence, between *biē* and *mētis*, is one that runs

120 Force and Discourse in the Funeral Games

throughout the Homeric and Hesiodic traditions.[26] It is important to note that in Detienne's account, physical force is understood as the simple and unmarked category, in contrast with *mētis* as a particularly marked and complex phenomenon. According to Detienne, physical ability, expressed as *biē* in Nestor's speech, determines the "natural outcome of the encounter," while the intelligence of *mētis* achieves the opposite effect. Yet, as we have seen in the preceding chapters, physical force is by no means a simple or straightforward concept in early Greek poetry, especially Homer. There is in fact as much polyvalence to physical force as there is to concepts of intelligence, and this is reflected in the multiplicity of terms designating "force." Thus, the very fact of the multiplicity of terms for force makes it such that the use of *biē* in opposition to *mētis* is itself marked. Metrical arguments aside, we must consider why *biē* is used in this particular instance and not one of the many other force terms.

Above all other terms designating some type of force, *biē* may be understood as the most physical, and could even be interpreted as a type of "violence."[27] Indeed, the semantic range of *biē*, along with its cognates, indicates points of commonality with other force terms, but it also takes on its own unique cultural semantic sphere. Like other terms such as *kratos* and *alkē*, *biē* too can be an object given by the gods.[28] But unlike other terms, *biē* generally has a more physical, less abstract quality associated with the body.[29] Such physicality is indicated by the term's frequent formulaic use in relation to the "hands" of both warriors and gods.[30] And perhaps the most important and most unique aspect of the term *biē* is its association with the singular subject. Often in early Greek hexameter, one will find the periphrastic use of *biē* along with the name of person in the genitive or in adjectival form as a stand-in for the person in question.[31] This phraseology applies most often to Heralces, that semi-divine hero best known for his physical force, presented either as *biē Hērakleiē* or *biē*

---

[26] For application to Hesiod, see Vernant's discussion in *Cunning Intelligence* (Detienne and Vernant 1978: 55–130). For the role of the *mētis/biē* opposition in Homer and esp. the *Iliad*, see Nagy 1979: 42–58.

[27] Thus, for instance, Chantraine suggests that *biā* (*biē*) "se distingue des autres noms de la force par le fait que *biā* exprime volontiers la violence, se rapporte à une acte de violence" (Chantraine 2009: 174).

[28] See, for instance, *Iliad* 7.205, 7.289.

[29] On only two occasions, *biē* refers to the force of wind, but it is the same simile used in reference to bodily force: *Iliad* 16.213, *Iliad.* 23.71.

[30] See *Theogony* 490, 649, 677; *Works and Day* 148, 321; *Shield of Heracles* 75; *Iliad* 3.431, 12.135, 15.139, 15.181; *Odyssey* 12.246, 21.315, 21.373.

[31] Snell 1953: 19–20; Schmitt 1967: 109–11; Nagy 1979: 318–19; Chantraine 2009: 174.

Hērakléos, but the formula also applies to other warriors.[32] In this sense, the *biē* of the warrior is constitutive of his identity.[33] At the same time, *biē* has implications for mortality, and this is evident from the common formula "would that my force were fixed" (βίη δέ μοι ἔμπεδος εἴη).[34] The adjective in this "optative of wish" expression, *empedos*, has the original meaning of "on/in the ground" and then takes on the more abstract sense of "constant." Hence the formula expresses a desire for physical force to be firm as though fixed in the ground and not subject to the flux of change.[35] Alex Purves has demonstrated that in Homer, the loss of being *empedos* implies the "loosening of limbs" that comes with falling and/or death.[36] Most importantly, in the *Iliad*, the *biē empedos* formula is limited in reference to the figure of Nestor. It is first uttered by Agamemnon in reference to Nestor in *Iliad* 4, while calling the warriors to fight.[37] Then the same formula is uttered by Nestor when reproaching the other Greeks for not standing against Hector.[38] He also utters the same phrase to Patroclus when lamenting Achilles' absence and recalling his own battle against the Eleans.[39] And lastly, he makes use of the same phrase recounting his previous athletic exploits, when Achilles awards him a prize after the chariot race of *Iliad* 23, even though Nestor did not compete.[40] In short, the formula "would that my force were fixed" (βίη δέ μοι ἔμπεδος εἴη) becomes a type of tag line in the *Iliad* specific to the figure of Nestor, the one major Greek warrior whose force must reside in speech because of the failings of his mortal body.

Nestor's use of *biē* in opposition to *mētis* in his speech to Antilochus can therefore be seen to have a double motivation. First, we might consider the opposition to be a function of Nestor's obsession with loss of his own *biē*.[41] At the same time, unlike other force terms, *biē* is associated with the warrior subject in his singularity, such that *biē* can be considered one of the

---

[32] The "force of Heracles": *Iliad* 2.658, 2.666, 5.638, 11.690, 15.640, 18.117, 19.98; *Odyssey* 11.601; *Theogony* 289, 315, 332, 943, 982; *Shield of Heracles* 52, 69, 115, 349, 416. Figures other than Heracles: *Iliad* 3.105, 13.771, 13.781, 17.24, 20.307.

[33] Snell 1953: 19–20; Nagy 1979: 318; D. Stocking 2007: 62–6.

[34] *Iliad* 4.314, 7.157, 11.670, 23.629; *Odyssey* 14.468, 14.503.

[35] *LfgrE* ad loc.: "From the lit. meaning 'standing firmly on (in?) the ground' (πέδον) developed on the one hand to *unchanged, undisturbed*, (still) *present* (1a), on the other to (metaph.) *firm, reliable* (1b); sometimes w. a temp. connot.: *continuous* (1c)."

[36] Purves 2006: 190–1.   [37] *Iliad* 4.314.   [38] *Iliad* 7.157.

[39] *Iliad* 11.670.   [40] *Iliad* 23.629.

[41] Dunkle 1987: 3 suggests that Nestor's lack of *biē* may be a motive for overvaluing *mētis* in his advice to Antilochus.

122   Force and Discourse in the Funeral Games

major means by which a warrior attains identity and reputation.[42] And so Nestor's praise of *mētis* presents an alternative to force as a type of instrument by which one attains reputation and status.[43]

In general, Nestor's opening speech of *Iliad* 23 and his formulation of the *mētis-biē* dichotomy has been taken at face value and considered to be "good advice" for Antilochus.[44] Yet, in the previous chapter, we have already seen how Nestor's first major speech from *Iliad* 1 on the difference between Achilles and Agamemnon (*karteros* vs. *pherteros*) was greatly misguided. Similarly, if we compare Nestor's advice with the outcome of the race, we are presented with several major difficulties. The first problem is whether Antilochus actually follows Nestor's advice. After praising *mētis*, Nestor then gives specific advice on how to approach the turn as the best means for passing the other warriors in the race.[45] Antilochus does manage to pass Menelaus in the race, finishing second rather than third. Yet the text explains that he passed at a point where there was a "narrowing of the course," although the turn itself is never actually described in *Iliad* 23.[46] Following the bT scholia, some consider this place in the road to be just after the turn, or the turn itself, such that Antilochus was true to his father's advice.[47] Yet it could be that Antilochus' bravado in passing Menelaus at this point was not the act of *mētis* Nestor had in mind.[48] Hanna Roisman suggests a solution to this interpretive problem by focusing on the fact that *mētis* itself is of a variegated nature, *pantoiē* (*Iliad* 23.314), such that Antilochus follows the basic principle of flexibility in *mētis* rather than the exact details of his father's advice.[49] But I would further point out that Nestor's focus on the turn is self-contradictory even according to the speech itself. For Nestor begins the speech to his son by

---

[42] With regard to the relationship between *biē* and reputation, Nagy 1979: 318–19 notes that the *biē*-naming constructions are used in conjunction with warriors whose name employs the *kleos* root: Hereacles, Iphikles, Eteokles, Patroclus. Thus Nagy concludes, "The heroic resource of *biē* then has a distinctly positive aspect as a key to the hero's *kleos*" (Nagy 1979: 319).

[43] On the relationship between *mētis* and *kleos*, particularly in reference to Odysseus and the Odyssean tradition, see Pucci 1987: 216–19.

[44] On the general inconsistency between Nestor's reputation and the results of his advice, see Roisman 2005.

[45] *Iliad* 23.334–48.

[46] *Iliad* 23.420. On interpretation of the "narrow road" in the scholia, see Rousseau 1992. On the "narrow road" as an oral-formulaic theme marker for occasions of interpretive debate within the Homeric tradition, see Elmer 2015.

[47] bT 420a. See Detienne and Vernant 1978: 15–16; Gagarin 1983; Forte 2019.

[48] Dunkle 1987: 6; Clay 2007: 71; Rousseau 2010: 29–43; Buchan 2012: 101–2.

[49] Roisman 1988: 117–18. A similar emphasis on the variegated nature of *mētis*, as described by Nestor, is given in Detienne and Vernant 1978: 15.

Nestor's Advice to Antilochus 123

stating "you know well how to drive the turn" (οἶσθα γὰρ εὖ περὶ τέρμαθ᾽ ἐλισσέμεν·) (*Iliad* 23.309). And yet he then gives him advice precisely on the turn, thus rendering his focus on the turn even more curious.[50] But even if we accept that Antilochus follows a more general principle of *mētis*, there remains a central point of difficulty. In Nestor's presentation of the conditions of the race there are only two factors to consider: the physical quality of the horses and the skill of the chariot driver relative to other chariot drivers and their horses. In other words, the race becomes a matter of reconciling the *mētis* of the chariot driver with the *biē* of the horses, and in Nestor's reckoning, superior use of one's own *mētis* can overcome another's superior *biē*.[51] If Nestor's advice was accurate and reliable, then Antilochus' use of *mētis* would have earned him second place, and he would have taken the prize without question. But, in fact, Antilochus' second place prize is doubly challenged and threatened. First, it is threatened by Achilles, who suggests giving second place to Eumelus because he has the reputation as best but crashed as a result of the intervention of Athena.[52] In a manner that mirrors Achilles himself from *Iliad* 1, Antilochus threatens to become angry, to have *cholos*, if he is deprived of his prize.[53] That first minor crisis over second prize is averted when Achilles agrees with Antilochus and gives Eumelus a prize from his personal store of goods. But immediately after this initial settlement,

---

[50] It is because of advice on the turn that the analyst tradition viewed Nestor's speech as a whole as an interpolation. See, for instance, Leaf ad loc. The focus on the turn in Nestor's speech may be topical, as that part of the race with the most intrigue, as seen in later descriptions such as Sopocles, *Electra* 720–2, 743–8, on which see Dunkle 1987: 3; Roisman 1988: 120. Frame 2009: 133–9 sees the focus on the turn as a type of reaction to Nestor's own win in a chariot race, which he narrates briefly when he is given a prize by Achilles (*Iliad* 23.638–42). Phillipe Rousseau 1992: 176–9; 2010: 125 suggests that the inconsistency regarding the mention of the turning post in Nestor's speech compared to the narrative should be interpreted metapoetically, especially because the turn is marked by a *sēma* of a deceased person from a prior age. Buchan 2012: 102–3 views Antilochus' approach versus Nestor's advice as a difference in the two characters' attitudes towards death. For an extension and more detailed account of the ways in which the chariot race has metapoetic resonance, see Martin 2019: 383–405.

[51] This is a basic principle, which can be shown to operate throughout early Greek literature, especially in Hesiod's *Theogony* and also in the Cyclops episode of the *Odyssey* (*Odyssey* 9.406, 408), on which see, among others, Reinhardt 1960: 67; Segal 1962: 34; Austin 1975: 143–50; Detienne and Vernant 1978: 93n.2; Clay 1983: 112–25; Schein 2016: 34–5.

[52] *Iliad* 23.536–8. See further Kelly 2017: 94, who suggests that Achilles' motivation comes from a belief that "the 'best' is always and everywhere to have a privileged access to material reward."

[53] *Iliad* 23.543–54. The parallel between Antilochus and Achilles in this episode was already noted by Eustathius. See further Martin 1989: 188–9; Lohmann 1992: 309–10; Richardson 1993: 228–9; Kitchell 1998: 165; Beck 2005: 241; Kelly 2017: 98. For the special significance of *cholos* as an oral poetic theme dealing with the deprivation of *timē* more generally, see Walsh 2005.

124 Force and Discourse in the Funeral Games

Antilochus' second place prize is threatened yet again, this time by Menelaus. The basis of the challenge is not simply that Antilochus "cheated," but something more abstract. Menelaus claims:

ἤσχυνας μὲν ἐμὴν ἀρετήν, βλάψας δέ μοι ἵππους
τοὺς σοὺς πρόσθε βαλών, οἵ τοι πολὺ χείρονες ἦσαν.

Iliad 23.571-2

You have shamed my *aretē*, having hindered my horses
by casting yours in front, which were by far inferior.

What we see from these lines is that the physical ability or *biē* of the horses is not simply important for determining which prize one might receive in the race, but it is also indicative of the horse owner's *aretē*, that is, his particular position and status within society.[54] In other words, Menelaus claims that during that critical moment in the race, at the narrowing of the road, when Antilochus should have committed an act of deference by giving way to Menelaus, his social superior, he instead committed an act of defiance against him.

In sum, even though Nestor's advice seems to provide a solution to Antilochus' dilemma, i.e. the inferior ability of Antilochus' horses, by providing a neat, structural definition of *mētis* in opposition to *biē*, it also opens up the problem of force more generally. We see that the outcome of the contest is far more complicated and contentious than Nestor could have predicted. The conclusion of the chariot race reveals a twofold complexity to the very phenomenon of *biē*, as represented in the *Iliad*. First, with the case of Eumelus, it shows how physical ability itself can be adversely affected by divine intervention, well beyond the realm of human agency. This is a factor not considered by Nestor in his speech to Antilochus. Second, even though *biē* usually comes to represent the warrior's individual subjectivity, the race shows how the question of one's force can extend beyond the limits of the warrior's physical body to also

---

[54] Although there are many debates on the historical semantic development of *aretē*, most agree that within Homer it refers primarily to one's social position. Thus, Adkins 1960: 36: "There is an inevitable tendency for [*agathos* and *aretē*] to be used solely with reference to social position, irrespective of other qualities." Similarly, Finkelberg 1998: 20: "*Aretē* as such is envisaged in the Homeric poems as determined by birth and wealth rather than as ought to be proved in fair competition; accordingly, the translation 'breeding' would fit the majority of such contests." For the verb of "shame" in this context as an extension of physical disfigurement, see Cairns 1993: 57. On the etymology of *aretē* and its semantics as related to social "fitness," see most recently Massetti 2013/2014.

Menelaus' Quarrel with Antilochus **125**

include one's horses. As such, even *biē*, the most purely physical and subjective form of force, cannot be disentangled from broader issues of social and political status. Indeed, not only did Nestor fail to factor in the role of the gods, but Nestor's advice also failed to consider the role of social hierarchy in the contest over prizes. Thus, contrary to Detienne's comments in *Cunning Intelligence*, there is no natural outcome to the contest, at least not one that is predicted by physical strength alone. This is because the force of *biē* for mortals can never be objective or *empedos*, neither for Nestor nor for anyone else. Rather, like other forms of force already discussed, the chariot race reveals that *biē* is also doubly contingent. It is contingent both upon the gods and upon intersubjective social relations among mortals. It is the fact of its contingency, its failure to be *empedos*, that makes the uniquely subjective nature of *biē* as a determinant of identity and social status so problematic.

Foucault and the Funeral Games: Menelaus' Quarrel with Antilochus

To my knowledge, few Classical scholars have addressed this basic problem concerning the contingency of physical force and its relationship to subjective identity and social hierarchy in *Iliad* 23. This very topic, however, was addressed, albeit indirectly, by the historian and philosopher Michel Foucault. Although Foucault's treatment of antiquity is most well known in reference to his last major work, the *History of Sexuality* (1976–84, 2018), Foucault takes up an analysis of the funeral games on several occasions in order to explore the "the will to truth" as an occasion for promoting discontinuous models of history.[55] Foucault's most in-depth discussion of the funeral games appears in a recently published series of

---

[55] Foucault's first discussion of the funeral games appears in his first lecture series at the Collège de France, *Lectures on the Will to Know* (1970–1). As described in his inaugural lecture, "The Discourse on Language" (*L'ordre du discours*), Foucault explains: "It will involve seeing whether the will to truth is not as profoundly historical as any other system of exclusion; whether it is not as arbitrary in its roots as they are; whether it is not as modifiable as they are in the course of history…In short, it is a matter of seeing what real struggles and relations of domination are involved in the will to truth" (Foucault 2013: 2). Foucault's analysis of the relationship between domination and will to truth is inherited from Nietzsche (see Foucault 2013: 214–19). The historical dimension of the project may be viewed as a more practical application of the principles regarding the analysis of history through discourse with a focus on points of rupture and discontinuity, as set out in Foucault's *Archaeology of Knowledge*, published just one year prior to his inaugural lectures in 1969.

126   Force and Discourse in the Funeral Games

lectures delivered at the Catholic University of Louvain in 1981 titled *Wrong-Doing, Truth-Telling*.[56]

In the Louvain lectures, Foucault's objective is not simply to discuss the history of truth in broad terms, but in relationship to a very precise mode of speech, which he refers to as "avowal." At the outset of *Wrong-Doing, Truth-Telling*, Foucault defines an avowal as follows:

> Avowal is a verbal act through which the subject affirms who he is, binds himself to this truth, places himself in a relationship of dependence with regard to another, and modifies at the same time his relationship to himself.

> **(Foucault 2014: 17)**

Foucault's concept of avowal can be seen as an outgrowth of his work on the history of madness and the prison, wherein the act of confession and the means of procuring a confession play a prominent role in defining the patient as "mad" or the inmate as "guilty." In addition, Foucault's account of avowal may be viewed as a subtype in Emile Benveniste's broader theory of discourse and *énonciation*. Indeed, Foucault himself acknowledged the influence of Benveniste on his own particular approach to the problems of language and society.[57] As discussed in Chapter 1, unlike the speech act theory of Austin, Benveniste had originally discussed performative aspects of language in reference to the construction of a speaking subject: "The 'Ego' is he who says 'ego'."[58] Above all other modes of speech performance, the avowal seems to give an especially strong emphasis on that speaking *egō*. And Benveniste further noted that every act of enunciation must necessarily have a dialogic context: "Consciousness of self is only possible if experienced by contrast. I use *I* only when I am speaking to someone who will be a *you* in my address."[59] For Foucault, avowal is a special case of such dialogic performance because it does not just establish a communicative relationship, but a *power* relationship, i.e. one in which the speaking subject takes up a position of *inferiority* relative to the addressee. As such,

---

[56] Foucault's lecture in Brazil, "Truth and Juridical Forms," which also addresses the funeral games, acts in some sense as a shortened form of his initial Collège de France lecture series. For discussion of the Brazil lecture, see Leonard 2005: 75–80. The lectures at Louvain, however, give far greater attention to the funeral games and with a slightly different focus from the earlier lectures.

[57] See esp. Foucault's recently published essay "Linguistics and Social Sciences" (Foucault 2022), delivered at the Centre d'études et de recherches économiques et sociales of the University of Tunis in March 1968.

[58] Benveniste 1971: 224.   [59] Benveniste 1971: 224.

the notion of avowal serves in many respects as the basis for Foucault's broader theory of "power." In an essay published just one year after Foucault's *Wrong-Doing, Truth-Telling* lectures, Foucault defined power and its relationship to the subject in more general terms as follows:

> This form of power applies itself to immediate everyday life which categorizes the individual, marks him by his own individuality, attaches him to his own identity, imposes a law of truth on him which he must recognize and which others have to recognize in him. It is a form of power which makes individuals subjects. There are two meanings of the word "subject": subject to someone else by control and dependence; and tied to his own identity by a conscience or self-knowledge. Both meanings suggest a form of power which subjugates and makes subject.
>
> **(Foucault, 1982: 212)**

Foucault's broader theory of power and the subject matches nearly exactly with his earlier definition of avowal except for one difference. In the case of avowal, the two modes of subject construction, both the individual as subject and as subject to someone else, are brought about specifically through the self-reflexive act of speech performance. In *Wrong-Doing, Truth-Telling*, Foucault presents the funeral games of Patroclus, and the conflict between Menelaus and Antilochus in particular, as one of the first observable occasions of avowal in Western history. Thus, he situates the problem of the subject and speech performance squarely within the context of physical contest. And it is through Foucault's focus on the act of avowal that the problems regarding force and subjective identity for the funeral games become fully apparent.

In order to set up his argument on avowal in Homer, Foucault offers an extremely in-depth account of the chariot race of Book 23. One of Foucault's most important and unique observations on the chariot race concerns the initial description of the warriors when they volunteer. As Foucault notes, the order in which they volunteer is of paramount importance:

> And what do we see when they rise? First, there is Eumelus, who is said to be the strongest, and then there is Diomedes, who is said to be extremely strong; next is Menelaus with his fast horses, followed by Antilochus whose horses are slower; and finally there is Meriones, about whom almost nothing is said. The very adjectives attached to

128 Force and Discourse in the Funeral Games

their names reveal from the outset their respective strengths and the vigor of their teams. They are not at all considered equal from the beginning. To the contrary, they stand one by one according to their strength, in descending order from the one who must win to the one who has no chance of winning.

(**Foucault 2014: 38**)

Indeed, if the gods had not intervened and if Antilochus had not exercised his own *mētis*, then the order in which the warriors rose would have indicated the outcome of the race itself. For Foucault, this very fact is indicative that the *agōn* in Homer has a far different purpose compared with our own modern conceptions of competition. He explains:

The race has, as its function, to solemnly reveal, in a combat that is at the same time a ceremony, the heroes' different strengths. The race's real function is to put them in the order of their true value. Consequently, far from being a test in which equal individuals can distinguish themselves so that an unpredictable winner emerges, the race is nothing more than a liturgy of truth.

(**Foucault 2014: 39**)

As Foucault himself states in this first lecture, the concept of "truth" as a form of objective reality is not an overtly operative concept in the funeral games, nor in Archaic Greek poetry more generally.[60] Instead, the idea of "truth" to which Foucault refers is based on relational modes of power. In general, Foucault refers to the truth-power matrix as "regimes of truth," where any such "regime" is meant to construct and reflect the hierarchies of a given society.[61] In the case of the funeral games, Foucault observes, a particular hierarchy is in place prior to the chariot race, which is based on the chariot driver and his horses. And yet, as Foucault notes, the results of

---

[60] In fact, the term "truth" does occur in *Iliad* 23 once, as Foucault himself notes, in reference to Phoenix, who is placed at the turn in order to speak the truth (*Iliad* 23.360–1). But even during the quarrel between Antilochus and Menelaus, Phoenix is not called upon, on which see Foucault 2014: 40. The problem has also been noted by Classicists as early as Leaf if not before.

[61] See further note 22 above for Foucault's definition of a "regime of truth." In his account, Foucault is greatly influenced by Nietzsche's argument that a "will-to-truth" is nothing more than a "will-to-power" (Foucault 2013: 214–19). At the same time the notion of "regime" and also "hierarchy" or "order" implicit in Foucault's definition of "truth," and its close connection to the act of speech, is perhaps more directly derived from Dumézil's work on truth as "order" (Sanskrit *r̥tá-*), as discussed in *Servius et la fortune* (Dumézil 1943: 241–4). Foucault quotes from Dumézil's *Servius* in the first lecture of *Wrong-Doing, Truth-Telling* (Foucault 2014: 28), discussed below.

Menelaus' Quarrel with Antilochus **129**

the race do not correspond to that presupposed hierarchy. Thus, Foucault considers the events of the chariot race as a depiction of a "crisis of truth," that is, a crisis in social hierarchy. We might also interpret it as a crisis, which reflects the very contingency of force (*biē*) and its failure to match social expectation with contest result.

For Foucault, this crisis of "truth" in the funeral games is made manifest when Menelaus challenges Antilochus for the second-place prize. Beginning with Louis Gernet, many scholars have treated the quarrel between Menelaus and Antilochus as one of the first instances of juridical practice in early Greek history.[62] And for Foucault, juridical practice itself is largely dependent on "truth-telling," such that juridical practice itself is one of the primary areas in which one can observe a transformation in the very concept of truth in the Western tradition.[63] Thus, following the work of Gernet, Foucault uses the funeral games as an instance of "pre-law," which in turn also reflects a pre-philosophic and pre-rational mode of "truth."[64] In Gernet's analysis of the funeral games, it is the ritual gestures in the distribution of prizes, the "geste de la main," and the status of the prize as a *res nullius*, a good belonging to no one, which give the strongest indication of a connection with early juridical practice.[65] Foucault, by contrast, gives far greater attention to the verbal exchange in the episode. In particular, Foucault pays special attention to Menelaus' double call for justice against Antilochus. After Menelaus has explained that Antilochus "shamed" his *aretē* (*Iliad* 23.571), he states:

ἀλλ' ἄγετ' Ἀργείων ἡγήτορες ἠδὲ μέδοντες
ἐς μέσον ἀμφοτέροισι δικάσσατε, μὴ δ' ἐπ' ἀρωγῇ,
μή ποτέ τις εἴπῃσιν Ἀχαιῶν χαλκοχιτώνων·
Ἀντίλοχον ψεύδεσσι βιησάμενος Μενέλαος
οἴχεται ἵππον ἄγων, ὅτι οἱ πολὺ χείρονες ἦσαν
ἵπποι, αὐτὸς δὲ κρείσσων ἀρετῇ τε βίῃ τε.

Iliad **23.573–8**

---

[62] See Wolff 1946, Gernet 1955: 9–18; Gagarin 1986: 36–8; Thür 1996; Papakonstantinou 2008: 19–37.

[63] Foucault's interest in the "prehistory" of truth, especially in Archaic Greece, is no doubt influenced by Marcel Detienne's *Masters of Truth*, published in 1967, three years prior to Foucault's first lecture series at the Collège de France, "Lectures on the Will to Know," where Foucault first took up the topic of truth in Homer, as well as in Hesiod. For Detienne's influence on Foucault, see Detienne's comments (1996: 19) as well as Stocking 2017b.

[64] For Gernet's concept of pre-law, *prédroit*, as that which anticipates and reflects later formalized law, see Gernet 1968: 175–260.

[65] Gernet 1955: 11–13.

130 Force and Discourse in the Funeral Games

But come leaders and rulers of the Argives,
judge between us in the middle, but not for the sake of aid,
lest someone of the bronze-clad Achaeans say that Menelaus
goes off with the horses, having overpowered Antilochus with lies,
since his horses were by far inferior, but he himself was superior in *aretē*
and *biē*.

For Foucault, the significance of these lines rests in the fact that Menelaus first calls upon the rest of the Argives to judge the dispute so that Menelaus' taking of the prize is not interpreted as an act of violence or falsehood (*Iliad* 23.576): "he wants the truth of his victory to be recognized without violence and in truth" (Foucault 2014: 34).

In addition, I would further add that the entire question of the "truth" of the event ultimately rests on the issue of *biē* between the two warriors. Menelaus does not want others to claim that Antilochus is greater in social position and force, *aretē* and *biē*, despite having inferior horses (*Iliad* 23.578). Much like the dispute between Agamemnon and Achilles in *Iliad* 1, as described by Nestor, here too the conflict between Antilochus and Menelaus is based on that ambiguous question as to who is "stronger" (*Iliad* 23.578: *kreissōn*)—both socially and physically.[66]

Yet, Menelaus then makes a shift in his own approach, and the rest of the Greeks are never actually called to judge the quarrel.[67] Instead, Menelaus calls for an oath from Antilochus:

εἰ δ᾽ ἄγ᾽ ἐγὼν αὐτὸς δικάσω, καί μ᾽ οὔ τινά φημι
ἄλλον ἐπιπλήξειν Δαναῶν· ἰθεῖα γὰρ ἔσται.
Ἀντίλοχ᾽ εἰ δ᾽ ἄγε δεῦρο διοτρεφές, ἣ θέμις ἐστί,
στὰς ἵππων προπάροιθε καὶ ἅρματος, αὐτὰρ ἱμάσθλην
χερσὶν ἔχε ῥαδινήν, ᾗ περ τὸ πρόσθεν ἔλαυνες,
ἵππων ἁψάμενος γαιήοχον ἐννοσίγαιον
ὄμνυθι μὴ μὲν ἑκὼν τὸ ἐμὸν δόλῳ ἅρμα πεδῆσαι.

Iliad **23.579–85**

---

[66] On *kreissōn* as the comparative form proper of *kratos*, see Chantraine 2009: 556.

[67] Leonard 2005: 76–7 rightly notes the shift and further points out that Foucault glosses over the shift in his earlier lecture, "Truth and Juridical Forms." It should be noted that Foucault does in fact make that very observation in the later lecture series *Wrong-Doing, Truth-Telling* (Foucault 2014: 34), although that lecture series was not available to Leonard at the time of her writing.

Menelaus' Quarrel with Antilochus **131**

But come, I myself will pursue justice, and I claim that no one
else of the Danaans will challenge it. For it will be straight.
Divinely reared Antilochus, come here, as is custom,
standing before the horses and the chariot, take the slender
whip in hand, with which you drove the chariot before,
and grasping the horses, swear to the earth-moving earth-shaker
that you did not willingly constrain my chariot through treachery.

As Foucault notes, the semantics of *dikazō* in this early contest make it
impossible for Menelaus to "judge" the case in the typical modern sense.
That is to say, Menelaus is not an impartial third party in the dispute who
can preside over the conflict. As Foucault states, "The *dikē* that [Menelaus]
proposes is not justice. It is not a just sentence, but rather the just settlement of the dispute, of the conflict that opposes him to Antilochus."[68] The
oath itself becomes a means for settling the dispute. Indeed, this very call
for an oath is what Menelaus claimed he would demand, even as
Antilochus passed him during the race (see *Iliad* 23.441). Hence, the quarrel between Menelaus and Antilochus that occurs after the race may be
viewed as an extension of the athletic *agōn*. In this respect, Foucault follows Gernet and quotes him:

The law itself emanates from the life of the games. There is continuity
between the agonistic customs and the judicial customs. The question
of competence is settled by itself; the *agōn*, the combat, the milieu that
is preestablished for reaching a decision through competition, is also a
milieu favorable to reaching a decision by means of a sentence.
(Gernet 1955: 17–18 quoted in Foucault 2014: 37)

For Foucault, then, if "truth" is operative in the quarrel between Antilochus
and Menelaus, i.e., a "truth" which indicates a hierarchy that should determine how the race ought to have been, and if Antilochus honored
Menelaus' superior rank, then that truth is meant to be restored through
the "oath."

And yet what is most striking is that Antilochus does *not* accept
Menelaus' challenge and does *not* perform the oath. Instead, Antilochus
offers his own act of deference to Menelaus. Antilochus states:

---

[68] Foucault 2014: 34.

132 Force and Discourse in the Funeral Games

ἄνσχεο νῦν· πολλὸν γὰρ ἔγωγε νεώτερός εἰμι
σεῖο ἄναξ Μενέλαε, σὺ δὲ πρότερος καὶ ἀρείων.

Iliad 23.587-8

Hold on now. For I am much younger than you
Lord Menelaus, and you are older and better.

In these lines we see that Antilochus puts a halt to the judicial aspects of the challenge by directly addressing the very reason for Menelaus' displeasure.[69] As already noted above, the essential problem is not that Antilochus "cheated" per se, but rather that he engaged in a particular maneuver that did not show respect to Menelaus' superior social position. Antilochus' response to Menelaus avoids the issue of the "truth contest" of the oath by replacing that oath with a request for forgiveness. And that request also gives what Menelaus had demanded all along: an acknowledgement of Menelaus' superiority, as indicated in Antilochus' use of comparatives, "older and better" (πρότερος καὶ ἀρείων) (*Iliad* 23.588).[70]

Rather than provide an oath, Foucault suggests that Antilochus' response constitutes an avowal. But, as Foucault notes, the avowal of Antilochus does not consist in a confession. He does not admit a fault per se. And for Foucault, the reason for the lack of confession is because the entire conflict does not rest on an explicit violation of the "rules" of the race. Rather, the dispute centers on defining the proper relationship between Menelaus and Antilochus. Antilochus' act of avowal, his non-apology, does precisely that. For, according to Foucault, the "truth" of the event is simply the "proper" relationship between the two warriors. Thus, Foucault explains:

> In fact, the avowal consists of saying, "You were stronger; you were first; you were ahead of me (*proteros kai areiōn*—you were first; you were stronger)." This does not at all mean that Menelaus was ahead, that Menelaus's chariot was ahead of Antilochus's. It means that according

---

[69] As Beck 2005: 242 further notes, the resolution brought about by Antilochus greatly contrasts with the crisis of distribution between Achilles and Agamemnon with which the *Iliad* began.

[70] The comparative form *areiōn* as well as the superlative *aristos* may be etymologically related to *aretē*, for discussion of which see most recently Massetti 2013/2014. As such, Antilochus' response effectively answers Menelaus' complaint that Antilochus shamed his *aretē*.

Menelaus' Quarrel with Antilochus   133

to the order, in a sense, of their true strength, according to the order of their true status, according to the order of the brilliance of each hero, indeed, Menelaus was the *proteros*, he was the first. The role of the race was to ritualize this situation and this relationship; and what Antilochus did—and is now renouncing—was to try to extinguish, suffocate, weaken Menelaus's brilliance.

(Foucault 2014: 42)

In his explanation, Foucault picks up on a potential play in the meaning of *proteros* as it is used by Antilochus. The notion that Menelaus is "older" in age also means that he is socially superior, and so he should also be physically ahead or "prior" in the race. Of course, that did not happen in the race, and so Antilochus' speech compensates for his failure to acknowledge that fact. Indeed, I would add to Foucault's observation that in the foot race, which comes after the chariot race, it would appear that Antilochus makes a similar claim, as though he had in fact learned his lesson concerning the relative inequalities between warriors in terms of age, status, and ability. For in the foot race, Antilochus himself had come last, but he then delivers a speech after the event in order to explain the results. He states:

εἰδόσιν ὔμμ᾽ ἐρέω πᾶσιν φίλοι, ὡς ἔτι καὶ νῦν
ἀθάνατοι τιμῶσι παλαιοτέρους ἀνθρώπους.
Αἴας μὲν γὰρ ἐμεῖ᾽ ὀλίγον προγενέστερός ἐστιν,
οὗτος δὲ προτέρης γενεῆς προτέρων τ᾽ ἀνθρώπων·
ὠμογέροντα δέ μίν φασ᾽ ἔμμεναι· ἀργαλέον δὲ
ποσσὶν ἐριδήσασθαι Ἀχαιοῖς, εἰ μὴ Ἀχιλλεῖ.

Iliad 23.787–92

I will speak out to all of you who know, friends, since even now immortals honor the older men.
For Ajax is older than me by a little,
but that man [i.e. Odysseus] is from a prior generation of earlier men.
They say that he is of a raw old age. And it is grievous for the Achaeans to compete with him with their feet, except for Achilles.

Where Antilochus had to acknowledge that Menelaus was older and prior, *proteros*, in the post-event quarrel of the chariot race, he uses the same

134 Force and Discourse in the Funeral Games

reasoning, i.e., that Ajax and Odysseus are *proteroi*, to explain why those two warriors actually came prior to him in the foot race itself.[71]

Antilochus' avowal after the chariot race, like his speech after the foot race, is meant to allow the "truth" to come forth: it is a verbal performance that organizes the warriors within a hierarchy of relative inequality. Such a "truth" should have come to light in the execution of the race itself, had Antilochus not attempted to overcome that presupposed hierarchy in his first contest. The execution of the chariot race itself, therefore, does not reveal a "regime of truth" but only the unreliability of force (*biē*) to accurately predict such a regime. Antilochus' avowal thus compensates for the contingency of the competition.

To be sure, Foucault is not a trained Classicist and there remain several potential objections to his interpretation of the funeral games. In articulating and responding to these objections, however, we may ultimately see a deeper value in Foucault's unique approach to the contest. In the first place, we might wonder to what extent Foucault is projecting his own conception of "truth" onto the funeral games episode. To what extent is the conception and terminology of Archaic Greek "truth," rather than Foucauldian "truth," operative in the text? In *Wrong-Doing, Truth-Telling*, Foucault himself notes that the ancient Greek term for "truth" appears at only one moment in the games, when Achilles places Phoenix at the turn of the makeshift course for the chariot race "in order that he might recall the race and speak forth the truth" (ὡς μεμνέῳτο δρόμους καὶ ἀληθείην ἀποείποι) (*Iliad* 23.361).[72] This particular line is especially significant as far as the semantics of Archaic Greek truth are concerned. From a grammatical perspective, the "truth" of *alētheia* is a function of memory in so far as it is the alpha privative form of *lēthe*, forgetfulness.[73] Hence, truth is "that which is not forgotten." Within Archaic Greek contexts, memory often has associations with divine inspiration from the Muses, the

---

[71] See further Purves 2011: 536. The logic that men who are *proteroi* are superior follows a basic model of generational decline that is a general feature of ancient Greek perspectives on age and ability, one which is evident also in Hesiod, on which see Clay 2003: 82–5; Calame 2009: 84–5; Currie 2012. It is also the same principle that Nestor invokes in his first speech to Achilles and Agamemnon, on which see Chapter 1.

[72] This observation was not made in "Truth and Juridical Forms," and Leonard 2005: 75 offers the Phoenix episode as a counterpoint to Foucault's arguments in that essay. In *Wrong-Doing, Truth-Telling*, Foucault refers to Phoenix as *istōr*, a type of judicial expert (Foucault 2013: 74; Foucault 2014: 40). Yet, the term *istōr* is not used in the Phoenix episode, and Foucault is most likely applying this term based on Detienne's comments on the secularization of truth from its magico-religious aspects to the pre-political and judicial realm (Detienne 1996: 193–4n.73).

[73] Chantraine 2009: 594; Detienne 1996: 47–9; Cole 1983: 7–8.

Menelaus' Quarrel with Antilochus   135

children of Memory.[74] But in this example from the funeral games, we see how "memory" and "truth" are directly connected even without divine inspiration. Phoenix is positioned at the turn to observe the race, and it is his task to "recall the race" and "speak forth the truth," where "truth" is precisely that which he himself remembers (μεμνέῳτο...ἀληθείην ἀποείποι). In this one instance, the act of memory and the verbal act of speaking the truth are equivalent.[75] Yet, Foucault's point in making this observation on the sole occurrence of "truth" in the episode is that Phoenix is never called upon as a witness to enact his memory, to "speak forth the truth."[76] Instead, according to Foucault, a different type of truth is in question. The "truth" Foucault refers to is that of social valuation. As he states, "The race's real function is to put them in the order of their true value."[77]

This "true value" to which Foucault refers would thus reflect a different function of Archaic truth, namely the function of praise. In fact, for his explication of the funeral games, Foucault relies explicitly on Dumézil's account of the Indo-European relationship between "truth" and "praise" as described in *Servius et la fortune*. Foucault begins his lecture with the concluding comments of Dumézil from that work:

> As far back as we go in the behavior of our species, the 'true utterance' is a force to which few forces resist...Very early on the Truth appeared to men as one of the most effective verbal weapons, one of the most prolific seeds of power, one of the most solid foundations for their institutions.
>
> **(Dumézil 1943, 243–4 quoted in Foucault 2014: 28)**

Thus, prior to Foucault's broader historical theorization, Dumézil drew a fundamental connection between "truth" and "power" within Indo-European

---

[74] See Detienne 1996: 39–52.

[75] This instance provides a good example of *alētheia*, as described by Thomas Cole (1983), in which "truth" is defined in terms of the subjective constraints of perception and communication. Cole positions his own argument on Archaic truth as a response to Heiddeger but makes no mention of Detienne's work, although this is precisely how Detienne himself also defined his own approach (Detienne 1996: 26–8).

[76] Foucault 2014: 40: "And yet, during the debate between Antilochus and Menelaus, do they call upon this witness, the one who saw the event and was in a position to say 'Yes, such and such a thing happened?' Absolutely not; there is never any question of Phoenix nor the istōr throughout the debate, and it will never be brought up again. The public is also present, but it only intervenes when it is a question of deciding the validity of the procedures. The public does not intervene at all in the establishment of the facts, nor in the justice of the sentence."

[77] Foucault 2014: 39.

136   Force and Discourse in the Funeral Games

cultures, where that connection itself is established primarily through the verbal act of praise.[78] In this regard, Antilochus' avowal, the establishment of his own subjectivity, which also causes him to subject himself to Menelaus' superior status, is also an indirect mode of praise of Menelaus. In Dumézil's terms, the *force* of Antilochus' utterance compensates for his original failure to acknowledge Menelaus' own "excellence and force" (*Iliad* 23.578). That the "truth" of avowal is also tantamount to praise is made evident when Achilles responds to Antilochus' speech after the foot race. There too he arranged himself and the other heroes in a hierarchy, but with the addition that none could surpass Achilles. As a result, Achilles rewards him with an additional half talent of gold for his comment, which Achilles describes specifically as an *ainos*.[79] Thus, in response to the objection to Foucault's misuse of ancient Greek concepts of truth, we can say that even if the Greek term for "truth," *alētheia*, is not operative in the funeral games episode, its more general function, praise for the sake of reconfirming social hierarchy, does appear to be at work nevertheless.

A second, potential objection to Foucault's analysis, however, arises from the initial one concerning the status of truth in the games. Foucault himself believes that Antilochus' avowal achieves its purpose of restoring the "truth" of the race. Yet even though an Archaic principle of "truth" as social valuation may be at work in the chariot race episode, we might still wonder if Antilochus' response does actually restore the "true value" of the heroes who participate. One assumes that it is the very function of the prizes to reflect such "true value." Yet in the end, Menelaus does not walk away with the second-place prize, although Antilochus offers it to him. Antilochus concludes his "avowal" as follows:

τώ τοι ἐπιτλήτω κραδίη· ἵππον δέ τοι αὐτὸς
δώσω, τὴν ἀρόμην. εἰ καί νύ κεν οἴκοθεν ἄλλο
μεῖζον ἐπαιτήσειας, ἄφαρ κέ τοι αὐτίκα δοῦναι
βουλοίμην ἢ σοί γε διοτρεφὲς ἤματα πάντα
ἐκ θυμοῦ πεσέειν καὶ δαίμοσιν εἶναι ἀλιτρός.

Iliad 23.591–5

---

[78] According to Dumézil, such "praise" here is manifested primarily through the Indo-European root *kens-. Much of Dumézil's evidence comes from Indic and Roman material, but Detienne's *Masters of Truth* can be seen as a demonstration of many of the same principles at work in Archaic Greek culture, on which see Nagy 1979: 272.

[79] *Iliad* 23.795–6. On *ainos* as collective consent through praise, see Elmer 2013: 48–9.

Menelaus' Quarrel with Antilochus   137

And so let your heart endure. But I myself will give you
the horse, the one that I obtained. And even if you should
request something more from my home, I would wish to give it
to you right away rather than all of my days to fall from your favor,
you who are divinely reared, and to be at fault before divinities.

On one level, we might simply interpret the conclusion of Antilochus'
response as an extension of his avowal, since he claims that he would give
more than demanded of him in order to stay in good favor with Menelaus.
But at the same time, we can observe in Antilochus' words a reassertion of
his own position and right to the mare. As observed by Gernet and many
others after him, the prizes for the contest no longer belong to Achilles
once they are placed in the middle of the gathering, *es meson*. At that
moment, each prize becomes a *res nullius*.[80] As such, the results of the race
are meant to dictate who receives which prize without question, and this is
precisely why Antilochus challenged Achilles, when Achilles suggested
giving the second place prize to Eumelus (*Iliad* 23.539–54). In his response
to Achilles, Antilochus had already assumed ownership of the second-
place prize. When challenging Achilles' decision, Antilochus states "that
mare I will not give" (τὴν δ' ἐγὼ οὐ δώσω) (*Iliad* 23.553). The implication
is that the second-place prize is not Achilles' to give away. And after
Menelaus' challenge, Antilochus states, "I myself will give the horse"
(ἵππον δέ τοι αὐτὸς/ δώσω) (*Iliad* 23.591–2). By framing the gesture to
Menelaus as an act of "giving" on his part, he still assumes rightful ownership of the horse, just as he had in the beginning. And this is made obvious
by the additional detail Antilochus adds in his speech to Menelaus: "the
one which I obtained" (τὴν ἀρόμην) (*Iliad* 23.592). Thus, even though
Antilochus *seems* to give an avowal that places him in a position of inferiority to Menelaus, his speech concludes by indirectly reasserting his own
right to the second-place prize.[81] Indeed, the very fact that he suggests giving more to Menelaus from his own private store of goods (οἴκοθεν, *Iliad*
23.592) allows Antilochus to frame his deferral to Menelaus as an act of
generosity rather than a matter of *dikē*.

Of course, Menelaus picks up on Antilochus' subtle shift in language,
and he ends up giving the mare back to Antilochus! Menelaus explains:

---

[80]   Gernet 1955: 13. For further discussion, see B. K. M. Brown 2016: 58–60.
[81]   See Kelly 2017: 99, who also cites this as an agonistic claim.

138 Force and Discourse in the Funeral Games

$$\mathring{\eta}\delta\grave{\epsilon}\;\kappa\alpha\grave{\iota}\;\mathring{\iota}\pi\pi o\nu$$
$$\delta\acute{\omega}\sigma\omega\;\grave{\epsilon}\mu\acute{\eta}\nu\;\pi\epsilon\rho\;\grave{\epsilon}o\hat{\upsilon}\sigma\alpha\nu,\;\mathring{\iota}\nu\alpha\;\gamma\nu\acute{\omega}\omega\sigma\iota\;\kappa\alpha\grave{\iota}\;o\hat{\iota}\delta\epsilon$$
$$\acute{\omega}s\;\grave{\epsilon}\mu\grave{o}s\;o\mathring{\upsilon}\;\pi o\tau\epsilon\;\theta\upsilon\mu\grave{o}s\;\mathring{\upsilon}\pi\epsilon\rho\varphi\acute{\iota}\alpha\lambda os\;\kappa\alpha\grave{\iota}\;\mathring{\alpha}\pi\eta\nu\acute{\eta}s.$$

Iliad 23.609–11

And I will give (you) the horse, even though it is mine,
In order that these men may know that my *thumos* is never
overbearing and rough.

At first glance, the entire conclusion to the quarrel seems like a ridiculous episode of over-politeness. And we may interpret Menelaus' final statement, namely, that he not seem "overbearing and harsh," as an implicit contrast with Agamemnon's own treatment of Achilles in *Iliad* 1. At the same time, it should be noted that there remains a power struggle at play in the giving and giving back between the two warriors.[82] Just as Antilochus had claimed, "I will give the horse, which I obtained" ($\delta\acute{\omega}\sigma\omega$, $\tau\grave{\eta}\nu$ $\mathring{\alpha}\rho\acute{o}\mu\eta\nu$) (*Iliad* 23.592), so Menelaus' concluding remark can be viewed as a direct response to Antilochus: "I will give the horse, although it is mine" ($\delta\acute{\omega}\sigma\omega$ $\grave{\epsilon}\mu\acute{\eta}\nu$ $\pi\epsilon\rho$ $\grave{\epsilon}o\hat{\upsilon}\sigma\alpha\nu$) (*Iliad* 23.610). Thus, the quarrel over rightful possession of the second-place prize continues well after the contest, only by other means, that is, by means of symbolic domination through generosity.[83] Foucault, following Gernet, had pointed out that the judicial scene of challenge for the horse was merely a continuation and extension of the contest. And one can add to this that the contest still continues, even after the judicial scene is settled. The physical *agōn* gives way to a judicial *agōn*, which in turn is ultimately settled through agonistic exchange.[84]

And so, even though Foucault's individual observations provide tremendous insight into the chariot race, we may still question his ultimate conclusion, namely that Antilochus' avowal served the purpose of restoring the "true value" of the heroes. If the purpose of the avowal were to restore the "true value" of the heroes, the prize distribution itself would have ultimately matched the initial sequence of the rank of heroes as they first volunteered. But the final distribution of prizes does not match up with the expectations outlined by the original sequence. Although

---

[82] As observed by Allan and Cairns 2011: 135; Buchan 2012: 108–13; Kelly 2017: 100.

[83] On the ways in which generosity acts as a mode of symbolic domination, see Bourdieu 1977: 183–97.

[84] As Buchan 2012: 112 asserts, "The entire episode is a theoretical reflection on the nature of gift exchange." On agonistic exchange in early Greek culture more generally, see Beidelman 1989.

Antilochus should have been ranked fourth according to the initial sequence, he ultimately received the second-place prize. Perhaps, then, Antilochus was true to Nestor's original advice, even after the race had finished. For Nestor had commanded:

ἀλλ' ἄγε δὴ σὺ φίλος μῆτιν ἐμβάλλεο θυμῷ
παντοίην, ἵνα μή σε παρεκπροφύγῃσιν ἄεθλα.

Iliad 23.313–14

But come my dear place *mētis* of all sorts in your *thumos*
in order that the prizes may not escape you.

And the prize certainly did not escape Antilochus. Even after the race, he did not give up the prize. Instead, he shifted the discourse itself from one of justice to that of reciprocity. Thus, Foucault may be right in so far as Antilochus' response to Menelaus *appears* as an act of avowal and deferral to Menelaus, but its end result is far different. Perhaps the subtle turn in Antilochus' own verbal performance can be seen as yet another practice in the variegated ways of *mētis*.

Raising this objection to Foucault's analysis, however, does not mean that Foucault entirely misreads the chariot race episode, only that he did not read to the end. Foucault's incomplete and selective reading can be attributed to the fact that the funeral games serve a very specific purpose in his account. Foucault's concern is not with the role that funeral games play within the *Iliad*, but within a larger historical trajectory concerning the seemingly essential and eternal topics of "truth" and "justice." But this very effort to contextualize Foucault's own account brings us to our third and final objection: Can and should we interpret the funeral games of Patroclus within the historical framework Foucault provides?

According to Foucault, the agonism of justice and truth represented in Homer gives way to a new representation of truth and justice in Hesiod. In Hesiod, Foucault suggests, we find the beginnings of the "will-to-truth" expressed as a desire for objective truth and third-party arbitration. Once again relying on Louis Gernet, Foucault frames this new desire as an expression of a new kind of justice, the justice of *krinein*, which he contrasts with the justice of *dikazein*.[85] To highlight this contrast he cites the beginning of the *Works and Days*:

---

[85] Gernet 1955: 62–81; Foucault 2014: 45–6.

140 Force and Discourse in the Funeral Games

ἀλλ' αὖθι διακρινώμεθα νεῖκος
ἰθείῃσι δίκῃς, αἵ τ' ἐκ Διός εἰσιν ἄρισται.
ἤδη μὲν γὰρ κλῆρον ἐδασσάμεθ', ἄλλα τε πολλὰ
ἁρπάζων ἐφόρεις μέγα κυδαίνων βασιλῆας
δωροφάγους, οἳ τήνδε δίκην ἐθέλουσι δικάσσαι.

Works and Days 35–9

But come, let us settle our dispute with straight judgments,
with those from Zeus which are the best. For already,
we divided our inheritance, but you seized much and carried it off,
giving honor to the gift-devouring kings,
who wish to make judgment on a case such as this.

Foucault suggests that the justice of *dikazein* practiced by the "gift-devouring kings" is in some sense a continuation of Homeric procedures, as represented in the shield of Achilles (*Iliad* 18.497–508). In both cases, Foucault suggests, the judges or kings simply preside over the confrontation, and the judgment serves more or less simply to record the "outcome of the relations of force."[86] In contrast to *dikazein*, Foucault argues that the Hesiodic appeal to the justice of Zeus by way of *krinein*, served as a form of absolute arbitration beyond the realm of force relations.[87] According to Foucault, the decision reached by *krinein* is not dependent upon the performance of the two parties involved in the dispute, but rather it depends ultimately on an abstract notion of justice itself, *dikaion* and its personification *Dikē*. By elevating Justice to the status of a divinity, Hesiodic poetry gives a degree of immanence to the concept such that Justice has its own agency, which deals with practices that go beyond those of the parties involved in legal disputes. And ultimately, for Foucault, it is the abstraction of justice, separated out from its own performative context in legal disputes, that would in turn pave the way for a non-performative, objectivized concept of truth. Thus, Foucault explains that with Hesiod, "For the first time, it seems to me, there was a direct link between this *dikaion* and this *alēthes*, between the just and the true, which would become the problem, one could argue the constant problem, of the Western world."[88]

Foucault's analysis of the funeral games may therefore be viewed as part of a distinct historical analysis, which entails a broader periodization of Archaic Greek poetry, one that posits Homeric poetry as historically and

---

[86] Foucault 2014: 47.   [87] Foucault 2014: 45–7.   [88] Foucault 2014: 50.

Menelaus' Quarrel with Antilochus **141**

ideologically prior to Hesiodic poetry. Foucault's original intention in addressing Archaic Greek poetry on "justice" and "truth" was to undo "continuous models of history" by seeking breaks rather than points of continuity, where the Archaic Greek evidence indicated the clearest break with the modern era.[89] Yet the very periodization of Archaic Greek poetry that Foucault employs, from Homer to Hesiod, is by no means free from the implicit ideologies of continuous history. For Foucault, the break between Homeric and Hesiodic poetry pointed to a fundamental similarity between Hesiodic poetry and the present era, thereby introducing a connection between "justice" and "truth" as the "problem of the Western world."[90] Such positioning of Hesiodic after Homeric poetry thus reiterates a common historical model employed in the first half of the twentieth century to demonstrate how Hesiodic poetry occupied a transitional stage between poetry and philosophy, between *muthos* and *logos*, thereby anticipating the modern foundations of rational thought.[91] In other words, by positing a "break" between Homeric and Hesiodic poetry on the topic of "truth and justice," Foucault actually reiterates a model of continuous history, which simply begins with Hesiod rather than Homer. Yet, from a philological perspective, the chronology that posits Homeric poetry as prior to Hesiodic is by no means well established.[92] At the very least, we need not approach Homeric and Hesiodic poetry as two distinct historical time periods, since they can be seen to share common oral-poetic vocabulary and traditions.[93] In other words, perhaps we might identify two different and competing discourses on truth and justice between Homeric and Hesiodic poetry, but this difference in poetic representation does not presuppose a diachronic point of "transformation" from one to the other.[94] Foucault's account fails to take into consideration the diachronic

[89] See Foucault's inaugural lecture and first lecture series at the Collège de France (Foucault 2013), which seems to be his first foray into discussion of Archaic Greek poetry.
[90] See Foucault 2014: 50 quoted above.
[91] See Cornford 1912; Gigon 1945; Fränkel 1975; Havelock 1963. See further Stocking 2017b on the role of the *muthos-logos* dichotomy in the Classical scholarship of France in the second half of the twentieth century.
[92] See Janko 1982; Janko 2012; Koning 2010; West 2012. Detienne, in fact, sees the very opposite process of periodization occurring with regard to Archaic Greek "truth," namely that Hesiodic poetry presents an approach that is older and more akin to Indo-European associations between "truth" and magico-religious power, whereas the *agōn* of the funeral games represents the beginnings of the "secularization" of truth (Detienne 1996: 89–106).
[93] See, for instance, Nagy 1990b: 36–83; Muellner 1996: 52–93; Stocking 2017a.
[94] Even if we follow Foucault's periodized division between *dikazein* and *krinein*, one might still question whether there are in fact separate ways of thinking and speaking about judgment and settlement between Homer and Hesiod, since the act of *krinein* also appears in Homer. See, for instance, *Iliad* 7.291–2, when Hector explains that in a future battle, a *daimōn* will determine the outcome (*diakrinēi*) between himself and Ajax. Such an example very

142   Force and Discourse in the Funeral Games

complexities that the oral-poetic tradition creates. As such, Miriam Leonard's critique of Foucault's treatment of the funeral games in his lecture "Truth and Juridical Forms" also holds true for *Wrong-Doing, Truth-Telling*: "Foucault seems to have been overtaken by his narrative teleology in his treatment of the *Iliadic* material."[95]

Reversals in the "Regime of Truth": Eumelus and Ajax

Even though there are justifiable objections to Foucault's broader historical argument around the funeral games, this does not mean that we should dismiss Foucault's reading *tout court*. Indeed, as I shall point out, there remain two important conclusions one can draw from Foucault's own account, which remain vital for a deeper appreciation of the problematic relationship between force and social ranking as manifested in this foundational episode of competition. Indeed, although Foucault limited himself to the chariot race, his observations are in fact relevant to the funeral games as a whole. The first and most critical conclusion, which holds true, not just for the chariot race but for the games more generally, is that an *agōn* not only constructs a particular "regime of truth" or social hierarchy, but also provides an occasion for the undoing of such regimes. And the second related conclusion we can derive from Foucault's reading is the fact that such regimes or hierarchies within the *Iliad* cannot be fixed through physical contest alone, but they are ultimately settled through verbal performance and exchange.

Foucault's most important observation in the entire episode, I believe, is the fact that there is an expected outcome to the chariot race prior to the race's execution, where the expected outcome is represented by the order in which the warriors volunteer.[96] Based on that single observation, we should pay closer attention to one figure in the chariot race who has

---

much parallels the Hesiodic appeal to the justice of Zeus in *Works and Days* to settle the dispute between the poet and Perses.

[95] Leonard 2005: 79.

[96] As noted by Richardson 1993: 206, a parallel for warriors volunteering occurs in *Iliad* 7.162ff. Richardson also notes, "This listing seems to reflect the contestant's natural order of ability." See similarly, Clay 2007: 69. Bernadete 2000: 35 further frames the upsets of the funeral games in terms of a disruption of "nature": "Thus providence and art stand very close to one another: both change the order that 'nature' sets up and substitutes for it an unpredictable one." Of course, as already discussed in the previous chapter, the assumption of a concept of "nature" with autonomous and determinative power does not reflect an Archaic Greek perspective, since "nature" had not yet been theorized and ability itself is a multifaceted function

Eumelus and Ajax 143

received relatively little scholarly attention, but the one who in fact suffered the greatest loss: Eumelus.[97] The poet gives special attention to Eumelus' superiority in the race, when describing him as the first to volunteer:

ὦρτο πολὺ πρῶτος μὲν ἄναξ ἀνδρῶν Εὔμηλος
Ἀδμήτου φίλος υἱός, ὃς ἱπποσύνῃ ἐκέκαστο·

Iliad 23.288–9

By far the first, Eumelus lord of men rose,
the son of Admetus, who excelled in horsemanship.

There is a certain ambiguity in the phrasing of line 288. One might read *prōtos*, "first," simply in reference to the order alone, i.e. that Eumelus was first to rise. Yet, *prōtos* here is also modified by the adverb *polu*, "by far." From a formulaic perspective, *polu prōtos* occurs throughout early Greek hexameter as a reference not just to pure sequential order, but to an order, which also implies rank.[98] The fact that Eumelus is "first" to volunteer thus reflects the expectation that he should also be "first" to finish the race.[99]

Surprisingly, Eumelus plays no role whatsoever in the events of the *Iliad*. And his only other appearance is in another context of the ranking of warriors—only this time, it is not a simple ranking for the sake of a contest. Rather, it is a matter of the poet's divinely inspired, absolute ranking of all the Greeks who sailed to Troy at the end of the Catalogue of Ships. The poet concludes the catalogue with the following request to the Muse:

Οὗτοι ἄρ' ἡγεμόνες Δαναῶν καὶ κοίρανοι ἦσαν·
τίς τὰρ τῶν ὄχ' ἄριστος ἔην σύ μοι ἔννεπε Μοῦσα
αὐτῶν ἠδ' ἵππων, οἳ ἅμ' Ἀτρεΐδῃσιν ἕποντο.

Iliad 2.760–2

---

of different types of power and relations. And so the basis for ranking becomes entirely more problematic.

[97] For a parallel treatment of Eumelus, but from the perspective of "athletic losers," now see Dova 2020. The conclusions of Dova and those presented in this chapter were made entirely independent of each other, but we were both very happy to see the confluence in our perspectives.

[98] See *Iliad* 2.702, 8.256, 14.442; *Odyssey* 1.113, 8.197 (Odysseus' discus in the contest with Phaeacians), 9.449, 14.220, 17.31, 17.328.

[99] One has already observed a similar play on the adjective *proteros*, as used by Antilochus, which means both "older" and "earlier," such that older age also implies physical priority in the competition.

144 Force and Discourse in the Funeral Games

These then were the leaders and lords of the Danaans.
And you tell to me, Muse, who then was best of them
and of their horses, who followed with the sons of Atreus.

In part, the function of this question posed to the Muses might be to correct the fact that the poet assigned to Agamemnon, perhaps begrudgingly, the rank of "best" within the catalogue based strictly on the number of warriors he brought to Troy.[100] After listing the Greeks who sailed to Troy, the question posed to the Muses concerns who is best of the warriors. And yet, at the same time, the poet strangely asks not just who the best warrior is, but also who has the best horses.[101] And it is in fact Eumelus who is named as the warrior with the best horses:

> Ἵπποι μὲν μέγ᾽ ἄρισται ἔσαν Φηρητιάδαο,
> τὰς Εὔμηλος ἔλαυνε ποδώκεας ὄρνιθας ὣς
> ὄτριχας οἰέτεας σταφύλῃ ἐπὶ νῶτον ἐΐσας· (765)
> τὰς ἐν Πηρείῃ θρέψ᾽ ἀργυρότοξος Ἀπόλλων
> ἄμφω θηλείας, φόβον Ἄρηος φορεούσας.

Iliad **2.763–7**

The best horses were those of the son of Pheres,
whom Eumelus drove, swift like birds,
equal in coat, age, and by the level on their backs,
whom silver-bowed Apollo reared in Pieria
both mares, bringing with them the fear of Ares.

And in terms of men, the poet answers that it is Ajax who is best, but only when Achilles is absent:

> ἀνδρῶν αὖ μέγ᾽ ἄριστος ἔην Τελαμώνιος Αἴας
> ὄφρ᾽ Ἀχιλεὺς μήνιεν· ὃ γὰρ πολὺ φέρτατος ἦεν,

Iliad **2.768–9**

Of men, Telamonian Ajax was by far best,
while Achilles was in anger. For he was by far the mightiest

---

[100] *Iliad* 2.580: οὕνεκ᾽ ἄριστος ἔην, πολὺ δὲ πλείστους ἄγε λαούς, "Because he [Agamemnon] was the best (aristos), and he led the most numerous host." See Nagy 1979: 27; Sammons 2010: 175.

[101] Kirk 1985: 240 calls the mention of horses "awkwardly and gratuitously appended."

Eumelus and Ajax **145**

As Nagy notes, the entire invocation and response follows a ring composition, because the poet then adds additionally that it is in fact Achilles' horses that were also the best: "And the horses [were mightiest], who used to carry the blameless son of Peleus" (ἵπποι θ' οἳ φορέεσκον ἀμύμονα Πηλεΐωνα) (*Iliad* 2.770).[102] Ultimately, what we see from the ranking in *Iliad* 2 is that a warrior's status is not just determined by their own embodied singularity, but also in relationship to their horses as a marker of their social standing and as an extension of their own physical ability.[103] In that regard, Achilles represents the "total package" as it were. Indeed, the chariot race of *Iliad* 23 helps to motivate why the poet would mention the warrior's horses at all. It is precisely because a hero's status is entangled with his horses, thus extending the hero's identity itself beyond the individual physical body.[104] The *biē* of the horses helps determine the *biē* and *aretē* of the warrior. When Menelaus quarreled with Antilochus, it was because Antilochus endangered his own superior horses, and, by extension, threatened the very *aretē* of Menelaus himself (*Iliad* 23.571).

Furthermore, the ranking provided in *Iliad* 2 serves to highlight the very absence of Achilles.[105] And that absence of Achilles from the war in the beginning of the *Iliad* is reiterated by Achilles' absence from the competition in honor of Patroclus. For in *Iliad* 23, Achilles explains that he will not participate, not only because he is lamenting for his fallen friend Patroclus, but also because his own horses are immortal, and there would be no contest. Achilles explains:

ἦ τ' ἂν ἐγὼ τὰ πρῶτα λαβὼν κλισίην δὲ φεροίμην.
ἴστε γὰρ ὅσσον ἐμοὶ ἀρετῇ περιβάλλετον ἵπποι·
ἀθάνατοί τε γάρ εἰσι, Ποσειδάων δὲ πόρ' αὐτοὺς
πατρὶ ἐμῷ Πηλῆϊ, ὃ δ' αὖτ' ἐμοὶ ἐγγυάλιξεν.

Iliad 23.275–8

For I would take the first prizes and carry them to my tent.
For you know by how much my horses excel in *aretē*.
For they are immortal, and Poseidon gave them to
my father Peleus, who in turn gave them to me.

---

[102] Nagy 1979: 27.   [103] See further Brügger et al. 2010: 247.

[104] For modern arguments on interspecies subjectivity, as, for instance, with dogs and humans, see Haraway 2003; Haraway 2016.

[105] As Martin 2020: 401 notes: "The excellence of both Eumelus' mares and the hero Ajax is limited by time, constrained by an unexpressed but all-controlling anticipation, the universal wait for the return of Achilles."

146 Force and Discourse in the Funeral Games

Here, then, we see that the horses have a genealogy of their own that follows Achilles' genealogy, highlighting the divine implications of his family history, which, in turn, explains and justifies his superiority. The chariot race, then, is not to see who is best, but only who is best in the absence of Achilles.

Thus, based on the Muse-inspired ranking of *Iliad* 2, we see that when Eumelus rises first to compete, it is not only because he excels in horsemanship, but because he is ranked as best with his horses from a divinely inspired perspective, but still second to Achilles. And that ranking in turn is based on the relationship that the horses themselves have to the gods. Achilles' horses were a gift from Poseidon to Peleus (*Iliad* 23.276), while Eumelus' horses were raised by Apollo (*Iliad* 2.766). Thus, it is Eumelus' divinely inspired ranking as the one with the best, divinely reared horses that makes his loss in the race all the more shocking and unexpected.[106] And it should be further emphasized that the loss does not come from a fault of his own but is itself a function of divine intervention. For Apollo, we are told, is angry with Diomedes and, in the course of the race, prevents Diomedes from passing Eumelus by taking the whip from Diomedes' hand.[107] Yet, we then see Athena, who has favored Diomedes throughout the *Iliad*, come to Diomedes' rescue. She not only gives him back the whip but also causes Eumelus to crash (*Iliad* 23.388–97). Thus, Eumelus' loss demonstrates that even divinely inspired hierarchies can be overturned by the contingency of the actual events and the competing interests of different gods. The involvement of the gods in the chariot race, in other words, captures the way polytheism itself gives expression to the notion of "competing forces" in the universe. That is to say, the gods give expression to competing forces outside of human agency, which in turn have their effect on the competing embodied forces of humans.[108] In this regard, when

---

[106] Indeed, as Dova 2020 further notes, Eumelus' skill is well known from other epic traditions, and he is reported to have won the chariot race in the funeral games for Achilles according to the summary of the lost *Aethiopis*. See further Apollodorus *Bibl.* 5.5b.11 and Rengakos 2004: 17. For summary of the neoanalyst perspective that the funeral games for Patroclus should be seen as a variation of the games for Achilles, see Burgess 2001: 80–2.

[107] *Iliad* 23.383–4. Leaf 1900 ad loc. notes that Apollo's intervention against Diomedes might be motivated by the fact of Apollo's connection to the horses of Eumelus. For further discussion of the motives of the gods' intervention and the relation of such interventions to the *Iliad* as a whole, see further Rousseau 2010: 48–54 and Martin 2019: 383–405. For structural parallels between Eumelus and Achilles, see Dova 2020.

[108] On polytheism as an expression of competing "forces" in the external world according to early Greek thought, see Vernant 1988: 104. Kelly 2017: 96 is one of the few scholars to note the disruptive role of the gods in the social hierarchy of the contest: "The point is that one's abilities and resources do not automatically entitle one to victory. Other things may

Eumelus and Ajax 147

Achilles offers an additional prize to Eumelus, it is not just an act that is intended to avoid a physical confrontation with Antilochus. Rather, Achilles' gesture is an act of compensation with metaphysical implications. It is a human attempt to right the arbitrary wrongs done by the gods.[109] As an additional point, however, I would add that the poet of *Iliad* 23 also calls attention to the eventual disjunction between the expectation of the race and the actual results, even before the race begins. For after the warriors volunteer, Achilles shakes out lots for each warrior, presumably in order to determine starting position. The order and description for the drawing of lots is as follows:

ἂν δ' ἔβαν ἐς δίφρους, ἐν δὲ κλήρους ἐβάλοντο·
πάλλ' Ἀχιλεύς, ἐκ δὲ κλῆρος θόρε Νεστορίδαο
Ἀντιλόχου· μετὰ τὸν δ' ἔλαχε κρείων Εὔμηλος·
τῷ δ' ἄρ' ἐπ' Ἀτρεΐδης δουρὶ κλειτὸς Μενέλαος,
τῷ δ' ἐπὶ Μηριόνης λάχ' ἐλαυνέμεν· ὕστατος αὖτε
Τυδεΐδης ὄχ' ἄριστος ἐὼν λάχ' ἐλαυνέμεν ἵππους.

Iliad 23.352-7

They went into their chariots, and then they cast lots.
Achilles shook them, and out jumped the lot of the son of Nestor
Antilochus. After that the very mighty Eumelus obtained his.
And then the son of Atreus, Menelaus famed for his spear,
and then Meriones obtained his lot for driving the horses.
And last the son of Tydeus, who was best, obtained his lot to drive
the horses.

happen, things which interfere with the direct translation of personal quality into material or competitive supremacy."

[109] In Antilochus' objection to Achilles' original intention of awarding second prize to Eumelus, he claims that Eumelus "ought to have prayed to the gods, then he would not have come in last of all in the pursuit" (ἀλλ' ὤφελεν ἀθανάτοισιν/ εὔχεσθαι· τό κεν οὔ τι πανύστατος ἦλθε διώκων) (*Iliad* 23.546-7). It is in response to Antilochus' objection that Achilles gives Eumelus a gift from his personal store. Kelly 2017: 96 suggests that "[t]his disruptive potential [of the contest] is something that Achilles seems not to understand." But his actions may not necessarily bespeak an ignorance so much as a conscientious effort to counteract the disruptive potential of divine intervention. Achilles, above all other characters, is keenly aware of divine intervention and consciously fights against it, as in the case of Scamander in *Iliad* 21, and likewise, when he states to Apollo in *Iliad* 22.20: "I would take revenge on you, if I had the ability" (ἦ σ' ἂν τισαίμην, εἴ μοι δύναμίς γε παρείη). Nevertheless, Kelly is correct that Achilles' own attempts to smooth over these disruptions creates more problems than solutions, a point discussed further below.

148 Force and Discourse in the Funeral Games

As Richardson notes, the drawing of lots "conveniently confuses the natural order of excellence."[110] Of course that is true, provided we understand the "order of excellence" is not "natural" per se, but is rather the order that is socially expected and determined largely by the ability of one's horses.[111] I would further note that there is a correlation between the final distribution of prizes and how each warrior is described in the shaking out of lots.[112] Where Achilles had lamented about Eumelus that "the best man drives his horses last" (*Iliad* 23.536), the shaking of lots reveals that "the last shall be first," since Diomedes, whose lot is last, is also described being the "best" *aristos eōn*, and it is he who ultimately wins the race (ὕστατος... ἄριστος, *Iliad* 23.356–7). It is only here, and in *Iliad* Book 5, during his *aristeia*, that Diomedes actually receives the epithet of "best"— *aristos*.[113] Also, in the shaking out of the lots, Antilochus' comes out first. That outcome in lots may in fact anticipate the fact that Antilochus receives a prize that is superior to his expected position in the initial hierarchy. Furthermore, Antilochus' lot comes out before that of Eumelus, even though Eumelus clearly has the best horses and he "excelled at horsemanship" (*Iliad* 23.289). That very positioning in turn reflects Eumelus' loss in the race, but also his compensation at the hand of Achilles. For Achilles gives as a gift the armor of Asteropaeus (*Iliad* 23.558–63), a prize perhaps not as good as a pregnant mare, but presumably better than the third-place prize of a cauldron. And finally, Menelaus and Meriones are mentioned as the last two in the shaking out of lots, reflecting the prizes that they received.

Thus, even before the race begins, one is confronted with not one, but two sequences for the ranking of warriors. The first, when the warriors volunteer, is based primarily on the horses themselves, and it is for this reason that Eumelus is first. Yet the poet then provides a corrective through the shaking out of lots, and there we are presented with a sequence that seems to anticipate the chaotic logic of the final distribution of prizes. The shaking of lots does not predict the outcome but shows that an accurate prediction is impossible. It is impossible first because of divine intervention in the race and second because of human intervention as well, namely from the post-race quarrel and also from Achilles' own

---

[110] Richardson 1993: 213.

[111] On which see Clay 2007: 69–70.

[112] Pace Richardson 1993: 213, who simply sees it as a mere confusion of the "natural order."

[113] See Bernadete 2000: 34–58; Andersen 1977: 48–94; Nagy 1979: 30–1, who notes that both occasions when Diomedes is called *aristos* in *Iliad* 5 are "sinister."

intervention through compensatory prizes. Overall, the shaking of lots undoes the presupposed order even before the race is run. That additional relisting of the warriors thus reflects the tension between the status of the warriors (and their horses) and the broader field of interactions, human and divine, that are enacted through the contest.

Ultimately, the disruption of hierarchy is not limited to the chariot race, but such disruption reappears throughout the funeral games. This chapter, however, will not offer a blow-by-blow account of each event. Instead, we may turn back to the divinely inspired hierarchy pronounced in *Iliad* 2 as a guide for revisiting other key contests. As already stated above, the poet of *Iliad* 2 explains that Eumelus has the best horses, but Ajax, son of Telamon is the best of men after Achilles (*Iliad* 2.768–9). Indeed, Ajax has a fairly constant reputation throughout both the *Iliad* and the *Odyssey* as the "best after Achilles."[114] Such a reputation is especially significant for the funeral games, because Ajax enters more events than most of the other Greek warriors: the wrestling match (*Iliad* 23.700–39), the battle in armor (*Iliad* 23.797–825), and the weight throw (*Iliad* 23.826–49).[115] Given that Achilles willingly removed himself from competition, one would therefore assume that the best of the Greeks after Achilles would certainly win in any event he entered, and yet this does not actually happen. Through a focus on Ajax, we see even further how the funeral games problematize the operations of *biē* through a disruption of hierarchy.

Indeed, Ajax above all other warriors is especially known for his force, his *biē*. In the first episode to highlight Ajax's special status, his duel with Hector in *Iliad* 7, we see a special emphasis placed on his physical force. When Ajax learns that his lot is selected, he orders the Achaean warriors to pray silently to Zeus and then proclaims:

οὐ γάρ τίς με βίη γε ἑκὼν ἀέκοντα δίηται
οὐδέ τι ἰδρείη, ἐπεὶ οὐδ' ἐμὲ νήϊδά γ' οὕτως
ἔλπομαι ἐν Σαλαμῖνι γενέσθαι τε τραφέμεν τε.

Iliad 7.197–9

---

[114] See *Iliad* 17.279–80; *Odyssey* 11.467–70, 550–1, 24.15–18. He never receives the exact name of "second best," although his position amounts to as much, on which see O'Higgins 1989; Nagy 1979: 26–32; Whitman 1958: 169: "Constantly referred to as the greatest of the Achaeans after Achilles, he is nevertheless given no *aristeia* and no scene of distinction which is his alone."

[115] Meriones is the only other Greek warrior to enter three events and it is his final event, the spear throw, which also proves problematic. See discussion below.

150   Force and Discourse in the Funeral Games

For no one may willingly put me to flight against my will
either by force (*biē*) or by skill, since I do not deem myself
to have be born and raised in Salamis so ignorantly.

In his first boast, then, we see that Ajax considers it necessary to have both physical force (*biē*) and that to which it is commonly opposed, a type of nonphysical knowledge or intelligence, defined here as *idreiē*, but commonly glossed by scholars as *mētis*.[116] The poet then presents a typical prayer, which each Greek was said to have offered before the duel:

Ζεῦ πάτερ Ἴδηθεν μεδέων κύδιστε μέγιστε
δὸς νίκην Αἴαντι καὶ ἀγλαὸν εὖχος ἀρέσθαι·
εἰ δὲ καὶ Ἕκτορά περ φιλέεις καὶ κήδεαι αὐτοῦ,
ἴσην ἀμφοτέροισι βίην καὶ κῦδος ὄπασσον.

Iliad 7.202–5

O greatest and most glorious Zeus, ruling from Ida,
give victory to Ajax, and that he obtain a wondrous boast.
But even if you love Hector and you care for him,
grant *kudos* and equal force (*biē*) to both.

Here, we see in the prayer both an acknowledgement of divine intervention in human activity, as well as an anticipation of the eventual truce by which the duel is settled. But it is important to note here that the tie, anticipated in the prayer, is described as an equal match in personal and physical force between the two warriors (*Iliad* 7.205: ἴσην ἀμφοτέροισι βίην). And finally, when Hector requests to settle the duel with a truce, the *biē* of Ajax is emphasized yet a third time:

Αἶαν ἐπεί τοι δῶκε θεὸς μέγεθός τε βίην τε
καὶ πινυτήν, περὶ δ᾽ ἔγχει Ἀχαιῶν φέρτατός ἐσσι,
νῦν μὲν παυσώμεσθα μάχης καὶ δηϊοτῆτος   (290)
σήμερον· ὕστερον αὖτε μαχησόμεθ᾽ εἰς ὅ κε δαίμων
ἄμμε διακρίνῃ, δώῃ δ᾽ ἑτέροισί γε νίκην.

Iliad 7.288–92

---

[116] Aristarchus reads *idreiēi* (skill) against the manuscripts that have *aidreiēi* (folly). So it is the balance of both physical strength and intelligence that Dunkle 1987 insists is necessary for victory later on in the events of the funeral games. On the multiple associations and synonyms of *mētis* and its opposition to force, see Detienne and Vernant 1978: 18–21.

Ajax, since a god has given you size and force (*biē*)
and knowledge, and you are the strongest of the Achaeans with the spear,
now, let us stop our battle and fight today.
But later we will fight again until a *daimōn*
decides between us and gives victory to one or the other.

Thus, Ajax's force, his *biē*, is referenced in the episode three times over—from his own perspective, from that of the Greek warriors, and also from that of his opponent Hector. And yet, Ajax does not come away victorious in the duel despite his reputation for *biē*. Instead, they call a truce of sorts and exchange gifts (*Iliad* 7.299–302). The Greeks treat this conclusion as though it were a cause for celebration.[117] And yet the entire episode has tragic implications, since the gift Ajax received in this draw, the sword of Hector, is the very one which he will use to take his own life, according to later traditions.[118]

The tragic implications of the duel in the *Iliad* can also be observed by the continued reference to the gods in the episode. Ajax instructs the Greeks to pray to Zeus, and the Greeks themselves also pray. And finally, in Hector's request for a truce, he first explains that Ajax's force is not just a personal attribute, but a divine gift (*Iliad* 7.288: δῶκε θεός). And then Hector goes on to explains that a divinity will determine the outcome of their future combat (*Iliad* 7.290–1). The very focus on divine intervention is striking for two reasons. In the first place, no such divine intervention actually occurs in the battle between the two warriors. The emphasis on divine involvement only highlights its absence in the episode.[119] And second, such emphasis on the divine further calls attention to the fact that Ajax, compared with most other Greek heroes, receives little to no divine aid throughout the *Iliad*.[120] As such, the duel between Ajax and Hector offers a crystallization of the paradox of *biē*, along with its tragic

---

[117] Ajax is treated to a feast by Agamemnon, where he receives the special portions of meat, the chine, as a gift of honor, on which see Stocking 2017a: 44.

[118] Although Proclus' summary of the *Aithiopis* ends before the suicide of Ajax, a scholion to Pindar states that the *Aithiopis* did include his suicide (Bernabé 1996: fr. 5). On Ajax in the *Iliad* and the Epic cycle, see further Burgess 2001: 22, 142. On the tragic implications of the role of the sword in the *Iliad* and its relationship to Sophocles' Ajax, see most recently Finglass 2011: 380; Fletcher 2013; Mueller 2016: 19–35. On the blurred line between the materiality of Ajax's armor and his identity in Homer, see Purves 2015: 80–7.

[119] Unlike the duel between Menelaus and Paris (*Iliad* 3.373–82), for instance, the duel of *Iliad* 7 is interrupted first by the heralds (*Iliad* 7.277–82).

[120] See Van der Valk 1952: 272.

152 Force and Discourse in the Funeral Games

consequences for Ajax. There is no question that Ajax is superior in force when Achilles is absent. The poet of *Iliad* 2 described Achilles as the one who is truly "mightiest" *phertatos* (*Iliad* 2.769), and Hector applies that same term to Ajax in the absence of Achilles (*Iliad* 7.289).[121] At the same time, the gods are acknowledged to be the source of such force. But for Ajax, the gods do not come, not in the duel, nor in the battle more generally. Similarly, in the funeral games, Ajax does not receive divine aid, and victory eludes him despite his *biē*.

The first event of the funeral games in which Ajax competes is the wrestling match with Odysseus (*Iliad* 23.700–39). Like the duel, this contest also seems to gesture towards the post-Iliadic tragedy of Ajax, which began with the contest between Odysseus and Ajax over the arms of Achilles.[122] And in this event, perhaps more so than in the chariot race, we see the operations of force and deception, *biē* and *mētis* at work. Ajax is described with his common epithet *megas*, "great," while Odysseus is also described with his equally common epithet *polumētis*, "possessing much cunning." In general, one might assume that the epithet of Odysseus would not necessarily carry much semantic weight because it is so common.[123] Yet, of all eighty-six occurrences, it almost always occurs at line end after the hephthemimeral caesura, except on five occasions, two of which are in the funeral games, where it occurs before the third foot caesura (*Iliad* 23.709; 23.755). Thus, its use here is metrically marked. In addition, the semantic significance of this epithet of Odysseus is further glossed with the phrase *kerdea eidōs*, "knowing profit," at line end (*Iliad* 23.709), which is a singular occurrence of the phrase, further highlighting Odysseus' deceptive nature.[124]

At the outset of the match, the two heroes are locked in a standstill, which appears based on an equal match in their physical force. The poet offers the following description:

---

[121] This particular superlative form, *phertatos*, has an extremely limited distribution. Of its seven occurrences, it applies four times in reference the figure of Achilles (*Iliad* 2.769, 16.21, 17.205, 19.216) and once to Zeus (*Iliad* 1.581), once to Ajax (*Iliad* 7.289), and once to the Trojan Dolops (*Iliad* 15.525), who was struck from behind by Menelaus.

[122] See Whitman 1958: 263–4; Kullmann 1960: 335; Willcock 1973: 5; Schein 1984: 25.

[123] The epithet occurs a total of eighty-six times for Odysseus in the *Iliad* and the *Odyssey*. Within the *Odyssey*, the phrase is specific to contexts in which Odysseus speaks (see Austin 1975: 28–9), and Bakker sees, then, a significance in this formula as an indication that "Odysseus is staged as the man full of *mētis* precisely and almost exclusively when he takes the floor in order to speak" (Bakker 2013: 163).

[124] For Odysseus' interest in "profit," *kerdea*, and his reputation for deception, see, among others, Clay 1983: 186–212; Redfield 1983; Roisman 1990.

Eumelus and Ajax 153

ἀγκὰς δ' ἀλλήλων λαβέτην χερσὶ στιβαρῇσιν
ὡς ὅτ' ἀμείβοντες, τούς τε κλυτὸς ἤραρε τέκτων
δώματος ὑψηλοῖο βίας ἀνέμων ἀλεείνων.

Iliad 23.711–13

The two held each other in their arms with their strong hands
like rafters of a high house, which a renowned craftsman joined,
avoiding the force of the winds.

Here we find one of two occurrences of the use of *biē* in reference to environmental forces, where such *biē* is not internal to the body but understood as an external force pushing against a house.[125] Yet this "house" in the simile is composed of two warriors pushing against each other's bodies, such that the notion of "avoiding the force of the winds" is tantamount to saying that force itself fails to move the warriors one way or another. That stalemate in "force" is expressed just a few lines later when the poet states:

οὔτ' Ὀδυσεὺς δύνατο σφῆλαι οὔδει τε πελάσσαι,
οὔτ' Αἴας δύνατο, κρατερὴ δ' ἔχεν ἲς Ὀδυσῆος.

Iliad 23.719–20

Neither was Odysseus able to make him fall and bring him to the ground,
nor was Ajax able, but the dominant force of Odysseus held.

The verb *dynamai* itself, as an expression of potential, may be considered part of the repertoire of terms for force.[126] Here in the wrestling match, the repetition οὔτ'...δύνατο, with different subjects as the agent of action, gives expression to the reciprocal, yet ineffective, force that each acts upon the other. And in addition, we find yet another term to add to the repertoire, since Odysseus as agent who withstands the efforts of Ajax is defined

---

[125] The same simile is used at *Iliad* 16.213 to describe the compactness of the Myrmidon soldiers marching out to battle. The use of the simile at *Iliad* 23.711–13 is interesting in so far as similes are typically used by the narrator, as Ready 2011 has noted, in order to highlight one character over another evincing an agonistic orientation. In the *agōn* of the funeral games, however, this simile is used to give expression to the apparent stalemate in competition, and this is reflected in the description of how the separate bodies themselves also fuse into a single comparandum of the well-built house.

[126] So Benveniste 2016: 362. Surprisingly, this verb and its noun forms are almost always expressed in the negative or in optative constructions in the *Iliad*, as a mark of the limits of one's potential. See the appendix under *dynamis* for citations.

154 Force and Discourse in the Funeral Games

by yet another term for force: *(w)is* (*Iliad* 23.720).[127] This term has a semantic range and usage that overlaps with *biē* as well as *sthenos*.[128] Like *sthenos*, it can refer to bodily strength as well as nonhuman forces. Its most common usage in the *Iliad*, however, is in the instrumental form *iphi*, and it is almost always accompanied by a verbal action.[129] That is to say, the noun *(w)is* seems to be more often associated with specific events and may therefore have a type of punctual aspect, whereas *biē*, however impermanent it may be, nevertheless has a more durative aspect. In this regard, it would be a mistake to assume that the "force," *(w)is*, of Odysseus at *Iliad* 23.720 is equivalent to the use of *biē Heraklēos*.[130] In the latter, the force of *biē* is definitive of the character of Heracles, whereas in the former, the "force of Odysseus" in the wrestling match refers not just to his name but is also relevant to the specific moment in the match when he is able to withstand Ajax. Indeed, compared to his typical associations with *mētis*, Odysseus described as the "force of Odysseus" is especially marked.[131]

Within the context of this stalemate in force, Ajax addresses Odysseus with the following words:

διογενὲς Λαερτιάδη πολυμήχαν' Ὀδυσσεῦ
ἤ μ' ἀνάειρ', ἢ ἐγὼ σέ· τὰ δ' αὖ Διὶ πάντα μελήσει.

Iliad 23.723–4

Divine-born son of Laertes, much contriving Odysseus,
either you lift me, or I lift you. All these things will be a concern for Zeus.

---

[127] At *Iliad* 23.720, the digamma is not respected, although it does occur frequently elsewhere in Homer, on which see Chantraine 2009: 469.

[128] The term has a limited distribution in the *Iliad* compared with the *Odyssey*. Like *sthenos*, it can refer to bodily strength, as at *Iliad* 11.669; *Iliad* 12.320, as well as to animals as well as "force of nature" at *Iliad* 17.730, *Iliad* 21.356. In the *Odyssey*, it seems to take on a function equivalent to *biē* as a periphrasis for the identity of an individual warrior, as in the formula ἲς Τηλεμάχοιο at *Odyssey* 2.409, 16.476, 18.60, 18.405, 21.101, 21.130, 22.354.

[129] It is normally in one of three formulas: ἶφι ἀνάσσ-: *Iliad* 1.38, 1.452, 6.478, 12.367; *Odyssey* 11.284, 17.443; ἶφι μάχεσθαι: *Iliad* 1.151, 2.720, 4.287, 5.606, 12.367, 18.14, 21.486; ἶφι δαμ-: *Iliad* 19.417, 21.208; *Odyssey* 18.57, 18.156.

[130] A line from the *Theogony* demonstrates as much, since we have the noun *(w)is* along with a genitive *biē* naming formula in reference to Heracles conquering the Nemean lion: *Theogony* 332 ἀλλά ἑ ἲς ἐδάμασσε βίης Ἡρακληείης "The strength of the force of Heracles conquered him." The first "force" term is in reference to the specific event, while the second relates to Heracles' identity more generally. Otherwise, that particular line would take the logic of simple periphrasis to an absurd conclusion.

[131] Note the "strength of Odysseus" is further glossed with the adjective *kraterē* (*Iliad* 23.720), thus doubling the association of force with the figure of Odysseus. Such doubling may act as a type of verbal compensation for his ability to withstand Ajax. That the role of "force" is somewhat problematically invoked in this episode is further indicated by the fact that the bT scholia on these lines explain that the contest is not won through *biē*.

Eumelus and Ajax 155

Why Ajax utters these words here is difficult to say. It may simply be to express his frustration, or it may also be a formal request for each to let his guard down so that the contest can proceed.[132] Regardless, the request speaks to Odysseus' own unique abilities in wrestling. The first line of address to Odysseus is entirely formulaic, yet it is not devoid of semantic content. For immediately after Ajax addresses Odysseus, the poet describes how Ajax lifted Odysseus, but then "Odysseus did not forget a trick" ($\delta \acute{o}\lambda o\upsilon$ δ' $o\grave{\upsilon}$ $\lambda \acute{\eta}\theta \epsilon \tau$' '$O\delta \upsilon \sigma \sigma \epsilon \acute{\upsilon}s$) (*Iliad* 23.725). And so in the match, Odysseus enacts his general reputation as *polumēchanos*, "much contriving."[133] Yet, the general structure of Ajax's verbal gesture here is also significant. In his frustration, he expresses an either/or scenario, and insists that the outcome will ultimately be determined by Zeus. In some sense, we can see this verbal gesture itself as an anticipation of his own failure to achieve victory both in the wrestling match and in the contest of arms. In the first place, Ajax's speech is not a boast, but a statement that admits the possibility of defeat.[134] Secondly, as in the duel with Hector, he ultimately appeals to Zeus as the one who will determine the outcome. And yet, as with the duel, here too no divine intervention is apparent.

In place of divine intervention, it is Achilles himself who stops the contest short, with the following proclamation:

$\mu\eta\kappa\acute{\epsilon}\tau$' $\grave{\epsilon}\rho\epsilon\acute{\iota}\delta\epsilon\sigma\theta o\nu$, $\mu\grave{\eta}$ $\delta\grave{\epsilon}$ $\tau\rho\acute{\iota}\beta\epsilon\sigma\theta\epsilon$ $\kappa\alpha\kappa o\hat{\iota}\sigma\iota\cdot$
$\nu\acute{\iota}\kappa\eta$ δ' $\grave{\alpha}\mu\phi o\tau\acute{\epsilon}\rho o\iota\sigma\iota\nu\cdot$ $\grave{\alpha}\acute{\epsilon}\theta\lambda\iota\alpha$ δ' $\hat{\iota}\sigma$' $\grave{\alpha}\nu\epsilon\lambda\acute{o}\nu\tau\epsilon s$
$\acute{\epsilon}\rho\chi\epsilon\sigma\theta$', $\acute{o}\phi\rho\alpha$ $\kappa\alpha\grave{\iota}$ $\acute{\alpha}\lambda\lambda o\iota$ $\grave{\alpha}\epsilon\theta\lambda\epsilon\acute{\upsilon}\omega\sigma\iota\nu$ $A\chi\alpha\iota o\acute{\iota}$.

***Iliad* 23.735-7**

May you two no longer struggle. Do not wear yourselves out with troubles.
Victory belongs to you both. Go, having taken equal prizes
in order that other Achaeans may compete for prizes.

---

[132] The bT scholia refer to Ajax's comment as a call for what is later known in competition as a *labē*, wherein there is an undefended exchange of efforts. Leaf cites the later example of the boxers Kreugas and Daxomenes as a parallel. Still, that might be an anachronistic projection of later agonistic practice, and the precise rules of what constitutes a victory in this wrestling match are unclear. In later practice of wrestling, the entire objective was to throw the opponent to the ground three times. On the technical difficulties with this episode, see Poliakoff 1987: 40.

[133] Throughout Greek history, wrestling is understood to be a sport that matches skill and force, on which see Poliakoff 1987: 33–53.

[134] In generalizing about Greek vs. Trojan styles of speech, Hilary Mackie has observed that "[o]n the whole, Trojan talk suggests an ambivalent and uncertain attitude toward the future" (Mackie 1996: 63). Such ambivalence can also be observed in the figure of Ajax.

156 Force and Discourse in the Funeral Games

Both figures obey Achilles, and it seems like a happy enough resolution, which avoids the harsh, zero-sum perspective on competition: both are victors. Yet the resolution is ultimately unsatisfactory on several fronts. Most importantly, it has been noted since the time of the scholia that the very idea of "equal prizes" here seems like an impossibility.[135] Indeed, prior to the event, the inequality of prizes is specifically emphasized. First place is a tripod worth twelve oxen, and second place is a woman skilled in work, set at a value of four oxen.[136] Not only is there a significant discrepancy between first- and second-place prizes in terms of their explicit "value," but both "objects" are individual and truly indivisible. In addition, the "tie" in the wrestling match is not necessarily the only version of the outcome of this contest. According to the mythic retelling of the funeral games of Patroclus in Hyginus, we learn that Ajax is in fact the victor of the wrestling match.[137] That outcome would make sense, given his general reputation for superiority in *biē*. Hence, the tie itself in the *Iliad* is especially marked, and Achilles' effort to create a happy resolution to the wrestling match seems fairly specious. Adrian Kelly sees this as but one example of Achilles' tenuous control over the games.[138] There is also a broader point to be made here when it comes to the language and practice of force relations. Achilles' language is internally consistent. In order for there to be two victors, there must be equal prizes as signs of that double victory. Yet that language does not match up with the reality of the prizes themselves. The prizes cannot be divided equally, and Ajax ought to have won, not just according to an alternate tradition, but by virtue of the fact that he is acknowledged to be the "best of the Achaeans" after Achilles. In practical terms, therefore, the language of double victors amounts to a loss for the figure of Ajax.

In Ajax's second competition, the battle in arms with Diomedes (*Iliad* 23.797–825), we find a structural parallel to both the wrestling match and his earlier duel with Hector. The battle itself and its rules have posed some problems for scholars, as to how and when a victor would be

---

[135] The bT scholia offer the following possibilities: that Odysseus gets first prize and second is divided, or that an additional gift is given from Achilles' private store of goods, as in the case of Eumelus. Scodel 2008: 40 agrees with this possibility of an additional prize. But the text makes no indication of this procedure. Taplin 1992: 258 sees this lack of resolution as another instance of the non-seriousness of the games. Kelly 2017: 102 sees it as an example of Achilles' ineptitude as commander in the games.

[136] As Richardson notes, this seems like a low value for a skilled woman slave (Richardson 1993: 247). On the valuation of slaves in Homer, see Seaford 2004: 25.

[137] Hyginus *Fab.* 273, on which see Willis 1941: 394.

[138] Kelly 2017: 102.

Eumelus and Ajax **157**

determined.[139] Unlike the duel with Hector, where Ajax himself was demonstrating superiority, in the duel with Diomedes it seems as though Diomedes has the advantage. And unlike the wrestling match, it is not just Achilles, but all the Greeks who fear for Ajax and call for an intervention:

καὶ τότε δή ῥ' Αἴαντι περιδείσαντες Ἀχαιοὶ
παυσαμένους ἐκέλευσαν ἀέθλια ἶσ' ἀνελέσθαι.
αὐτὰρ Τυδεΐδῃ δῶκεν μέγα φάσγανον ἥρως
σὺν κολεῷ τε φέρων καὶ ἐϋτμήτῳ τελαμῶνι.

Iliad 23.822–5

And then, fearing for Ajax, the Achaeans commanded them,
after stopping, to take equal prizes.
But the hero gave to the son of Tydeus the great sword,
carrying it with its scabbard and well-cut strap.

As in the wrestling match, there is yet another call for "equal prizes" to be seized. In this case the prizes are the arms of Sarpedon and the sword of Asteropaeus. Achilles offers a unique prescription for the distribution of these prizes. He declares that the arms of Sarpedon are to be shared in common (*Iliad* 23.809: *xunēia*) and that a feast, a *dais*, is to be held for them both (*Iliad* 23.810). Inherent in the very etymology of the feast is the notion of "division," *daiesthai*.[140] The division of the material arms between the two contestants will thus match the division and sharing of food.[141] And so unlike the wrestling match, the "equal division" of the prizes is entirely possible for the battle in arms. Yet, we have the addendum at *Iliad* 23.824–5 that Achilles awarded the sword nevertheless to Diomedes. Those lines were athetized by Aristophanes and Aristarchus because the awarding of the additional prize seems to directly contradict the idea that the fight was ended prematurely. But if we accept these lines, then the effect is precisely the same as that in the first event. The apparent tie

---

[139] Many consider the contest overly brutal, especially if the goal of the contest, described as ψαύσῃ δ' ἐνδίνων (*Iliad* 23.806), means "touch the entrails" according to the A scholia, or it could simply mean touch what is inside the armor. See Leaf ad loc.; Chantraine 2009: 30; Whitman 1982: 97–8; Richardson 1993: 260.

[140] Chantraine 2009: 237–8.

[141] Feasts themselves can often be seen as competitive events, where the "equality" is not literal, but proportional, on which see Stocking 2017a: 8–19; Nagy 1979: 128; Saïd 1979: 17–9; Bakker 2013: 38–42. In the case of this duel, however, emphasis seems to be placed on the communality created between the two warriors after their hostile encounter, as suggested in Plutarch's *Moralia* (736D), on which see Richardson 1993: 261.

158 Force and Discourse in the Funeral Games

amounts to a loss for Ajax. There may even be an additional irony since it is not only the prized sword that is described but also the scabbard and its strap, the *telamōn* (*Iliad* 23.825), the very term from which Ajax's father derives his name.[142] It would appear as though Ajax and his patriline are signaled even as the first-place prize goes to another warrior.

The final event in which Ajax competes, the weighted throw, is far less dramatic than both the wrestling match and the battle in arms. In the contest, Ajax is third to compete and his throw far outstrips the others:

τὸ τρίτον αὖτ᾽ ἔρριψε μέγας Τελαμώνιος Αἴας
χειρὸς ἄπο στιβαρῆς, καὶ ὑπέρβαλε σήματα πάντων.

Iliad 23.842-3

Then third, the great son of Telamon, Ajax, threw it
from his strong hand, and it exceeded the marks of all.

Line 843 was athetized by Aristarchus on the grounds that it seems to have been "transferred" from the episode of the Phaeacian games in the *Odyssey*, wherein Odysseus cast the discus, and he too exceeded the "marks of all" (σήματα πάντων) (*Odyssey* 8.192). Leaf and others, of course, have pointed out that the athletic context of the phrase in the *Iliad* is entirely appropriate, since there seems to have been a procedure by which different throws were marked and differentiated in the field.[143] Aristarchus, however, was right to point out that the phrase "marks of all" (σήματα πάντων) is by no means a common formula. In fact, the formula appears in only these two episodes. From an oral-formulaic perspective, such limited distribution is significant, marking an "interformulaic" connection between the two episodes.[144] As Bakker explains, "The scale of interformularity does not code what is for the modern reader or scholar...the likelihood of allusion or quotation, but what is for the epic poet and his audience *specificity of the similarity of scenes to each other.*"[145] Clearly there is a fundamental similarity between Ajax's weighted throw and Odysseus' throw of the discus. And yet, as Bakker further notes, "similarity points up multiple reversals and ironies."[146] That is certainly the

---

[142] It is generally assumed that the name Telamon refers in general to the notion of endurance, but at its root, *tel-e₂ refers to that which carries or supports.
[143] For technical details on the discus throw in later Greek competition and its role in the problem of determining a victor in the pentathlon, see Lee 2001; Egan 2007.
[144] Bakker 2013: 157–69.   [145] Bakker 2013: 159, italics in original.
[146] Bakker 2013: 159, italics in original.

Eumelus and Ajax 159

case in comparing the throws of Ajax and Odysseus. In the first place, the very notion that the throw would exceed the "marks of all" should be an indication of a clear victor. Such is the case in Odysseus' contest with the Phaeacians. After Odysseus' throw, the disguised Athena comments that even a blind man could distinguish the mark, and she further states:

ἀλλὰ πολὺ πρῶτον. σὺ δὲ θάρσει τόνδε γ' ἄεθλον·
οὔ τις Φαιήκων τόν γ' ἵξεται οὐδ' ὑπερήσει.

Odyssey 8.197–8

But it is by far the first. But you take courage in this contest.
No one of the Phaeacians will reach it or exceed it.

Certainly the same expectation is implicit in the description of Ajax's throw in the *Iliad*. But unlike Odysseus, Ajax does not come away from the contest "by far the first" despite his performance. For the poet then goes on to describe how a relatively insignificant warrior named Polupoites "threw beyond the entire competition" (παντὸς ἀγῶνος ὑπέρβαλε) (*Iliad* 23.847).

Once more, in his final competition, a test of force in which Ajax above all others ought to have excelled, we find that the possibility of victory is presented and then once more taken from him. And the very fact that the description offers an ironic comparison with Odysseus further highlights the implicit tragedy in Ajax's agonistic efforts.

Thus, in every competitive context in which Ajax is able to demonstrate his personal and presumably superior physical force, his *biē*, for which he is so well known, he nevertheless fails to obtain a clear victory. Furthermore, each contest either directly or indirectly calls attention to the results of Ajax's final contest with Odysseus over the arms of Achilles. The duel with Hector highlights Ajax's *biē* but ends in a truce, and through that truce he obtains the sword by which he will end his own life. The wrestling match with Odysseus presents a physical confrontation that anticipates the contest over the arms, in so far as it highlights the "cunning intelligence" of Odysseus and introduces us to a fundamental problem regarding the "division" of prizes between the two warriors. The duel with Diomedes is another contest over armor, where the possibility of equal division is made a real possibility, and yet, even so, Ajax fails to "win" per se. And lastly, Ajax's victory is snatched from him in the weight throw, the one contest whose outcome would seem to be entirely determined by physical force. And there too, we have an implicit, interformular contrast

160 Force and Discourse in the Funeral Games

with the ever-victorious Odysseus. It is in the Nekuia episode of the *Odyssey*, furthermore, that we see Odysseus regret the price of victory and his own "winning ways" when confronted with the *psychē* of Ajax. He exclaims:

ὡς δὴ μὴ ὄφελον νικᾶν τοιῷδ' ἐπ' ἀέθλῳ·
τοίην γὰρ κεφαλὴν ἕνεκ' αὐτῶν γαῖα κατέσχεν,
Αἴανθ', ὃς περὶ μὲν εἶδος, περὶ δ' ἔργα τέτυκτο
τῶν ἄλλων Δαναῶν μετ' ἀμύμονα Πηλεΐωνα.

Odyssey **11.548–51**

Would that I had not won for the sake of such a prize
for it is because of those arms that the earth has held such a person,
Ajax, who in form and deeds was deemed superior
to all other Danaans, after the blameless son of Peleus.

The tragedy of Ajax, which we find implicit in the epic tradition, is not simply his death, but the lack of cohesion between Ajax's social valuation and the failure to manifest that value through success in competition. Such lack of cohesion in the contest over the armor of Achilles is anticipated in the funeral games of the *Iliad*. For no warrior takes part in more events of the funeral games of Patroclus than Ajax, and yet Ajax does not come away from a single event as the clear and pre-eminent victor. Even though Ajax has the clear reputation as best of the Greeks after Achilles, it would seem that he is forever relegated to "second best."[147] Ajax, known for his size and strength, is ultimately and tragically the "biggest loser."

Thus, the original observation made by Foucault on the discrepancy between initial social ranking and the results of competition in the chariot race applies just as much to the other events. The divinely inspired hierarchy of *Iliad* 2, which ranks Eumelus as the one with the best horses and Ajax as best of warriors after Achilles, holds a key to the true drama of the funeral games. That drama unfolds not simply in the contests but in the way the characters themselves must come to terms with the lack of cohesion between social reputation and contest results. Such lack of cohesion can be expressed furthermore as the failure of force (*biē*) to reliably predict agonistic success.

---

[147] Purves 2019: 88 contrasts Ajax's eternally second-place position with Odysseus: "While Ajax always seems to be trapped in his ranking of 'second to Achilles,' Odysseus––whether he is overtaking or being overtaken––always manages to win."

That very failure itself can be further viewed as a function of the paradoxical nature of *biē* as a form of what we might term interdependent subjectivity. As we have already noted, of all the terms for force, it is *biē* which is constitutive of a warrior's identity. And yet, a warrior's *biē* is also indicated by other beings and objects beyond the warrior's own physical body, whether one's identity and power is entangled with horses or other material objects.[148] Such interdependence also applies to the involvement of the gods. For although *biē* represents a warrior's subjectivity, it is also conceptualized as a "gift" from the gods, and the gods can easily intervene in the enactment of such force. Such was the case with Eumelus and his horses.[149] Yet in the case of Ajax, the gods do not intervene, despite Ajax's own continued reference to Zeus. There, instead, we simply observe a more general failure of force, wherein Ajax's own performance simply falls short of his reputation. In this sense, Ajax's own results in the contest reiterate Nestor's point at the beginning of the funeral games, that force is not fixed, *biē* is not *empedos*.

Resolution through Discourse: Achilles' Interventions and the End of the *Agōn*

Lastly, the inherent contingency of physical force in the funeral games and the problems it poses to social rank brings us to our final useful observation we might derive from Foucault's reading, namely the critical role that speech itself plays in the funeral games. Much of Foucault's analysis of the funeral games revolved around the notion that the act of speech presents a "means of modifying relations of power among those who speak, and finally as an element within an institutional structure."[150] Indeed, the funeral games of Patroclus show that the *agōn* does not just modify such relations of power through physical competition alone, but equally so through speech. Although Foucault himself focused on the speech interactions between Antilochus and Menelaus, it is in fact Achilles, above all

---

[148] On the entanglement between objects and persons in Homer, see Grethlein 2008; Whitley 2013.

[149] Such intervention is equally present in the foot race. There we see Odysseus pray to Athena, and "she made his limbs light" (*Iliad* 23.772), and also caused Oilean Ajax to slip on the remains of previously slaughtered cattle so that Odysseus himself could secure victory. One message, if there is any, that the funeral games seem to convey is that one does not win by individual effort alone, but through divine intervention, which directly affects an athlete's physical body.

[150] Foucault 2014: 28.

162 Force and Discourse in the Funeral Games

other characters in the games, who makes use of the power of speech. For in many of the events, Achilles himself interrupts the physical performance of the competition with his own efforts at verbal command in order to compensate for the potential upsets in the contests. His very first intervention, however, occurs in a quarrel among spectators, between Oilean Ajax and Idomeneus, who are engaged in their own battle of words, and they call for Agamemnon to serve as an *istor* in their argument (*Iliad* 23.486).[151] Before the dispute is deferred to Agamemnon, however, Achilles is able to take charge and utters a *muthos* (*Iliad* 23.491) for them to stop and simply observe the race (*Iliad* 23.492–8).[152] Yet, observation of the actual results does not settle anything. And Achilles presents a second verbal intervention after the race, when he exclaims, "In last place, the best man drives the single-footed horses" (λοῖσθος ἀνὴρ ὤριστος ἐλαύνει μώνυχας ἵππους·) (*Iliad* 23.536), and then suggests that Eumelus receive second place, to which the Achaeans agree. And yet that verbal intervention on Achilles' part is the basis for the series of verbal quarrels that follow.[153] In the case of Eumelus, Achilles' speech is ineffective. Achilles' second speech intervention, however, in the wrestling match, is more effective, since the poet tells us that both Ajax and Odysseus "heard and obeyed" (κλύον ἠδὲ πίθοντο) (*Iliad* 23.738), although it remains a problem as to how precisely Achilles' command of equal division is to be executed. And in the semi-mock battle between Ajax and Diomedes, Achilles' speech is absent, since it is the Greeks and not Achilles who command the warriors to stop the fight and share the prize (*Iliad* 23.823), while Achilles awards the first-place prize to Diomedes only afterwards. In both the wrestling match and the battle in arms, as we have noted, Ajax appears as though he is about to lose before both contests are called short. Thus, where divine intervention would seem to cause an undoing of social hierarchy, human intervention seems to attempt to reconstitute that hierarchy, or at least prevent a total inversion of expectation. Yet, as Adrian Kelly has noted, each of Achilles' own efforts at command ultimately falls short of its

---

[151] Surprisingly, Foucault gives a great deal of attention to the concept of the *istor* and wrongly applies the term to Phoenix (on which see discussion above), when the term is in fact used in this other verbal quarrel between Oilean Ajax and Idomeneus, which Foucault entirely passes over.

[152] On Achilles' intervention here as an assertion of his own authority, see Kitchell 1998: 165–6; Scodel 2008: 56–7; Allan and Cairns 2011: 135–6; Kelly 2017: 93.

[153] On the act of communal approval in the funeral games, see Elmer 2013: 1–2, 187–97; as well as Kelly 2017: 95, who argues against Elmer's reading of *Iliad* 23.539: "Thus he spoke, and all would have approved as he commanded" (Ὣς ἔφαθ', οἳ δ' ἄρα πάντες ἐπῄνεον ὡς ἐκέλευε).

Achilles' Interventions and the End of the *Agōn* 163

goal and leaves more problems than answers.[154] In other words, Achilles is not as effective as one would hope in bridging the gap between social hierarchy and the outcome of the contests.

Indeed, the most problematic of Achilles' verbal interventions is the final event, the spear throw. Here, however, Achilles does not even allow for the possibility of an unexpected result. Rather than end the competition prematurely, he simply prevents the event from taking place at all and awards prizes to the two competitors, Agamemnon and Meriones.[155] As with the wrestling match and battle in arms, the end result here proves problematic. This is the only event in which the two prizes, a cauldron and spear, are not assigned a "place value," neither by the poet nor by Achilles.[156] Instead, Achilles addresses Agamemnon and proposes the following distribution of prizes:

Ἀτρεΐδη· ἴδμεν γὰρ ὅσον προβέβηκας ἁπάντων
ἠδ᾽ ὅσσον δυνάμει τε καὶ ἥμασιν ἔπλευ ἄριστος·
ἀλλὰ σὺ μὲν τόδ᾽ ἄεθλον ἔχων κοίλας ἐπὶ νῆας
ἔρχευ, ἀτὰρ δόρυ Μηριόνῃ ἥρωϊ πόρωμεν,
εἰ σύ γε σῷ θυμῷ ἐθέλοις· κέλομαι γὰρ ἔγωγε.

Iliad 23.890–4

Son of Atreus, we know how much you have excelled all others
and by how much in ability and with the spear you were best.
But you go with this prize, to the curved ship, but let us give the spear
to Meriones, if you should wish in your *thumos*, for I command it.

Scholars are in constant debate as to whether Achilles is here genuinely praising Agamemnon and giving him the first-place prize to match his supposed standing as "best," *aristos*, or if he is giving Agamemnon the second-place prize, and so therefore implicitly insulting him. However, such arguments may mistakenly apply the logic of competition and value after the fact. Rather than try to assign place value to those prizes, I suggest we take the lack of naming of first and second prize as highly significant in and of itself. Without naming which is first and which is second,

---

[154] On Achilles' general deficiency as an *agōnothetēs*, see Kelly 2017: 108.
[155] On progressive shortening of each of the events, see Kelly 2017: 106–7.
[156] For debates on the place value of the prizes and Achilles' intervention as either positive or negative, see, among others, Willcock 1973: 2; Lohmann 1992: 314–15; Postlethwaite 1995; Scodel 2008: 153–7; Wilson 2002: 125–6; Allan and Cairns 2011: 136; Kelly 2017: 104–6.

164 Force and Discourse in the Funeral Games

the logic of the *agōn* as a competition for prizes and therefore status simply cannot be enacted. And this lack of naming of the place value of the prize fits perfectly with Achilles' prevention of the competition from taking place at all. As mentioned above, the athletic prize may be considered a *res nullius*, and the victor has automatic rights to that prize. This was, after all, the very cause of Antilochus' conflict with both Achilles and Menelaus. But without the competition occurring, no one can legitimately claim either prize for himself. Thus, in this final event, Achilles completely transfers his own role from *agōnothetēs*, one who oversees the games and distributes prizes according to competition results, to a larger political function as distributor of material goods based strictly on social valuation. In other words, it is in this last event that Achilles entirely abandons the pretext of the *agōn* and fully appropriates the role previously reserved for Agamemnon.

Most importantly, Achilles' gestures toward Agamemnon in this final event, both verbal and nonverbal, are precisely the opposite of what he himself experienced at the hands of Agamemnon. First, one may wonder to what extent Achilles' statement about Agamemnon's superiority is meant to be ironic. The claim to Agamemnon's superiority is anchored in communal knowledge—"we know" (ἴδμεν) (*Iliad* 23.890). On the one hand, such a focus on the social acknowledgment of superiority, of course, may speak to a discrepancy with the reality of Agamemnon's own skill.[157] On the other hand, the social acknowledgement of Achilles' own reputation as the best, *aristos*, is precisely what Agamemnon challenged in *Iliad* 1.[158] The second most important point here is not whether Agamemnon receives a prize of inferior value, but that Achilles is able to make Agamemnon himself *complicit* in the very distribution of the prizes. As the final line states, "If you are willing in your *thumos*, for I at least command it" (εἰ σύ γε σῷ θυμῷ ἐθέλοις· κέλομαι γὰρ ἔγωγε) (*Iliad* 23.894). This verbal gesture, which requests an agreement to attend the command, is entirely different from Agamemnon in *Iliad* 1, since Agamemnon had insisted that he would take the prize of another, whether that warrior was willing or not (*Iliad* 1.135–9). From an enunciative perspective, Achilles' final pronouncement here is of an entirely different order from his earlier interventions in the funeral games. As many scholars have noted, Achilles' initial intervention in the chariot race makes him similar to Agamemnon, in so far as Achilles' speech evokes a response of *cholos* from Antilochus.[159]

---

[157] As pointed out by Postlethwaite 1995.   [158] See *Iliad* 1.185–7, Scodel 2008: 137.
[159] See note 53 above.

Conclusion **165**

In that first event of the games, Achilles' intervention failed to acknowledge the other participants involved. In this final performative "command," however, he takes full account of his addressee, and recruits him into his own effort. The final line is framed in distinctly dialogic terms, "you...I" (εἰ σύ...ἔγωγε) (*Iliad* 23.894).[160] Unlike his initial interventions, Achilles is entirely effective in his last speech performance. Here, Achilles gives perfect expression to the dialogism that Benveniste had noted was necessary in establishing the authority of the speaker.[161] Achilles' effectiveness can be measured by Agamemnon's response: "Thus he spoke, nor did the lord of men Agamemnon disobey" (Ὣς ἔφατ᾽, οὐδ᾽ ἀπίθησεν ἄναξ ἀνδρῶν Ἀγαμέμνων) (*Iliad* 23.895).

Conclusion

Overall, it seems quite clear that Achilles' own ability as an *agōnothetēs* is questionable, if we agree that the *agōnothetēs* should not have the ability to arbitrarily assign prizes in a contest.[162] I would add, however, that Achilles' failure as an *agōnothetēs* may be viewed as a function of the more general failure of the operations of force to accurately predict a correspondence between social value and competition results. If those who were publicly acknowledged as "best" consistently won, then there would have been no need for Achilles to intervene in the first place. Indeed, from a philological perspective, the funeral games problematize the very naming of who is "best," *aristos*. For even though the term *aristos* constitutes a major theme throughout the *Iliad*, the usage of this term clusters specifically in *Iliad* 23.[163] But each occurrence of this term *aristos* in *Iliad* 23, intending to designate masculine singular supremacy, introduces us to problems and qualifications of that very term. In the drawing of lots for the chariot race, Diomedes, whose lot is drawn last, is described as "best," while Achilles describes Eumelus as the "best" who came in last (cf. *Iliad* 23.357, 23.536). Thus, with both usages, we are introduced to the problem of rank versus sequence in the competition, as well as an unanswered problem as to who is *aristos* in horsemanship, Eumelus or Diomedes. The third occurrence

---

[160] See Benveniste 1971: 224–5 on the dialogic I/you formulation in *énonciation*.

[161] "Consciousness of self is only possible if experienced by contrast. I use *I* only when I am speaking to someone who will be a *you* in my address" (Benveniste 1971: 224).

[162] On this point, see further B. K. M. Brown 2016: 206; Kelly 2017: 108.

[163] Of the twenty-five occurrences in the nominative singular referring to heroes, five are in *Iliad* 23, whereas otherwise it is only used once per book at most.

166 Force and Discourse in the Funeral Games

applies to the boxing match, where Epeius boasts to be *aristos*, but then immediately acknowledges his deficiency in the practice of war (*Iliad* 23.669)—hence another mode of qualifying and compromising superlative status.[164] And finally, there is the appellation of Agamemnon himself as "best," which remains a constant problem of the *Iliad* and is the source of the initial quarrel in *Iliad* 1.[165] Each use of the term *aristos* in the funeral games thus invites us to question that very designation. Overall, it is presumed that the athletic contest will reveal "the truth," in Foucault's terms, namely that the *aretē* of each warrior will shine forth (cf. *Iliad* 23.374–5) and ultimately determine who is "best," *aristos*, but no such revelation occurs.[166] Thus, in this final "non-contest" of the games, I suggest, we see Achilles completely abandon the very logic of competition as a means for determining or representing social value. Prior to the final event, Achilles had attempted simply to supplement the shortcomings of the contest in determining who was "best." In this final event, Achilles entirely replaces the function of the *agōn* with his own verbal performance.

If we return then to the question with which we began this chapter— "Does the very physicality of the *agōn* provide a way of determining a form of force that exists beyond language?"—the final event of the funeral games provides a clear and resounding answer: No. The power and rank derived from different types of force cannot be conceived without those modes of verbal performance that actively construct speaking subjects, while also subjecting those speaking subjects to the consent of their addressees. In Homer's *Iliad*, there is no force without discourse.

---

[164] On Epeius' social status in the *Iliad*, see Golden 2008: 51 and Scanlon 2018: 6–11. Indeed, Scanlon sees the victory of Epeius as emblematic of the problem of social status more generally in *Iliad* 23. As he states, "In sum, the contests with Epeius to a degree call into question the elite status upheld in the other contests of *Iliad* 23—for example, the status of Achilles as host and of other victors given honorary prizes" (Scanlon 2018: 10).

[165] Consider, for instance, the poet's qualification of Agamemnon as "best" because he commands the most men in the Catalogue of Ships, on which see Nagy 1979: 26–7; Sammons 2010: 174.

[166] On the potential, etymological relationship between *aretē* and *aristos*, see Chantraine 2009: 107. Because in this episode, the question of *aretē* and the determination of who is *aristos* relates to rank, one can observe it being potentially derived from the notion of "fitness" and the verb *arariskō*, on which see Vine 1998: 61 and Massetti 2013/2014.

4
The "Force that Kills"

Simone Weil and the Problem of Agency in the *Iliad*

In the previous three chapters, we have seen how the complex language of force in the *Iliad* is deployed predominantly in the context of speech performance. When the language of force is invoked, it typically applies to genealogy, political power, and the *agōn*. In each of these cases, the different types of force, and the relations they imply, are understood to be attributes of a given person, although the source for that force is typically assumed to derive from outside the person, usually from a god. And as each chapter has further shown, every time a speaker makes a claim to force as a predictor of personal superiority, all such claims are continually undermined by the narrative events of the poem.

Overall, then, the multiplicity of terms and complexity of expression on force seem to take us quite far from that original and profound proclamation first articulated by Simone Weil. That is to say, the language of Homeric force seems to have little to do with the type of violence that Weil describes as the central focus of the *Iliad*. And so one cannot help but ask, does Simone Weil's notion of "the force that kills" in the *Iliad* find expression in the specific language of Homeric poetry?

There is in fact a specific term that fully expresses "the force that kills" in the *Iliad*. That term, however, is not found in the laundry list of words for force mentioned by Bruno Snell or Emile Benveniste.[1] The closest equivalent to Weil's concept of force, I suggest, is expressed through the verbs *damazō/damnēmi* in Homer.[2] At the core of this verbal notion is a basic sense of "subjugation," which occurs within a semantic sphere that

---

[1] According to Snell 1953: 20, the terms for force are *menos, sthenos, bie, ikhus, is kratos, alke, dynamis*. And Benveniste (2016: 362) provides a similar list: *kratos, bia, is, iskhus, sthenos, alkē, dynamis*. See the introduction for further discussion.

[2] On the relationship of the Homeric verbal forms *damazō* and *damnēmi* from the root *demh₂-*, see Beekes 2010: 301; Chantraine 2009: 251; Chantraine 1948: 301. The basic meaning can be found in the Hittite *damaš-* "to do violence, subjugate."

Homer's Iliad *and the Problem of Force*. Charles H. Stocking, Oxford University Press.
© Charles H. Stocking 2023. DOI: 10.1093/oso/9780192862877.003.0005

168 Simone Weil and the Problem of Agency in the *Iliad*

covers both male and female, human and nonhuman.[3] For the verb takes three distinct objects in the *Iliad*, and the meaning is slightly altered accordingly. With animals as the object, the verbal root refers to the act of "taming" or "breaking." With women and in domestic contexts, it means to "subjugate" in reference to marriage or enslavement.[4] And finally, with regard to men as object, the verb takes on its most physical and final sense as "to kill."[5] The use of this verbal root thus speaks to the problematic sexual politics of Archaic Greece that often equates women and animals. At the same time, such domestic forms of dominance are further connected to the act of killing itself as the ultimate expression of subjugation.

Yet the significance of this verbal complex for the *Iliad* goes far beyond basic semantics. Indeed, a contextual study of the verbs *damazō/damnēmi* in the *Iliad* speaks directly to the issue of force that is central to Simone Weil's thought—namely, the problem of force and the human subject. What we find in the Iliadic role of these verbal forms is both convergence with and divergence from Simone Weil's views. On the one hand, uses of the verbs *damazō/damnēmi* in the *Iliad* corroborate Weil's notion that violent force is a process by which the active human subject becomes a passive object. Indeed, philology converges with philosophy on this point because humans in the *Iliad* are predominantly treated grammatically as the accusative object or the passive subject in those verbal expressions.[6] And when humans are actively involved in the process of force described by the verbal root *dam-*, and not merely as objects, human agency itself seems to be explicitly problematized. For the majority of occurrences of these verbs in the *Iliad* downgrade the role of human activity from subjective agent to instrument.[7] On the other hand, the Iliadic episodes that deploy *damazō/damnēmi* also introduce us to an alternative model of human subjectivity quite distinct from that of Weil. Where Weil's account of force in the *Iliad* is informed by a Judeo-Christian view of the individual human subject as "soul," a reading of the *Iliad* more attuned to philological detail indicates that subjectivity in the *Iliad* is better understood as a form

---

[3] It should be noted, however, that the English verb "dominate," from Latin *dominus*, is actually derived from the IE root, **domh₂-o-*, different from the root **demh₂-*, on which see Benveniste 2016: 239–50. Nevertheless, English "dominate" does capture the range of meanings for the root **demh₂-* in Homeric Greek.

[4] For this meaning, see further discussion in Chapter 4.

[5] See Cunliffe ad loc. as well as H. W. Nordheider's entry for *damnēmi* in in *LfgrE*, pp. 212–15 for the general distinctions in meaning.

[6] There are only eight occurrences in the *Iliad* of a human subject as the nominative agent of the verbal root in the active, on which see the appendix under *damazō/damnēmi*.

[7] See, for instance, the formulaic uses χερσί/χείρεσσιν δαμ- listed under II in the appendix.

of "co-agency" that is shared between mortals and immortals. In this respect, the force represented by the verbal root *dam-* underscores the permeability of the human and its interactions with all that is external to it.[8] Indeed, the subject/object/instrument relations of force shared between mortals and immortals are best illustrated in the three most iconic deaths of the *Iliad*: those of Sarpedon, Patroclus, and Hector. Ultimately, the role of force expressed in these three episodes through *damazō/damnēmi* demonstrates that the "force that kills" in the *Iliad* is one that allows the poem as a whole to problematize the very notion of the human subject as an autonomous agent.

Simone Weil on Force and the Subject in Homer and History

Before engaging in a direct study of the verb *damazō* in the *Iliad*, we should first delve deeper into Weil's own particular understanding of force. To be sure, much of what Weil proclaims in her essay *L'Iliade ou le poème de la force* is so powerfully written that it appears self-explanatory. But there is in fact a rich and complex history to her thought on force. When one analyzes Weil's discussions of the *Iliad* prior to *L'Iliade ou le poème de la force*, it becomes clear Weil's thinking on Homer and force has a double source. As many have pointed out, the first and most obvious source is the events of war in the early twentieth century, which Weil herself experienced. Those experiences are reflected in her essay "Ne recommençons pas la guerre de Troie," published in 1937.[9] Less obvious, however, is the fact that Weil's thinking on force and the *Iliad* seems to be equally influenced by her involvement in the labor movement, reflected in her work *Oppression et liberté*, the majority of which was written in 1934, but first published in 1940. In both works, Weil discusses the *Iliad*, not in relation to "force" per se, but in relation to the connected concept of power, French *pouvoir*. At the same time, however, we may observe in *Oppression et liberté* how Weil begins to outline a universal concept of "force" that is

---

[8] For "co-agency" in the *Iliad*, see Brouillet 2019. Brouillet's concept and its relevancy for Iliadic death will be discussed in greater detail below.

[9] Weil had spent time in the militia during the Spanish Civil War, and she writes about that war as well as World War I and the events prior to World War II in "Ne recommençons pas la guerre de Troie." The essay was first published in *Nouveaux cahiers* in 1937. It was published in English as "Words and War" in 1946 in the journal *Politics*, one year after "*Iliad* or the Poem of Force" was published in English in that same journal.

170 Simone Weil and the Problem of Agency in the *Iliad*

only fully developed in *L'Iliade ou le poème de la force*. Understanding the genealogy of Weil's thought on force will therefore help us to appreciate the nuance and broader significance of Weil's claims on the nature of force as it applies to the *Iliad*, and it will further help us to understand how the *Iliad* itself diverges from Weil's particular views.

The main premise of Weil's first published essay on Homer, "Ne recommençons pas la guerre de Troie," was the unreal nature of the cause of war. Weil proclaims that modern warfare has a more unreal cause than even that of the Trojan war:

> At the center of the Trojan war, there was at least a woman, a woman perfectly beautiful. For our contemporaries, words adorned with capital letters play the role of Helen.
>
> **(Weil 1960: 42)**[10]

Those words in capital letters include terms such as Democracy, Dictatorship, Communism, Capitalism, and Anarchy, among others, and they were especially relevant to the violent events of 1930s Europe. But Weil insists that despite the unreal and abstract basis for the cause of war there remains a material reality to war: the materiality of death. She explains:

> The man on the right and the man on the left both forget that long months of civil war have gradually brought an almost identical regime on both sides. Each of the two has lost his ideal without noticing it, by replacing it with an empty entity; for each of the two, the victory of what he still calls his idea can no longer be defined except by the extermination of the adversary; and each of the two, if one speaks to him of peace, will reply with contempt by the blunt argument, the argument of Minerva in Homer, the argument of Poincaré in 1917: "The dead do not want it."
>
> **(Weil 1960: 41)**

The "argument of Minerva" in this passage from Weil is a reference to *Iliad* 2.[11] When the Greeks are about to flee Troy, after Agamemnon's "Testing Speech," Athena says to Odysseus:

---

[10] Translations from the French for this essay are my own.

[11] Earlier in the essay Weil refers to the same episode as the "argument of Minerva and Ulysses": "In order to shame the Greeks, who propose to return to their homes, Minerva and Ulysses believed they found a sufficient argument in the suffering of their dead comrades" (Weil 1960: 41).

Force and the Subject in Homer and History 171

κὰδ δέ κεν εὐχωλὴν Πριάμῳ καὶ Τρωσὶ λίποιτε
Ἀργείην Ἑλένην, ἧς εἵνεκα πολλοὶ Ἀχαιῶν
ἐν Τροίῃ ἀπόλοντο φίλης ἀπὸ πατρίδος αἴης;

Iliad 2.176–8

You would leave behind as a boast to Priam and the Trojans
Argive Helen, for whose sake many Achaeans
died in Troy, far from their beloved fatherland?

Thus, in Weil's view, the apparent cause of war, whether Helen or an abstract political concept, is merely a pretext, while those who have died in the war provide an even stronger motive, not for the commencement of war, but for its perpetuation. In *L'Iliade ou le poème de la force*, Weil brings up this same passage from *Iliad* 2, and asks "What indeed is Helen to Ulysses?...Troy and Helen are important only as causing bloodshed and tears for the Greeks" (Weil 2003: 59). And she follows this passage with Achilles' fateful decision to re-enter the war after the death of Patroclus, when Achilles proclaims, "May I die then at once, since fate has not allowed me to protect my dead friend" (*Iliad* 18.98–9). Weil concludes:

The man possessed by this double appetite for death belongs, so long as he does not change, to a race quite unlike the race of the living.

(Weil 2003: 60)

The "double appetite for death" is a compulsion to kill and be killed, which Weil sees equally present in the *Iliad* and in modern Europe. This causes Weil to conclude that the act of killing perpetuates itself, and those human subjects who engage in the act of killing will ultimately negate themselves.[12]

In "Ne recommençons pas la guerre de Troie," Weil ultimately comes down on the idea of "power," rather than "force," as the final cause of war more generally. She first explains:

All the absurdities which make history look like a long delirium have their roots in an essential absurdity, the nature of power. The need for

---

[12] Doering 2010: 23–9 summarizes this notion as "self-perpetuating force," although it should be noted that "force" is not articulated as such in the essay "Ne recommençons pas la guerre de Troie."

172   Simone Weil and the Problem of Agency in the *Iliad*

> power is tangible, palpable, because order is essential to existence; but the attribute of the power is arbitrary ... however, it must not appear as arbitrary, without which there is no longer any power. Prestige, that is to say illusion, is thus at the very heart of power.
>
> **(Weil 1960: 51–2)**

Here Weil is rather vague on what power is, except for the fact that the "need" for it is real and depends on a second level of unreality—prestige. In *L'Iliade ou le poème de la force*, Weil further comments that "For prestige that is three-fourths of force consists of magnificent indifference of the strong towards the weak" (Weil 2003: 57). And yet prestige, as the feeling of indifference towards the weak, is ultimately an illusion for Weil because all will eventually be placed in that very position of weakness.

Although Weil does not go into great detail on her sense of what "power" means in "Ne recommençons pas la guerre de Troie," she does offer a more complete account of power in reference to the *Iliad* in her earlier work on the labor movement, *Oppression et liberté*. In the main essay of that work, "Réflexions sur les causes de liberté et oppression," written in 1934, Weil explicitly links the *Iliad* not just with modern war, but with modern production and labor. She states:

> The only proper character to this regime [of capitalism] is that the instruments of industrial production are at the same time the principal arms in the race for power. But always the means in the race for power, whatever they may be, subsume men by the same frenzy and impose themselves on them as absolute ends. It is the reflection of this frenzy, which gives an epic grandeur to works such as the *Comédie humaine*, Shakespeare's *Histories*, the *Chansons de geste*, or the *Iliad*.
>
> **(Weil 1955: 67)** [13]

Immediately after equating the plight of industrial production with these several literary works, Weil offers a summation of the *Iliad*, stating:

> The true subject of the *Iliad* is the grip of war on warriors, and through them, on all humans.
>
> **(Weil 1955: 67)**

---

[13] Translations from the French are my own.

Force and the Subject in Homer and History   **173**

Here, then, we have an early version of Weil's famous opening to *L'Iliade ou le poème de la force*. And yet, in her earlier version, she explicitly links the *Iliad* not with force, but with power. She first states:

> Thus in this ancient and wonderful poem there already appears the essential evil for humanity, the substitution of means for ends.
>
> **(Weil 1955: 67)**

For she explains that it is the focus on means that may be viewed as the essential attribute of power:

> Power, by definition, consists only of a means; or to put it better, to possess power, that is simply to possess the means of action which exceed the limited force that a single individual has at his disposal on his own. But the search for power, because it is essentially unable to seize hold of its object, excludes all consideration of an end, and finally comes, through an inevitable reversal, to take the place of all ends. It is this reversal of the relationship between means and end, it is this fundamental folly that accounts for all that is senseless and bloody throughout history.
>
> **(Weil 1955: 68)**

Thus, for Weil, power, as a focus on means rather than ends, leads to the oppression of humanity in two separate spheres of human action, both war and production, and the *Iliad* stands as a testament to the historical constant of violence and oppression in both realms.

Given Weil's focus on power in *Oppression et liberté* and "Ne recommençons pas la guerre de Troie," and given that these earlier essays serve as a type of draft for her later essay on the *Iliad*, one could very well imagine the opening to her essay dedicated strictly to the *Iliad* to read as follows: "Le vrai héros, le vrai sujet, le centre de *l'Iliade*, c'est *pouvoir*." Indeed, her earlier writings compel us to consider whether there is in fact a substantial difference for Weil between the notions of "force" and "power," and why she ultimately chose the term "force" as the key to her interpretation of the *Iliad*.

There is, I believe, a significant and theoretically motivated reason for Weil's focus on "force" rather than "power" in *L'Iliade ou le poème de la force*. That reason can be found in *Oppression et liberté*.[14] For the main

---

[14] Gold 2016 notes that *Oppression et liberté* may be seen as a precursor to *L'Iliade ou le poème de la force* but does not expand on the suggestion.

174 Simone Weil and the Problem of Agency in the *Iliad*

thrust of *Oppression et liberté* is a critique of Marxism, and her critique gives special attention to one of the main principles of Marxist philosophy—the principle of "productive forces." In *Oppression et liberté*, one can observe Weil begin to outline her own account of "force," formulated as a response to Marx. But it is an account that is not fully articulated until *L'Iliade ou le poème de la force*.

In *German Ideology*, Marx and Engels describe the notion of "productive forces," *Produktivkräfte* in German, as one of the main principles of history.[15] The idea of productive force reflects a basic human drive for the production of life in procreation that is coextensive with the drive for the production of the means of life through labor.[16] Furthermore, it is the drive of productive forces that ultimately leads to ever higher levels of production and the eventual exploitation of labor such that those productive forces become destructive forces with the formation and oppression of the working class. Hence, according to Marx and Engels, it is the premise of productive forces that facilitates the progress of history as a history of ever-increasing oppression. At the same time, however, it is that history of ever-increasing oppression, driven by productive forces, which will ultimately lead to the Communist revolution.[17] Hence, for Marx and Engels, the notion of "productive forces" becomes the historical cause for both oppression and deliverance from that oppression.

In one of her later essays in *Oppression et liberté*, "Is there a Marxist doctrine?," Simone Weil first praises Marx for the attention given to the idea of "force." Weil states:

> Marx was the first and, unless I am mistaken, the only one—for his researches were not continued—to have the double idea of taking society as the fundamental human fact and of studying therein, as the physicist does in matter, the relationships of force.
>
> **(Weil 1955: 159)**

But in that same essay, Weil criticizes Marx for only applying the notion of force to production:

---

[15] It is not clear whether Weil would have read Marx in German or in a French translation, but significantly, the standard translation of *Produktivkräfte* is *les forces productives* in French, and this motivates her shift from "*pouvoir*" to "*force*" in her writings, as explained below.

[16] See under "History: Fundamental Conditions" in Marx and Engels 2004: 48–51.

[17] See "Contradictions of Big Industry: Revolution" in Marx and Engels 2004: 91–6.

Force and the Subject in Homer and History   175

> [Marx] forgot that [production] is not the only necessity, and this is the cause of a further foolishness—the belief that production is the sole factor in relationships of force. Marx purely and simply forgets war.
>
> **(Weil 1955: 174)**

For Weil, it is the very fact of war and the exercise of a force that is *non-productive* that stands as the clearest objection to the truth value of "productive force" as the first principle of history.

In "Réflexions sur les causes de liberté et oppression," Weil goes into greater detail in her criticism of Marx on productive forces. In particular, she criticizes its "mythological" character and suggests that it is "devoid of any scientific reason," because the idea that production must ever increase is assumed as a necessity without being analyzed in its own right.[18] And so in response to Marx and Engels, Weil claims humans are engaged in not one but two constant struggles. The first is a struggle against nature for the means of life and livelihood, as Marx and Engels described. But Weil further points that even though humans may achieve a relative degree of success in this initial struggle against nature, primarily achieved through surplus production, a second order of struggle is also at play that is also part of the basic conditions of existence, the "competition of organisms of the same species," that is to say "man against man."[19] For Weil, this second struggle is one and the same as the struggle against nature because "oppression is exercised by force, and in the long run, all force originates in nature."[20] In this way, Weil seems to combine a Marxist view of "productive force" and its pertinence to social oppression with a more Hobbesian-type perspective on the state of nature as a state of war of all against all.[21]

Weil's critique of Marx and her revision of force has major implications for an understanding of human agency and its role or lack thereof in the *Iliad*. Marx and Engels refer to human agency as "self-activity," a notional condition in which "definite individuals, living under definite relationships, can alone produce their material life and what is connected with it."[22] Yet this concept remains notional, because the history of productive forces ultimately makes the conditions of self-activity impossible: "We have a

---

[18] Weil 1955: 14–16.   [19] Weil 1955: 59.   [20] Weil 1955: 62–3.

[21] To my knowledge, Weil did not directly address the work of Hobbes, but she comes close to paraphrasing him on several occasions in *Oppression et liberté*. Her view on the two orders of human struggle against nature and against themselves corresponds to her critique that Marx "forgets war," quoted above (Weil 1955: 174–5).

[22] See "Forms of Intercourse" in Marx and Engels 2004: 86–8.

176   Simone Weil and the Problem of Agency in the *Iliad*

totality of productive forces, which have, as it were, taken on a material form and are for the individuals no longer the forces of the individuals."[23] This absence of self-activity is especially pertinent for the working class, for whom "the only connection which still links them with the productive forces and with their own existence—labor—has lost all semblance of self-activity and only sustains their life by stunting it."[24] For Marx and Engels, only a Communist society has the ability to restore self-activity to humans.[25]

Weil builds on Marx and Engel's argument on the inverse relationship between force and human agency, but with far bleaker prospects. For Weil, the regime of force appears as a historical constant without remit. This is because the effects of force, according to Weil, are not a function of production alone but are a function of "nature." She asserts:

> Humanity finds itself as much the plaything of the forces of nature, in the new form that technical progress has given them, just as it ever was in primitive times.
>
> **(Weil 1955: 80)**

Contrary to Marx, humans do not lose their agency, their "self-activity," as a function of the productive forces alone, but as a function of force more generally because force is fundamental to the human condition. In making this assertion, she further points out the numerous failures of Communism to deliver humans from the oppressive effects of force, including both small-scale cooperatives and the Russian Revolution, and she concludes: "It would seem that man is born a slave, and that servitude is his natural condition."[26] Where Marx and Engels view the absence of human agency as an effect of the history of production, Weil understands this absence of agency as a transhistorical state.

Thus, if we consider Weil's earlier writing on both the *Iliad* and Marxism, we may better understand how and why Weil arrives at the idea of "force" as the central theme of the *Iliad*. Where Weil had earlier asserted that "power" was the major theme of the *Iliad*, her shift to "force" gives

---

[23] Marx and Engels 2004: 92.   [24] Marx and Engels 2004: 92.

[25] Thus, Marx and Engels claims that with Communism "[s]ociety regulates the general production and thus makes it possible for me to do one thing today and another tomorrow, to hunt in the morning, fish in the afternoon, rear cattle in the evening, criticize after dinner, just as I have in mind, without ever becoming hunter, fisherman, herdsman or critic" (Marx and Engels 2004: 52).

[26] Weil 1955: 80.

Force and the Subject in Homer and History   177

greater attention to the problem of human agency and history. Indeed, if we compare her two summary accounts on the significance of the *Iliad*, that shift in focus becomes apparent. As mentioned above, in *Oppression et liberté*, Weil had stated:

> The true subject of the *Iliad* is the grip of war on warriors, and through them, on all humans.
>
> (Weil 1955: 40)

Whereas in *L'Iliade ou le poème de la force*, she proclaimed:

> The true hero, the true subject, the center of the *Iliad* is force.
>
> (Weil 2003: 45)

Although the phrasing is nearly identical, Weil makes the subtle addition of "the true hero" to her second version. This addition of "the true hero" thus creates a double play on the term "subjet." Force takes on meaning not just as the main topic of the poem, but also as the only *active agent* in the poem.[27] Weil further elaborates on this point throughout her essay, claiming: "As pitilessly as force annihilates, equally without pity it intoxicates those who possess or believe they possess it. In reality, no one possesses it."[28]

Marx and Engels believed the lack of human agency or lack of "self-activity" was merely a temporary historical condition that could be reversed with the Communist revolution, but Weil's reading of the *Iliad* suggests otherwise. Thus, in her opening paragraph of *L'Iliade*, she further states:

> For those who have supposed that force, thanks to progress, now belongs to the past, have seen a record of that in Homer's poem. Those wise enough to discern the force at the center of all human history, today as in the past, find in the *Iliad* the most beautiful and flawless mirror.
>
> (Weil 2003: 40)

---

[27] Here I part slightly from Holoka's translation, which renderes the French "sujet" as "subject matter" (Weil 2003: 45). The more simple translation "subject" captures the double meaning of French "sujet" as both "subject as topic" and "subject as person/agent."

[28] Weil 2003: 51.

178 Simone Weil and the Problem of Agency in the *Iliad*

Those to whom Weil is referring would be none other than adherents to the Marxist principle of "productive forces," who, in Weil's time, believed that the oppressive progress of force would eventually lead humanity to revolution and a return to "self-activity."[29] Indeed, Weil's transhistorical perspective on the effects of force was observed already in her earlier essays. Regarding the effects of capitalist production, she had already noted in *Oppression et liberté*:

> Human history is only the history of the enslavement which makes men, both oppressive and oppressed, the simple toy of the instruments of domination which they have made themselves, and thus swallows up the living humanity to be the thing of inert things.
>
> **(Weil 1955: 68)**

And it is precisely this view that she finds expressed equally so in the *Iliad*, when she famously states:

> Exercised to the extreme, [force] makes the human being a thing quite literally, that is, a dead body.
>
> **(Weil 2003: 40)**

Yet Weil is also quick to add that the condition of "thingness" does not merely apply to the corpse, but it is also a condition for the living, that is, for the enslaved:

> But there are still more miserable beings who, without dying, have become things for life.
>
> **(Weil 2003: 48)**

For Weil, then, the ancient warrior and slave, victor and victim are all deprived of their active agency in their subjection to force in the very same way as humans today are subjugated by modern warfare and production.[30]

---

[29] Thus, in "Is There a Marxist Doctrine?" Weil comments on Marx, "He took refuge in a dream wherein social matter itself takes charge of the two functions that it denies man, namely, not only to accomplish justice, but to conceive it" (Weil 1955: 176).

[30] In a certain way, Weil's argument on force anticipates Foucault's argument on "subjugated subjects." See Foucault 1982: 212, discussed in the previous chapter. Where Weil insists that subjugation deprives humans of subjectivity, Foucault argues that the effects of subjugation, whether direct or indirect, are what constitute subjectivity. For the relationship between Weil and Foucault, see further Ritner 2017.

Subjects of Force in the *Iliad* **179**

Given Weil's own reaction to Marx and her insistence on "servitude as man's natural condition," it would be safe to extend Weil's initial claim. For Weil, force is not simply the "true hero," that is, the only active subject of the *Iliad*, but such "force" is the only active subject of human history itself.

Subjects of Force in the *Iliad*

The genealogy of Weil's thought helps to explain why the idea of force must take on a universal quality in her reading of the *Iliad*. That universalism is meant to counteract the equally universal claims about force proposed by Marx and Engels. This is perhaps why Weil glosses over and subsumes the many meanings of force that I have discussed throughout this book under a single category. But despite Weil's universalist approach, her particular understanding of force in the *Iliad*—force as that which deprives humans of active subjectivity—does in fact have a very precise correspondence in Homeric vocabulary. For this notion of force, which we might summarize as "the subjugation of the human subject," is clearly designated in the *Iliad* by the verbs *damazō/damnēmi*.

First the subjugating quality of force is expressed in the semantics of these verbs and their Indo-European root, $*demh_2$-. The basic sense of the root in Indo-European is "to tame" or "subdue," related to Sanskrit *damayati*. This basic meaning of the root is found on several occasions in the *Iliad*. Perhaps most significantly, it is used in reference to the horses of Achilles, whom none other than Achilles himself is said to be able to subdue. Thus, at *Iliad* 10.403, Odysseus tells Dolon that the horses of Achilles are difficult for mortals to control. And the formula concerning the horses of Achilles is repeated at *Iliad* 17.77 by the disguised Apollo when speaking to Hector after Patroclus has been killed:

οἳ δ' ἀλεγεινοὶ
ἀνδράσι γε θνητοῖσι δαμήμεναι ἠδ' ὀχέεσθαι
ἄλλῳ γ' ἢ Ἀχιλῆϊ, τὸν ἀθανάτη τέκε μήτηρ.
Iliad **10.402–4;** *Iliad* **17.76–8**

They are difficult for mortal men to tame and to be driven,
for anyone other than Achilles, whom an immortal mother bore.

On the one hand, the idea demonstrated here is that Achilles' own superior physical force, which is a function of his half-immortal genealogy, is

180   Simone Weil and the Problem of Agency in the *Iliad*

what allows him to be able to handle the immortal horses. After all, it was Achilles' matrilineal genealogy that was claimed as the basis for his physical superiority by Nestor, Agamemnon, and others, as discussed in Chapter 1. And yet, there is also a second, socially motivated basis for Achilles' ability to control these horses, based on his matriline. For the horses themselves are said to have been given to Achilles' father Peleus by Poseidon as a wedding gift for his marriage to Thetis. And Peleus in turn gave them to Achilles.[31] Thus, Thetis provides both the physical and social logic for why Achilles is able to tame and drive the immortal horses.

The wedding of Thetis and Peleus also provides an example of the second-level meaning for the root *$demh_2$- in Homer's *Iliad*. For the verbal root does not just apply to animals, but, disturbingly, it also applies to women. The most iconic example of this usage is when Thetis goes to Hephaestus to obtain a new set of arms for Achilles, and laments her forced marriage to Peleus:

Ἥφαιστ᾽, ἦ ἄρα δή τις, ὅσαι θεαί εἰσ᾽ ἐν Ὀλύμπῳ,
τοσσάδ᾽ ἐνὶ φρεσὶν ᾗσιν ἀνέσχετο κήδεα λυγρὰ
ὅσσ᾽ ἐμοὶ ἐκ πασέων Κρονίδης Ζεὺς ἄλγε᾽ ἔδωκεν;
ἐκ μέν μ᾽ ἀλλάων ἁλιάων ἀνδρὶ δάμασσεν
Αἰακίδῃ Πηλῆϊ, καὶ ἔτλην ἀνέρος εὐνὴν
πολλὰ μάλ᾽ οὐκ ἐθέλουσα.

Iliad **18.429–34**

Hephaestus, of all the goddesses on Olympus,
is there any who has endured so many terrible griefs in her heart,
as Zeus the son of Cronus has given to me as a source of pain?
From the rest of the sea goddesses, he subjected me
to Peleus, son of Aeacus, and I endured the bed of a man,
very much against my will.

From a mythological perspective, Thetis' description of her marriage to Peleus as an act of violent subjugation, as an act of "taming," is not merely metaphorical. In later accounts, both poetic and iconographic, Peleus physically subdued Thetis in order to marry her, wrestling her as she transformed into various monsters and animals.[32] Although Thetis' own

---

[31] *Iliad* 23.277–9.
[32] See Pindar, *N.* 3.32–6, *N.* 4.62–5. Thetis is not the first female Peleus wrestled, but his match against Atalanta is also a popular motif in Greek art. See Barringer 1996; Scanlon 2002: 175–98.

Subjects of Force in the *Iliad*   181

status as a sea goddess is what allows her to transform from human to animal, the episode also conjures a broader association in Greek thought between maidens and wild animals, where marriage itself is understood to involve the process of "taming."[33] An "untamed girl," designated by the terms *admēs* or *admētos*, refers specifically to a woman who is not married.[34] Regarding the visual evidence for Peleus' pursuit of Thetis, Sourvinou-Inwood thus concludes, "The notion of the girl as a wild thing to be captured and tamed through marriage... is expressed emphatically in the paradigm of Thetis."[35]

But despite the physical violence entailed in Thetis' own marriage, it is clear that the marriage was not simply a direct function of Peleus' own will. Indeed, Laura Slatkin focused on Thetis' speech to Hephaestus in order to call attention to the stark contrast between Thetis' perceived helplessness in the *Iliad* and the innate power of birth she possessed, which brought her to that very state of helplessness.[36] Interestingly, in Pindar's *Isthmian* 8, where we learn that Thetis' power rests on the fact that she will bear a son "stronger than the father," it is the goddess Themis who is responsible for assigning the sea goddess to Peleus (Pindar *I.* 8.36–45). By contrast, in Thetis' speech in the *Iliad*, it is Zeus who is the active subject that forces her upon the mortal Peleus (δάμασσεν: *Iliad* 18.431). Thetis' words make certain that her own unhappy condition has a cause that is higher than mortal action. How else would an immortal goddess actually submit to a mortal man?

Yet, beyond the mythological and quasi-metaphorical accounts of marriage as a "taming" ritual, the verbal root *dam-* also entails the problem of actual violence against women in the *Iliad*. When Menelaus and Paris are about to duel and thereby put an end to the Trojan war, a sacrifice is made, and both Greeks and Trojans make the following private prayer:

> Ζεῦ κύδιστε μέγιστε καὶ ἀθάνατοι θεοὶ ἄλλοι
> ὁππότεροι πρότεροι ὑπὲρ ὅρκια πημήνειαν
> ὧδέ σφ' ἐγκέφαλος χαμάδις ῥέοι ὡς ὅδε οἶνος
> αὐτῶν καὶ τεκέων, ἄλοχοι δ' ἄλλοισι δαμεῖεν.

Iliad **3.298–301**

---

[33] See, among others, Loraux 1978: 59–69; Calame 1997: 238–43.
[34] *Odyssey* 6.109, 228; *Homeric Hymn to Aphrodite 133.*
[35] Sourvinou-Inwood 1987: 138.
[36] Slatkin 1991: 55–7.

182 Simone Weil and the Problem of Agency in the *Iliad*

Zeus, most exalted and greatest, and the other immortal gods,
whoever should first break the oaths,
may their brains and those of their children flow to the earth like this wine
and may their wives be subjected to other men.

The last line of this prayer presents a double register for the effect of force on women. On the one hand, as already noted, the process of marriage is itself understood as a form of "taming" or subjugation for women. On the other hand, in the context of war, women are threatened with a second order of subjugation, where the wives of men may then become slaves to other men. This very sentiment is further expressed when Hector says to his wife that his greatest fear is the day "when some one of the bronze-clad Achaeans leads you away in tears and takes away the day of freedom" (6.454–5). These lines from Hector were used by Weil to account for the logic of force as that which transforms the living into things, even while they still live:

> This thing aspires at all times to be a man or a woman, and never attains the goal. This is a death that extends throughout life, a life that death has frozen long before putting an end to it.
>
> **(Weil 2003: 48–9)**

As *Iliad* 3.301 makes clear, women, perhaps more so than others, become "things" as double objects of force, first subjected to husbands, and at the same time always threatened to be re-subjected to others. Even Hector, in his pity for Andromache, uses her own enslavement as an occasion for his glory. Hence, upon the death of Hector, Andromache herself will become a "thing" in a double capacity, both as a slave and as the living monument of her husband.[37] It is the verbs *damazō/damnēmi* that succinctly articulate both philosophically and grammatically the ever-present subject-object status of women in the *Iliad*. When the verb is active, even female figures as powerful as Thetis herself are the grammatical object of force, but when women take on the grammatical position of the nominative, then they too are only passive subjects.[38]

---

[37] See Canevaro 2018: 184; Scodel 1992: 59: "Like a monument, she provokes a response in those who see her"; Graziosi and Haubold 2010 *ad Iliad* 6.460–1: "Andromache functions as a σῆμα, a living memorial of Hector's past achievements in war."

[38] Of course, it must be further noted that there are numerous ways, in both the *Iliad* and the *Odyssey*, by which women are able to transcend their subject-object status, on which see especially Canevaro 2018.

Subjects of Force in the *Iliad* **183**

The occurrences of the verbal root *dam-* applied to animals and women are, nevertheless, relatively rare in the *Iliad*. It is in reference to warriors that this verbal complex occurs most frequently. And it is in reference to warriors that it designates the paramount form of subjugation, the act of killing. But even in the case of male-on-male violence on the battlefield, subjective human agency is greatly de-emphasized. Of all the occurrences of the verbs *damazō* and *damnēmi* in the *Iliad*, only eight out of ninety-six uses appear in the active form with a mortal agent as the subject.[39] Far more frequently, the verbal complex is presented with the victim of force as the passive subject, and the killer's role is expressed in strictly instrumental terms. Thus, a common formulaic variation presents a warrior killed "by the spear" of another warrior.[40] And perhaps equally significant are variations where a warrior is killed "at the hands" of another warrior.[41] Thus, formulaically, we can observe an easy alternation between spears and hands, between inanimate and animate instruments of force.[42] In these episodes, following Simone Weil, we may assert that humans are reduced to "things" not only as objects, but also as the mere means or instruments of force. Such a sentiment can be found in *Oppression et liberté*, when Weil equates the plight of warriors in the *Iliad* with factory workers, explaining that history makes humans "the plaything of the instruments of domination they themselves have made" (Weil 1955: 68). What the *Iliad* demonstrates is that these mortal "instruments of domination" are not simply a function of the "means of production" in the Marxist sense, but the category applies equally to the tools of war produced as a means for destruction.

Thus, with the verbs *damazō/damnēmi*, we see that there are three types of beings—animals, women, and men—who are subjected to force in separate, but related capacities. And even in the case of male violence, we see humans relegated to the realm of instruments rather than subjective agents. In this regard, we might be able to better understand how and why Weil is able to assert that force itself is the only "true hero" or "true subject" of the *Iliad*—because humans themselves are never the sole agents of the force that kills.

And yet, when it comes to human subjectivity itself, it should be noted that Weil operates with a view of the person that is quite anachronistic and

---

[39] See *Iliad* 9.496, 10.210, 10.411, 11.98, 12.186, 20.400, 21.90, 21.226. The full list of occurrences for this verbal complex is presented in the appendix.

[40] See the appendix under *damazō/damnēmi*, I, III, IV.

[41] See the appendix under *damazō/damnēmi*, II.

[42] On the relationship between hands and weapons in the *Iliad*, see Holmes 2010: 74–6.

184 Simone Weil and the Problem of Agency in the *Iliad*

distinct from Homeric representation. As Seth Schein has noted, Weil "substitutes her own spiritual categories and values for those of the epic, which she views through highly idiosyncratic and anachronistic Platonic and Christian lenses."[43] In particular, she discusses human subjectivity in reference primarily to "the soul." Weil thus describes the warrior as a victim of force as follows:

> He is living, he has a soul; he is nonetheless a thing. Strange being—a thing with a soul. Strange situation for the soul!
>
> **(Weil 2003: 46)**

Similar descriptions of this body-soul dichotomy occur throughout her essay.[44] But of course, as Bruno Snell had first argued in *Entdeckung des Geistes*, Homeric poetry had not yet conceptualized the notion of "soul" as synonymous with the identity of the human subject. And even though Snell's own argument about the advent of soul as self in Greek history is deeply flawed, Christopher Gill, Matthew Clarke, Brooke Holmes, Anthony Long, and others have clearly shown how the notion of "self" in Homer does not operate according to the body-soul binary that was only introduced sometime in the Classical era.[45]

Even though Weil's own view on the self is inappropriate and anachronistic for Homeric poetry, we need not reject the idea that human subjectivity in Homer is impacted by the operation of force, especially with regard to the verbal root *dam-*. Indeed, when we focus on the deployment of *damazō/damnēmi* in Homer, an alternative model of subjective agency emerges. In place of a modern paradigm of the self as autonomous agent, the *Iliad* gives expression to a concept of "co-agency" shared between the human and nonhuman.

Relying on comparative anthropology, Manon Brouillet (2019) offered up the notion of "co-agency" in order to account for Agamemnon's famous pseudo-apology to Achilles and the Greeks at *Iliad* 19.86–96, when Agamemnon famously claimed, "I am not responsible" (ἐγὼ δ'οὐκ αἴτιος εἰμι) (*Iliad* 19.86). That particular episode in the *Iliad* has become a major scholarly crux for discussing the relationship between human and divine

---

[43] Schein 2016: 153.
[44] See further Ferber 1981: 75–6; Schein 1984: 68–9, 83.
[45] See Gill 1996; Clarke 1999; Holmes 2010; Long 2016. For further discussion on Snell's view, see discussion in the conclusion to this book.

Subjects of Force in the *Iliad* **185**

responsibility in Greek thought.[46] But as Versnel has observed, many of the interpretations of this episode rely on modern categories of philosophical analysis pertaining to agency and causation, and so he concludes that one should stop "feeding red herrings to Homer."[47] Instead, Versnel used this episode to explain more generally how, when confronted with catastrophe, the Greeks believed that "there is *not* one universal and monolithic principle of causation, or if there is, that no single definition would suffice in a world of great complexity."[48] Brouillet builds on Versnel's observations by demonstrating how Agamemnon's attribution of cause in his actions to Zeus, Moira, the Erinyes, and Atē is consistent with a more general tendency in the Homeric poems for Greek heroes to share their agency with gods. For Brouillet, a notion of "co-agency" between humans and gods is underscored by the conceptual conditions for the production of epic poetry itself and the close link between poet and Zeus.[49]

At first glance, the concept of "co-agency" may seem to be one and the same as "double motivation" or "double determination," most notably described by Albin Lesky (1961). The two concepts do indeed present close approximation, but there remains a subtle, but fundamental difference. The arguments around double motivation are concerned primarily with the psychological attributes of human cognition and decision making, so that one may determine whether the *cause* of events and actions can be attributed to human or divine will.[50] As Hayden Pelliccia (2011) has noted, however, the model of "double motivation" ultimately presupposes the anachronistic arguments on "free will vs. determinism," which presuppose a single cause for every action. The concept of "co-agency" sidesteps these issues by focusing the discussion not on the psychological *cause* of action but simply on how characters in the *Iliad* view themselves as sites of co-participation in action.

The verbs *damazō* and *damnēmi* contribute significantly to arguments on co-agency in the *Iliad* at both a grammatical and a conceptual level. For this verbal complex shows how characters see the process of killing as a single process that nearly always has two aspects. For example, before the

---

[46] For a summary of the major views, especially those of E. R. Dodds 1951, Hugh Lloyd-Jones 1971, and Bernard Williams 1993, see Versnel 2011: 160–79.

[47] Versnel 2011: 173.   [48] Versnel 2011: 162.

[49] Brouillet 2019: 7–9. Similarly, Pietro Pucci (2018) has thoroughly discussed the complex ways in which the narrative of the *Iliad* interacts with the rather opaque "will of Zeus." See esp. Brouillet 2019: 9–10.

[50] Lesky's argument is presented concisely in English in his essay "Divine and Human Causation in the Homeric Epics" in Lesky 2001.

186 Simone Weil and the Problem of Agency in the *Iliad*

duel between Menelaus and Paris, Menelaus prays to Zeus to "kill him with my hand" (ἐμῆς ὑπὸ χερσὶ δάμασσον) (*Iliad* 3.352). And Hector says to Helen that he does not know whether "the gods may kill me at the hands of the Achaeans" (μ' ὑπὸ χερσὶ θεοὶ δαμόωσιν Ἀχαιῶν) (*Iliad* 6.368). Agamemnon prays to Zeus, "do not allow the Greeks to be killed by the Trojans" (μηδ' οὕτω Τρώεσσιν ἔα δάμνασθαι Ἀχαιούς) (*Iliad* 8.244). And with regard to Achilles, Agamemnon had asserted, "since [Zeus] has now honored [Achilles] and subjugated the Achaean people" (ὡς νῦν τοῦτον ἔτισε, δάμασσε δὲ λαὸν Ἀχαιῶν) (*Iliad* 9.118). The narrator also describes how co-agency between Zeus and Trojans stopped Ajax in battle: "The mind of Zeus and noble Trojans subjugated him" (δάμνα μιν Ζηνός τε νόος καὶ Τρῶες ἀγαυοί) (*Iliad* 16.103). In these and many other examples, we see that the "force" of killing expressed through *damazō/damnēmi* does not strictly constitute its own self-perpetuating subject, as Weil had asserted. Rather, it is Zeus, as well as the other gods, who are the ultimate subjective agents of violent force, while humans nevertheless contribute either as co-participants or as mere instruments.

Simone Weil was aware of the ways in which force was expressed specifically in reference to the divine in the *Iliad*. But despite this awareness, she actively dismissed the significance of the gods in Homer. In *Oppression et liberté*, regarding the heroes in the *Iliad*, she states:

> None of them knows why each sacrifices himself and all his family to a bloody and aimless war, and that is why, all through the poem, it is the gods who are credited with the mysterious influence which nullifies peace negotiations, continually revives hostilities, and brings together again the contending forces urged by a flash of good sense to abandon the struggle.
>
> **(Weil 1955: 67)**

For Weil, the violence of war perpetuates itself, but this self-perpetuating character is entirely opaque to human participants. Thus, the gods, in Weil's account, are merely a narrative device for psychologically justifying the irrational continuation of violence.

But if we are to take the role of force in the *Iliad* seriously, at a poetic and philological level, and not merely as a paradigm for modern violence, then we must take seriously the role of the Iliadic gods in the perpetuation of force.[51] Indeed, when we focus specifically on the verbs *damazō* and

---

[51] The need to take the Homeric gods seriously is grounded in the anthropological principle of "taking indigenous thought seriously." See further Viveiros de Castro 2014: 194–6. As

damnēmi in the *Iliad*, we find that these verbs take on a prominent and interconnected role in the three most iconic deaths of the *Iliad*: those of Sarpedon, Patroclus, and Hector. And it is in those episodes where we find the greatest emphasis placed on co-agency between mortal and immortal. As will be made clear, the co-agency expressed through verbs in the root **demh$_2$-* functions not merely as a religious and metaphysical assumption. Rather, occurrences of the verb *damazō* and related forms serve as a means to actively *problematize* the notion of autonomous human agency from within the narrative of the poem.

Force, Fate, and Death: Sarpedon, Patroclus, and Hector

As soon as Achilles allows Patroclus to enter the battle at the beginning of *Iliad* 16, a new wave of violence and death commences, highlighted by the deaths of Sarpedon, Patroclus himself, and Hector. This causal sequence is one that will ultimately lead to the death of Achilles himself.[52] And as so many scholars have noted, Patroclus' initial act of entering the battle raises a central question on human responsibility: who is to blame for the death of Patroclus? But the question is not necessarily one that is meant to be answered. Instead, it is generally argued, the episode lends an overall tragic effect to the nature of human activity as such in Homer.[53] Here, I would like to contribute to that larger discussion by calling attention to how the problem of responsibility in this particular sequence of deaths is

---

Viveiros de Castro 2014: 196 explains: "Keeping the values of the Other implicit does not mean celebrating whatever transcendent mystery it supposedly keeps enclosed in itself. It consists in refusing to actualize the possibles expressed by indigenous thought, making a decision to maintain them, infinitely, as possibles—neither derealizing them as fantasies of the other nor fantasizing that they are actual for us." Thus, we must accurately describe the operations of the divine in the *Iliad* but refuse the general tendency to either dismiss or identify with those operations. On the need to take the Homeric gods seriously, see further Gagné and Jáuregui 2019.

[52] See Janko 1992: 312: "These parallels [between the death of Sarpedon, Patroclus, and Hector] underline the causal nexus linking the three major deaths in the poem with the yet greater one outside it, Akhilleus', which must soon follow Hektor's." Furthermore, Patroclus' own death may very well parallel that of Achilles, on which see further Burgess 2009: 79–81. And this may very well be a function of Patroclus as a ritual substitute and double of Achilles, on which see: Nagy 1979: 292–3; Nagy 1990b: 129–30; Nagy 2012: 48–57; and Nagy 2013: 146–68. And as Pucci 2018: 91 argues, Patroclus' request causes a break between Achilles and his double, which precipitates the death of both.

[53] See, among others, Adkins 1960: 14–15; Janko 1992 ad loc.; Redfield 1994; Karakantza 2014; Allen-Hornblower 2016: 18–93; Pucci 2018: 103–17.

188 Simone Weil and the Problem of Agency in the *Iliad*

explicitly linked to the enactment of force at both a thematic and a grammatical level through the *damazō/damnēmi* verbal complex. The issue of force is made especially apparent in the death of Sarpedon at the hands of Patroclus. First, Sarpedon's own decision to fight against Patroclus is brought about when he witnesses the enactment of force against his Lycian companions:

Σαρπηδὼν δ' ὡς οὖν ἴδ' ἀμιτροχίτωνας ἑταίρους
χέρσ' ὕπο Πατρόκλοιο Μενοιτιάδαο δαμέντας, @1
κέκλετ' ἄρ' ἀντιθέοισι καθαπτόμενος Λυκίοισιν
αἰδὼς ὦ Λύκιοι· πόσε φεύγετε; νῦν θοοὶ ἔστε.
ἀντήσω γὰρ ἐγὼ τοῦδ' ἀνέρος, ὄφρα δαείω
ὅς τις ὅδε κρατέει καὶ δὴ κακὰ πολλὰ ἔοργε
Τρῶας, ἐπεὶ πολλῶν τε καὶ ἐσθλῶν γούνατ' ἔλυσεν

Iliad 16.419–25

But when Sarpedon saw his freely clad companions
killed at the hands of Patroclus son of Menoetius,
He called out accosting the Lycians, equal to the gods:
For shame, Lycians. Where do you flee? Now be quick.
For I will meet that man, in order that I may learn
who is overpowering the Trojans and has caused much evil,
since he has loosened the limbs of many good men.

Sarpedon's decision to face the as yet unknown warrior results from the fact that his own companions are "killed at the hands of Patroclus, son of Menoetius" (χέρσ' ὕπο Πατρόκλοιο Μενοιτιάδαο δαμέντας) (*Iliad* 16.420), where being "killed at the hands of X warrior" is a common formulaic variation.[54] Sarpedon further glosses this account by asserting that this warrior has *kratos*, indicating that Sarpedon is aware of divine inspiration involved in Patroclus' rampage.[55] It is the witnessing of force that compels Sarpedon to make a decision to meet that force and eventually his own death.[56]

---

[54] See formula II in the appendix for *damazō/damnēmi*.

[55] On *kratos* as a gift from the gods, see the appendix. Furthermore, Patroclus seems to be divinely possessed as soon as he puts on the armor of Achilles, on which see Collins 1998: 15–45.

[56] As Clay 2009: 36 states, "The stark simplicity of these lines marks the critical moment for every hero: the moment when he chooses to face death rather than to flee." On the decision of the hero, see further Clay 2002.

Force, Fate, and Death: Sarpedon, Patroclus, and Hector 189

Immediately after Sarpedon's fateful decision, however, we are presented with a possible alternative, when Zeus contemplates an intervention in Sarpedon's eventual death:

ὤ μοι ἐγών, ὅ τέ μοι Σαρπηδόνα φίλτατον ἀνδρῶν
μοῖρ' ὑπὸ Πατρόκλοιο Μενοιτιάδαο δαμῆναι.
διχθὰ δέ μοι κραδίη μέμονε φρεσὶν ὁρμαίνοντι,
ἤ μιν ζωὸν ἐόντα μάχης ἄπο δακρυοέσσης
θείω ἀναρπάξας Λυκίης ἐν πίονι δήμῳ,
ἦ ἤδη ὑπὸ χερσὶ Μενοιτιάδαο δαμάσσω.

Iliad 16.433–8

Ah me, because Sarpedon, the most beloved of men for me,
is fated to be killed by Patroclus, son of Menoetius,
the heart in my chest has remained divided as I contemplate this,
whether I snatch him up still alive far from battle
and place him in the rich land of Lycia,
or whether I kill him at the hands of the son of Menoetius.

Perhaps most striking in Zeus' speech is the apparent conflict between Zeus' own emotions and the "fate," *moira*, of his dear son. It is generally understood that the fate of humans is beyond the decision-making power of the immortals.[57] But, as Pietro Pucci has noted, it was Zeus' earlier decision to have Achilles re-enter the battle that also sealed the fate of Sarpedon.[58] For Zeus himself proclaimed the major sequence of deaths as follows:

ὃ δ' ἀνστήσει ὃν ἑταῖρον
Πάτροκλον· τὸν δὲ κτενεῖ ἔγχεϊ φαίδιμος Ἕκτωρ
Ἰλίου προπάροιθε πολέας ὀλέσαντ' αἰζηοὺς
τοὺς ἄλλους, μετὰ δ' υἱὸν ἐμὸν Σαρπηδόνα δῖον.
τοῦ δὲ χολωσάμενος κτενεῖ Ἕκτορα δῖος Ἀχιλλεύς.

Iliad 15.64–8

[Achilles] will rouse his companion
Patroclus. And with his spear, shining Hector will kill him,
Patroclus, who will have killed many other strong men

---

[57] See Brügger 2016 ad loc. 16.433–8 with references. There is a social function to "fate" being independent of the gods' involvement, as Graziosi and Haubold 2005: 91 point out: "Harmony among the gods…can only be ensured if all mortals are abandoned to their fate."
[58] Pucci 2018: 34.

190 Simone Weil and the Problem of Agency in the *Iliad*

far from Troy, and among them, my divine son Sarpedon.
And in anger for Patroclus, divine Achilles will kill Hector.

What emerges, then, is a contradiction in the poem between the emotion of Zeus and his very own action. As Pucci explains, "The *Iliad* wants to show that a positive mythical deployment is possible... Yet this admission is real only in principle, for as a matter of fact Zeus cannot suspend Sarpedon's death that he himself has announced and decreed."[59]

This ambiguity is perfectly expressed at a philological level in Zeus' double usage of the verb *damazō* when he contemplates Sarpedon's future. For Zeus first comments, with the impersonal phrase that "it is *fated* that Sarpedon be killed by Patroclus son of Menoetius" (μοῖρ' ὑπὸ Πατρόκλοιο Μενοιτιάδαο δαμῆναι) (*Iliad* 16.434), but he concludes his speech by contemplating in a more personal manner, "whether *I* shall kill him at the hands of the son of Menoetius" (ἦ ἤδη ὑπὸ χερσὶ Μενοιτιάδαο δαμάσσω) (*Iliad* 16.438). Thus, we quickly learn that what is "fated" is something that is actively accomplished by Zeus himself. Furthermore, the same formulaic phrase occurs first when Sarpedon himself witnessed his companions "killed at the hands of Patroclus, son of Menoetius" (χέρσ' ὕπο Πατρόκλοιο Μενοιτιάδαο δαμέντας) (*Iliad* 16.420).

Thus, the events leading to Sarpedon's death are highlighted by formulaic repetitions of the verbal root *dam-*, and that repetition highlights the problem of agency and violence in the sequence of deaths:

χέρσ' ὕπο Πατρόκλοιο Μενοιτιάδαο δαμέντας

(*Iliad* 16.420)

"[companions] killed at the hands of Patroclus, son of Menoetius"
μοῖρ' ὑπὸ Πατρόκλοιο Μενοιτιάδαο δαμῆναι

(*Iliad* 16.434)

"It is fate that [Sarpedon] be killed by Patroclus, son of Menoetius"
ἦ ἤδη ὑπὸ χερσὶ Μενοιτιάδαο δαμάσσω

(*Iliad* 16.438)

"Or will I kill him at the hands of the son of Menoetius"

In the first two repetitions of this formula, we have passive constructions. Both Sarpedon's companions and Sarpedon himself are treated as objects

---

[59] Pucci 2018: 35.

Force, Fate, and Death: Sarpedon, Patroclus, and Hector   191

of subjugation. These first two formulaic repetitions speak directly to the cycle of violence, which Simone Weil referred to as the "double appetite for death," the desire to kill and be killed, which is elicited by the memory and witness of violence against one's own people.[60] Weil discussed this double appetite and action in reference to Achilles, but it applies just as much to Sarpedon. He witnessed his companions "killed by Patroclus," and his own decision to meet Patroclus means that he too will be "killed by Patroclus." But in the final repetition of this formula, spoken by Zeus, we move from a passive to an active use of the verb. And yet, in this active construction, the mortal agent Patroclus retains the very same instrumental role as in the previous two occurrences. It is Zeus himself who takes up the subjective role as nominative agent. Zeus' phrase at 16.438 thus gives precise grammatical expression to the operation of co-agency between mortals and immortals. It is a form of agency that also implies a hierarchy. The gods retain the position of subjective agency, and mortals function as mere instruments.

With Sarpedon's death, however, we also bear witness to the opacity of force when it comes to the strictly mortal perspective in the poem. Although Zeus contemplates whether he will actively kill Sarpedon, and Hera too tells Zeus to "allow" Sarpedon to be killed by Patroclus (*Iliad* 16.452), Glaucus, who first comments on the death of Sarpedon, presents one more variation of the *dam-* formula. For Glaucus calls to Hector to protect the body of Sarpedon and states: "Bronze Ares killed [Sarpedon] at the hands of Patroclus with his spear" (τὸν δ᾽ ὑπὸ Πατρόκλῳ δάμασ᾽ ἔγχεϊ χάλκεος Ἄρης) (*Iliad* 16.543). In Glaucus' speech, we have another active use of the verb, but in place of Zeus as the subject, Glaucus provides the deity "bronze Ares," which serves here as a periphrasis for "war."[61] Earlier, Glaucus did acknowledge that Zeus did not protect his son, the best of men (*Iliad* 16.521–2), but he does not go so far as to accuse Zeus of actively killing his son. At the same time, Glaucus will not give Patroclus full credit and responsibility for the death of Sarpedon, but relegates him to the role of instrumental agent, just as the gods had done.[62] Glaucus may be ignorant of divine operations, but his variation of the *damazō* formula still

---

[60] See Weil 2003: 60.

[61] Such forms of periphrasis thus reiterate Jean-Pierre Vernant's famous claim that "the Greek gods are powers not persons" (Vernant 1988: 328). Vernant had been attempting to distinguish cultic worship from the literary treatment of the gods, but such distinctions are not always so absolute. On the treatment of warriors in the *Iliad* as both servants and victims of Ares, see Nagy 1979: 289–308.

[62] Glaucus' attribution of agency to the personification of war, Ares, is a verbal expression that can also be observed in Archaic grave monuments such as that of the famous Kroisos Kouros from the National Museum of Archaeology in Athens.

192   Simone Weil and the Problem of Agency in the *Iliad*

limits human agency, perhaps in part as a rhetorical strategy to downgrade the success of the enemy.

Nowhere, however, is the question of agency and force between mortals and immortals more explicit than in the death of Patroclus himself. Patroclus has been well characterized as a proto-tragic figure, one who is possessed by *Atē* in his attempt to sack Troy and thereby transcend the limits of his own destiny.[63] Remarkably, the gods do not simply stop Patroclus by way of humans, but Apollo confronts Patroclus directly. In Patroclus' first series of attempts to scale the wall of Troy, we are told:

> τρὶς δ᾽ αὐτὸν ἀπεστυφέλιξεν Ἀπόλλων
> χείρεσσ᾽ ἀθανάτῃσι φαεινὴν ἀσπίδα νύσσων.

> ***Iliad* 16.703–4**

> Three times Apollo beat him back
> with immortal hands striking against his shining shield.

These immortal hands of Apollo may be explicitly contrasted with the mortal "hands of Patroclus." For just prior to Apollo's intervention, the poet states:

> Ἔνθά κεν ὑψίπυλον Τροίην ἕλον υἷες Ἀχαιῶν
> **Πατρόκλου ὑπὸ χερσί**, περὶ πρὸ γὰρ ἔγχεϊ θῦεν,
> εἰ μὴ Ἀπόλλων Φοῖβος ἐϋδμήτου ἐπὶ πύργου
> ἔστη τῷ ὀλοὰ φρονέων, Τρώεσσι δ᾽ ἀρήγων.

> ***Iliad* 16.698–701**

> Then the sons of the Achaeans would have seized high-gated Troy
> **at the hands of Patroclus**, for he ran far before them with his spear,
> if Phoebus Apollo had not been standing on the strong built tower
> thinking destructive thoughts against him, while protecting the Trojans.

---

[63] As the narrator comments at *Iliad* 16.685–6: "he was greatly deluded, the fool" (καὶ μέγ᾽ ἀάσθη/ νήπιος). On the one hand, Patroclus clearly does not heed the commands of Peleus, but at the same time, it becomes clear that this is not strictly a function of Patroclus' own responsibility but also a function of Zeus' own greater plan, since the narrator then comments that "the mind of Zeus is always stronger than that of men" (ἀλλ᾽ αἰεί τε Διὸς κρείσσων νόος ἠέ περ ἀνδρῶν) (*Iliad* 16.688). Pietro Pucci thus calls this the "conspiracy against Patroclus" (Pucci 2018: 103–18). On the proto-tragic character of Patroclus, see Holmes 2010: 52.

Force, Fate, and Death: Sarpedon, Patroclus, and Hector **193**

And as we have already noted, it was the "hands of Patroclus" which were often invoked in the *dam-* formulas used to describe the destruction of many Trojans, including Sarpedon. Thus, Apollo's own immortal hands serve as the counterpoint to those of Patroclus. They serve as a means to prevent human action from moving beyond what the gods will allow.

As Brooke Holmes has commented, Apollo's intervention against Patroclus is both supremely physical and at the same time invisible.[64] It is in Apollo's second attack against Patroclus, the one that brings to Patroclus "the end of life" (βιότοιο τελευτή) (*Iliad* 16.787), where this physical invisibility is most emphasized. For the narrator comments that Patroclus "did not notice" (οὐκ ἐνόησεν) (*Iliad* 16.789) Apollo coming because of a mist. Then Apollo "meets" Patroclus not head on, but by standing behind him:

στῆ δ' ὄπιθεν, πλῆξεν δὲ μετάφρενον εὐρέε τ' ὤμω
χειρὶ καταπρηνεῖ, στρεφεδίνηθεν δέ οἱ ὄσσε.

Iliad 16.791–2

He stood behind him, and struck him on the back and broad shoulders with down-turned hand, and his eyes spun round.

In his capacity as the "far-shooter," Apollo's attacks against mortals are almost always invisible.[65] At the same time, this particular attack is unique. Alex Purves has noted that Apollo's position, standing behind Patroclus, στῆ δ' ὄπιθεν, presents the same formula used when Athena stands behind Achilles and prevents him from drawing his sword (*Iliad* 1.197).[66]

What both Athena and Apollo accomplish is a form of divine, physical intervention in mortal activity. In both cases, the warrior is stopped from executing on his own intentions. As discussed in Chapter 1, Athena stated that she came to stop the *menos* of Achilles (*Iliad* 1.207). And in *Iliad* 16, the narrator describes how Apollo's blow *loosened* the armor of Achilles from Patroclus' body (*Iliad* 16.804: λῦσε δέ οἱ θώρηκα), and with that his "limbs were *loosened*" (*Iliad* 16.805: λύθεν δ' ὑπὸ φαίδιμα γυῖα). The "loosening of limbs" formula is synonymous with the formula for "loosening" or "releasing" *menos* at the moment of a warrior's death.[67] In both

---

[64] Holmes 2010: 52–8.
[65] As Holmes 2010: 53 comments, "After all, how does one meet in combat (ἀντιβολέω) the one who strikes from afar (ἑκατηβόλος)?" Thus, Holmes demonstrates how the attack may be compared to the pestilence of *Iliad* 1, where the attack of Apollo can really only be measured by the symptoms it produces.
[66] Purves 2019: 134–5.   [67] See formulas XV and XVI under *menos* in the appendix.

194　Simone Weil and the Problem of Agency in the *Iliad*

instances, therefore, we have an unseen epiphany, an epiphany where the god does not appear in front of the warrior but behind him, and that invisible appearance of the god has a direct effect, stopping the physical force of the warrior.[68]

Apollo, however, is not the final cause of Patroclus' death, even if his blow anticipates that eventual outcome. Instead, Apollo's act makes way for more visible, mortal violence against Patroclus, first by the relatively obscure Trojan Euphorbus, who also strikes him in the back with a spear and then returns into the crowd (*Iliad* 16.806–15), and finally by Hector himself, who deals the final blow and vaunts over Patroclus' dying body (*Iliad* 16.818–42). The figure of Euphorbus has attracted great scholarly attention, precisely because his involvement in the death of Patroclus seems excessive.[69] Even according to the model of co-agency, all that would be needed is one deity and one mortal: Apollo and Hector would suffice for the killing of Patroclus. But, as William Allan has argued, the supplemental function of Euphorbus clearly serves to doubly emphasize the hollowness of Hector's own victory over Patroclus.[70] This fact is made most evident when Patroclus responds to Hector's boast:

ἤδη νῦν Ἕκτορ μεγάλ' εὔχεο· σοὶ γὰρ ἔδωκε
νίκην Ζεὺς Κρονίδης καὶ Ἀπόλλων, **οἵ με δάμασσαν**
ῥηιδίως· αὐτοὶ γὰρ ἀπ' ὤμων τεύχε' ἕλοντο.
τοιοῦτοι δ' εἴ πέρ μοι ἐείκοσιν ἀντεβόλησαν,
πάντές κ' αὐτόθ' ὄλοντο **ἐμῷ ὑπὸ δουρὶ δαμέντες.**
ἀλλά με μοῖρ' ὀλοὴ καὶ Λητοῦς ἔκτανεν υἱός,

---

[68] Furthermore, in the second attack of the god Apollo against Patroclus, as in the first, we find emphasis on the hand of the god. As Holmes has noted, the precise description of the "down-turned hand" is rare but appears in the *Odyssey* when Poseidon strikes the ship of the Phaeacians (*Odyssey* 13.164). See also Lowenstam 1981: 68–73. The point of comparison further underscores the difference between mortal and immortal agency and the degree of devastation that gods can achieve compared with mortals.

[69] Mühlestein 1972, following in the neo-analytic tradition, proposed that Euphorbus was a doublet of Paris, thereby assimilating the death of Patroclus to the death of Achilles. Although others have not followed a neo-analytic method, there has been significant agreement on Mühlestein's conclusion, on which see, among others, Janko 1992: 410, 415; Scodel 2002: 96; M. L. West 2003b: 5n.22. Nickel 2002 offers a novel reading where Euphorbus is a double of Achilles such that Euphorbus' attack on Patroclus is equivalent to Achilles killing himself. Allan 2005 parts from these earlier trends by offering an interpretation of Euphorbus based on the internal logic of the narrative.

[70] See Allan 2005. As Allan further points out, Euphorbus is the brother of Polydamas, who is the only Trojan prince to censure Hector for his over-confidence, and so Allan astutely notes, "Euphorbus functions like his brother Polydamas in questioning Hector's wisdom on the battlefield" (Allan 2005: 5).

Force, Fate, and Death: Sarpedon, Patroclus, and Hector 195

ἀνδρῶν δ' Εὔφορβος· σὺ δέ με τρίτος ἐξεναρίζεις.
ἄλλο δέ τοι ἐρέω, σὺ δ' ἐνὶ φρεσὶ βάλλεο σῇσιν·
οὔ θην οὐδ' αὐτὸς δηρὸν βέῃ, ἀλλά τοι ἤδη
ἄγχι παρέστηκεν θάνατος καὶ μοῖρα κραταιὴ
χερσὶ δαμέντ' Ἀχιλῆος ἀμύμονος Αἰακίδαο.

Iliad 16.844–54

Now go and boast greatly, Hector. For Zeus, son of Cronus
and Apollo have granted you victory, **they who killed
me easily.** For they themselves took the armor from my shoulders.
For if twenty such men as you had come against me,
all would have been destroyed, **killed by my spear.**
But destructive fate and the son of Leto killed me,
and among men, it was Euphorbus. But you strip my armor, in third place.
And I will tell you something else and put it in your mind.
You yourself will not last long, but already
death and mighty fate stand near you,
killed by the hands of blameless Achilles.

As has been widely recognized, the question of agency is the central point in Patroclus' dying words. But what has not been emphasized enough is how the problem of agency is expressed specifically through the repetition of the verb *damazō* in Patroclus' speech (*Iliad* 16.845, 848, 854).

The repetitions of the verbal root *dam-* make Patroclus' speech directly comparable with Zeus' speech concerning the fate of Sarpedon. First, in Zeus' speech about Sarpedon, the repetition of the verb *damazō* only indirectly addressed the question of co-agency, as the speech moved from passive to active construction. In the final lines of Zeus' speech, Zeus himself took responsibility for the death of Sarpedon, when he contemplated, "Or will I kill him at the hands of the son of Menoetius" (ὑπὸ χερσὶ Μενοιτιάδαο δαμάσσω) (*Iliad* 16.438). Patroclus too, in his last breaths, recognizes the ultimate agency of the gods in the act of subjugation, when he asserts that it was Zeus and Apollo "who killed me easily" (οἵ με δάμασσαν/ῥηιδίως) (*Iliad* 16.845). Second, in Zeus' speech, we observed how fate, *moira*, was equivalent to Zeus' own action. That same synonymous function between Zeus and fate can be observed in Patroclus' reckoning. For Patroclus first claims that Zeus and Apollo are the two deities who subdued him. And then he further states that "destructive fate and the son of Leto killed me" (ἀλλά με μοῖρ' ὀλοὴ καὶ Λητοῦς ἔκτανεν υἱός) (*Iliad* 16.849). In this regard,

196 Simone Weil and the Problem of Agency in the *Iliad*

the first order of co-agency in the death of Patroclus occurs at the divine level, since Apollo does not act alone, but he acts together with Zeus/fate. And then, the second order of co-agency occurs between Apollo and Euphorbus—both are unseen and attack Patroclus "from behind" (*Iliad* 16.791; *Iliad* 16.806). And the narrator's own description of the death of Patroclus confirms Patroclus' account when the poet states, "Patroclus subjugated by the strike of the god and by the spear" (*Πάτροκλος δὲ θεοῦ πληγῇ καὶ δουρὶ δαμασθεὶς*) (*Iliad* 16.816). In this regard, Patroclus' use of the verb *exenarizō* to describe the action of Hector at the end of his speech may also be significant, since the primary meaning of the verb is not to kill per se, but to strip the armor.[71] Patroclus is thus denying Hector the act of ultimate subjugation, that is, he denies him the act of killing proper.

Patroclus' use of the verb *damazō* further underscores the cycle of violent force to which all are victim. In the Sarpedon episode, we saw how Sarpedon's witnessing of his companions "killed at the hands of Patroclus" ultimately led to Sarpedon himself "killed at the hands of Patroclus." Patroclus himself explains that if it weren't for divine intervention many more Trojans would be "killed by my spear" (*ἐμῷ ὑπὸ δουρὶ δαμέντες*) (*Iliad* 16.848). But he concludes that the killing does not end with Patroclus' own death, since Hector is already "killed at the hands of blameless Achilles, son of Aeacides" (*χερσὶ δαμέντ' Ἀχιλῆος ἀμύμονος Αἰακίδαο*) (*Iliad* 16.854). Thus, like Sarpedon, Patroclus too is but one more victim in the cycle of subjugating force expressed through the verbal root *dam-*. Trojans were killed by Patroclus, including Sarpedon, but Patroclus is in turn killed by Zeus, Apollo, and Euphorbus. But Hector in turn will be killed by Achilles.

And, lastly, as the divine horses of Achilles make clear, Achilles too will be subjected to this same cycle of violence. For in their own denial of blame for the death of Patroclus, the horses of Achilles also predict the death of Achilles himself. Miraculously, they speak to Achilles and state:

$$οὐδέ τοι ἡμεῖς$$
$$αἴτιοι, ἀλλὰ θεός τε μέγας καὶ μοῖρα κραταιή.$$

Iliad 19.409–10

We ourselves are not to blame, but a great god and mighty fate.

---

[71] See Cunliffe ad loc.

Force, Fate, and Death: Sarpedon, Patroclus, and Hector   197

On the one hand, the horses' denial of blame echoes precisely the words of Agamemnon, in his own apology to Achilles. At the same time, the horses insist on a double level of co-agency in the death of Patroclus, which mirrors Patroclus' own account. First, in both we see an insistence on a type of co-agency between fate and a god (*Iliad* 19.409; 16.849). The horses too specify that the god in question is Apollo as the one that is truly responsible for the death of Patroclus, while Apollo granted *kudos* to Hector (*Iliad* 19.414), and the narrator had given the same account in *Iliad* 16 (*Iliad* 16.730). And most importantly, the horses predict the death of Achilles by a similar process:

> ἀλλὰ σοὶ αὐτῷ
> μόρσιμόν ἐστι θεῷ τε καὶ ἀνέρι ἶφι **δαμῆναι**.

Iliad 19.416-17

But it is fated for you to be killed forcefully by god and a man.

That Achilles will die in the Trojan war is, of course, not news to Achilles himself, since he had already announced the acceptance of his death to his mother Thetis (*Iliad* 18.98–100).[72] But what the horses specify is the precise manner of death for Achilles: to be killed, δαμῆναι, through co-agency between human and god (*Iliad* 19.417), thereby mirroring the death of his companion Patroclus.[73] Thus, the repetitions of the verb *damazō* in *Iliad* 16, and those that come after, ultimately reflect a continuous cycle of violence in which all characters in the *Iliad* are engaged, and for which mortals themselves are only partially involved.

Although the cycle of violence and subjugating force will presumably end with Achilles, it reaches its climax in the *Iliad* with the death of Hector in *Iliad* 22. Like Sarpedon and Patroclus, the killing of Hector is also represented as a direct result of co-agency between human and god, Athena and Achilles. But before Hector's direct confrontation with the mortal-immortal pair, the *Iliad* also presents Hector's death as if it were a function of his own behavior. As Hector awaits Achilles outside the walls of Troy, Hector quickly regrets the position he finds himself in, and furthermore blames himself for it. In his soliloquy while awaiting Achilles he acknowledges, "Now I have destroyed my people by my own recklessness"

---

[72] On Achilles' own knowledge of his death, presumably from Thetis, see Burgess 2009: 43–55.
[73] See further Edwards 1991: 283; Coray 2009: 176.

198 Simone Weil and the Problem of Agency in the *Iliad*

(*Iliad* 22.104). In this regard, Hector, perhaps more so than Patroclus, is understood as the quintessential proto-tragic figure, whose own choices and limited knowledge lead to his demise.[74] Indeed, one of the major causes of oversight is the overconfidence he has had in his force. While outside the walls of Troy, Hector imagines that someone less noble than he (*Iliad* 22.104: *kakōteros*) will chastise him, saying:

Ἕκτωρ ἧφι βίηφι πιθήσας ὤλεσε λαόν.

Iliad 22.106

Hector, obeying his might and force, has destroyed his people.

This statement is in immediate reference to the fact that Hector did not listen to Poulydamas, who had advised him to lead himself and the Trojan warriors into the gates of Troy (*Iliad* 22.100–1; cf. *Iliad* 18.293–4). Hector acknowledges, "I did not *obey* him" (ἀλλ᾽ ἐγὼ οὐ πιθόμην) (*Iliad* 22.104), and instead, he "*obeyed* his might and force" (ἧφι βίηφι πιθήσας) (*Iliad* 22.106). Indeed, before his soliloquy, the narrator had already confirmed the role that Hector's own force would play in his death, stating:

ὣς Ἕκτωρ ἄσβεστον ἔχων μένος οὐχ ὑπεχώρει
πύργῳ ἔπι προὔχοντι φαεινὴν ἀσπίδ᾽ ἐρείσας·

Iliad 22.96–7

Since Hector, with unquenchable *menos*, did not yield,
Leaning his shining shield on the jutting bastion.

Where Hector imagines some lesser man might attribute Hector's situation to force in its most basic form of violence, as *biē*, the poet specifies that it is, ironically, Hector's own *menos* that keeps him outside the walls of Troy.

    Menos has in fact played an important role for Hector throughout the poem, leading to the moment of his death. As we have already noted, *menos* may refer more specifically to a hero's "life force" in so far as it is a source for movement and action, and it leaves the body upon death.[75] And according to Hector's own wife, Andromache, Hector has a superabundance of *menos*. When Andromache hears the lamentation of the

---

[74] See Redfield 1994: 128–59.
[75] See discussion in Chapter 1 and formula XV under *menos* in the appendix.

Force, Fate, and Death: Sarpedon, Patroclus, and Hector 199

Trojan women, after Hector has been slain, she correctly fears for the life of Hector, stating:

> ἀλλὰ μάλ' αἰνῶς
> δείδω μὴ δή μοι θρασὺν Ἕκτορα δῖος Ἀχιλλεὺς
> μοῦνον ἀποτμήξας πόλιος πεδίονδε δίηται,
> καὶ δή μιν καταπαύσῃ ἀγηνορίης ἀλεγεινῆς
> ἥ μιν ἔχεσκ', ἐπεὶ οὔ ποτ' ἐνὶ πληθυῖ μένεν ἀνδρῶν,
> ἀλλὰ πολὺ προθέεσκε, **τὸ ὃν μένος οὐδενὶ εἴκων**.

Iliad 22.454–9

But I am terribly afraid that divine Achilles pursues brave Hector,
toward the plain, alone, having cut him off from the city,
and that he will bring an end to Hector's pain-causing pride
which used to possess him, since he never remained among the numbers of men
but ran far out in front, **yielding his *menos* to no one.**

Andromache's fear and her characterization of Hector speak directly to the prophetic words Andromache uttered to her husband in *Iliad* 6. When she first saw Hector, she pronounced:

> δαιμόνιε **φθίσει σε τὸ σὸν μένος**, οὐδ' ἐλεαίρεις
> παῖδά τε νηπίαχον καὶ ἔμ' ἄμμορον, ἣ τάχα χήρη
> σεῦ ἔσομαι

Iliad 6.407–9

Blessed one, your *menos* will cause your demise,
nor do you pity your tender child and ill-fated wife,
who will soon be your widow.

Because *menos* is understood as a source of life and action, it causes warriors like Hector to go out in the front ranks and to stand apart from the rest of the warriors. As the *Iliad* described over and again, it is a warrior's *menos* that is roused when he goes into battle.[76] But Andromache realizes the tragic irony inherent in the role that *menos* plays in a warrior's life cycle: *That which animates a warrior's body and gives it life will also cause*

---

[76] See formulas VII–XI under *menos* in the appendix.

200   Simone Weil and the Problem of Agency in the *Iliad*

the warrior to die. Andromache's pronouncement to Hector thus takes Weil's argument on force to its absolute extreme: the "force that kills" is not simply external to the human subject, but it is inherent in the very life of the human subject.

More specifically, in Andromache's words, Hector's *menos* is not just the force that will kill him, but it will cause his *decay*, for she uses the verb *phthinein* to describe Hector's inevitable death by *menos*. The root *phthi-* presents a notion of demise associated specifically with the vegetal cycle, and it is most clearly expressed in its negative sense with the adjective *aphthitos*. As Gregory Nagy has demonstrated, the adjective *apthitos* in epic "conveys... the growing and wilting of plants, and also by extension, the life and the death of mortals."[77] The adjective itself is most commonly associated with the phrase *kleos aphthiton*, "imperishable glory," a phrase with an Indo-European inheritance.[78] The phrase occurs only once in Homeric epic, but in the most iconic speech of the poem, when Achilles reveals his mother's prophecy about his own life, where he must choose between a return home, *nostos*, or death in battle. The return home would be to Achilles' native Phthia, a place whose very name incorporates the root pertaining to the vegetal cycle.[79] But if he does not return to Phthia and dies in battle instead, he would receive *kleos aphthiton*, "imperishable fame" (*Iliad* 9.413). In Achilles' choice, one that can be extrapolated to the warrior's condition more generally, the choice between *nostos* and *kleos* is a choice between life and death. But Andromache's own prophecy to Hector offers a more tragic vision of the warrior's lot, one that complicates the either-or choice between life and death, and it does so for one simple reason: the source of life itself for a warrior, his *menos*, is precisely that which precipitates his death.

In this regard, Andromache had perfectly predicted the death of Hector as we watch it unfold before the walls of Troy. For it is Hector's "unquenchable *menos*" that prevents him from retreating (*Iliad* 22.96). And after Hector projects the reproach of others, claiming that he has destroyed his people by means of his strength, only then, with no other option, does he entertain the possibility of *kleos*, stating:

---

[77] Nagy 1979: 184.

[78] On the Indo-European heritage of the phrase *kleos aphthiton* see Kuhn 1853: 467; Schmitt 1967: 61–102; Nagy 1974: 140–9; Nagy 1981; Nagy 1990a: 122–7; Watkins 1995: 173–8. For arguments against *kleos aphthiton* as part of an Indo-European poetics see Finkelberg 1986; Olson 1995: 224–7. For the most recent developments in this long-standing argument see Volk 2002 and Finkelberg's response to Volk in Finkelberg 2007.

[79] Nagy 1979: 184–5.

Force, Fate, and Death: Sarpedon, Patroclus, and Hector   201

ἐμοὶ δὲ τότ’ ἂν πολὺ κέρδιον εἴη
ἄντην ἢ Ἀχιλῆα κατακτείναντα νέεσθαι,
ἠέ κεν αὐτῷ ὀλέσθαι ἐϋκλειῶς πρὸ πόληος.

Iliad **22.108-10**

Far better would it be for me
either to go before Achilles and kill him
or to be killed by him with *kleos* before the city.

Hence, the warrior's *menos*, his life force, may cause the warrior to die, and therefore partake in the vegetal cycle, as Andromache predicts. But in facilitating the warrior's death, it also enables him to transcend that very life-death cycle by way of the *kleos* that follows death.

Nevertheless, despite Hector's own apparent resolution to accept his warrior-fate, he resists facing Achilles because, as Jenny Strauss Clay has commented, "dying is hard to do."[80] Not only does he try to reason his way out of confronting Achilles during his soliloquy (*Iliad* 22.111–28), but even after he decides to do so, fear seizes him and he runs. The pursuit itself is described as an agonistic race for the *psyche* of Hector (*Iliad* 22.131–66).[81] Thus, if a warrior's *menos* has a paradoxical impulse, as a force that is the source of both life and death for a warrior, that paradox is captured in the protracted nature of *Iliad* 22, with its multiple starts and stops in Hector's reasoning and actions as he approaches his own end.

Hector's own life force, his *menos*, however, is not the final cause of his demise. For Hector does not die until Zeus and the gods decide to subjugate him. The foot race that keeps Hector alive momentarily does not come to an end until Zeus, as a spectator of the event, considers Hector's fate.[82] Thus, Zeus comments on Hector's piety and asks:

ἀλλ’ ἄγετε φράζεσθε θεοὶ καὶ μητιάασθε
ἠέ μιν ἐκ θανάτοιο σαώσομεν, ἠέ μιν ἤδη
Πηλεΐδῃ Ἀχιλῆϊ δαμάσσομεν ἐσθλὸν ἐόντα.

Iliad **22.174-6**

---

[80] Clay 2002.

[81] *Iliad* 22.131–66. See Purves 2019: 75–80 on the relationship between running and death in this episode. The race is also compared to a chariot race, with an emphasis on the horses in a way that also signifies the death of both Hector and ultimately Achilles, on which see Bakker 2017; Myers 2019: 191–7.

[82] On Zeus and the gods as spectators of Hector's death and in the *Iliad* more generally, see Myers 2019, esp. 191–7.

202 Simone Weil and the Problem of Agency in the *Iliad*

Come, gods, speak out and consider whether we will save him
from death, or if we will kill him, noble though he is,
through Achilles, son of Peleus.

Here we see Zeus contemplate the life of Hector with language that parallels precisely the contemplation of the fate of his son Sarpedon. Just as Zeus asked whether he will kill Sarpedon at the hands of Patroclus (*Iliad* 16.438: δαμάσσω), so he asks the same with regard to Hector (*Iliad* 22.176: δαμάσσομεν). In both cases, it is Zeus who is the active subject of the verb *damazō*, while the mortals take on only an instrumental role. At the same time, there remains a significant difference between the Sarpedon episode and that of Hector. With Sarpedon, Zeus pondered his son's fate only from his own first-person singular perspective, and he was quickly chastised for it by Hera. But with Hector, he immediately turns to a communal decision before the gods, actively incorporating them into the subjugation of Hector.[83]

Ultimately, Hector's fate is expressed through the famous image of Zeus' golden scales.[84] The motion of the scales, the sinking of Hector's own fate and the rising of Achilles, is paralleled by the inverted physical movement of their respective patron gods, Apollo and Athena:[85]

ῥέπε δ᾽ Ἕκτορος αἴσιμον ἦμαρ,
ᾤχετο δ᾽ εἰς Ἀΐδαο, λίπεν δέ ἑ Φοῖβος Ἀπόλλων.
Πηλεΐωνα δ᾽ ἵκανε θεὰ γλαυκῶπις Ἀθήνη

Iliad 22.213–14

The fated day of Hector fell,
it went to the house of Hades, and Phoebus Apollo left him,
And the grey-eyed goddess Athena came to the son of Peleus.

---

[83] On the significant difference in the episodes of Sarpedon and Hector regarding Zeus and the counsel of the gods, see Pucci 2018: 49–55. On the metapoetic significance of the debates about the fate of both Sarpedon and Hector among the community of the gods, see Elmer 2013: 151–3.

[84] On the significance of the golden scales in the *Iliad*, see, among others, Reinhardt 1961: 166–7; Vermeule 1979: 39–41; Morrison 1997. Pucci sees the scales in a literal rather than metaphorical manner: "The Golden Scales are not a metaphor or an allegory, but a real instrument of measurement that tells the will of Zeus in an impassive and visible form and sign" (Pucci 2018: 55).

[85] On the significance of Athena and Apollo as ritual antagonists in the mortal conflicts of the *Iliad*, see Nagy 1979: 144.

Force, Fate, and Death: Sarpedon, Patroclus, and Hector   203

The sinking of Hector's fate on the scale is accompanied by Apollo leaving, and presumably rising to Olympus, while the rise in Achilles' fate is accompanied by Athena descending into the realm of mortal action. Prior to this moment, it was Apollo's physical intervention in the body and movement of Hector that had kept him alive. As the two warriors ran around the city of Troy, the narrator comments:

πῶς δέ κεν Ἕκτωρ κῆρας ὑπεξέφυγεν θανάτοιο,
εἰ μή οἱ πύματόν τε καὶ ὕστατον ἤντετ᾽ Ἀπόλλων
ἐγγύθεν, ὅς οἱ ἐπῶρσε μένος λαιψηρά τε γοῦνα;

Iliad 22.202–4

How then could Hector have escaped the fate of death,
if Apollo had not come to him, this last and final time,
nearby, and roused his *menos* and light knees.

In that fateful race, the momentary preservation of Hector's life would not have been possible were it not for intervention of the gods.[86] As has been made clear throughout our philological study of the different force terms, *menos*, like other types of force, is understood to be given or supplemented by the gods, and here, Apollo is responsible for the additional physical effort that Hector is able to exert. This is not the first time that Apollo has supplied Hector with *menos*.[87] But when the scales tip in Achilles' favor, it is critical that this motion be accompanied by a change of deities who intervene in the action. Thus, the scales for the fates of Hector and Achilles are also scales of co-agency. With the sinking of Hector's fate, he loses the "life support" that Apollo had provided.

Hector himself only becomes fully aware of the gods' involvement when he realizes that the mortal companion, his brother Deiphobus, whom he believed came to help him in the fight against Achilles, was in fact Athena in disguise. It is at that moment, when Hector is finally and totally alone, that he sees the role the gods have played in his own fate all along. Hector thus speaks to himself:

ἀλλ᾽ ὃ μὲν ἐν τείχει, ἐμὲ δ᾽ ἐξαπάτησεν Ἀθήνη.
νῦν δὲ δὴ ἐγγύθι μοι θάνατος κακός, οὐδ᾽ ἔτ᾽ ἄνευθεν,
οὐδ᾽ ἀλέη· ἦ γάρ ῥα πάλαι τό γε φίλτερον ἦεν

---

[86] See Leaf ad loc.; Richardson 1993: 129–30.   [87] See also *Iliad* 15.59–60, 15.262.

204 Simone Weil and the Problem of Agency in the *Iliad*

Ζηνί τε καὶ Διὸς υἷι ἑκηβόλῳ, οἵ με πάρος γε
πρόφρονες εἰρύατο· νῦν αὖτέ με μοῖρα κιχάνει.

Iliad 22.299–303

But [Deiphobus] is inside the wall, Athena deceived me.
Now evil death is near me and no longer far away,
nor is there escape. For this was preferable a long time ago
for Zeus and the far-shooter son of Zeus, who previously
protected me eagerly. But now fate has seized me.

To be sure, Hector has always been defined by his piety, and he was certainly
aware of the gods' involvement in his life. But this last realization is tantamount to a confession of sorts regarding his own miscalculations when it
comes to mortal-immortal action.[88] Indeed, Hector's final realization here
contrasts markedly with his boast of autonomy over the corpse of Patroclus.
With the death of Patroclus, he proclaimed his own preeminence:

ἔγχεϊ δ' αὐτὸς
Τρωσὶ φιλοπτολέμοισι μεταπρέπω, ὅ σφιν ἀμύνω
ἦμαρ ἀναγκαῖον·

Iliad 16.834–6

With the spear, I myself am preeminent among the war-loving Trojans,
since for them I ward off the day of compulsion.

With the death of Patroclus, Hector made no reference to the divine aid or
favor that Patroclus insisted was operative, and instead Hector focused on
himself (*Iliad* 16.834: *autos*). Now in his final moments, Hector is aware
that the necessity of death, his fate, was unavoidable.

Conclusion: Achilles' Awareness

In contrast to Hector and nearly all other humans in the *Iliad*, Achilles is
distinctly aware of mortal-immortal co-agency and his own limited role in
the enactment force. Perhaps this is because Athena had appeared to him

---

[88] It is this miscalculation that makes Hector a tragic figure, on which see Redfield
1994: 147–59.

from the very beginning of the poem, where she herself physically stopped Achilles' *menos*, when he was about to kill Agamemnon. And once again, Athena appears to Achilles directly before the walls of Troy to explain that she will bring about the fight between him and Hector. She states:

νῦν δὴ νῶι ἔολπα Διὶ φίλε φαίδιμ' Ἀχιλλεῦ
οἴσεσθαι μέγα κῦδος Ἀχαιοῖσι προτὶ νῆας
Ἕκτορα δηώσαντε μάχης ἄατόν περ ἐόντα.

Iliad 22.216–18

Shining Achilles, dear to Zeus, now I expect
great *kudos* will be brought by us to the Achaeans before the ships,
when we slay Hector, though he is insatiable in battle.

Grammatically, Athena makes the role of co-agency between herself and Achilles obvious through the use of the dual form of the participle (*Iliad* 22.218: δηώσαντε). And before the physical confrontation, Achilles makes the role of co-agency all the more apparent when he proclaims to Hector:

οὔ τοι ἔτ' ἔσθ' ὑπάλυξις, ἄφαρ δέ σε Παλλὰς Ἀθήνη
ἔγχει ἐμῷ δαμάᾳ·

Iliad 22.270-1

There will not be any escape for you, but Pallas Athena
will kill you with my spear.

Here we see Achilles employ the same grammatical construction with the verb *damazō* that was used to describe the deaths of Sarpedon and Patroclus. The god takes on the active role of nominative subject while Achilles attributes to himself only an instrumental role in the killing of Hector. This statement too contrasts with Hector's boast over Patroclus. And even after Achilles has slain Hector, we find that Achilles does not make an ipsocentric boast like Hector but instead gives credit to the gods, stating "since the gods have granted that this man be killed" (ἐπεὶ δὴ τόνδ' ἄνδρα θεοὶ δαμάσασθαι ἔδωκαν) (*Iliad* 22.379).

Finally, Achilles' strictly instrumental role is further reiterated when the poet comments on Andromache's preparation for the return of Hector that would never take place:

206 Simone Weil and the Problem of Agency in the *Iliad*

νηπίη, οὐδ' ἐνόησεν ὅ μιν μάλα τῆλε λοετρῶν
χερσὶν Ἀχιλλῆος δάμασε γλαυκῶπις Ἀθήνη.

Iliad **22.445–6**

Fool, nor did she realize that, far from the baths,
grey-eyed Athena subjugated him at the hands of Achilles.

These very lines are most often quoted in reference to Simone Weil's interpretation of the *Iliad*, where she comments on the stark contrast between the world of war and the domestic sphere. For Weil, Hector's situation is emblematic of all warriors:

> Truly, he was far from the warm baths, that hapless man. Nor was he alone. Nearly all of the *Iliad* takes place far from warm baths. Nearly all human life has always taken place far from warm baths.
>
> **(Weil 2003: 46)**

Weil's own emphasis on these lines has served to further emphasize the ever-present, but often suppressed female perspective on war in the *Iliad,* a perspective that lends deep emotion to the poem.[89] Furthermore, it is in reference to these lines in the *Iliad* that Simone Weil claims:

> The force that kills is summary and crude.
>
> **(Weil 2003: 46)**

On the one hand, through the use of the same verb for subjugation and death, *damazō*, that occurred in reference to Sarpedon and Patroclus, this episode is representative of the "force that kills." Hector's death at Achilles' hands confirms the self-perpetuating cycle of force and death acted upon the heroes of the *Iliad*. On the other hand, from a more literal and grammatical perspective, it is not force that is the subject of action here but rather the goddess Athena. Yet Simone Weil did not attribute full grammatical agency to Athena in this episode. For Weil translated *Iliad* 22.445–6 in French as follows:

---

[89] Canevaro's study of women and objects in the *Iliad* thus begins with a reformulation of Weil with the introductory chapter, "How Far Are We from a Hot Bath?" (Canevaro 2018). See further Gold 2016, who discusses how Weil's status as a woman author is the most significant aspect of appreciating her work on the *Iliad*.

Conclusion: Achilles' Awareness   207

La naïve! Elle ne savait pas que bien loin des bains chauds
Le bras d'Achille l'avait soumis, à cause d'Athèna aux yeux vert.

(Weil 2003: 20)

In her rendition, Weil treats the arms/hands of Achilles as the grammatical subject that subjugates Hector, and she makes Athena merely the source or reason for the action. Although Weil has been accused of willfully mistranslating the *Iliad*, scholars have not commented on these lines as a cause for offense. And yet Weil's grammatical shift does not accurately reflect how the poet or the audience would understand the event. Grammatically, and phenomenologically, Athena is not merely the cause of the action, but the primary agent. This grammatical shift in Weil's translation ultimately reflects Weil's own refusal to take the Homeric gods seriously, as discussed above. In Weil's reckoning, the fact that agency is attributed to the gods in the *Iliad* reflects a basic and universal irrationality present in the enactment of war and violent force, since any will to self-preservation or even communal preservation would compel one to act otherwise. Certainly, Weil's dismissal of the gods in the *Iliad* is no doubt a result of her own Christianized religious views on the ontological status of the person as a "soul," applied equally to the *Iliad* and to modernity.[90] But if we take the grammatical constructions of force in Homer at face value, we are better able to appreciate how the verbal expressions themselves reflect on the poem's broader religious and philosophical implications and its significance for the narrative. Within the context of *Iliad* 22, the attribution of agency to Athena in this specific episode actively downplays that of Achilles. Achilles' own view on his limited agency is thus consistent with the narrator's perspective, and it contrasts starkly with Hector's own misguided belief in himself and his divine favor.

The attribution of agency to the gods does not merely reflect on the irrationality of war within the *Iliad*, as Weil suggests, but it directly highlights human *ignorance*. The poet described Andromache as "foolish," *nēpiē* (*Iliad* 22.445), a word that occurs in the poem when humans act with expectations that are contrary to what is or will happen. Patroclus too was addressed by the poet as *nēpie* in his effort to sack Troy (*Iliad* 16.686). And then, once Patroclus had been conquered, Hector too addressed Patroclus as *nēpie* (*Iliad* 16.833). And once Hector was slain, Achilles too addressed Hector as *nēpie*, for not realizing that Achilles would avenge the

---

[90] See Schein 2016: 153–4.

208 Simone Weil and the Problem of Agency in the *Iliad*

death of Patroclus (*Iliad* 22.333). Thus, the cycle of subjugating force is one that is specifically attended by a lack of knowledge on the part of mortal actors.

In contrast to all these figures, Achilles alone has knowledge of both his fate and the gods' involvement in it. Just as Achilles' horses had predicted his fate and manner of death to him, so Hector, in his moment of death, does the same thing, saying that Paris and Apollo, a mortal and immortal, will act together to kill Achilles (*Iliad* 22.359–60). And just as Achilles had accepted his fate pronounced by his horses, so he does the same with Hector. Thus, ironically, Achilles, as the one character who has the greatest capacity to kill, is also the one most keenly aware of his own limited agency. And above all others, Achilles is the one most keenly aware that he too will be a victim of the force that kills.

Conclusion
Homeric Forces and Human Subjects Reconsidered

When we read the *Iliad* with a focus on the vocabulary of force, what becomes most apparent is the inherent contingency of human life and action in the poem. That contingency can be observed most especially through the dynamic interaction between speech and narrative. Throughout the *Iliad*, the different types of force are invoked in speech in order to create and recreate hierarchies between the various characters. That is to say, various forms of force are appealed to as standards by which permanent and preeminent status and personhood should be achieved. And yet, at every instance in which a character attempts to establish such hierarchies of force, other characters or the narrative action of the poem itself undo those very efforts.

Thus, in *Iliad* 1, Athena abruptly brings to a halt Achilles' own enactment of force, his *menos*, against Agamemnon. What proceeds, however, in the subsequent quarrel and aftermath is a basic misassessment of the significance of Achilles' own force, status, and genealogy. In order to mitigate the effects of the quarrel, Nestor intervenes and creates a "scale of superiority." He asserts that the Lapiths are the "most superior," *kartistoi*, Agamemnon is *pherteros*, "more superior," and Achilles is merely "superior" in the positive, *karteros* (*Iliad* 1.254–84). As discussed in Chapter 2, *kratos* already implies a degree of comparison by virtue of its basic semantics, implying "superiority" in a contest such that superlative or comparative grammatical forms of *kratos* would appear redundant. But the grammatical forms employed by Nestor only make sense from a pragmatic perspective, when the characters who receive those designations are compared with each other from within the speech. From a rhetorical perspective, the effect is that Nestor too, though no longer able to demonstrate physical force, is nevertheless associated with the most superior, lost generation of Lapiths (*Iliad* 1.269–73). Nestor's intention in creating this scale is to create a

---

Homer's Iliad *and the Problem of Force*. Charles H. Stocking, Oxford University Press.
© Charles H. Stocking 2023. DOI: 10.1093/oso/9780192862877.003.0006

210 Conclusion

delicate social balance concerning who is "best of the Achaeans" by maintaining the authority of Agamemnon while still attempting to appease Achilles. And yet despite Nestor's good intentions, the arrangement he proposes fails precisely because Nestor fails to take into account the genealogical implications in Achilles' own birth. Nestor is ignorant of the "power of Thetis" and her intimate ties with Zeus. Because the power of Thetis is always latent, as noted by Laura Slatkin, we never see the power of Thetis made manifest. As I have argued in Chapter 1, even Achilles himself fails to acknowledge the full impact of the power of his matrilineal genealogy (*Iliad* 21.184–91).

Once the authority of Agamemnon has been challenged, and the Achaean camp is on the verge of dissolution, Odysseus, in a manner similar to Nestor's first intervention, attempts to reconstitute the authority of Agamemnon, specifically through his two iterative speeches, one to the *basileis* and the other to the *dēmos* (*Iliad* 2.189–206). Like Nestor, Odysseus invokes comparative language, claiming that the *basileis* are *pherteroi* (*Iliad* 2.201) and, perhaps most controversially, that Agamemnon should be considered the one *basileus* for the Greeks by virtue of his connection to Zeus (*Iliad* 2.205–6). But unlike Nestor in *Iliad* 1, Odysseus' efforts appear to have nominal success in reconstituting the Greek army under the singular authority of Agamemnon. Indeed, Odysseus' violent act of beating Thersites with the scepter of Agamemnon may be viewed as a clear reuniting of physical force and political power. And yet the larger narrative context of *Iliad* 2 ultimately *contradicts* Odysseus' own logic and actions. As discussed in Chapter 2, Odysseus' insistence that Zeus loves Agamemnon (*Iliad* 2.197) can be considered somewhat ironic in light of the fact that *Iliad* 2 begins with Zeus sending the destructive dream to Agamemnon in order to deceive him. This irony is further captured in the semiotics of Agamemnon's "testing speech" to the Greek army, when Agamemnon claims that the *kratos* of Zeus is greatest and, because of this, he has been deceived by Zeus (*Iliad* 2.110–41). Agamemnon believes what he says is false, when it is actually true. And finally, that rupture between divine and mortal kings is expressed in terms of ritual failure, when Agamemnon offers a sacrifice to Zeus, in which the narrator comments that he accepted the sacrifice but did not grant his prayers (*Iliad* 2.411–20). Hence, from *Iliad* 2 we see that the *kratos* of Zeus supplies the logic of mortal hierarchies at the same time that it serves as the basis for undermining them.

It is not until *Iliad* 9 that Zeus' own deception of the Greeks becomes apparent, when Agamemnon redelivers a version of his "testing speech" from *Iliad* 2 in all sincerity (*Iliad* 9.17–28). And it is Diomedes' own

Homeric Forces and Human Subjects Reconsidered   **211**

rebuke of Agamemnon that solidifies in speech what was demonstrated in the narrative of *Iliad* 2 (*Iliad* 9.32–49). Contrary to the efforts of both Nestor and Odysseus to unify physical force and political power under the authority of Agamemnon, Diomedes uses the words of Agamemnon himself in order to show that what Zeus gives is always variable and divided, *diandicha* (*Iliad* 9.37). In place of a unified notion of force and political power, Diomedes places emphasis once more on the physical value of force in battle, *alkē* (*Iliad* 9.39). And yet, despite the communal approval that Diomedes receives for his rebuke, he does not have the final say. Once again, in the service of maintaining an authoritative hierarchy, Nestor intervenes. Similar to his first speech from *Iliad* 1, Nestor characterizes Diomedes, like Achilles before him, in positive terms as *karteros* (*Iliad* 1.280, *Iliad* 9.53). And similar to his first speech, Nestor also claims superiority in age (*Iliad* 1.259, *Iliad* 9.60). And finally, Nestor ultimately contrasts Diomedes' positive quality of force as *karteros* with Agamemnon's own absolute political authority, defining Agamemnon this time in the superlative, as "most kingly," *basileutatos* (*Iliad* 9.69). Historians often make note of Nestor's speech in order to account for the fluid political structures of the Geometric and Archaic periods, where there may be varying degrees of "kingliness."[1] But Nestor's use of the superlative form of kingship can only make sense in light of his own rhetorical practices—employing positive, comparative, and superlative adjectives of force and authority. This comparative practice is clear when one compares his speeches in *Iliad* 1 and *Iliad* 9. Nevertheless, despite Nestor's own efforts to publicly uphold Agamemnon's authority, Nestor also goes against his own initial valuation of Agamemnon relative to Achilles when, in private, Nestor claims that Agamemnon has dishonored Achilles, "the most superior man," *pheristos*, whom the gods themselves honor (*Iliad* 9.110–11).

Thus, from *Iliad* 1 to *Iliad* 9, one can trace a sequence of speeches which make use of the language of force for the sake of establishing social hierarchies. These interconnected speeches reveal the ways in which physical force and political power are problematically entangled with issues of social valuation. Most importantly, the episodes discussed here show how the relations supposedly dictated by force, both physical and political, are entirely dependent on performative speech, while speech itself fails to firmly establish such relations. Such is the case even with the gods when Zeus and Poseidon indirectly confront each other through speech, by way

---

[1] See, for instance, Finley 1954: 76; Hall 2014: 129.

212 Conclusion

of Iris, as to who is "stronger," *pherteros*. Although Poseidon does not take up a physical challenge against Zeus, he still denies Zeus' claim to superiority and reminds Zeus of his own dependence on the other gods (*Iliad* 15.158–217).

The funeral games of *Iliad* 23 provide a type of limit case for the contingency of force and its dependence on speech in the *Iliad*. One would assume that nowhere else could the execution of force be more indicative of rank than in the physical *agōn* proper. Yet, as I have argued in Chapter 3, each of the contests reveals the ways in which contest results occur contrary to expectation, requiring the intervention of Achilles. This is made most apparent when we compare the divinely inspired hierarchy of Greek warriors spoken by the narrator in *Iliad* 2 with the contest results of *Iliad* 23. When the poet asks who was the best, *aristos*, of men together with their horses who came to Troy (*Iliad* 2.760–2), the poet responds that when Achilles is absent, Eumelus is best in terms of his horses and Ajax best of men (*Iliad* 2.763–8), but it is ultimately Achilles who is best or strongest, *phertatos* on both counts (*Iliad* 2.769). First and foremost, one must note the strange addition of horses that is paired with men in establishing social rank. Such an addition might seem perplexing from a strictly humanist perspective, but it speaks precisely to the ways in which personhood extends beyond the bounded biological human, much in the way that Donna Haraway discusses symbiotic life with "companion species." One's social value, one's *aretē*, is implicated at the intersection of the human with animal and object. It is for this very reason that Menelaus contests Antilochus in the chariot race (*Iliad* 23.570–85). Most importantly, Eumelus plays no other role in the entire *Iliad* except in the chariot race, where he ought to have won but loses because Athena caused his chariot to crash. In the case of the chariot race, divine intervention actually disrupts the Muse-inspired hierarchy from *Iliad* 2, in which Eumelus was pronounced as the man with the best horses after Achilles. Similarly, it is Ajax who is pronounced as the best of men after Achilles, and Ajax competes in more physical contests in the funeral games than any other Greek warrior. Yet Ajax fails to ever achieve a clear victory. Unlike Eumelus, no god disrupts Ajax's contests, and it is simply the case that others surpass him. Furthermore, as many have noted, each contest hints at the final contest of Ajax for the arms of Achilles and its tragic end. And even though Achilles attempts to intervene in each of the contests, his own efforts prove problematic. This is most evident in the final event, the spear throw, when Achilles abandons the idea of contest entirely. Thus, the funeral games demonstrate the ultimate failure of force to properly establish the

Homeric Forces and Human Subjects Reconsidered   213

relationship between acknowledged social rank and contest result. The futility of such agonistic executions of force is further underscored after the *agōn*, when Achilles engages in his own private chariot race of sorts around the *sēma* of Patroclus, dragging the corpse of Hector behind him. Desiring the life force (*menos*) of his fallen companion (*Iliad* 24.6), he attempts to erase the embodied memory of Patroclus' killer Hector through mutilation—but even then, Achilles' efforts prove ineffective because of the gods' interventions.[2]

It should be noted that the terms for Homeric force and their deployment in the poem pertain mostly to relations among the Greeks in the *Iliad*. One may wonder to what extent the same contingencies of force apply to the violence between Greek and Trojan in the act of killing. As I have argued, the *Iliad* gives its most supreme expression on the contingency of enacted force in the description of the killing of Sarpedon, Patroclus, and Hector in *Iliad* 16 and *Iliad* 22. For all three deaths center on the problem of agency, speech, and action expressed grammatically through the verbs *damazō* and *damnēmi*. Zeus himself has decided the sequence of deaths, which are all causally linked (*Iliad* 15.64–8). And when Zeus contemplates the death of Sarpedon, we see a grammatical alteration between fate as the active agent and Zeus himself (*Iliad* 16.434, 16.438). Similarly, the issue of speech and action is most especially problematized in the death of Patroclus, which involves Apollo and two mortals, Euphorbus and Hector. But Hector claims the death of Patroclus and pronounces his own preeminence, without reference to divine aid (*Iliad* 16.834). And so in his last breaths, Patroclus' corrects Hector with a further emphasis that it was first Zeus and Apollo who subjugated him (16.845) and then Euphorbus, while Hector was merely third in the sequence (16.850). And Patroclus' own account here is further corroborated by the narrator, who explains that it was the strike of Apollo's hand and the spear of Euphorbus that conquered Patroclus (*Iliad* 16.816: Πάτροκλος δὲ θεοῦ πληγῇ καὶ δουρὶ δαμασθείς). And finally, we observe how Hector himself is abandoned by the gods and slowly gains awareness of his own imminent death. In contrast with Hector, who must come to his own realization of divine factors in the narrative of his own fate, Achilles

---

[2] Thus, regarding this episode, Simon Goldhill 1991: 90 states, "The *Iliad*'s dominant question of the limits of power in the relations of exchange between humans is raised in starkest form by the unchecked expression of violence towards a bare body, which even—especially—when a dead body, is covered by the restraints of social discourse." On the unique role of the corpse as *soma*, especially Hector's, and its preservation related to human subjectivity, see further Holmes 2010: 32–7.

214 Conclusion

has been made aware of the divine operations from the beginning. And Achilles' awareness is expressed grammatically in his threat to Hector, when he pronounces, "But Athena will kill you with my spear" (ἄφαρ δέ σε Παλλὰς Ἀθήνη/ ἔγχει ἐμῷ δαμάᾳ) (*Iliad* 22.270–1). And unlike Hector, Achilles readily accepts the various pronouncements of his own death that will also be at the hands of mortal and immortal combined. When it comes to the act of killing, therefore, the Homeric language of force does not merely give expression to contingency, but it further emphasizes varying degrees of human ignorance when it comes to the destructive events in which mortals as such are involved.

What we find throughout the *Iliad*, therefore, is that the contingencies of force, in its various forms, are directly tied to issues of speech performance. It is for this reason that Homeric force became a topic discussed by the structuralist thinkers Bourdieu, Derrida, and Foucault, who, each in their own way, are predominantly concerned with the relationship between language and human subjectivity. Indeed, Bourdieu, Derrida, and Foucault can each be seen to continue the problem of Homeric force and the subject inaugurated by Simone Weil and Bruno Snell. As we have seen, the observations of each of these thinkers prove vital for a better appreciation of the role that Homeric forces play within the larger narrative structure. To be sure, as I have indicated, there remain problems with their particular interpretations of Homer, which prevent the simple *application* of their observations and arguments to the poem as a whole.[3] Rather, their arguments require philological interventions that help us to arrive at broader philosophical implications of the *Iliad*, which move beyond even what each of those thinkers presupposes. Thus, Bourdieu used Homeric speech and the scepter in order to argue against J. L. Austin's arguments concerning the linguistic basis of the "illocutionary force" of speech. What we have seen, however, is that the invocation of physical forces often occurs in speech itself. Hence, the seemingly externalized justification of the authority of speech performance in Homer by way of physical force rests on very shaky ground. That is to say, the external conditions of what Bourdieu calls "symbolic power" can never be entirely separated from the verbal performances that reproduce those conditions. Through a similar mode of inquiry, Jacques Derrida argued that *kratos*, as a form of political force, operates as a self-justifying phenomenon, which he termed "ipso-centrism." And yet, here too, the *Iliad*'s narrative intricacies seem to

---

[3] On the problems of merely "applying" the work of structuralists and other continental philosophers to Classical texts, see Miller 2003; Miller 2015b.

Homeric Forces and Human Subjects Reconsidered   215

contradict any arguments presented by speakers in the poem for the political self-justification of force. That contradiction is evidenced by the fact that the narrative of the *Iliad* undermines the very role that the *kratos* of Zeus might play in justifying the political power of Agamemnon. And indeed, even though Zeus himself asserts and attempts to justify his behavior in absolute terms as a function of *kratos*, the speeches and actions by Athena, Hera, and Poseidon remind both Zeus and the audience that Zeus' own force and power exists relationally and in no way as the transcendent "sign" of sovereignty. Unlike Bourdieu and Derrida, however, Michel Foucault does not presuppose that physical force is a self-justifying phenomenon. Instead, through his own detailed analysis of the chariot race in the funeral games of Patroclus, Foucault demonstrates how speech performance can either reconfirm or deconstruct presupposed hierarchies of force. And as I have argued, Foucault's observations apply to the funeral games as a whole and especially to the ways in which Achilles' own speech performance supplemented the infelicities of the physical contests themselves. Thus, despite some difficulties and infelicities with these earlier "structuralist" interpretations of Homer, each helps us to better appreciate the ways in which the problem of force in Homer is inseparable from the problem of speech performance and language meaning more generally.

Lastly, one might suppose that the destructive aspects of force—what Simone Weil referred to as "the force that kills"—is the most supremely physical and final enactment of force. And one might surmise that Weil's rendition of Homeric force should exist beyond the interpretive contingencies of speech and language. But as I have argued in Chapter 4, even the act of killing is subjected to the linguistic problems of interpretation from within the poem. The linguistic contingencies of force can be most especially observed in the verbs *damazō/damnēmi*. Humans seldom if ever take on the linguistic role of nominative active agent with these verbs of domination and killing. Instead, humans appear only as the objects of such force or, at best, its mortal instruments, while the gods and "fate" retain the grammatical and metaphysical role as nominative, subjective agents. As such, the enactment of the "force that kills" is presented in the poem as a problem of human interpretation. Such a problem is most clearly expressed when Hector is corrected by Patroclus as to who served as the true active subject in Patroclus' death. On the one hand that act of killing, expressed through the verbs *damazō* and *damnēmi*, gives clear expression to the notion of the "subjugation of the subject" as expressed by Weil. That is to say, humans as subjects are only defined by virtue of being subjected by force. And even though humans will assert particular

216   Conclusion

relations of force as *speaking* subjects, those efforts on the part of speakers almost always prove false. At the same time, however, these forces in the *Iliad* are not merely self-perpetuating in the way that Weil and others have asserted. In the *Iliad*, the true, active subjects of force are the gods themselves.

Ultimately, when taking into account the variety of Homeric forces, expressed through speech and narrative throughout the *Iliad*, what becomes most salient is the *contingency* of such forces, which is itself a function of the assumed interdependence between mortal and immortal. Simone Weil gave little room for discussion of the gods in *L'Iliade ou le poème de la force*, and in an earlier essay she dismissed the divine perspective as a mere superstition meant to explain away the irrationality of human behavior.[4] Bruno Snell, however, did identify mortal-immortal interdependence as an essential feature of Homeric force. And for Snell, it was this aspect of Homeric forces that distinguished it from modern presuppositions. He states:

> We believe that a man advances from an earlier situation by an act of his own will, through his own power. If Homer, on the other hand, wants to explain the source of an increase in strength, he has no course but to say that the responsibility lies with a god.
>
> **(Snell 1953: 20)**

And Snell further observed that Homeric forces are viewed as a "fitting donation from the gods" (Snell 1953: 21). But what Snell failed to notice is that the attribution of force from the gods is most often pronounced by speakers, whose own knowledge of human-divine interaction is severely limited.

For Snell, the understanding of force as something external to human agency was a basic indicator of "primitive" thought. As Snell asserted in the conclusion to his chapter on Homer: "Homeric man has not yet awakened to the fact that that he possesses in his own soul the source of his powers."[5] This statement from Snell is curious indeed—as though "Homeric man" should be aware of a reality beyond what is represented in the poems themselves.[6] It should be further noted that in the German, Snell does not stress any notion of "facts" per se but insists rather that

---

[4] Weil 1955: 67.   [5] Snell 1953: 21.

[6] On the problem of psychologizing Homeric characters beyond poetic representation, see Williams 1993: 22.

Homeric men have not awakened to the "consciousness" of their own powers—*Bewußtsein*.[7] For Snell, this conscious reality is the autonomous individual. Indeed, even though it has been acknowledged that Snell's notions of "Mind/Spirit" and "Consciousness," *Geist* and *Bewußtsein*, are indebted to Hegel, few scholars have noted that such a perspective relies ultimately on the German ideological assumptions of individuality.[8] Yet, in one of the key passages from *The Phenomenology of Spirit* (*Phänomenologie des Geistes*), Hegel asserts:

> The task of leading the individual from his culturally immature standpoint up to and into science had to be taken in its universal sense, and the universal individual, the world spirit (*Weltgeist*)/self-conscious spirit (*selbstbewußte Geist*),[9] had to be examined in the development of its cultural education (*Bildung*).
>
> **(Hegel 2018: 18, Preface, paragraph 28)**

In these lines, we see that "world spirit" or "self-conscious spirit" is one and the same as the "universal individual," and the mechanism by which this is realized is not merely historical progression, but "development" or "cultural education"—*Bildung*.[10] It is this Hegelian perspective which informs Snell and thus deeply implicates his observations on Homer in a much broader German ideological discourse related not just to *Geist*, but also to "consciousness" and "cultural education," *Bewußtsein* and *Bildung*. Anglophone scholars who argue with Snell often take up the issue of whether rationality and individuality are historical or ahistorical, but the idea of individuality itself, so strongly promoted in German philosophic thought, is seldom called into question in and of itself.[11]

---

[7] Snell 2009: 29: "Die homerischen Menschen sind noch nicht zu dem Bewußtsein erwacht, in der eigenen Seele den Ursprungsort eigener Kräfte zu besitzen."

[8] On Hegel's influence on Snell, see Austin 1975: 81–5; MacCary 1982: 3–15; Gill 1996: 35–6; Lohse 1997: 1–2. On the role of individuality in the history of German philosophical thought, see, among others, Lukes 1971; Lukes 1973; Dumont 1986; Dumont 1994; Church 2012.

[9] The "self-conscious spirit," *selbstbewusste Geist*, is offered as a gloss, Hegel 1987: 28.

[10] On the ideology of *Bildung* in German thought, see, among others, Dumont 1994: 69–198; Bollenbeck 1994; Horlacher 2016.

[11] Thus for instance, Vernant adhered generally to Snell's developmental view because it corresponded, in part, to his own approach, which was broadly defined as both "historical psychology" and "historical anthropology," although that method had a separate intellectual genealogy related to the work of Ignace Meyerson. See Vernant 1973. Nevertheless, Vernant still insisted that the Homeric warrior was to be understood as an individual (Vernant 1991: 320–4). A notable exception in Classical Studies to this assumption of individuality is Porter and Buchan 2004. See also Holmes 2010, who takes a nonunified view of Homeric embodiment and traces the history of the individually conceptualized body or *soma*, inspired by but

218 Conclusion

From recent posthumanist perspectives, as well as not so recent anthropological work, however, the very notion of the autonomous "individual" has ceased to be an assumed reality. The anthropological and posthumanist perspectives may therefore prove useful in reconsidering what Homeric terms for force say about early Greek views on subjectivity itself. Like so many concepts and arguments in anthropology, Marcel Mauss was perhaps the first to call into question the status of the individual as a historical constant and cultural universal with his essay "A Category of the Human Mind: The Notion of Person, the Notion of Self."[12] In the French tradition, Mauss's project was continued most notably by Louis Dumont, first in his work on the Indian caste system, *Homo Hierarchicus* (first published in 1966), and also in other works, especially *Essays on Individualism* (first published in 1983) and *German Ideology* (first published in 1991). Dumont sketched out a historical ideological development of individualism in western thought which began with the "outworldly individual," seen especially with Indian and Christian ascetics, which in turn gave way to the "individual-in-the world" as a political and philosophical category from the thirteenth century onward. In short, for Dumont, what defined the individual historically was how a person's relationship to society was conceptualized. Building on and responding to Dumont's work, Marilyn Strathern proposed the notion of the "dividual" in order to explain how Melanesians of the Papua New Guinea highlands understood personhood from a synchronic rather than historical perspective. Strathern thus explains:

> While it will be useful to retain the concept of sociality to refer to the creating and maintaining of relationships, for contextualizing Melanesians' views we shall require a vocabulary that will allow us to talk about sociality in the singular as well as the plural. Far from being regarded as unique entities, Melanesian persons are as dividually as they are individually conceived. They contain a generalized sociality

---

distinct from Snell's model. And now see Holmes's recent essay on Snell's *Enteckung des Geistes* as an "undead text" (Holmes 2020), which situates Snell's argument in relationship to broader issues of the Classical tradition in pre- and postwar Germany along with the text's influence in the traditions of the UK and France. Most importantly, Holmes gives a compelling account of how and why Snell's own problematic methods and presuppositions still persist through the value invested in Classical Studies today.

[12] Mauss 1985. This was his last essay, first published in 1938 in the *Journal of the Royal Anthropological Institute*.

Homeric Forces and Human Subjects Reconsidered   219

within. Indeed, persons are frequently constructed as the plural and composite site of the relationships that produced them.

(Strathern 1988: 13)

The works of Dumont and Strathern have continued to influence anthropological research up to the present.[13] Complementary with these anthropological discourses is the more recent work on posthumanism, broadly construed. Indeed, Michel Foucault's famous quote from *The Order of Things* (*Les mots et les choses*)— "Man is an invention of recent date. And one perhaps nearing its end"[14]— has operated as a type of battle hymn for posthumanism. One might just as easily replace Foucault's term "man" with "the individual." In the twentieth and twenty-first centuries, there have been innumerable ways in which the notion of person has been thought beyond the category of the bounded individual, especially from the perspectives of gender, technology, and species symbiosis—just to name three categories of inter- and intra-relationality among infinite possibilities.[15]

One particular scholar who has especially influenced the direction of posthumanism but disavows the category, Donna Haraway, has leveled a major attack against the idea of the individual from a biological perspective in her work *Staying with the Trouble: Making Kin in the Chthuluscene* (2016).[16] In that work, Haraway asks:

What happens when human exceptionalism and bounded individualism, those old saws of Western philosophy and political economics, become unthinkable in the best sciences, whether natural or social? Seriously unthinkable: not available to think with.

(Haraway 2016: 30)

In accounting for this unthinkability of the individual, Haraway describes the numerous ways in which one might define humans as a becoming with all species—animal, insect, and bacterial.[17] In this regard, she grounds her

---

[13] For the most recent application and reappraisal of dividuality, see volume 5.1 (2015) of the journal of ethnographic theory, *HAU*.

[14] Foucault 2002: 422.

[15] The bibliography on these topics is immense, but for accounts of the intellectual history of posthumanism as a category of analysis, see, among others, C. Wolfe 2010; Nayar 2013: 22–52; Braidotti 2013: 13–104; Braidotti 2018.

[16] For Haraway's discomfort with the category and term posthumanism, see Gane 2006: 140.

[17] As such the work is a continuation of Haraway 2003.

220   Conclusion

own work in major scientific research, and she gives special attention to one particular paper, "A Symbiotic View of Life," by Gilbert, Sapp, and Tauber, which has the telling subtitle "We Have Never Been Individuals."[18] That essay contrasts the early history of science, organized around the principle of individuality, with the most current work in microbiology and the relationships between microscopic and macroscopic life. Gilbert, Sapp, and Tauber thus summarize:

> Symbiosis is becoming a core principle of contemporary biology, and it is replacing an essentialist conception of "individuality" with a conception congruent with the larger systems approach now pushing the life sciences in diverse directions. These findings lead us into directions that transcend the self/nonself, subject/object dichotomies that have characterized Western thought.
>
> **(Gilbert, Sapp, and Tauber 2012: 326)**

In this regard, biologists are carrying out at the microbial level precisely what anthropologists and historians have been exploring at the sociological level.

Work in anthropology and posthumanism therefore offers an ideal occasion to reevaluate Snell's account of the Homeric person. Because Snell situated his observations on Homeric "mind," "body," and "force" within an ideological discourse of *Bildung*, the "Homeric View of Man" will necessarily be interpreted as deficient, presenting a type of failed individuality that also promises the individual-to-come.[19] Yet if we follow Haraway's claim that "we have never been individuals," then the Homeric perspective on the nonunitary person is not so much a sign of primitivism, but constitutes an alternate anthropological category, one that is also structurally parallel with the most current scientific research.

It is precisely the contingency and relationality implied by the various operations of Homeric forces that allow us to rethink the Homeric person, not simply as a failed self-conscious individual, but as an *intersubjective dividual*, one constituted by human-divine symbiosis.[20] As an example,

---

[18] Gilbert, Sapp, and Tauber 2012. See Haraway 2016: 67,

[19] On the "primitivism" of Homer "als unser Anfang" in Snell's writing, see Burkert 2004: 173–4; Schmitt 2012: 265–6.

[20] Describing the Homeric person according to the anthropological category of "dividual" was first suggested briefly by Whitley 2013 in a discussion of human-thing entanglements in the Homeric poems and Iron Age Greece. This notion of dividual finds parallel with Gill's argument for the "divided self" (Gill 1996: 175–239). Furthermore, Pelliccia (1995: 261)

Homeric Forces and Human Subjects Reconsidered   221

this interactive and interdependent status is perfectly expressed in the role that *biē* plays in the identity of the warrior. As already noted, the *biē* naming formula stands as a periphrasis for the person as agent throughout the Homeric epics.[21]

At the same time, *biē* is precisely one of those forms of force that can be given by the gods.[22] Thus, with *biē*, we see how force defines a warrior in terms of his identity at the same time that the warrior's own force is not a function of autonomous agency but is subject to the gods. A similar perspective can be seen in the function of *menos* as a warrior's "life force." That "life force" propels a warrior forward, and it is what causes a warrior such as Hector to fight in the front ranks. And because of this, Andromache tragically comments that Hector's own *menos*, his "life force," will also be the cause of his death (*Iliad* 6.407). But as we see in *Iliad* 22, Hector is not the one who is in full control of his *menos*, since it is supplemented variously by Zeus and Apollo. And in the end, Hector realizes it is those same gods who supplied him with his force that will also precipitate his death. Unlike Hector, who only realizes the tragic implications of human-divine interdependence at the moment of his death, Achilles seems to be continuously aware of that symbiotic relation. That awareness is made most evident in his own death threats to Hector, when he pronounces, "But Athena will subjugate you with my spear" (ἄφαρ δέ σε Παλλὰς Ἀθήνη/ ἔγχει ἐμῷ δαμάᾳ) (*Iliad* 22.270–1). Achilles, it would seem, above others, is aware of his own role as an instrument of force and never as an autonomous agent.

But even though the operation of Homeric forces seems to run contrary to the concept of the autonomous individual, we cannot go so far as Donna Haraway and insist that the individual is "unthinkable" for Homeric poetry. The "individual," i.e., a person whose status and agency is independent of gods and others, was perhaps not possible but still remained thinkable. It is this thinkable possibility of the individual agent that is expressed in the Homeric vocabulary of force. Indeed, although Bruno Snell was keen to observe that different force relations are understood as "gifts from the gods," it is not the case that all such terms are expressed as

---

notes how the "divided self" occurs by way of interaction on the part of both gods and organs. Such views of intersubjectivity also extend well beyond Archaic Greek poetry. It is applicable, for instance, to the Stoic concept of sympathy, which Holmes 2019 explains in terms of "cosmobiology," based in part on Haraway's notion of "becoming with" (Haraway 2007; Haraway 2016).

[21] This applies most often to Heracles, on which see discussion in Chapter 3 as well as Nagy 1979: 317–19; D. Stocking 2007: 63–4; and item I under *biē* in the appendix.

[22] See item XIV under *biē* in the appendix.

222 Conclusion

such. In particular, the noun *dynamis* and verb *dynamai* are never presented for humans as objects given by the gods. For the noun and verb give expression to a notion of force as potential or ability. But in the *Iliad*, the noun and verb are used primarily to describe the *limits* of human potential and framed almost always in the negative.[23] That negative potential and its relation to the gods is well expressed by Achilles, after Apollo has lured him away from the fighting. When Achilles realizes the deception, he proclaims:

νῦν δ' ἐμὲ μὲν μέγα κῦδος ἀφείλεο, τοὺς δὲ σάωσας
ῥηϊδίως, ἐπεὶ οὔ τι τίσιν γ' ἔδεισας ὀπίσσω.
ἦ σ' ἂν τισαίμην, εἴ μοι δύναμίς γε παρείη.

Iliad 22.18–20

And now you have robbed me of my *kudos*, and you saved them easily, since you did not fear retribution hereafter.
But I would take vengeance on you, if I were able.

As we have already noted, Achilles, above all others, is aware of human-divine interdependence when it comes to the enactment of force. But that very awareness does not prevent him from expressing his own personal *desire* to exert his force separate from the gods and even *against* a god. And yet, in expressing that desire as such, he simultaneously admits that his own personal force or potential, his *dynamis*, would fail to achieve such an end.

And so, just as the *Iliad* gives expression to human dependence upon the gods by way of different force relations, those same force relations also bely an unfilled desire that it could be otherwise.[24] That impossible desire is expressed in another manner with the recurring formula in the *Iliad*: "Would that my force were fixed" (βίη τέ μοι ἔμπεδος εἴη) (*Iliad* 4.314, 7.157, 11.670, 23.629). As discussed in Chapter 3, each occasion of this formula is in reference to or uttered by Nestor. Hence the formula becomes Nestor's tagline and serves as a constant refrain throughout the *Iliad*. Because it is uttered by Nestor, who is also the most loquacious of the Greeks, the formula's use and contexts therefore speak to the ways in which contingencies of force are inextricable from speech performance

---

[23] On the negative role of *dynamis* in the *Iliad*, see discussion in the introduction and appendix.
[24] On the problematic of desire more generally in the *Iliad*, see Buchan 2012.

Homeric Forces and Human Subjects Reconsidered 223

itself throughout the *Iliad*. The contingency of speech performance is one and the same as the Homeric warrior's performance in life. The force of a warrior, expressed as *biē*, can never be firmly established and permanent, just as the life of a warrior can never be so. The desire that force be *empedos* is one and the same as a warrior's desire to attain a permanent sense of being.

Furthermore, the general view of Iliadic force implied by Nestor's refrain presents a stark contrast with the *Odyssey*. The question of force in the *Odyssey* is beyond the scope of this book and deserves its own study.[25] Here, however, one cannot help but comment on a variation of Nestor's *biē* formula pronounced in the *Odyssey*. Just as the *Iliad* nears its conclusion with a funerary *agōn*, so the *Odyssey* concludes with the wedding contest of the bow.[26] At the moment when the disguised Odysseus strings the bow, he says "my *menos* is still *empedon*" (ἔτι μοι μένος ἔμπεδόν ἐστιν) (*Odyssey* 21.426). The implicit interformulaic contrast made between the *Iliad* and the *Odyssey* here is threefold.[27] First, Odysseus himself twice utters the Iliadic "Nestor formula" —βίη τέ μοι ἔμπεδος εἴη—when in disguise and speaking to Eumaeus the swineherd (*Odyssey* 14.468, 14.503). Hence, Odysseus' last proclamation after stringing the bow contrasts with the desire for fixed force when disguised as an aged beggar. Second, in his final pronouncement, we see that *biē* in the more popular formula is replaced with *menos*—the difference is telling. *Biē* stands both for violent force and for the intersubjective identity and status of a human. *Menos*, on the other hand, in both the *Iliad* and the *Odyssey*, comes to stand for a type of "life force." In the *Iliad*, *menos* has paradoxically tragic implications since this "life force" propels men into battle, precipitating their own deaths. Here in the *Odyssey*, however, Odysseus' life force, his *menos*, will precipitate the death of the suitors. Third, variations of the *biē empedos* formula are strictly in the negative or contrafactual optative (optative of wish). By contrast, Odysseus asserts that his *menos* is indeed *empedos* in factually

---

[25] See further Collins 1998 for the changing significance and value of *alkē* in the *Odyssey* compared to the *Iliad*. The appendix on Homeric terms for force presented in this book may provide the foundations for such work. As is made clear from the appendix, distribution of the terms for force in the *Odyssey* is fairly limited to specific themes and contexts, especially with regard to the suitors, the Cyclops episode, and Odysseus' own person.

[26] On the contest of the bow and its potential connections to the Indo-European poetics of wedding contests, see Jamison 1999. On the contest of the bow and its logic within the narrative of the *Odyssey*, see Ready 2010. For the structural parallel in the two *agōnes* as it pertains to politics and death, see Buchan 2012: 103–8.

[27] On intertextual relations between the *Iliad* and *Odyssey* and the contrasts that such connections make more generally, see Pucci 1987.

224 Conclusion

indicative terms. Such a claim speaks to the miraculous fact that Odysseus returns ten years after the Trojan war apparently ageless, thanks to the intervention of Athena.[28] Thus the transformation of Nestor's *biē empedos* formula into a statement about the permanence of Odysseus' own *menos* further underscores the negative ideological import of Homeric forces for the *Iliad* as a whole.

Lastly, in returning to the *Iliad*, we can see this impossible desire associated with various types of force in reference to Achilles himself. In the very beginning of the *Iliad*, Agamemnon comments upon the impossible desire of Achilles as the reason that he will not obey Nestor's advice. Agamemnon states:

ἀλλ᾽ ὅδ᾽ ἀνὴρ ἐθέλει περὶ πάντων ἔμμεναι ἄλλων,
πάντων μὲν κρατέειν ἐθέλει, πάντεσσι δ᾽ ἀνάσσειν

Iliad 1.287-8

But that man wishes to be above all others,
he wishes to have *kratos* over all, to rule over all

To have *kratos* over all is to desire to exist and act in absolute terms without recourse to others, human or divine. But, as the narrative of the *Iliad* demonstrates, what Agamemnon criticizes in Achilles is true also for Agamemnon. And we have seen that Zeus himself gives expression to that same desire for absolute superiority (*Iliad* 8.5–27), even though the gods continuously challenge him on that very assertion of independence.

In this regard, each assertion of force in the *Iliad*, through its different terms and in its different relational modes, actively problematizes what it means to be a subject, a subject utterly dependent on others both human and divine. At the same time, it presents such interdependent subjects desiring to live and exert force in absolute terms. And so when we closely analyze the language of Homeric force in its plurality and contingencies, the *Iliad* ultimately presents itself as a meditation on the very impossibility of immanent individuality.

---

[28] Athena does employ a negative version of this formula against Odysseus in his battle with the suitors as a form of rebuke and a type of test of Odysseus (*Odyssey* 22.226). Finally, the only other occurrence of the formula is by Eurucleia promising Odysseus that she can keep quiet about his identity (*Odyssey* 19.493). All three occurrences therefore concern Odysseus' revenge on the suitors, as does Odysseus' use of the *biē empedos* formula when speaking to Eumaeus. For comparison of usages, side by side, see the appendix under *menos*.

APPENDIX

Force in Early Greek Hexameter

This appendix provides a basic account of the semantics of the seven "force" terms listed by Bruno Snell (1953: 20) and Émile Benveniste (2016: 362). Those terms include *kratos, alkē, menos, sthenos, biē, (w)is,* and *dynamis.*[1] And I have included an eighth entry pertaining to the *damazō/damnēmi* verbal complex. The purpose of this appendix is to provide a list of all citations of the eight terms and their related cognates in early Greek hexameter poetry, including the *Iliad,* the *Odyssey,* as well as the *Theogony, Works and Days,* and the *Homeric Hymns.* For the purposes of this book, Iliadic usages are provided first and the rest are provided thereafter. Following the initial comments of Snell and Benveniste, this appendix considers the ways in which the semantics of each term differ, while also noting key instances of overlap. The main purpose, however, is not simply to provide a strictly lexical semantic account of each term but also to consider each term's more specific deployment within the poetic contexts of early Greek hexameter. Usages are therefore grouped and organized first according to formulaic context, where the formula here is treated as the syntactic grouping of co-occurring lexical items (without strict reference to metrical position).[2] After formulaic groupings, occurrences are categorized according to broad trends in pragmatic usage, followed by specific instances that cannot be classified under formulaic or generic categorization. Occurrences of each of these terms are far greater in the *Iliad* and *Odyssey* than in the rest of the Greek hexameter corpus. Where possible, general differences in usage are noted. It is hoped that this appendix may provide the ground for further research on Homeric concepts of force and its potential impact on later phases of Greek and Roman history.

Kratos

This noun does not mean physical "force" per se. Rather it refers to a sense of "dominance" or "superiority" and therefore the term always implies a contest between two or more people (Snell 1953: 21; Benveniste 2016: 363–71; *LfgrE* ad loc.). Furthermore, *kratos* as superiority may be seen to operate as a central, organizing principle for other forms of force, such as when Diomedes claims that "*alkē*

---

[1] The noun *kikus,* listed by Snell, is omitted because it only occurs twice (*Odyssey* 11.393, *Hymn to Aphrodite* 237), and similarly, *ischus,* listed by Benveniste, is also omitted because it only occurs three times in the Hesiodic corpus (*Theogony* 146, 153, and 823).

[2] For the oral-poetic approach to Homeric lexical items, see, among others, Muellner 1976; Martin 1989; Wilson 2002; Walsh 2005. For a concise history of the various and competing accounts of Homeric formulas, see Russo 1997. For an understanding of Homeric formulas in terms of their semantic constituency and referentiality, see especially Foley 1991: 13–33; Bakker 2013: 157–69.

226 Appendix: Force in Early Greek Hexameter

(fighting force) is the greatest *kratos*" (*Iliad* 9.39; Benveniste 2016: 364). The sense of *kratos* as "superiority" may be semantically opposed to *achos*, grief, in the epic tradition (Nagy 1979: 85–90). Because *kratos* conveys a notion of "dominance" or "superiority" in a contest, there is a comparative dimension already built into its semantics, which is simply reiterated in the positive (*krateros/karteros*), comparative (*kreissōn*), and superlative (*kartistos*) forms. Yet the use of the forms differs in pragmatic function (see discussion in Chapter 1 on Nestor's use of comparative and superlatives). *Kratos* has an especially strong association with Zeus, and *kratos* is also conceived as an object given by the gods, primarily by Zeus. Thus, the use of *kratos* further underscores the contingency of competition and the reliance on a larger economy shared between humans and gods. The sense of "superiority" may be understood in either political or physical terms, and this bi-valence is especially captured in the used of the verb *krateein*.

Part I. *Kratos* in the *Iliad*

   I. κράτος ἐστὶ μέγιστον, "[which/whose] *kratos* is the greatest"
      Formula primarily associated with Zeus in the *Iliad*.
      Speech: *Iliad* 2.118; *Iliad* 9.25; *Iliad* 9.39; *Iliad* 24.293, 24.311
      Narrative: *Iliad* 13.484

   II. κράτος ἐγγυαλίζω, "place *kratos* in the hand/to give *kratos*"
      Speech: *Iliad* 11.192; *Iliad* 11.207; *Iliad* 11.753; *Iliad* 17.206
      Narrative: *Iliad* 17.613

   III. κράτος δίδωμι, "give *kratos*"
      Speech: *Iliad* 9.254; *Iliad* 13.743; *Iliad* 15.216; *Iliad* 16.524; *Iliad* 17.562; *Iliad* 20.121

   IV. κράτος φέρειν, to carry *kratos*, to be "superior" and therefore victorious in the encounter
      The language of "carrying kratos" seems to be related to the agonistic context of carrying away a prize, as seen in *Iliad* 23.413, Hesiod, *Theogony* 437, Hesiod, *Works and Days* 657. Chantraine (2009: 1146) also considers this formula to be the basis for the comparative adjective *pherteros*. See Chapter 1 for further discussion.
      Speech: *Iliad* 13.486; *Iliad* 18.308

   V. κάρτεϊ καὶ σθένεϊ, "in/with dominance and strength"
      For further discussion of *sthenos*, see discussion in the appendix under *sthenos*.
      Speech: *Iliad* 15.108; *Iliad* 17.322; *Iliad* 17.329

   VI. ἠνορέῃ πίσυνοι καὶ κάρτεϊ χειρῶν
      "trusting in their manliness and the dominance of their hands"
      Narrative: *Iliad* 8.226, *Iliad* 11.9

   VII. Additional, non-formulaic instances of *kratos*
      Speech: *Iliad* 1.509–10; *Iliad* 6.387; *Iliad* 12.214; *Iliad* 17.623; *Iliad* 7.142; *Iliad* 16.54

Appendix: Force in Early Greek Hexameter 227

Adjective: καρτερός/κρατερός, -ή, -όν
This is the positive adjectival form not to be confused with comparative adjectives ending in -teros. Thus it means to be in possession of kratos. Because kratos conveys a sense of "superiority," however, the positive adjective nevertheless has comparative connotations. See discussion of the adjectival form in Chapter 1.

VIII. εἰ καρτερός + verb "to be," "If perhaps he/she/you have kratos..."
Used primarily in concessive clauses, where possession of kratos proves ultimately insufficient.
Speech: Iliad 1.178; Iliad 1.280; Iliad 13.483; Iliad 5.410; Iliad 5.645; Iliad 9.53; Iliad 13.316

IX. κρατερός περ ἐών, "Though he has kratos"
This formula takes the same concessive force as the formula above and is related also to the formula "good though he be," ἀγαθός περ ἐών. See discussion in Chapter 1, especially regarding usage in Iliad 15.
Speech: Iliad 15.164; Iliad 15.195; Iliad 16.624

X. κρατερός as part of line-end epithet
In reference to Diomedes:
Narrative: Iliad 4.401; Iliad 4.411; Iliad 5.143; Iliad 5.251; Iliad 5.286; Iliad 5.814; Iliad 7.163; Iliad 10.369; Iliad 10.446; Iliad 11.316; Iliad 11.361; Iliad 11.384; Iliad 11.660; Iliad 16.25; Iliad 23.290; Iliad 23.472; Iliad 23.812
Speech: Iliad 8.53; Iliad 10.536
Narrative: Iliad 5.151 in reference to Diomedes, not at line end
As line-end epithet of other characters:
Speech: Iliad 5.385 (Ephialtes); Iliad 5.393 (Heracles); Iliad 6.130 (Lykourgos); Iliad 12.182 (Polupoites)

XI. κρατερὸν δ᾽ ἐπὶ μῦθον ἔτελλε, "he uttered an authoritative speech/command"
Narrative: Iliad 1.25; Iliad 1.326; Iliad 1.379; Iliad 16.199

XII. κρατερὸν μένος, "dominant life force"
For further discussion of semantics, see discussion in the appendix under menos.
Speech: Iliad 7.38; Iliad 10.479
Narrative: Iliad 16.189; Iliad 17.742; Iliad 23.837; Iliad 13.60

XIII. ἀμύμονά τε κρατερόν τε, "blameless and dominant"
Narrative: Iliad 4.89, Iliad 5.169; Iliad 21.546
Speech: Iliad 18.55

XIV. κρατερὸν μήστωρα φόβοιο, "dominant driver of fear"
Speech: Iliad 6.97; Iliad 6.278
Narrative Iliad 12.39

XV. τοῦ δὴ ἑταῖρον ἔπεφνες ἐνηέα τε κρατερόν τε, "he killed his gentle and mighty companion."
There is irony in this formula since krateros means to possess superiority. But if one is killed then that superiority failed.
Speech: Iliad 17.204; Iliad 21.96

228   Appendix: Force in Early Greek Hexameter

XVI. κρατερὰς ὑσμίνας, "difficult encounter"
Here adjectival usage may be the sense of *krat-* related to *kratús*, hard, as discussed by Benveniste and Chantraine.
Accusative plural:
Narrative: *Iliad* 2.40
Speech: *Iliad* 2.345; *Iliad* 5.200; *Iliad* 5.530; *Iliad* 12.347; *Iliad* 12.360; *Iliad* 15.562; *Iliad* 17.543
Dative singular:
Narrative: *Iliad* 4.462; *Iliad* 36 5.712; *Iliad* 7.18; *Iliad* 16.648; *Iliad* 16.788; *Iliad* 19.52
Speech: *Iliad* 11.468; *Iliad* 13.522; *Iliad* 16.451; *Iliad* 16.567; *Iliad* 21.207
Genitive singular:
Speech: *Iliad* 16.447; 16.645
Narrative: *Iliad* 18.243
Accusative singular:
Narrative: *Iliad* 5.84; *Iliad* 5.627
Speech: *Iliad* 7.14; *Iliad* 11.190, *Iliad* 11.205
Narrative: *Iliad* 13.383; *Iliad* 14.448; *Iliad* 16.764; *Iliad* 17.15; *Iliad* 17.289

XVII. λαβὼν κρατεροῖσιν ὀδοῦσιν, "taking with strong teeth"
Here, as in other cases, adjectival usage may be the sense of *krat-* related to *kratús*, hard as discussed by Benveniste.
Narrative: *Iliad* 11.114; *Iliad* 11.175; *Iliad* 17.63

XVIII. Adverb: κρατερῶς
Speech: *Iliad* 8.29; *Iliad* 9.431; *Iliad* 9.694; *Iliad* 11.410; *Iliad* 13.56; *Iliad* 15.666; *Iliad* 16.501; *Iliad* 17.559
Narrative: *Iliad* 4.344; *Iliad* 17.135

Comparative adjective: κρείσσων, -ον
The comparative grammatical form conveys the sense of being "superior" in the context of competition between two or more people.

XIX. ἀλλ᾽ αἰεί τε Διὸς κρείσσων νόος, "mind of Zeus is superior"
Speech: *Iliad* 16.688; *Iliad* 17.176

XX. ὁππότερος δέ κε νικήσῃ κρείσσων τε γένηται, "whoever wins and is superior"
Speech: *Iliad* 3.71; *Iliad* 3.92

XXI. Non-formulaic uses of comparative κρείσσων
Speech: *Iliad* 1.80; *Iliad* 21.486; *Iliad* 19.217; *Iliad* 20. 334; *Iliad* 21.190–1; *Iliad* 23.578

Superlative adjective: κάρτιστος, -η, -ον
The superlative form is semantically equivalent to the positive form, but has a different pragmatic function. Where the positive adjective *karteros/krateros* is often used in a concessive context, the superlative is used in strictly positive assertions within explicitly comparative contexts.

XXII. Non-formulaic uses of the superlative
Speech: *Iliad* 1. 266–7; *Iliad* 6.98; *Iliad* 7.155; *Iliad* 8.17; *Iliad* 9.558; *Iliad* 20.243
Narrative: *Iliad* 21.253

Appendix: Force in Early Greek Hexameter **229**

Adjective: κράταιος, -η, -ον

Benveniste had suggested that this adjective is semantically related to *kratus*, "hard," rather than to *kratos* referring to dominance or superiority. Still, the occurrences of the adjective do seem to suggest "dominant" or "superior." For further discussion of the formation of the adjective, see Nagy 1979: 349–54.

XXIII. μοῖρα κραταιή, "dominant fate," "overpowering fate"

The adjective is used primarily to describe "fate," *moira*, as it pertains to conquering warriors and bringing death. Here differences between speech and narrative are noted.

Narrative: *Iliad* 5.83; *Iliad* 5.629; *Iliad* 16.334; *Iliad* 16.853; *Iliad* 19.410; *Iliad* 20.477

Speech: *Iliad* 21.110; *Iliad* 24.132; *Iliad* 24.209; *Iliad* 6.458

XXIV. Verb: κρατέειν

The verb can be used in the very physical sense, describing the ability to prevail in a conflict or to dominate. But it can also take on a much more political sense related to ruling over others. In the *Iliad*, there is equal distribution between political and physical senses, while in the *Odyssey* it takes on a strictly political connotation. On the general dichotomy between political and physical force, see especially Chapter 2.

Speech: *Iliad* 1.79; *Iliad* 1.288; *Iliad* 16.172; *Iliad* 16.424; *Iliad* 21.214; *Iliad* 21.315

Part II. *Kratos* in the *Odyssey*

XXV. κράτος ἐστὶ μέγιστον, "whose *kratos* is greatest"

Odyssey 1.70; *Odyssey* 5.4

XXVI. κράτος ἔστ᾽ ἐνὶ οἴκῳ, "(my) *kratos* is in the house."

Odyssey 1.359; *Odyssey* 21.353

Related phrase: κράτος ἔστ᾽ ἐνὶ δήμῳ, "(my) *kratos* is among the people" *Odyssey* 11.353: used by King Alcinous in reference to his decision to send Odysseus home

XXVII. κάρτος τε βίη τε, "dominance and violent force"

This formula is specific to the *Odyssey*.

Odyssey 4.415; *Odyssey* 6.197

XXVIII. βίη καὶ κάρτεϊ εἴκων, "yielding to *biē* and *kratos*"

Odyssey 13.143; *Odyssey* 18.139

XIX. κράτος δοῦναι, "give *kratos*"

Odyssey 21.280: θεὸς δώσει κράτος, ᾧ κ᾽ ἐθέλῃσιν, "a god will give *kratos*, to whomever he wishes"

XXX. Individual use of *kratos*, *Odyssey* 3.370

Adjective: καρτερός/κρατερός, -ή, -όν

XXXI. εἰ καρτερός + verb "to be"

Odyssey 8.139; *Odyssey* 22.13

XXXII. κρατερός περ ἐών, "though he has *kratos*" (only once in *Odyssey*)

Odyssey 11.265

230 Appendix: Force in Early Greek Hexameter

XXXIII. κρατερὴ ἀνάγκη, "strong/harsh necessity"
Odyssey 10.273

XXXIV. καρτερὸς ἀνὴρ, "a dominant man"
Used strictly in the *Odyssey* in reference to Odysseus. The line end of the nominative *anēr* thus corresponds formulaically to line beginning accusative *andra*, also in reference to Odysseus, on which see Kahane (1994: 58–9).
Odyssey 4.242; *Odyssey* 4.271; *Odyssey* 20.393

XXXV. κρατέρ' ἄλγεα, having/suffering "strong/harsh pains." Occurs strictly at line end. Semantically, this adjectival usage may be the sense of *krat-* related to *kratus*, "hard," as discussed by Benveniste.
Odyssey 5.13; *Odyssey* 5.395; *Odyssey* 11.593; *Odyssey* 15.232; *Odyssey* 17.142; one occurrence in the *Iliad* at *Iliad* 2.721.

XXXVI. κρατερῆφι βίηφιν, "through dominant force"
Odyssey 9.476; *Odyssey* 12.210; One occurrence in the *Iliad* at *Iliad* 21.50.

XXXVII. καρτερός/κρατερός as line end epithet in the *Odyssey*
Odyssey 4.11; *Odyssey* 15.122; *Odyssey* 9.407, *Odyssey* 9.446

XXXVIII. Comparative adjective: κρείσσων, -ον
Odyssey 6.182; *Odyssey* 18.46; *Odyssey* 18.83; *Odyssey* 21.345; *Odyssey* 22.167; *Odyssey* 22.353

XXXIX. Superlative adjective: κάρτιστος, -η, -ον
Odyssey 12.120

XL. Verb: κρατέειν
Odyssey 11.485; *Odyssey* 13.275; *Odyssey* 15.274; *Odyssey* 15.298; *Odyssey* 16.265; *Odyssey* 24.431

Part III. *Kratos* and related forms in *Theogony*, *Works and Days*, and *Homeric Hymns*

XLI. κράτος + βίη, "dominance and force"
Theogony 437: νικήσας δὲ βίη καὶ κάρτει; *Theogony* 385: Children of Styx

XLII. κρατερός περ ἐὼν, "though he has *kratos*"
Hymn to Hermes 386; *Theogony* 465

XLIII. κρατερὴ ἀνάγκη: "strong/harsh necessity"
Hymn to Aphrodite 130; *Theogony* 517

XLIV. καρτερός/κρατερός as part of line-end epithet
Hymn to Demeter 404, 430
Formula: ἀμύμονά τε κρατερόν τε, "blameless and dominant" (several times in *Iliad*)
Theogony 1013

XLV. Comparative adjective, κρείσσων, -ον
Works and Days 210; *Works and Days* 217; *Hymn to Apollo* 267

Appendix: Force in Early Greek Hexameter   231

XLVI. Formula: οὐδὲ βοῶν ἐλατῆρι κραταιῷ φωτὶ ἔοικα, "I am not similar to a
mighty driver of cattle"
Hymn to Hermes 265, 377

XLVII. Verb: κρατέειν
Hymn to Apollo 426; *Theogony* 403

Alkē

Alkē may be translated generally as "fighting force," i.e., the type of force that is
specific to the context of attack and defense in battle. Benveniste (2016: 363) provided the following definition: "To face up to danger without flinching, not to yield
under attack, to stand firm in the fray" (see similar account in *LFgrE* ad loc: *Kraft,
die Feindliches abwehrt*). Collins (1998: 14) defines *alkē* as follows: "Stylized as the
organizing principle of the military world in Homeric poetry. Not merely one in a
series, *alkē* defines the man who has committed his total being to war." As such,
Collins also finds fault with Benveniste's strictly defensive definition and sees the
concept as both defensive and aggressive force in war. Like all other forms of force,
it too is understood to be given from the gods. And similar to *menos*, *alkē* has a
distinctly mental component related to thinking (*mēdomai*), remembering
(*mimnēskomai*), forgetting (*lanthanō*), desiring (**mao/memona* related to *menos*),
and trust (*peithō*). According to Collins, the mental components are because "[a]
warrior's ability to fight, and thereby to survive and triumph in war, depends upon
the vigilant command that he maintains over his own mental resources" (Collins
1998: 103). What makes *alkē* unique compared to other terms for force is the conceptualization as a type of outer layer which the warrior wears, reflected in its use
with verbs such as "putting on" (*duō*) and "clothed in" (*epiennumi*). As such, it may
function as a type of "immortal armor" that further reflects a unique form of
divine possession (on which see Collins 1998: 15–45). Lastly, it should be noted
that there is marked difference in the distribution of *alkē* between the *Iliad* and the
Odyssey. Common formulas in the *Iliad* are rare in the *Odyssey* and vice versa. In
the *Odyssey*, there is an especially strong theme of *alkē* related to paternal inheritance between Telemachus and Odysseus, and the uses of *alkē* appear especially
marked because of the ways in which divinely possessed fighting force is deployed
in non-military or civilian contexts (on which see Collins 1998: 118).

Part I. *Alkē* in the *Iliad*

I. *Alkē* from Zeus and the other gods
Speech: *Iliad* 8.140; *Iliad* 15.490; *Iliad* 9.38–40

II. δύω ἀλκήν, "putting on *alkē*"
Speech: *Iliad* 9.231; *Iliad* 19.36

III. ἐπιέννυμι ἀλκήν, "clothed in *alkē*"
Narrative: *Iliad* 7.164; *Iliad* 8.262; *Iliad* 18.157; *Iliad* 20.381

232 Appendix: Force in Early Greek Hexameter

- IV. μήδομαι ἀλκῆς, "thinking upon *alkē*"
  Speech: *Iliad* 4.418; *Iliad* 5.718
- V. μιμνήσκω ἀλκῆς, "remembering *alkē*"
  Speech: *Iliad* 6.112; *Iliad* 8.174; *Iliad* 11.287; *Iliad* 13.48; *Iliad* 15.487;
  Iliad 15.734; *Iliad* 16.270; *Iliad* 17.185
  Narrative: *Iliad* 11.566
- VI. λανθάνω ἀλκῆς, "forgeting *alkē*"
  Speech: *Iliad* 6.265; *Iliad* 11.313; *Iliad* 13.269; *Iliad* 22.282
  Narrative: *Iliad* 13.836; *Iliad* 15.322; *Iliad* 16.357; *Iliad* 16.602
- VII. μεθίημι ἀλκῆς, "release/letting go of *alkē*"
  Speech: *Iliad* 4.234; *Iliad* 12.409; *Iliad* 13.116
- VIII. παύω ἀλκῆς, "ceasing from *alkē*"
  Speech: *Iliad* 15.250
- IX. *μάω/μέμονα ἀλκῆς, "eager for *alkē*"
  Speech: *Iliad* 17.181; *Iliad* 20.256
  Narrative: *Iliad* 13.197
- VI. πείθω ἀλκί, "trusting/confident in *alkē*"
  Narrative: *Iliad* 5.299; *Iliad* 13.471; *Iliad* 17.61; *Iliad* 17.728; *Iliad* 18.158
- VII. πίμπλημι ἀλκῆς, "fill with *alkē*"
  Speech: *Iliad* 17.499
  Narrative: *Iliad* 17.212
- XII. φευγόντων δ᾽ οὔτ᾽ ἄρ κλέος ὄρνυται οὔτε τις ἀλκή
  "For those who flee, neither *kleos* nor *alkē* arises."
  Speech: *Iliad* 5.530; *Iliad* 15.564
- XIII. Food and wine to restore *menos* and *alkē*
  Speech: *Iliad* 9.706; *Iliad* 19.161
- XIV. *Alkē* used in similes for warriors
  Narrative: *Iliad* 4.253; *Iliad* 13.330; *Iliad* 17.281; *Iliad* 18.154
- XV. Non-formulaic occurrences in the nominative
  Speech: *Iliad* 3.45; *Iliad* 4.245; *Iliad* 16.157
  Narrative: *Iliad* 5.740; *Iliad* 16.753; *Iliad* 21.528
- XVI. Non-formulaic occurrences in the accusative
  Speech: *Iliad* 9.34
- XVII. Non-formulaic occurrences in the genitive
  Speech: *Iliad* 11.710; *Iliad* 13.786; *Iliad* 17.42
  Narrative: *Iliad* 15.527; *Iliad* 21.578

Adjective: ἄλκιμος
- XVIII. Adjective as predicate nominative
  Speech: *Iliad* 6.522; *Iliad* 15.570
- XIX. Adjective modifying spears/tools of war
  εἵλετο δ᾽ ἄλκιμον + [tool]
  Narrative: *Iliad* 3.338; *Iliad* 10.135; *Iliad* 11.43; *Iliad* 14.12; *Iliad* 15.482;
  Iliad 16.139
- XX. Modifying "heart," ἄλκιμον ἦτορ
  Speech: *Iliad* 5.529; *Iliad* 16.209; *Iliad* 16.264
  Narrative: *Iliad* 17.111; *Iliad* 20.169; *Iliad* 21.572

Appendix: Force in Early Greek Hexameter   233

XXI. Modifying men/warriors
Speech: *Iliad* 13.278; *Iliad* 17.177; *Iliad* 21.586
Narrative *Iliad* 11.483; *Iliad* 16.689

XXII. Modifying "son," ἄλκιμος υἱός
Predominantly applied to Patroclus, on which see Collins (1998: 15–45).
Speech: *Iliad* 10.110; *Iliad* 12.349, *Iliad* 12.362; *Iliad* 18.12; *Iliad* 18.455; *Iliad* 19.24
Narrative: *Iliad* 6.437; *Iliad* 11.605; *Iliad* 11.814; *Iliad* 11.837; *Iliad* 12.1; *Iliad* 16.278;
Iliad 16.307; *Iliad* 16.626; *Iliad* 16.665; *Iliad* 16.827; *Iliad* 17.429

Part II. *Alkē* in the *Odyssey*

XXIII. ἐπιέννυμι ἀλκήν, "clothed in *alkē*"
Odyssey 9.214; *Odyssey* 9.514

XXIV. μιμνήσκω ἀλκῆς, "remember *alkē*"
Odyssey 4.527

XXV. πείθω ἀλκί, "trusting/confident in *alkē*"
Formula is common in the *Iliad*, especially with animal similes, but
used only once in the *Odyssey* at *Odyssey* 6.130.

XXVI. Individual occurrences of *alkē* in the *Odyssey*
Odyssey 2.61; *Odyssey* 12.120; *Odyssey* 17.365; *Odyssey* 22.226; *Odyssey*
22.237; *Odyssey* 22.305; *Odyssey* 23.128; *Odyssey* 24.509

Adjectival use: ἄλκιμος

XXVII. Predicate nominative
Odyssey 1.302; *Odyssey* 3.200; *Odyssey* 10.553; *Odyssey* 22.138; *Odyssey*
22.232

XXVIII. εἵλετο δ᾽ ἄλκιμον [spear], "he seized a strong spear/spears"
Odyssey 1.99; *Odyssey* 15.551; *Odyssey* 17.4; *Odyssey* 22.25; *Odyssey*
22.125; *Odyssey*
20.127
Non formulaic occurrence: *Odyssey* 21.34

Part III. *Alkē* and Related Forms in *Theogony*, *Works and Days*, and *Homeric Hymns*

Hymn to Artemis, 9; *Hymn to Hermes* 101; *Theogony* 526; *Theogony* 876; *Theogony*
950–1; *Works and Days* 201; *Shield of Heracles* 320

Biē

This noun is often understood as the prototypical term for "force" and indicates
physical or violent action (see Chantraine 2009: 174–5). It is often discussed in

234 Appendix: Force in Early Greek Hexameter

structural opposition to the concept of *mētis*, "wily intelligence," both within the context of Greek culture (Detienne and Vernant 1978, esp. 9–26) and within the context of the epic tradition more specifically (Nagy 1979: 42–50). Because of the naming formula, most often used with Heracles, *biē* is also predominantly associated with the subjective identity and agency of a warrior and is understood as one of the primary means by which a warrior secures reputation (see Nagy 1979: 317–19; D. Stocking 2007: 63–4). This notion of force also gives expression to contingency and human mortality, primarily through the formula βίη τέ μοι ἔμπεδος εἴη, "Would that my force were fixed"—a tag-line for the figure of Nestor in particular. At the same time, like other types of force, *biē* can be given by the gods. And furthermore, one's own status can be determined by the *biē* of one's horses, as discussed in Chapter 3 on the funeral games of Patroclus. Thus, because *biē* is foundational to the identity of a warrior and also dependent upon gods and other beings, this term gives expression to a notion of Homeric interdependent subjectivity. That is to say, the usages of *biē* help to confirm how force and subjectivity exist beyond the notion of the individual autonomous agent in Homeric poetry, on which see discussion in Chapter 4, conclusion. Unlike the *Iliad*, where usage occurs throughout and is understood in generally positive terms, usage of *biē* in the *Odyssey* is primarily restricted to the Cyclops episode and in reference to the suitors, thus revealing a difference in valuation between contexts of war and non-war.

Part I. *Biē* in the *Iliad*

   I. Naming formula: *biē* + name in adjectival form or in genitive singular
   This is often a periphrasis for the name of the hero in question. The "force" aspect does take on a salient quality in certain contexts. The formula is used predominantly of Heracles. For further discussion of this formulaic construction, see Chapter 3.
   Referring to Heracles:
   Speech: *Iliad* 2.658; *Iliad* 2.666; *Iliad* 5.638; *Iliad* 11.690; *Iliad* 15.640; *Iliad* 18.171;
   Iliad 19.98
   Non-Heracles, *biē* formula:
   Speech: *Iliad* 3.105; *Iliad* 13.770; *Iliad* 13.781; *Iliad* 17.24; *Iliad* 20.307; *Iliad* 23.859
   Narrative: *Iliad* 4.385–6; *Iliad* 5.781; *Iliad* 13.758; *Iliad* 17.187; *Iliad* 22.323
   II. βίη + ἔμπεδος + verb form of "to be"
   Used primarily in optative of wish constructions, and spoken primarily by Nestor.
   "Would that my force were fixed." See Chapter 3 for further discussion.
   Speech: *Iliad* 4.314; *Iliad* 7.157; *Iliad* 11.670; *Iliad* 23.629
   Compare with *Iliad* 8.103, σὴ δὲ βίη λέλυται, "your force has been lost" (Diomedes speaking to Nestor)

Appendix: Force in Early Greek Hexameter 235

III. Superior force relations, $\beta i\eta$ (dative/instrumental/accusative) + $\varphi\epsilon\rho\tau\epsilon\rho\rho\varsigma$ and related
forms
Speech: *Iliad* 3.431; *Iliad* 7.288–9; *Iliad* 15.165; *Iliad* 15.181

IV. Superior force relations, $\beta i\eta$ (dative/instrumental/accusative) + $\dot{\alpha}\mu\epsilon i\nu\omega\nu$ and related
forms
Speech: *Iliad* 1.404; *Iliad* 6.478–9; *Iliad* 11.787; *Iliad* 15.139; *Iliad* 23.315
Additional, related uses of *biē* + comparative forms
Speech: *Iliad* 9.498; *Iliad* 23.577–8
$\pi\epsilon i\theta\omega\ \beta i\eta\varphi\iota$, "confident/trusting in force"
Speech: *Iliad* 4.325; *Iliad* 12.135; *Iliad* 22.107
Narrative: *Iliad* 12.153; *Iliad* 12.256

VII. *Biē* used in reference to "lack of willingness"
Speech: *Iliad* 1.430; *Iliad* 7.197
Narrative: *Iliad* 13.572

VIII. Formula, "force of the winds" house simile
$\delta\dot{\omega}\mu\alpha\tau\sigma\varsigma\ \dot{\nu}\psi\eta\lambda\sigma\hat{\iota}\sigma\ \beta i\alpha\varsigma\ \dot{\alpha}\nu\dot{\epsilon}\mu\omega\nu\ \dot{\alpha}\lambda\epsilon\epsilon i\nu\omega\nu$, "of a tall house, warding off the force of the winds"
Narrative: *Iliad* 16.213; *Iliad* 23.713

IX. $\mu\epsilon\theta\hat{\eta}\kappa\epsilon\ \beta i\eta\varsigma$, "let go of force" (used once in *Iliad*, once in *Odyssey*)
Narrative: *Iliad* 21.177

X. $\kappa\dot{\alpha}\rho\tau\sigma\varsigma\ \tau\epsilon\ \beta i\eta\ \tau\epsilon$- "superiority and force"
See under *kratos* in the appendix.
Denominative verb, $\beta\iota\alpha\zeta$- + $\beta\epsilon\lambda\dot{\epsilon}\epsilon\sigma\sigma\iota$, "overpowered by arrows," used only in reference
to Ajax
Speech: *Iliad* 11.589
Narrative: *Iliad* 11.576; *Iliad* 15.727; *Iliad* 16.102

XII. Non-formulaic uses of *biē*
Speech: *Iliad* 3.45; *Iliad* 7.204–5; *Iliad* 12.341; *Iliad* 15.106; *Iliad* 18.34; *Iliad* 21.315–16; *Iliad* 21.500–1; *Iliad* 24.42
Narrative: *Iliad* 11.561; *Iliad* 15.613–14; *Iliad* 16.386–7; *Iliad* 16.826; *Iliad* 17.569; *Iliad* 21.366–7

XIII. Non-formulaic denominative verbal form $\beta\iota\dot{\alpha}\zeta\omega$, "to overpower"
Speech: *Iliad* 21.451–2; *Iliad* 22.229; *Iliad* 23.576

Part II. *Biē* in the *Odyssey*

XIV. Naming formula, *biē* + name in adjectival form or in genitive singular
Heracles *biē* naming formula: *Odyssey* 11.601
Non-Heracles, *biē* naming formula:
Odyssey 11.296 for Iphicles; *Odyssey* 11.290 for Iphicles

236 Appendix: Force in Early Greek Hexameter

XV. βίη + ἔμπεδος + verb form of "to be" (in *Iliad*, used strictly of Nestor)
Odyssey 14.468; *Odyssey* 14.503
Compare with *Odyssey* 21.426, when Odysseus, in disguise, strings the bow and states that his *menos* is *empedos*. (Discussed under *menos* in the appendix.)

XVI. Superior force relations, βίη (dative/instrumental/accusative) + φέρτερος, etc.
Odyssey 6.6; *Odyssey* 12.246; *Odyssey* 18.234; *Odyssey* 21.134; *Odyssey* 21.371

XVII. πείθω βίηφι, "confident/trusting in force"
Odyssey 21.315

XVIII. *Biē* used in reference to "lack of willingness"
Odyssey 1.403–4; *Odyssey* 4.646

XIX. μεθῆκε βίης, "let go of force" (used once in *Iliad*, once in *Odyssey*)
Odyssey 21.126

XX. Formula for vengeance, used only in the *Odyssey* τίς δ᾽ οἶδ᾽ εἴ κέ ποτέ σφι βίας ἀποτείσεται ἐλθών, "Someone knows whether he coming back will pay back to them their acts of force."
Odyssey 3.216; *Odyssey* 11.118; *Odyssey* 16.255; *Odyssey* 17.540

XXI. τῶν ὕβρις τε βίη τε, "violence and force" at line beginning, only in the *Odyssey*
Odyssey 15.329; *Odyssey* 17.565

XXII. βίας ὑποδέγμενος ἀνδρῶν, "receiving/enduring violence of men"
Only in the *Odyssey*
Odyssey 13.310; *Odyssey* 16.189

XXIII. Non-formulaic uses of *biē* in the nominative
Odyssey 18.4

XXIV. Non-formulaic uses of *biē* in the accusative
Odyssey 4.668; *Odyssey* 22.219; *Odyssey* 23.31

XXV. Non-formulaic uses of *biē* in the genitive
Odyssey 4.422; *Odyssey* 10.200; *Odyssey* 20.379; *Odyssey* 21.185

XXVI. Non-formulaic uses of *biē* in the dative
Odyssey 15.231; *Odyssey* 21.128

XXVII. Non-formulaic uses of *biē* in the instrumental
Odyssey 9.406–8; *Odyssey* 9.475–6; *Odyssey* 12.209–10

XXVIII. Non-formulaic adjectival and adverbial forms, *biai-*
Odyssey 2.236; *Odyssey* 2.237; *Odyssey* 22.37

XXIX. Non-formulaic denominative verbal forms—βιάζω, "to overpower"
Odyssey 7.278; *Odyssey* 9.410; *Odyssey* 21.348

Part III. *Biē* in *Theogony*, *Works and Days*, and *Homeric Hymns*

XXX. Naming formula: *biē* + name in adjectival form or in genitive singular
Referring to Heracles, *biē* naming formula:
Theogony 289; *Theogony* 315; *Theogony* 332; *Theogony* 943; *Shield of Heracles* 115, 149, 416, 452

Appendix: Force in Early Greek Hexameter   **237**

XXXI. Superior force relations, βίη (dative/instrumental/accusative) + φέρτερος, etc.
Hymn to Apollo 336-8

XXXII. Biē used in reference to "lack of willingness"
Hymn to Demeter 124-5; Hymn to Demeter 413

XXXIII. Non-formulaic uses of biē
Theogony 146; Theogony 385; Theogony 489-90; Theogony 649-50; Theogony 677; Theogony 669-70; Works and Days 148; Works and Days 275; Works and Days 321

Menos

The meanings of menos seem to vary greatly within different contexts (see LfgrE ad loc.), but in the epic tradition, menos seems to primarily connote a notion of "vital force," associated with the living, animate body. Other translations, "anger," "urge," "violence," etc., may be derived from this basic idea. Like other terms for force, menos may be an object given by the gods, especially in the context of fighting. It is especially related to embodied action (see Clarke 1999: 112-13). Unlike other terms, however, the force of menos may also be "breathed" into the warrior by a god, further underscoring its relationship to human vitality. In this regard it is associated with the "hot breath" or thumos of a warrior. It is also that which leaves the warrior, together with the psychē (also a form of breath/air), at the moment of death. And menos is a form of force with which a warrior is "filled," which makes it a type of interiorized substance. Similar operations can be found for alkē and sthenos, but occur less frequently. As a vital substance related to "air" and "movement," it may also be used to describe nonhuman forces including fire, wind, and rivers. In the Iliad, menos occurs a great deal in narrative contexts, specifically because of its role in battle narratives. Similar to biē, menos may be used in naming formulas with the name of the person in the genitive, yet in those cases, menos seems to take on a quality salient to specific occasions compared with the biē naming formula. Although less common in the Iliad, the menos naming formula is very common and refers almost strictly to Alcinous in the Odyssey, where Alcinous' name, "force" (alkē) + "mind" (noos), is captured in the etymological semantics of menos as force and mind, *mens-. On the mental aspects of menos and its root, see further Beekes 2010: 930-1; Chantraine 2009: 685; Bakker 2008: 67-73; Collins 1998: 111-12; Nagy 1974: 266-8. More general differences between the Iliad and the Odyssey are reflected in other formulaic uses of menos, where common formulas in the Iliad are extremely rare in the Odyssey and vice versa. Lastly, such formulaic differences also have thematic consequences. A particularly striking contrast between the Iliad and the Odyssey is revealed through the specific formula "μοι μένος ἔμπεδόν ἐστιν," "my force is fixed," used twice in reference to Odysseus (Odyssey 21.426, 22.226), which contrasts greatly with the refrain from the Iliad used primarily of Nestor, βίη δέ μοι ἔμπεδος εἴη, "would that my force were fixed" (Iliad 4.314, 7.57, 11.670, 23.629). The Odyssey may therefore be seen to offer a positive assertion on the permanence of force in opposition to the Iliad's insistence on its impermanence. Such difference is further reflected in the lexical difference of "force" in the two

238 Appendix: Force in Early Greek Hexameter

formulas, between *menos* as vital force and *biē* as violent force (see Chapter 4 conclusion for further discussion).

Part I. Menos in the *Iliad*

I. παύω μένος, "stop *menos*"
A formula with limited distribution. For the importance of this phrase, especially as it applies to *Iliad* Book 1, see discussion in Chapter 1.
Speech: *Iliad* 1.207; *Iliad* 1.282; *Iliad* 21.340
Narrative: *Iliad* 21.384–5

II. μένος ἔμπεδον + verb "to be"—"force is fixed"
This formula seems to be a variation of the formula used with *biē*, which is more common. The *biē empedos* formula is used primarily as an optative of wish, demonstrating how "force is not fixed," especially for the figure of Nestor. The *menos empedon* formula occurs only with indicative verb, reflecting a more positive notion. The formula is used only once in the *Iliad*, three times in the *Odyssey*.
Speech: *Iliad* 5.254

III. *Menos* as an object given by the gods, δίδωμι μένος, "give *menos*"
Narrative: *Iliad* 5.1–2

IV. *Menos* as an object given by the gods, ἵημι μένος, "cast *menos* in"
Speech: *Iliad* 5.125; *Iliad* 19.37; *Iliad* 23.390
Narrative: *Iliad* 20.79–80

V. *Menos* as an object given by the gods, βάλλω μένος, " throw/place *menos* in"
Speech: *Iliad* 17.451
Narrative: *Iliad* 5.512–13; *Iliad* 10.366; *Iliad* 16.529

VI. *Menos* as an object given by the gods, τίθημι μένος, "place *menos* in"
Narrative: *Iliad* 21.145–6; *Iliad* 23.399–400

VI. *Menos* given by the gods, ἐμπνέω μένος, "breathing *menos*" into a warrior
Here we see the specifically corporeal and internal aspects of *menos* associated with the living being.
Speech: *Iliad* 15.262; *Iliad* 17.456; *Iliad* 19.159; *Iliad* 20.110
Narrative: *Iliad* 10.482; *Iliad* 15.59–60

VIII. "Speaking thus, he/she roused *menos* …," Ὣς εἰπὼν ὄτρυνε μένος
Narrative: *Iliad* 5.470; *Iliad* 5.792; *Iliad* 6.72; *Iliad* 11.291; *Iliad* 13.155; *Iliad* 15.500;
Iliad 15.514; *Iliad* 15.667; *Iliad* 16.210; *Iliad* 16.275
Speech: *Iliad* 17.423

IX. Variants of the rousing *menos* formula
Speech: *Iliad* 7.37–8; *Iliad* 12.266; *Iliad* 13.78; *Iliad* 20.93
Narrative: *Iliad* 5.563; *Iliad* 8.335; *Iliad* 22.203–4

X. *Menos* as rousing agent with person as object
Speech: *Iliad* 24.198–9
Narrative: *Iliad* 20.174–5

Appendix: Force in Early Greek Hexameter 239

XI. Awakening *menos*, ἐγείρω μένος
Speech: *Iliad* 15.232
Narrative: *Iliad* 15.594

XII. Not relaxing one's *menos*, οὐ λήγω μένος
Narrative: *Iliad* 13.424; *Iliad* 21.305

XIII. "force and invincible hands," μένος καὶ χεῖρες ἄαπτοι
This formula demonstrates the way this embodied force is specifically associated with action.
Speech: *Iliad* 8.450–1; *Iliad* 12.166; *Iliad* 13.317–18
Narrative: *Iliad* 7.309; *Iliad* 17.638

XIV. "Force and hands," μένος καὶ χεῖρες
Speech: *Iliad* 6.501–2; *Iliad* 13.105; *Iliad* 13.287; *Iliad* 14.73; *Iliad* 15.509–10

XV. "*Psyche* and *menos* were released," λύθη ψυχή τε μένος τε
Describing the moment of death.
Narrative: *Iliad* 5.296; *Iliad* 6.27; *Iliad* 8.122–3; *Iliad* 8.315

XVI. Other moments of death described with the loss of *menos*
Speech: *Iliad* 8.358–9; *Iliad* 17.29
Narrative: *Iliad* 13.444; *Iliad* 16.613; *Iliad* 17.529; *Iliad* 17.298

XVII. Naming formula, *menos* + name of warrior in genitive
Similar to the *biē* formula but seems to have more contextual salience in its usage. It is far less frequent. In the *Odyssey*, it becomes a standard formula specifically associated with Alcinous.
Narrative: *Iliad* 11.268; *Iliad* 11.272; *Iliad* 14.418; *Iliad* 16.189; *Iliad* 23.836–8

XVIII. *Menos* of fire
Speech: *Iliad* 6.182; *Iliad* 16.620–1; *Iliad* 17.565; *Iliad* 22.96; *Iliad* 23.177; *Iliad* 23.190–1; *Iliad* 23.237–9

XIX. Menos paired with *alkē*
See *alkē* in the appendix for further discussion of semantic pairing.
Speech: *Iliad* 9.706; *Iliad* 19.161
Narrative: *Iliad* 16.602

XX. "filled with *menos*," πίμπλημι μένεος
Speech: *Iliad* 9.678–9
Narrative: *Iliad* 1.103; *Iliad* 13.59–61; *Iliad* 22.312

XXI. "forgetting force," λανθάνω + μένεος/ἀλκῆς
The connection between "force" and "memory" is implied by the etymology of *menos*.
For further discussion, see Collins 1998 and Bakker 2008.
Speech: *Iliad* 6.264–5; *Iliad* 22.282

XXII. "encounter my force," ἀντιόω μένει
Speech: *Iliad* 6.127; *Iliad* 21.151; *Iliad* 21.430–1

XXIII. Non-formulaic usages in the nominative
Speech: *Iliad* 2.387; *Iliad* 5.472; *Iliad* 5.891–2; *Iliad* 6.100–1; *Iliad* 6.260–2; *Iliad*

240 Appendix: Force in Early Greek Hexameter

6.407; *Iliad* 7.457; *Iliad* 8.177–8; *Iliad* 8. 360–1; *Iliad* 10.479–80; *Iliad* 13.634–5; *Iliad* 15.493; *Iliad* 17.20; *Iliad* 17.156–7; *Iliad* 17.475; *Iliad* 17.502–3; *Iliad* 18.264; *Iliad* 19.202; *Iliad* 20.372; *Iliad* 21.410–11; *Iliad* 21.481–2; *Iliad* 21.488; *Iliad* 22.346; *Iliad* 22.459; *Iliad* 23.467–8
Narrative: *Iliad* 3.294; *Iliad* 5.506; *Iliad* 5.515–16; *Iliad* 5.523–5; *Iliad* 7.209–10;
Iliad 12.17–18; *Iliad* 17.742; *Iliad* 20.171–2; *Iliad* 20.374; *Iliad* 23.524–5; *Iliad* 24.6

Part II. *Menos* in the *Odyssey*

XXIV. μένος ἔμπεδον + verb "to be," "force is fixed/firm"
This formula seems to be a variation of the formula used with *biē*, which is more common. The *biē empedos* formula is used primarily as an optative of wish, demonstrating how "force is not fixed," especially for the figure of Nestor. The *menos empedon* formula occurs only with the positive indicative verb, reflecting the opposite sentiment of the more common formula. The formula is used only once in the *Iliad*, three times in the *Odyssey*.
Odyssey 19.493; *Odyssey* 21.426; *Odyssey* 22.226

XXV. *Menos* as a gift from the gods, placed inside the person
All four occurrences of *menos* as a gift in the *Odyssey* are by Athena, specifically with regard to paternal *menos*. See discussion in Collins 1998: 111–12; Bakker 2008.
Odyssey 1.88–9; *Odyssey* 1.321; *Odyssey* 2.270–1; *Odyssey* 24.520

XXVI. "pursuing their own *menos*," ἐπισπόμενοι μένεϊ σφῷ
Odyssey 14.262; *Odyssey* 17.431; *Odyssey* 24.183–4

XXVII. "unchecked in menos," μένος ἄσχετος
Odyssey 2.85; *Odyssey* 2.303; *Odyssey* 3.103–4; *Odyssey* 17.406; *Odyssey* 20.19

XXVII. Naming formula: *menos* + genitive name, used almost strictly of Alcinous. *Menos* means both "force" and is etymologically related to "mind" (*men-*). Hence the semantics of "force" and "mind" are also captured by Alcinous' very name.
μένος Ἀλκινόοιο at line end: *Odyssey* 7.167; *Odyssey* 7.178; *Odyssey* 8.2; *Odyssey* 8.4; *Odyssey* 8.385; *Odyssey* 8.421; *Odyssey* 8.423; *Odyssey* 13.20; *Odyssey* 13.24; *Odyssey* 13.49; *Odyssey* 13.64; *Odyssey* 18.34
Odyssey 8.359 (in reference to Hephaestus)

XXVIII. "Rousing *menos*"
Used only once in the Odyssey, many times in the *Iliad*.
Odyssey 8.15

XXIX. "fill with *menos*," πίμπλημι μένεος
Odyssey 4.661–662

XXX. "force and invincible hands," μένος καὶ χεῖρες ἄαπτοι
Used once in *Odyssey*, many times in the *Iliad*.
Odyssey 11.502

Appendix: Force in Early Greek Hexameter **241**

XXXI. "Nor could the wet *menos* of blowing winds penetrate it"
οὔτ᾽ ἀνέμων διάη μένος ὑγρὸν ἀέντων
Odyssey 5.478; *Odyssey* 19.440
XXXII. Non-formulaic uses of *menos*
Odyssey 7.2; *Odyssey* 9.457–8; *Odyssey* 10.160; *Odyssey* 11.220; *Odyssey* 11.270;
Odyssey 11.515; *Odyssey* 11.561–2; *Odyssey* 12.279; *Odyssey* 13.386–7; *Odyssey* 22.203; *Odyssey* 24.319

Part III. *Menos* in Hesiodic Poems and the *Homeric Hymns*

Theogony 324; *Theogony* 492–3; *Theogony* 562–3; *Theogony* 687–8; *Theogony* 832; *Theogony* 853; *Theogony* 869; *Theogony* 896; *Works and Days* 414; *Works and Days* 625; *Hymn to Demeter*, 239–40; *Hymn to Demeter* 361; *Hymn to Demeter* 368;
Hymn to Apollo 371–2; *Hymn to Apollo* 374; *Hymn to Aphrodite* (Hymn 6) 3–4; *Hymn to Ares* 14–15; *Shield of Heracles* 343; *Shield of Heracles* 446; *Shield of Heracles* 23; *Shield of Heracles* 364; *Shield of Heracles* 429

Sthenos

Sthenos may refer to a type of force that is less specifically tied to events and actions such as *biē* and *alkē* are, and it is also less directly tied to the vitality of life in the same way as *menos*. Overall, the term *sthenos* seems to refer to a more generic quality of strength (see *LfgrE* ad loc.; A. Nussbaum 1998). It is the general quality of strength that allows it to be paired with the more specific terms, including *kratos* and *alkē*, which entail more specific contexts and events, namely competition and battle. Sthenos is often used in reference to animals. The seemingly tautological formula, σθένος οὐκ ἀλαπαδνόν, "*sthenos* is not feeble" is used two out of three times in the *Iliad* in reference to animals in similes, and it takes on this same use in the *Odyssey* and Hesiod. In addition, three out of the five instances of the formula σθένεϊ βλεμεαίνων, "exulting in *sthenos*" are also in reference to animals. Unlike other terms for force, *sthenos* also refers to environmental entities such as rivers as well as Orion and Ocean. In this regard, *sthenos* might even be seen to convey a sense of "natural strength." To be sure, *alkē* is used of animals, but specifically those that are attacking or being attacked, and *menos* refers to elements of nature, but more specifically in reference to their activities. At the same time, however, *sthenos* cannot simply mean "natural strength" because it also refers to the presence of strength in non-biological beings such as the golden maidens of Hephaestus (*Iliad* 18.420). And like all other terms for force, *sthenos* is also an object given by the gods in specific instances, reflecting its role in the embodied economy shared between humans and gods. Thus, as I argue in Chapter 1, the uses of *sthenos*, along with *menos*, both convey a general quality of strength under the rubric of "nature-culture." This paradigm for *sthenos* is most present in *Iliad* 21 in Achilles' confrontations with both Asteropaeus and the river Scamander. *Sthenos* in the *Odyssey*,

242 Appendix: Force in Early Greek Hexameter

Hesiod, and the *Homeric Hymns* is consistent with its usage in the *Iliad*, often making use of the same formulas.

Part I. *Sthenos* in the *Iliad*

I. A god places *sthenos* in someone, ἐμβάλλω σθένος
   Narrative: *Iliad* 11.11; *Iliad* 14.151; *Iliad* 21.304

II. "Their force is not feeble," σθένος οὐκ ἀλαπαδνόν
   This formula would appear as though it were a tautology, but *sthenos* refers to the general notion of force, which may in turn have degrees of strength or weakness. It may also refer to a consistency of force which does not diminish. Hence, it is a claim for *sthenos* as a type of permanent condition.
   Speech: *Iliad* 8.463
   Narrative: *Iliad* 5.783; *Iliad* 7.257

III. "exulting (?) in force" [βλεμεαίνω of unknown meaning]
   Speech: *Iliad* 17.22
   Narrative: *Iliad* 8.337; *Iliad* 9.237; *Iliad* 12.42; *Iliad* 17.135; *Iliad* 20.36

IV. Formula, *kratos* and *sthenos* in dative
   Speech: *Iliad* 15.108; *Iliad* 17.329
   Narrative: *Iliad* 17.322

V. Filled with *alkē* and *sthenos*, πίμπλημι ἀλκῆς καὶ σθένεος
   Narrative: *Iliad* 17.211–12; *Iliad* 17.499

VI. "with great *sthenos*," σθένεϊ μεγάλῳ
   Speech: *Iliad* 12.224
   Narrative: *Iliad* 13.193

VII. "*sthenos* rises," σθένος ὄρνυμι
   Speech: *Iliad* 2.451; *Iliad* 11.827
   Narrative: *Iliad* 5.139

VIII. Naming formula, *sthenos* + name in genitive
   This is the rarest variant of the naming formula, used only twice in the Homeric corpus.
   Speech: *Iliad* 13.248
   Narrative: *Iliad* 23.827

IX. *Sthenos* of environmental figures
   Speech: *Iliad* 21.195
   Narrative: *Iliad* 18.486; *Iliad* 18.607

X. Non-formulaic occurrences of *sthenos*
   Speech: *Iliad* 8.32; *Iliad* 9.351–2; *Iliad* 13.678; *Iliad* 16.542; *Iliad* 17.751; *Iliad* 18.274; *Iliad* 20.361; *Iliad* 21.308
   Narrative: *Iliad* 18.419–20; *Iliad* 15.359

XI. Adjective: σθεναρός, -ή, -όν
   Speech: *Iliad* 9.505

XII. Adjective ἐρισθενή, "of great *sthenos*"
   Epithet of Zeus in the *Iliad*.
   Speech: *Iliad* 13.54; *Iliad* 21.184
   Narrative: *Iliad* 19.355

Appendix: Force in Early Greek Hexameter **243**

Part II. *Sthenos* in the *Odyssey*

XIII. Non-formulaic uses
Odyssey 8.135–6; *Odyssey* 8.289; *Odyssey* 18.373; *Odyssey* 21.282; *Odyssey* 22.237

Part III. *Sthenos* in Hesiodic Poems and the *Homeric Hymns*

XIV. Non-formulaic uses
Theogony 4; *Works and Days* 62; *Works and Days* 416; *Works and Days* 437; *Works and Days* 598; *Works and Days* 615; *Works and Days* 619; *Homeric Hymn to Apollo* 268; *Shield of Heracles* 97; *Shield of Heracles* 420

(W)is

(W)is is cognate with Latin *vis*, although the digamma is not always respected in early Greek hexameter (Chantraine 2009: 469; Beekes 2010: 598). It can refer to both bodily strength and occasionally environmental forces (*LfgrE* ad loc.). Both *(w)is* and *dynamis* are terms for force that are not expressly said to be given from the gods. Thus, *(w)is* is closest to a "natural" or "innate" notion of force. It most likely has a separate etymology from *(w)is*, *inos* referring to sinews or tendons (see Chantraine 2009: 468–9; Beekes 2010: 598–9), yet this does not prevent both roots from being associated with each other in Homeric poetry (on which see further Clarke 1999: 111–13). In the *Iliad*, the instrumental form appears with verbs of fighting, ruling, and domination, thus giving further indication to the alternate modes of power, physical and political. Other usage in the *Iliad* is generally non-formulaic and sparse. By contrast, in the *Odyssey*, *(w)is* appears with far greater frequency, with many of the same uses as in the *Iliad*. In addition, it occurs most frequently in the *Odyssey* as a naming formula, strictly in reference to Telemachus. Each of the moments of speech marked by the naming formula are unique occasions when Telemachus asserts himself, such that one is able to read the sequence of naming formulas as part of Telemachus' coming of age in the course of the *Odyssey*.

Part I. *(W)is* in the *Iliad*

I. Force of the winds, ἲς ἀνέμου/ἀνέμοιο
Narrative: *Iliad* 15.382–3; *Iliad* 17.739
II. Formula "unmeasurable force," ἲν᾽ ἀπέλεθρον
Speech: *Iliad* 5.245
Narrative: *Iliad* 7.269
III. Instrumental formula, "fighting with force," ἶφι μάχεσθαι
Speech: *Iliad* 1.151; *Iliad* 4.287; *Iliad* 5.606; *Iliad* 12.367; *Iliad* 18.14; *Iliad* 21.486
Narrative: *Iliad* 2.719–20

244   Appendix: Force in Early Greek Hexameter

    IV. Instrumental formula, "to rule with force," ἶφι ἀνάσσειν
        Speech: *Iliad* 1.37–8; *Iliad* 1.451–2; *Iliad* 6.477–8
    V. Formula, to conquer/be conquered with force, ἶφι δαμῆναι
        Speech: *Iliad* 19.416–17
        Narrative: *Iliad* 21.207–8
    VI. Non-formulaic uses of *(w)is*
        Speech: *Iliad* 11.668–9 *Iliad* 12.319–20; *Iliad* 21.356
        Narrative: *Iliad* 3.374–5; *Iliad* 23.719–20
    VII. Adjectival formula: "strong flocks," ἴφια μῆλα
        Speech: *Iliad* 8.505; *Iliad* 9.406; *Iliad* 9.466
        Narrative: *Iliad* 5.556; *Iliad* 8.545; *Iliad* 23.166

Part II. *(W)is* in the *Odyssey*

    VIII. Naming formula, "the sacred force of Telemachus," ἱερὴ ἴς Τηλεμάχοιο·
         Odyssey 2.409; *Odyssey* 16.476; *Odyssey* 18.60; *Odyssey* 18.405; *Odyssey*
         21.101
         Odyssey 21.130; *Odyssey* 22.354
    IX. Force of the winds, ἴς ἀνέμου/ἀνέμοιο
        Odyssey 9.71; *Odyssey* 13.276; *Odyssey* 19.186
    X. "unmeasurable force," ἶν᾽ ἀπέλεθρον (only once in the *Odyssey*)
        Odyssey 9.538
    XI. Instrumental formula, "rule with force," ἶφι ἀνάσσειν
        Odyssey 11.284; *Odyssey* 17.443
    XII. Instrumental formula, "conquer with force," ἶφι δαμῆναι
        Odyssey 18.57; *Odyssey* 18.156
    XIII. Non-formulaic occurrences of *(w)is* in the *Odyssey*
        Odyssey 11.393; *Odyssey* 12.175–6; *Odyssey* 18.3–4; *Odyssey* 21.281–2
    XIV. Adjectival formula, "strong flocks," ἴφια μῆλα
        Odyssey 11.108; *Odyssey* 12.128; *Odyssey* 12.263; *Odyssey* 12.322; *Odyssey*
        18.278; *Odyssey* 20.51; *Odyssey* 23.304

Part III. *(W)is* in the Hesiodic Poems and *Homeric Hymns*

    XV. Non-formulaic occurrences
        Theogony 332; *Theogony* 951; *Works and Days* 517–18; *Works and Days*
        541; *Shield of Heracles* 11
    XVI. Adjectival formula, "strong flocks," ἴφια μῆλα
        Hymn to Aphrodite 169

Dynamis

This term does not express physical force per se, but rather conveys the sense of
ability or potential (*LfgrE* ad loc.). This is made most obvious in the verb *dynamai*,

Appendix: Force in Early Greek Hexameter   245

which is far more frequent than the related noun form in early Greek hexameter. As "ability" or "potential," it is conceived as inherently limited and specific to the person. It is not supplemented by the gods in the same way as *kratos*, *biē*, *alkē*, and *sthenos*. At the same time, this fact also results in a more general trend where the expression of ability or potential in Homer, Hesiod, and the *Homeric Hymns* almost always occurs in the negative, explaining how someone is not able to do something. In the *Iliad*, the noun and verb are used in the negative forty-three times, only three times in the positive, and six times in conditional or independent optative constructions. Similarly, in the *Odyssey* the noun and verb are used thirty times in the negative, twelve times in the positive, and seven times in conditional or independent optative constructions. In Hesiod and the *Hymns*, it is used seven times in the negative and six times in the positive. Most of the positive expressions relate to the ability of the gods to accomplish all, in contrast to humans, especially in the *Odyssey*. As such, this overall trend in the verb *dynamai* and noun *dynamis* for expressing potential underscores an inherently negative outlook on the relationship between force and the human condition in early Greek hexameter.

Note: Because grammatical use has a significant impact on the overall semantics of *dynamis* and *dynamai*, occurrences here are categorized according to syntax.

Part I. *Dynamai, dynamis* in the *Iliad*

    I. Verb, negative indicative statements
       Speech: *Iliad* 1.241–2; *Iliad* 1.562–3; *Iliad* 1.588–9; *Iliad* 2.342–3; *Iliad* 3.236;
       Iliad 5.475; *Iliad* 6.100–1; *Iliad* 8.299; *Iliad* 9.351–2; *Iliad* 9.551–2; *Iliad* 13.729; *Iliad* 15.399–400; *Iliad* 15.416–17; *Iliad* 17.643; *Iliad* 18.62; *Iliad* 18.443; *Iliad* 19.136–7; *Iliad* 19.163–4; *Iliad* 21.357; *Iliad* 22.46–7; *Iliad* 23.462–3; *Iliad* 24.403–4
       Narrative: *Iliad* 3.451–2; *Iliad* 11.116–17; *Iliad* 11.120; *Iliad* 13.436; *Iliad* 13.510–11; *Iliad* 13.552–3; *Iliad* 13.607; *Iliad* 13.647; *Iliad* 13.687–8; *Iliad* 15.617; *Iliad* 16.107–8; *Iliad* 16.141–2; *Iliad* 16.509; *Iliad* 16.520–5; *Iliad* 18.161–2; *Iliad* 21.175; *Iliad* 21.218–20; *Iliad* 22.199–200; *Iliad* 23.719–20
    II. Verb, positive indicative statements
       Iliad 16.515–16; *Iliad* 23.465–6
    III. Verb, conditional statements
       Speech: *Iliad* 1.393–4; *Iliad* 14.196; *Iliad* 18.427; *Iliad* 20.360–1; *Iliad* 21.191–3
    IV. Verb, independent optative constructions
       Speech: *Iliad* 18.464–5
    V. Noun, *dynamis*, used in negative context
       Speech: *Iliad* 13.787–8; *Iliad* 8.294–5
    VI. Noun, *dynamis*, used in positive context
       Speech: *Iliad* 23.890–1
    VII. Noun, *dynamis*, used in conditional context
       Speech: *Iliad* 22.20

246 Appendix: Force in Early Greek Hexameter

Part II. *Dynamai, dynamis* in the *Odyssey*

VIII. Verb, negative indicative statements
Odyssey 1.78–9; *Odyssey* 1.250; *Odyssey* 2.191; *Odyssey* 3.89; *Odyssey* 3.235–8; *Odyssey* 4.373–4; *Odyssey* 4.467; *Odyssey* 4.558; *Odyssey* 5.15; *Odyssey* 5.319–20; *Odyssey* 9.27–8; *Odyssey* 9.304–5; *Odyssey* 10.246; *Odyssey* 10.291; *Odyssey* 12.232; *Odyssey* 12.392–3; *Odyssey* 13.331; *Odyssey* 14.445; *Odyssey* 16.126–7; *Odyssey* 16.238–9; *Odyssey* 17.303; *Odyssey* 17.144; *Odyssey* 18.230; *Odyssey* 18.241–2; *Odyssey* 19.157–8; *Odyssey* 19.478; *Odyssey* 21.171; *Odyssey* 21.246–7; *Odyssey* 21.253–6; *Odyssey* 21.403; *Odyssey* 23.106; *Odyssey* 24.159; *Odyssey* 24.170–1

IX. Verb, positive indicative statements
Odyssey 4.237; *Odyssey* 4.612; *Odyssey* 4.827–8; *Odyssey* 5.25; *Odyssey* 10.69; *Odyssey* 10.306; *Odyssey* 16.208; *Odyssey* 20.237; *Odyssey* 21.202; *Odyssey* 23.11; *Odyssey* 23.128

X. Verb, conditional statement
Odyssey 2.62; *Odyssey* 5.90; *Odyssey* 16.256–7

XI. Verb, independent optative constructions
Odyssey 4.388; *Odyssey* 4.644; *Odyssey* 9.523

XII. Participle construction, positive statement
Odyssey 1.276; *Odyssey* 11.414

XIII. Noun, *dynamis*
Odyssey 3.205

Part III. *Dynamai, dynamis* in the Hesiodic Poems and Homeric Hymns

XIV. Verb, negative indicative statement
Works and Days 214–15; *Hymn to Demeter* 329; *Hymn to Apollo* 192–3; *Hymn to Aphrodite* 7; *Hymn to Aphrodite* 33; *Hymn to Aphrodite* 234; *Hymn to Dionysos* (Hymn 7) 17–18

XV. Verb, positive indicative statements
Hymn to Hermes 175; *Hymn to Ares* 11

XVI. Noun, positive statements
Theogony 419–20; *Works and Days* 336; *Hymn to Hermes* 117; *Shield of Heracles* 354–5

Damazō/damnēmi

The basic sense in this verbal complex refers to the act of "subjugation" at varying social and physiological levels. It can be traced back to the Indo-European root *demh₂-*, hence it must be distinguished historically from the Indo-European root *domh₂-o-*, which is related to English "dominate" (Beekes 2010: 301; Benveniste

Appendix: Force in Early Greek Hexameter **247**

2016: 239–50; Chantraine 2009: 251; Chantraine 1948: 301). Unlike the other terms for force, occurrences of this root in the *Iliad* are equally distributed between narrative action and verbal performance. This more even distribution seems to be logical given the role of violence in the action of the *Iliad* as a whole. Furthermore, one may observe variations on the meaning of the verbal root in reference to subjugation, based on the object of the act of subjugation. Thus, when the verb applies to animals, subjugation refers to the act of "taming" or "breaking" the animal (see, for instance, *Iliad* 10.402–3, 17.76–7, 20.266). When women are the object, the act refers to general subjugation as in marriage or in enslavement (on which see *Iliad* 3.301, 18.432). And when the object of the verbal action is a male, it predominantly refers to the act of killing, but may occasionally refer to physical conquest that does not result in death (for the distinctions in meaning see Cunliffe ad loc. and *LfgrE* ad loc.). Furthermore, the grammatical uses of this verbal complex speak to a general perspective on the role of human agency in acts of subjugation and killing. The majority of uses appear in the passive form. When the active form of the verb is used, there are only eight occurrences where the nominative subject is a human agent of the act of subjugation (*Iliad* 9.496, 10.210, 10.411, 11.98, 12.186, 20.400, 21.90, 21.226). Otherwise, it is often a god expressed as the active subject of the verb with the human role in the act of killing relegated to an instrumental role. This is most clearly expressed in the speech of Zeus concerning the fate of Sarpedon (*Iliad* 16.433–8), in Patroclus' dying words to Hector (*Iliad* 16.844–54), and also in Achilles' threat to Hector when he claims, "Athena will kill you with my spear" (ἄφαρ δέ σε Παλλὰς Ἀθήνη/ ἔγχει ἐμῷ δαμάᾳ·) (*Iliad* 22.270–1). Thus on the one hand, this verb speaks to a broader theme of "co-agency" between human and divine in the poem. At the same time, this verbal root for violence also demonstrates in philological terms what both Simone Weil and Michel Foucault after her referred to as the "subjection of the human subject." See Chapter 4 for further discussion.

Part I. Verbal Root *dam-* in the *Iliad*

I. Formula: δουρὶ δαμ-, "killed by the spear," most often occurring at line end
Speech: *Iliad* 3.436; *Iliad* 5.653; *Iliad* 11.444; *Iliad* 11.749; *Iliad* 11.821; *Iliad* 16.848; *Iliad* 22.246
Narrative: *Iliad* 4.479; *Iliad* 16.816; *Iliad* 17.303

II. Flexible formula: χερσὶ/χείρεσσιν δαμ-, "killed by the hand"
The hand is used as the instrument of killing as a way to express agency of human involvement.
Speech: *Iliad* 3.352; *Iliad* 6.368; *Iliad* 10.310; *Iliad* 10.397; *Iliad* 10.452; *Iliad* 20.94; *Iliad* 20.143; *Iliad* 23.675
Narrative: *Iliad* 2.860; *Iliad* 2.874; *Iliad* 5.559; *Iliad* 5.564; *Iliad* 8.344; *Iliad* 15.2; *Iliad* 16.420; *Iliad* 16.438; *Iliad* 16.458; *Iliad* 16.854; *Iliad* 22.446

III. Flexible formula: ἔγχεϊ + δαμ-, "killed by the spear"
Variant of δουρὶ δαμ-.
Speech: *Iliad* 16.542; *Iliad* 22.270–1

248   Appendix: Force in Early Greek Hexameter

IV. Flexible formula: βέλος + δαμ- "the arrow/projectile killed…"
Speech: *Iliad* 5.278
Narrative: *Iliad* 5.10; *Iliad* 11.478 (ὀϊστός); *Iliad* 14.439; *Iliad* 16.811–12

V. Formula: ἀναλκείῃσι δαμ-, "overcome by weakness"
Speech: *Iliad* 17.337
Narrative: *Iliad* 6.74; *Iliad* 17.32

VI. Formula: οἳ δ᾿ ἀλεγεινοὶ/ ἀνδράσι γε θνητοῖσι δαμήμεναι ἠδ᾿ ὀχέεσθαι,
"[The horses] are difficult for mortal men to break and drive"
In reference to the horses of Achilles.
Speech: *Iliad* 10.402–3; *Iliad* 17.76–7
Narrative: *Iliad* 20.266

VII. Formula: μηδ᾿ οὕτω Τρώεσσιν ἔα δάμνασθαι Ἀχαιούς, "Do not allow the
Achaeans to be killed by the Trojans"
Speech: *Iliad* 8.244; *Iliad* 15.376

VIII. Flexible formula: Τρωσὶν/ Τρώεσσι δαμ-, "killed by the Trojans"
Speech: *Iliad* 13.98; *Iliad* 18.461
Narrative: *Iliad* 13.16; *Iliad* 13.353; *Iliad* 13.668; *Iliad* 17.2

IX. Formula: δαμάσαντό γ᾿ Ἀχαιούς, "killed the Achaeans"
Speech: *Iliad* 10.210; *Iliad* 10.411

X. Formula: δάμασσε δέ μιν μεμαῶτα, "he killed him in his fury"
Narrative: *Iliad* 11.98; *Iliad* 12.186; *Iliad* 20.400

XI. Flexible formula: μοῖρα δαμ-, "fate kills"
Speech: *Iliad* 16.433; *Iliad* 16.853–4; *Iliad* 17.421; *Iliad* 18.119

XII. Formula: θυμὸν ἐνὶ στήθεσσι φίλον δαμάσαντες ἀνάγκῃ, "having conquered the spirit in our chests by necessity"
Speech: *Iliad* 18.112; *Iliad* 19.65; *Iliad* 9.495 (flexible variant)

XIII. Formula: ἶφι δαμ-, "killed with force"
Speech: *Iliad* 19.417
Narrative: *Iliad* 21.208

XIV. Flexible formula: Πηλεΐωνι/ Πηλεΐδῃ δαμ-, "killed by the son of Peleus"
Speech: *Iliad* 20.294; *Iliad* 20.312; *Iliad* 22.39; *Iliad* 22.175

XV. Flexible formula: Διὸς μάστιγι δαμ-, "broken by the whip of Zeus"
Speech: *Iliad* 13.812
Narrative: *Iliad* 12.37

XVI. Formula: ὑπὸ γούνατ᾿ ἐδάμνα, "conquered the knees"
Narrative: *Iliad* 21.52; *Iliad* 21.270

XVII. Formula: βριθὺ μέγα στιβαρόν, τῷ δάμνῃσι στίχας ἀνδρῶν, "a great heavy
spear, with which she kills the ranks of men"
Narrative: *Iliad* 5.745; *Iliad* 8.389

XVIII. Non-formulaic occurrences of δαμ-
Speech: *Iliad* 1.61; *Iliad* 3.301; *Iliad* 3.429; *Iliad* 5.191; *Iliad* 5.391; *Iliad*
5.893; *Iliad* 6.159; *Iliad* 7.72; *Iliad* 9.118; *Iliad* 9.545; *Iliad* 12.403; *Iliad*
14.199; *Iliad* 14.316; *Iliad* 16.561; *Iliad* 16.845; *Iliad* 18.432–3; *Iliad* 19.9;
Iliad 19.203; *Iliad* 21.90; *Iliad* 21.226; *Iliad* 21.291; *Iliad* 22.55; *Iliad* 22.379
Narrative: *Iliad* 5.138; *Iliad* 13.434; *Iliad* 13.603; *Iliad* 14.353; *Iliad*
15.476; *Iliad* 15.522; *Iliad* 16.103; *Iliad* 16.326; *Iliad* 16.826; *Iliad* 21.383;
Iliad 21.401; *Iliad* 21.578; *Iliad* 23.655

Appendix: Force in Early Greek Hexameter **249**

Part II. Verbal Root δαμ- in the *Odyssey*

XIX. Formula: ἀλλ' ὁ μὲν ἤδη κηρὶ δαμεὶς Ἀϊδόσδε βεβήκει, "but he already killed by fate, went to Hades"
Odyssey 3.410; *Odyssey* 6.10

XX. Formula: βριθὺ μέγα στιβαρόν, τῷ δάμνησι στίχας ἀνδρῶν
Odyssey 1.99
See also *Iliad* 5.746; *Iliad* 8.398

XXI. Formula: πολλοὶ μὲν γὰρ τῶν γε δάμεν, πολλοὶ δὲ λίποντο, "many were killed, and many left behind"
Odyssey 4.495. Compare with *Iliad* 12.13

XXII. Formula: νηυσὶ δαμ-, "conquered at the ships"
Odyssey 4.499. Compare with *Iliad* 7.71

XXIII. Flexible formula: θυμόν δαμ-, "conquer spirit"
Compare with *Iliad* 9.495; 18.112; 19.65
Odyssey 5.468; *Odyssey* 11.562

XXIV. Formula: δαμ- Ἀχαιούς, "kill the Achaeans" at line end
Odyssey 9.59. Compare with *Iliad* 6.368; 8.244; 10.210; 10.411; 15.376

XXV. Formula: εἴ χ' ὑπ' ἐμοί γε θεὸς δαμάσῃ μνηστῆρας ἀγαυούς, "if god kills the haughty suitors for me"
Odyssey 19.488; *Odyssey* 19.496; *Odyssey* 21.213
See also *Odyssey* 24.100

XXVI. Flexible formula: εἴ... δάμη, "if he was killed"
Odyssey 1.237; *Odyssey* 3.90

XVII. Flexible formula: μοῖρα δαμ-
Odyssey 3.269. Compare with *Iliad* 16.433; 16.853; 17.421; 18.119

XVIII. Flexible formula: πληγῇσιν δαμ-, " conquered by blows"
Odyssey 4.244; *Odyssey* 18.54

XXIX. Formula: ἶφι δαμ-, "conquered/killed by force"
Odyssey 18.57; *Odyssey* 18.156

XXX. Formula: ὑπὸ μνηστῆρσιν δαμ-, "killed by the suitors"
Odyssey 4.790; *Odyssey* 17.252

XXXI. Non-formulaic occurrences of δαμ- in the *Odyssey*
Odyssey 4.397; *Odyssey* 4.637; *Odyssey* 9.454; *Odyssey* 11.220–1; *Odyssey* 14.367; *Odyssey* 14.487–8; *Odyssey* 17.24–5; *Odyssey* 23.310

Part III. δαμ- in Hesiod and the *Homeric Hymns*

XXXII. Formula: χερσὶ δαμ-, "conquered/killed at the hands"
Theogony 490; *Works and Days* 152; *Shield of Heracles* 11

XXXIII. Flexible formula: πληγῇσιν δαμ-, "conquered by blows"
Theogony 857

XXXIV. Non-formulaic occurrences of δαμ- in Hesiod and the *Homeric Hymns*
Theogony 122; *Theogony* 464; *Theogony* 865; *Hymn to Aphrodite* 17; *Hymn to Aphrodite* 251

References

Acampora, C. 2013. *Contesting Nietzsche*. Chicago.

Adkins, A. W. H. 1960. *Merit and Responsibility: A Study in Greek Values*. Oxford.

Adkins, A. W. H. 1970. *From the Many to the One: A Study of Personality and Views of Human Nature in the Context of Ancient Greek Society, Values, and Beliefs*. London.

Adkins, A. W. H. 1975. "Art, Beliefs, and Values in the Later Books of the *Iliad*." *Classical Philology* 70: 239–54.

Alden, M. 2000. *Homer beside Himself: Para-Narratives in the Iliad*. Oxford.

Allan, W. 2005. "Arms and the Man: Euphorbus, Hector, and the Death of Patroclus." *The Classical Quarterly* 55.1: 1–16.

Allan, W. and D. Cairns. 2011. "Conflict and Community in the *Iliad*." *Competition in the Ancient Word*, ed. N. Fisher and H. van Wees. Swansea: 113–46.

Allen-Hornblower, E. 2016. *From Agent to Spectator: Witnessing the Aftermath in Ancient Greek Epic and Tragedy*. Berlin.

Andersen, Ø. 1977. *Die Diomedesgestalt in der Ilias*. Oslo.

Angermüller, J. 2014. *Poststructuralist Discourse Analysis: Subjectivity in Enunciative Pragmatics*. New York.

Angermuller, J. 2015. *Why There Is No Poststructuralism in France: The Making of an Intellectual Generation*. London.

Arthur [Katz], M. 1982. "Cultural Strategies in Hesiod's *Theogony*: Law, Family, and Society." *Arethusa* 15: 63–82.

Austin, J. L. 1962. *How to Do Things with Words*. Oxford.

Austin, N. 1975. *Archery at the Dark of the Moon: Poetic Problems in Homer's Odyssey*. Berkeley.

Bakker, E. 2005. *Pointing at the Past: From Formula to Performance in Homeric Poetics*. Cambridge, MA.

Bakker, E. 2008. "Epic Remembering." *Orality, Literacy, Memory in the Ancient Greek and Roman World*, ed. A. Mackay. *Orality and Literacy in Ancient Greece*, Vol. 7: 65–78.

Bakker, E. 2013. *The Meaning of Meat and the Structure of the Odyssey*. Cambridge.

Bakker, E. 2017. "Hector and the Race Horse: The Telescopic Vision of the *Iliad*." *The Winnowing Oar: New Perspectives on Homeric Studies*, ed. Chr. Tsagalis and A. Markantonatos. Berlin: 57–74.

Balibar, E. 2003. "Structuralism: A Destitution of the Subject?" *Differences: A Journal of Feminist Cultural Studies* 14.1: 1–7.

Baracchi, C. 2011. "Force." in Political Concepts, 1. <http://www.politicalconcepts. org/issue%201/force.>

Barker, E. 2009. *Entering the Agōn: Dissent and Authority in Homer, Historiography, and Tragedy*. Oxford.

Barringer, J. 1996. "Atalanta as Model: The Hunter and the Hunted." *Classical Antiquity* 15.1: 48–76.

252 References

Beck, D. 2005. *Homeric Conversation*. Washington, D.C.

Beck, D. 2012. *Speech Presentation in Homeric Epic*. Austin.

Beekes, R. 2010. *Etymological Dictionary of Greek*. Leiden.

Beidelman, T. O. 1989. "Agonistic Exchange: Homeric Reciprocity and the Heritage of Simmel and Mauss." *Cultural Anthropology* 4.3: 227–59.

Benardete, S. 2000. *The Argument of the Action: Essays on Greek Poetry and Philosophy*. Chicago.

Benfey, C. 2005. "Introduction." *War and the Iliad: Simone Weil and Rachel Bespaloff*, ed. C. Benfey. New York: vii–xix.

Bennington, G. 1993. *Jacques Derrida*. Chicago.

Bennington, G. 1999. *Jacques Derrida*. Chicago.

Benveniste, É. 1970. "L'appareil formel de l'énonciation." *Langages* 5.17: 12–18.

Benveniste, É. 1971. *Problems in General Linguistics*. Coral Gables, FL.

Benveniste, É. 2016. *Dictionary of Indo-European Concepts and Society*. Trans. E. Palmer. Chicago.

Bernabé, A., ed. 1996. *Poetae Epici Graeci. Testimonia et Fragmenta*. Vol.1. Leipzig.

Bernadete, S. 2000. *The Argument of the Action*. Chicago.

Bianchi, E., S. Brill, and B. Holmes, eds. 2019. *Antiquities beyond Humanism*. Oxford.

Bloch, R. S. 1997. "Bia." *Der Neue Pauly*, Band II. Stuttgart & Weimar: 615–16.

Bolens, G. 2000. *La logique du corps articulaire: les articulations du corps humain dans la littérature occidentale*. Rennes.

Bollenbeck, G. 1994. *Bildung und Kultur: Glanz und Elend eines deutschen Deutungsmusters*. Frankfurt.

Bonifazi, A. 2008. "Memory and Visualization in Homeric Discourse Markers." *Orality, Literacy, Memory in the Ancient Greek and Roman World*, ed. E. A. Mackay. Leiden: 35–64.

Bourdieu, P. 1977. *Outline of a Theory of Practice*. Cambridge.

Bourdieu, P. 1991. *Language and Symbolic Power*. Ed. J. B. Thompson, trans. G. Raymond and M. Adamson. Cambridge, MA.

Bouvier, D. 2002. *Le sceptre et la lyre: l'Iliade ou les héros de la mémoire*. Grenoble.

Braidotti, R. 2013. *The Posthuman*. Cambridge.

Braidotti, R. 2018. "A Theoretical Framework for Critical Posthumanities." *Theory Culture and Society. Transversal Posthumanities*. Special edition. May: 1–31.

Brouillet, M. 2016. *Des chants en partage: l'epopée homerique comme expérience religieuse*. Paris.

Brouillet, M. 2019. "Le discours d'un roi: de la dénégation de responsabilité à l'agentivité partagée dans les excuses d'Agamemnon." *Cahiers des mondes anciens* 12. <https://journals.openedition.org/mondesanciens/2227>

Brown, B. K. M. 2016. *The Mirror of Epic: The Iliad and History*. Berrima, NSW.

Brown, C. 1989. "Ares, Aphrodite, and the Laughter of the Gods." *Phoenix* 43: 283–93.

Brown, R. L. 1967. *Wilhelm von Humboldt's Conception of Linguistic Relativity*. Paris.

Brügger, C. 2016. *Homers Ilias*, Band IX: *Sechzehnter Gesang (Π)*, Faszikel 2: *Kommentar*. Berlin/Boston.

Brügger, C., M. Stoevesandt, and E. Visser. 2010. *Homers Ilias. Zweiter Gesang (B)*, Faszikel 2: *Kommentar*. Berlin/Boston.

Buchan, M. 2012. *Perfidy and Passion: Reintroducing the Iliad*. Madison, WI.

Buck, C. D. 1949. *A Dictionary of Selected Synonyms in the Indo-European Languages*. Chicago.

References **253**

Burckhardt, J. 1998. *The Greeks and Greek Civilization*. Ed. O. Murray, trans. S. Stern. London.

Burgess, J. S. 2001. *The Tradition of the Trojan War in Homer and the Epic Cycle*. Baltimore.

Burgess, J. S. 2009. *The Death and Afterlife of Achilles*. Baltimore.

Burgess, J. S. 2012. "Intertextuality without Text in Early Greek Epic." *Relative Chronology in Early Greek Epic Poetry*, ed. Øivind Andersen and Dag Haug. Cambridge: 168–82.

Burkert, W. 1985. *Greek Religion: Archaic and Classical*. Oxford.

Burkert, W. 1992. *The Orientalizing Revolution: Near Eastern Influences on Greek Culture in the Early Archaic Age*. Cambridge, MA.

Burkert, W. 2004. "Mikroskopie der Geistesgeschichte: Bruno Snells *Entdeckung des Geistes* im kritischen Rückblick." *Philologus* 148: 168–82.

Butler, J. 1997. *Excitable Speech: A Politics of the Performative*. New York.

Cairns, D. 1993. *Aidōs: The Psychology and Ethics of Honour and Shame in Ancient Greek Literature*. Oxford.

Cairns, D. 2017. "Homeric Values and the Virtues of Kingship." *The Homeric Epics and the Chinese Book of Songs: Foundation Texts Compared*, ed. F.-H. Mutschler. Newcastle: 381–409.

Calame, C. 1995. *The Craft of Poetic Speech in Ancient Greece*. Trans. J. Orion. Ithaca, NY.

Calame, C. 1997. *Choruses of Young Women in Ancient Greece*. Trans. D. Collins and J. Orion. Ithaca, NY.

Calame, C. 2009. *Poetic and Performative Memory in Ancient Greece: Heroic Reference and Ritual Gestures in Time and Space*. Trans. H. Patton. Washington, D.C.

Calame, C. 2016. "Sujet de désir et sujets de discours Foucauldiens: la sexualité face aux relations érotiques de Grecques et Grecs." *Foucault, sexualité, l'antiquité*, ed. S. Boehringer and D. Lorenzini. Paris: 99–118.

Canevaro, L. G. 2018. *Women of Substance in Homeric Epic: Objects, Gender, Agency*. Oxford.

Carlier, P. 1984. *La royauté en Grèce avant Alexandre*. Strasbourg.

Cartledge, P. 2009. *Ancient Greek Political Thought in Practice*. Cambridge.

Casali, S. 2010. "The Development of the Aeneas Legend." *A Companion to Vergil's Aeneid and its Tradition*, ed. J. Farrell and M. C. J. Putnam. Chichester, West Sussex: 37–51.

Casewitz, M. 1992. Sur le concept de "peuple." *La langue et les textes en grec ancien: actes du colloque Pierre Chantraine*, ed. F. Létoublon. Amsterdam: 193–200.

Cassin, B. 2016. *Nostalgia: When Are We ever at Home?* Trans. P.-A. Brault. New York.

Chantraine, P. 1948. *Grammaire homérique*. Paris.

Chantraine, P. 2009. *Dictionnaire étymologique de la langue grecque: histoire des mots*. Paris.

Christensen, J. 2009. "The End of Speeches and a Speech's End: Nestor, Diomedes, and the *telos muthōn*." *Reading Homer: Film and Text*, ed. K. Myrsiades. Cranbury, NJ: 136–162.

Christensen, J. 2015. "Reconsidering 'Good' Speakers: Speech-Act Theory, Agamemnon and the Diapeira of *Iliad* 2." *GAIA* 18.1: 67–81.

254 References

Christensen, J. and E. Barker. 2011. "On Not Remembering Tydeus: Agamemnon, Diomedes and the Contest for Thebes." *Materiali e Discussioni per l'Analisi dei Testi Classici* 66.1: 9–44.

Christesen, P. 2012. *Sport and Democracy in the Ancient and Modern Worlds.* New York.

Church, J. 2012. *Infinite Autonomy: The Divided Individual in the Political Thought of G. W. F. Hegel and Friedrich Nietzsche.* University Park, PA.

Clarke, M. 1999. *Flesh and Spirit in the Songs of Homer: A Study of Words and Myths.* Oxford.

Clay, J. S. 1983. *The Wrath of Athena: Gods and Men in the Odyssey.* Princeton, NJ.

Clay, J. S. 1989. *The Politics of Olympus: Form and Meaning in the Major Homeric Hymns.* Princeton, NJ.

Clay, J. S. 2002. "Dying Is Hard to Do." *Colby Quarterly* 38: 7–16.

Clay, J. S. 2003. *Hesiod's Cosmos.* Cambridge.

Clay, J. S. 2007. "Art, Nature, and the Gods in the Chariot Race of *Iliad* Ψ." *Contests and Rewards in the Homeric Epics: Proceedings of the 10th International Symposium on the Odyssey*, ed. M. Paizi-Apostopoulou, A. Rengakos, and C. Tsagalis. Ithaca, Greece: 69–75.

Clay, J. S. 2009. "How to Be a Hero: The Case of Sarpedon." *Antiphilēsis*, ed. E. Karamalengou and E. Makrygianni. Stuttgart: 30–8.

Cole, T. 1983. "Archaic Truth." *Quaderni Urbinati di Cultura Classica* 13.1: 7–28.

Collins, D. 1998, *Immortal Armor: The Concept of Alkē in Archaic Greek Poetry.* Lanham, MD.

Combellack, F. M. 1948. "Speakers and Scepters in Homer." *Classical Journal* 43: 209–17.

Considine, P. 1985. "The Indo-European Origin of Greek MHNIS." *Transactions of the Philological Society* 83.1: 144–70.

Cook, E. 2003. "Agamemnon's Test of the Army in *Iliad* Book 2 and the Function of Homeric *Akhos*." *American Journal of Philology* 124.2: 165–98.

Cook, E. 2009. "On the Importance of *Iliad* Book 8." *Classical Philology* 104.2: 133–61.

Cook, E. 2016. "Homeric Reciprocities." *Journal of Mediterranean Archaeology* 29: 94–104.

Coray, M. 2009. *Homers Ilias*, Band VI: *Neunzehnter Gesang (T)*, Faszikel 2: *Kommentar.* Berlin/Boston.

Coray, M. and M. Krieter-Spiro, eds. 2021. *Homers Ilias, Gesamt Kommentar*, Band XIV: *Einundzwanzigster Gesang.* Berlin/Boston.

Cornford, F. M. 1912. *From Religion to Philosophy. A Study in the Origins of Western Speculation.* London.

Cunliffe, R. J. 2012. *A Lexicon of the Homeric Dialect.* Norman, OK.

Currie, B. 2012. "Hesiod on Human History." *Greek Notions of the Past in the Archaic and Classical Eras*, ed. J. Marincola, L. Llewellyn- Jones, and C. Maciver. Edinburgh: 35–64.

Cusset, F. 2008. *French Theory: How Foucault, Derrida, Deleuze, & Co. Transformed the Intellectual Life of the United States.* Trans. J. Fort. Minneapolis.

Derrida, J. 1972. "Structure, Sign, and Play in the Discourse of the Human Sciences." *The Structuralist Controversy: The Languages of Criticism and the Sciences of Man*, ed. R. Macksey and E. Donato. Baltimore: 247–72.

References   255

Derrida, J. 1978. *Writing and Difference*. Trans. A. Bass. *Chicago*.

Derrida, J. 1981a. *Positions*. Trans. A. Bass. Chicago.

Derrida, J. 1981b. "Plato's Pharmacy." *Dissemination*, trans. B. Johnson. Chicago: 61–171.

Derrida, J. 1982. *Margins of Philosophy*. Trans. A. Bass. London.

Derrida, J. 1986. *Glas*. Trans. J. P. Leavey Jr. and R. Rand. Lincoln, NE.

Derrida, J. 1997. *The Politics of Friendship*. Trans. G. Collins. London.

Derrida, J. 2005. *Rogues: Two Essays on Reason*. Trans. P.-A. Brault and M. Naas. Stanford.

Derrida, J. 2009. *The Beast and the Sovereign*, Vol. 1. Trans. G. Bennington. Chicago.

Derrida, J. 2010. "We Other Greeks." *Derrida and Antiquity*, ed. M. Leonard, trans. M. Naas. Oxford: 17–42.

Descola, P. 2013. *Beyond Nature and Culture*. Trans. J. Lloyd. Chicago.

Descombes, V. 1980. *Modern French Philosophy*. Trans. L. Scott-Fox and J. M. Harding. Cambridge.

Dessons, G. 2006. *Émile Benveniste, l'invention du discours*. Paris.

Detienne, M. 1996. *The Masters of Truth in Archaic Greece*. Trans. J. Lloyd. New York.

Detienne, M. and J.-P. Vernant. 1978. *Cunning Intelligence in Greek Culture and Society*. Trans. J. Lloyd. Hassocks.

Dickson, K. 1995. *Nestor: Poetic Memory in Greek Epic*. New York.

Dietrich, B. C. 1979. "Views of Homeric Gods and Religion." *Numen* 26: 126–51.

Diller, Hans. 1956. "Der vorphilosophische Gebrauch von κόσμος und κοσμεῖν." *Festschrift Bruno Snell zum 60 Geburtstag am 18 Juni 1956 von Freuden und Schülern uberreicht*. Munich: 47–60.

Dodds, E. R. 1951. *The Greeks and the Irrational*. Sather Classical Lectures 25. Berkeley.

Doering, J. E. 2010. *Simone Weil and the Spectre of Self-Perpetuating Force*. Notre Dame, IN.

Donlan, W. 1985. "The Social Groups of Dark Age Greece." *Classical Philology* 80.4: 293–308.

Donlan, W. 2007. Kin-Groups in the Homeric Epics. *Classical World* 101.1: 29–39.

Dosse, F. 1997a. *History of Structuralism*, Vol. 1: *The Rising Sign*. Trans. D. Glassman. Minneapolis.

Dosse, F. 1997b. *History of Structuralism*, Vol. 2: *The Sign Sets*. Trans. D. Glassman. Minneapolis.

Dova, S. 2020. *The Poetics of Failure in Ancient Greece*. Routledge.

Dufaye, L. and L. Gournay, eds. 2013. *Benveniste après un demi-siècle: regards sur l'énonciation aujourd'hui*. Paris.

Dumézil, G. 1943. *Servius et la fortune: essai sur la fonction sociale de louange et de blâme et sur les éléments indo-européens du cens romain*. Paris.

Dumont, L. 1980. *Homo Hierarchicus: The Caste System and its Implications*. Trans. M. S. Sainsbury, L. Dumont, and B. Gulati. Chicago.

Dumont, L. 1986. *Essays on Individualism: Modern Ideology in Anthropological Perspective*. Chicago.

Dumont, L. 1994. *German Ideology: From France to Germany and Back*. Chicago.

Dunkle, R. 1981. "Some Notes on the Funeral Games, *Iliad* 23." *Prometheus* 7: 11–18.

Dunkle, Roger. 1987. "Nestor, Odysseus, and the μῆτις-βίη Antithesis: The Funeral Games, *Iliad* 23." *The Classical World* 81.1: 1–17.

256 References

Easterling, P. E. 1989. "Agamemnon's Skeptron in the *Iliad*: Images of Authority." *Papers Presented to Joyce Reynolds on the Occasion of her Seventieth Birthday*, ed. M. Mary Margaret and R. Charlotte. *Cambridge Philolological Society Supplement* 16: 104–21.

Ebert, J. 1969. "Die Gestalt des Thersites in der *Ilias*." *Philologus* 113.1: 159–75.

Edwards, M. 1987. *Homer, Poet of the Iliad*. Baltimore.

Edwards, M. 1991. *The Iliad: A Commentary*, V: *Books 17–20*. Cambridge.

Egan, R. 2007. "How the Pentathlon Was Won: Two Pragmatic Models and the Evidence of Philostratus." *Phoenix* 61.1: 39–54.

Elmer, D. 2010. "Kita and Kosmos: The Poetics of Ornamentation in Bosniac and Homeric Epic." *Journal of American Folklore* 123.489: 276–303.

Elmer, D. 2013. *The Poetics of Consent: Collective Decision Making and the Iliad*. Baltimore.

Elmer, D. 2015. "The 'Narrow Road' and the Ethics of Language Use in the *Iliad* and the *Odyssey*." *Ramus* 44.1–2: 155–83.

Erbse, H. 1986. *Untersuchungen zur Funktion der Götter im homerischen Epos*. New York.

Everett, C. 2013. *Linguistic Relativity: Evidence across Languages and Cognitive Domains*. Berlin.

Faraone, C. 2012. "The Many and the One: Imagining the Beginnings of Political Power in the Hesiodic Theogony." *Archiv für Religionsgeschichte* 13, special issue: *Imagined Beginnings: The Poetics and Politics of Cosmogonic Discourse in the Ancient World*, ed. C. Faraone and B. Lincoln: 37–50.

Faulkner, A. 2008. "The Legacy of Aphrodite: Anchises' Offspring in the Homeric Hymn to Aphrodite." *American Journal of Philology* 129.1: 1–18.

Ferber, M. 1981. "Simone Weil's *Iliad*." *Simone Weil: Interpretations of a Life*, ed. G. A. White. Amherst: 63–85.

Ferry, L. and A. Renaut. 1985. *La pensée '68: essai sur l'antihumanisme contemporain*. Paris.

Finglass, P. 2011. *Sophocles: Ajax*. Cambridge.

Finkelberg, M. 1986. "Is *Kleos Aphthiton* a Homeric Formula?" *Classical Quarterly* 36.1: 1–5.

Finkelberg, M. 1998. "*Timē* and *Aretē* in Homer." *The Classical Quarterly* 48.1: 14–28.

Finkelberg, M. 2007. "More on *Kleos Aphthiton*." *The Classical Quarterly* 57.2: 341–50.

Finley, M. 1954. *The World of Odysseus*. New York.

Fletcher, J. 2013. "Weapons of Friendship: Props in Sophocles' *Philoctetes* and *Ajax*." *Performance in Greek and Roman Theatre*, ed. G. Harrison and V. Liapis. Leiden: 199–215.

Foley, J. M. 1991. *Immanent Art: From Structure to Meaning in Traditional Oral Epic*. Bloomington, IN.

Ford, A. L. 1992. *Homer: The Poetry of the Past*. Ithaca, NY.

Forte, A. S. W. 2019. "The Disappearing Turn of *Iliad* 23.373." *Classical Philology* 114: 120–5.

Foucault, M. 1977. "The Political Function of the Intellectual." *Radical Philosophy* 17: 12–14.

Foucault, M. 1982. "The Subject and Power." *Michel Foucault: Beyond Structuralism and Hermeneutics*, ed. H. L. Drefuys and P. Rabinow. Chicago: 208–26.

References 257

Foucault, M. 1998. *Aesthetics, Method, and Epistemology: Essential Works of Foucault, 1954–1984.* Ed. J. D. Faubion. New York.

Foucault, M. 2000. "Truth and Juridical Forms." *Power: Essential Works of Foucault 1954–1984,* Vol. 3, ed. J. E. Faubian, trans. Robert Hurley. New York: 1–89.

Foucault, M. 2002. *The Order of Things: An Archaeology of the Human Sciences.* Trans. A. Sheridan. London.

Foucault, M. 2013. *Lectures on the Will to Know and Oedipal Knowledge: Lectures at the Collège de France 1970–1971.* Eds. D. Defert, A. I. Davidson, trans. G. Burchell. London.

Foucault, M. 2014. *Wrong-Doing, Truth-Telling: The Function of Avowal in Justice.* Eds. F. Brion and B. E. Harcourt, trans. S. W. Sawyer. Chicago.

Foucault, M. 2022. "Linguistics and Social Sciences." Trans. and ed. J. Schroeder. *Theory, Culture & Society.* https://journals.sagepub.com/doi/10.1177/02632764221091549.

Fraisse, S., ed. 1989. *Simone Weil: Oeuvres complètes,* II.3: *Écrits historiques et politiques.* Paris.

Frame, D. 1978. *The Myth of Return in Early Greek Epic.* New Haven.

Frame, D. 2009. *Hippota Nestor.* Washington, D.C.

Franco, Cristiana. 2014. *Shameless: The Canine and the Feminine in Ancient Greece.* Trans. M. Fox. Oakland, CA.

Frank, S. 2016. "The 'Force in the Thing': Mauss' Nonauthoritarian Sociality in *The Gift.*" *HAU: Journal of Ethnographic Theory* 6.2: 255–77.

Fränkel, H. 1975. *Early Greek Poetry and Philosophy.* Trans. M. Hadas and J. Willis. New York.

Gagarin, M. 1986. *Early Greek Law.* Berkeley.

Gagarin, Michael. 1983. "Antilochus' Strategy: The Chariot Race in *Iliad* 23." *Classical Philology* 78.1: 35–9.

Gagné, R. 2015. "Literary Evidence: Poetry." *Oxford Handbook of Ancient Greek Religion,* ed. E. Eidinow and J. Kindt. Oxford: 83–96.

Gagné, R. and M. H. de Jáuregui. 2019. "Sauver les dieux." *Les Dieux d'Homère,* Vol. 2. Liège: 7–42.

Gane, N. 2006. "When We Have Never Been Human, What Is to Be Done? Interview with Donna Haraway." *Theory, Culture, and Society* 23.7–8: 135–58.

García, J. F. 2002. "Symbolic Action in the Homeric Hymns: The Theme of Recognition." *Classical Antiquity* 21.1: 5–39.

Garcia, L. F. 2013. *Homeric Durability. Telling Time in the Iliad.* Washington, D.C.

García Ramón, José Luis. 2010. "Hethitisch *nakkī-* und homerisch $\varphi\acute{\epsilon}\rho\iota\sigma\tau\sigma\varsigma$: Avestisch [°]*bairišta-,* homerisch $\varphi\acute{\epsilon}\rho\tau\epsilon\rho\sigma\varsigma$, $\varphi\acute{\epsilon}\rho\tau\alpha\tau\sigma\varsigma$." *Investigationes Anatolicae: Gedenkschrift für Erich Neu,* ed. J. Klinger, E. Rieken, and C. Rüster. Wiesbaden: 73–89.

Gavrylenko, V. 2012. "The Body without Skin in the Homeric Poems." *Blood, Sweat, and Tears: The Changing Concepts of Physiology from Antiquity into Early Modern Europe,* ed. M. Horstmanshoff, H. King, and C. Zittel. Leiden: 479–502.

Geeraerts, D. 2010. *Theories of Lexical Semantics.* Oxford.

Gernet, L. 1955. *Droit et société dans la Grèce ancienne.* Paris.

Gernet, L. 1968. *Anthropologie de la Grèce antique.* Paris.

Gernet, L. and A. Boulanger. 1969. *Le genie grec dans la religion.* Paris.

258 References

Gigon, O. 1945. *Der Ursprung der griechischen Philosophie: Von Hesiod bis Parmenides*. Basel.

Gilbert, S., J. Sapp, and A. Tauber. 2012. "A Symbiotic View of Life: We Have Never Been Individuals." *The Quarterly Review of Biology* 87.4: 325–41.

Gill, C. 1996. *Personality in Greek Epic, Tragedy, and Philosophy: The Self in Dialogue*. Oxford.

Gill, C., N. Postlethwaite, and R. Seaford, eds. 1998. *Reciprocity in Ancient Greece*. Oxford.

Goffman, E. 1967. *Interaction Ritual: Essays in Face-to-Face Behavior*. Chicago.

Gold, B. 2016. "Simone Weil: Receiving the *Iliad*." *Women Classical Scholars: Unsealing the Fountain from the Renaissance to Jacqueline de Romilly*, ed. R. Wyles and E. Hall. Oxford: 359–76.

Golden, M. 2008. *Greek Sport and Social Status*. Austin.

Goldhill, S. 1991. *The Poet's Voice: Essays on Poetics and Greek Literature*. Cambridge.

Gossman, L. 2000. *Basel in the Age of Burckhardt*. Chicago.

Graziosi, B. 2016. "Theologies of the Family in Homer and Hesiod." *Theologies of Ancient Greek Religion*, ed. E. Eidinow, J. Kindt, and R. Osborne. Oxford: 35–61.

Graziosi, B. and J. Haubold. 2003. "Homeric Masculinity: $HNOPEH$ and $A\Gamma HNOPIH$." *The Journal of Hellenic Studies* 123: 60–76.

Graziosi, B. and J. Haubold. 2005. *Homer: The Resonance of Epic*. London.

Graziosi, B. and J. Haubold. 2010. *Homer, Iliad VI*. Cambridge.

Grethlein, Jonas. 2008. "Memory and Material Objects in the *Iliad* and the *Odyssey*." *Journal of Hellenic Studies* 128: 27–51.

Griffin, J. 1980. *Homer on Life and Death*. Oxford.

Griffin, J. 1986. "Homeric Words and Speakers." *Journal of Hellenic Studies* 106: 36–57.

Griffin, J., ed. 1995. *Homer. Iliad Book Nine*. Oxford.

Griffith, M. 1983. *Aeschylus: Prometheus Bound*. Cambridge.

Gschnitzer, F. 1976. "Politische Leidenschaft im homerischen Epos." *Studien zum antiken Epos*, ed. H. Görgemanns and E. A. Schmidt. *Beitrage zur Klassische Philologie* 72: 1–21.

Gumperz, J. and S. Levinson, eds. 1996. *Rethinking Linguistic Relativity*. Cambridge.

Guthenke, C. 2008. *Placing Modern Greece: The Dynamics of Romantic Hellenism, 1770–1840*. Oxford.

Guthrie, W. K. C. 1950. *The Greeks and their Gods*. Boston.

Haft, A. J. 1990. " 'The City-Sacker Odysseus' in *Iliad* 2 and 10." *Transactions of the American Philological Association* 120: 37–56.

Hainsworth, J. B. 1993. *The Iliad: A Commentary*. Vol. III: *Books 9–12*. Cambridge.

Hall, J. 2014. *A History of the Archaic Greek World, ca. 1200–479 BCE*. 2nd edition. Chichester, West Sussex.

Hammer, D. 1997. "Who Shall Readily Obey? Authority and Politics in the *Iliad*." *Phoenix* 15.1: 1–24.

Hammer, D. 2002. *The Iliad as Politics: The Performance of Political Thought*. Norman, OK.

Hammer, D. and M. Kicey. 2010. "Simone Weil's *Iliad*: The Power of Words." *The Review of Politics* 72.1: 79–96.

Haraway, D. 2003. *The Companion Species Manifesto: Dogs, People, and Significant Otherness*. Chicago.

References 259

Haraway, D. 2007. *When Species Meet*. Minneapolis.

Haraway, D. 2016. *Staying with the Trouble: Making Kin in the Chthulucene*. Durham, NC.

Harrell, S. E. 1991. "Apollo's Fraternal Threats: Language of Succession and Domination in the *Homeric Hymn to Hermes*." *Greek, Roman, and Byzantine Studies* 32.4: 307–29.

Haubold, J. 2000. *Homer's People: Epic Poetry and Social Formation*. Cambridge.

Havelock, E. A. 1963. *Preface to Plato*. Cambridge, MA.

Hegel, G. W. F. 1987. *Phänomenologie des Geistes*. Stuttgart.

Hegel, G. W. F. 2018. *The Phenomenology of Spirt*. Trans. and ed. T. Pinkard. Cambridge.

Heiden, B. 1997. "The Ordeals of Homeric Songs." *Arethusa* 30: 221–40.

Hesk, J. 2006. "Homeric Flyting and How to Read It: Performance and Intratext in *Iliad* 20.83–109 and 20.178–258." *Ramus* 35.1: 4–28.

Hitch, S. 2009. *King of Sacrifice: Ritual and Royal Authority in the Iliad*. Cambridge, MA.

Hobson, M. 2012. "The Final Seminars of Jacques Derrida: 'The Beast and the Sovereign'." *Paragraph* 35.3: 435–50.

Holmes, B. 2010. *The Symptom and the Subject: The Emergence of the Physical Body in Ancient Greece*. Princeton, NJ.

Holmes, B. 2015. "Situating Scamander: 'Natureculture' in the *Iliad*." *New Essays on Homer: Language, Violence, and Agency*, ed. S. Lindheim and H. Morales. *Ramus* 44.1–2: 29–51.

Holmes, B. 2017. "The Body of Western Embodiment: Classical Antiquity and the Early History of a Problem." *Embodiment: A History*, ed. J. E. H. Smith. Oxford: 17–49.

Holmes, B. 2019. "On Stoic Sympathy: Cosmobiology and the Life of Nature." *Antiquities beyond Humanism*, ed. E. Bianchi, S. Brill, and B. Holmes. Oxford: 239–70.

Holmes, B. 2020. "On Bruno Snell, *The Discovery of the Mind*." *Undead Texts and the Disciplines That Love to Hate Them*, ed. L. Daston and S. Marcus. *Public Culture* 32.2: 363–74.

Holoka, J. 2002. "Homer and Simone Weil: The *Iliad* sub specie violentiae." *Epea pteroenta: Beiträge zur Homerforschung. Festschrift für W. Kullmann zum 75. Geburtstag*, ed. M. Reichel and A. Rengakos. Stuttgart: 63–75.

Holoka, J. 2003. *Simone Weil's "The Iliad or the Poem of Force": A Critical Edition*. New York.

Hooker J. T. 1990. "The Visit of Athena to Achilles in *Iliad* 1." *Emerita* 58: 21–32.

Horlacher, R. 2016. *The Educated Subject and the German Concept of Bildung: A Comparative Cultural History*. New York.

Jameson, F. 1972. *The Prison-House of Language*. Princeton, NJ.

Jamison, S. 1999. "Penelope and the Pigs: Indic Perspectives on the *Odyssey*." *Classical Antiquity* 18.2: 227–72.

Janko, R. 1982. *Homer, Hesiod and the Hymns: Diachronic Development in Epic Diction*. Cambridge, MA.

Janko, R. 1991. "Review of Clay, *The Politics of Olympus*." *Classical Review* 41:12–13.

Janko, R. 1992. *The Iliad: A Commentary*, Vol. IV: *Books 13–16*. Cambridge.

260 References

Janko, R. 2012. "πρῶτόν τε καὶ ὕστατον αἰὲν ἀείδειν: Relative Chronology and the Literary History of the Early Greek Epos." *Relative Chronology in Early Greek Epic Poetry*, ed. Ø. Andersen and D. Haug. Cambridge: 20–43.

Judet de La Combe, P. 2012. "La crise selon l'*Iliade*." *Donum natalicium digitaliter confectum Gregorio Nagy…oblatum*, ed. L. Meullner. https://chs-harvard-edu. proxy1.lib.uwo.ca/CHS/article/display/4645.

Kahane, A. 1994. *The Interpretation of Order: A Study in the Poetics of Homeric Repetition*. Oxford.

Karakantza, E. 2014. "Who Is Liable for Blame? Patroclus' Death in *Iliad* 16." *Crime and Punishment in Homeric and Archaic Epic*, ed. M. Christopoulos and M. Paizē-Apostolopoulou. Ithaca, Greece: 121–40.

Katz, J. 2015. "Saussure at Play and his Structuralist and Post-Structuralist Interpreters." *Cahier Ferdinand de Saussure* 68: 113–32.

Kelly, A. 2007. *A Referential Commentary and Lexicon to Iliad VIII*. Oxford.

Kelly, A. 2011. "Scepter." *The Homer Encyclopedia*, ed. M Finkelberg. Chichester: 761.

Kelly, A. 2017. "Achilles in Control? Managing Oneself and Others in the Funeral Games." *Conflict and Consensus in Early Greek Hexameter Poetry*, ed. P. Bassino, L. G. Canevaro, and B. Graziosi. Cambridge: 87–108.

Kerschensteiner, J. 1962. *Kosmos: Quellenkritische Untersuchungen zu den Vorsokratikern*. Zetemata 30. Munich.

Kirk, G. S. 1985. *The Iliad: A Commentary*, Vol. I: *Books 1–4*. Cambridge.

Kitchell, K. F. 1998. "But the Mare I Will Not Give Up: The Games in *Iliad* 23." *Classical Bulletin* 74: 159–71.

Kitts, M. 2013. "What's Religious about the *Iliad*?" *Religion Compass* 7.7: 225–33.

Knudsen, R. 2014. *Homeric Speech and the Origins of Rhetoric*. Baltimore.

Koerner, E. F. K. 2000. "Towards a 'Full Pedigree' of the 'Sapir-Whorf Hypothesis': From Locke to Lucy." *Explorations in Linguistic Relativity*, ed. Pütz and Verspoor. Amsterdam: 1–25.

Koning, H. H. 2010. *Hesiod, The Other Poet: Ancient Reception of a Cultural Icon*. Leiden.

Kozak, L. A. 2014. "Oaths and Characterization: Two Homeric Case Studies." *Oaths and Swearing in Ancient Greece*, ed. A. H. Sommerstein and I. C. Torrance. Berlin: 213–29.

Kuhn, A. 1853. "Über die durch Nasale erweitertenVerbalstämme." *Zeitschrift für Vergleichende Sprachforschung* 2: 255–71.

Kullmann, W. 1956. *Das Wirken der Götter in der Ilias*. Berlin.

Kullmann, W. 1960. *Die Quellen der Ilias*. Wiesbaden.

Kyle, D. G. 1996. "Gifts and Glory: Panathenaic and Other Greek Athletic Prizes." *Worshipping Athena: Panathenaia and Parthenon*, ed. J. Neils. Madison: 106–36.

Kyle, D. 2015. *Sport and Spectacle in the Ancient World*. Malden, MA.

Lardinois, A. 2018. "Eastern Myths for Western Lies." *Mnemosyne* 71.6: 895–919.

Latacz, J., R. Nünlist, and M. Stoevesandt, eds. 2009. *Homers Ilias. Erster Gesang (A)*, Faszikel 2: *Kommentar*. Berlin/Boston.

Lateiner, D. 1997. "Homeric Prayer." *Arethusa* 30.2: 241–72.

Lattimore, Richmond, trans. 1951. *The Iliad*. Chicago.

Lavigne, D. 2017. "IROS IAMBIKOS: Archilochean Iambos and the Homeric Poetics of Conflict." *Conflict and Consensus in Early Greek Hexameter Poetry*, ed. P. Bassino, L. G. Canevaro, and B. Graziosi. Cambridge: 132–53.

References 261

Leaf, W. 1900. *The Iliad: Edited with General and Grammatical Introductions, Notes, and Appendices*. London.

Leavitt, J. 2011. *Linguistic Relativities: Language Diversity and Modern Thought*. Cambridge.

Lee, H. 2001. *The Program and Schedule of the Ancient Olympic Games*. Nikephoros Bd. 6. Hildesheim.

Leitao, D. 2012. *The Pregnant Male as Myth and Metaphor in Classical Greek Literature*. New York.

Leonard, M. 2000. "Politiques de l'amitié: Derrida's Greeks and a National Politics of Classical Scholarship." *Proceedings of the Cambridge Philological Society* 46: 45–78.

Leonard, M. 2005. *Athens in Paris: Ancient Greece and the Political in Postwar French Thought*. Oxford.

Leonard, M., ed. 2010a. *Derrida and Antiquity*. Oxford.

Leonard, M. 2010b. "Introduction: Today on the Eve of Platonism." *Derrida and Antiquity*, ed. M. Leonard. Oxford: 1–16.

Leonard, M. 2010c. "Derrida between 'Greek' and 'Jew'." *Derrida and Antiquity*, ed. M. Leonard. Oxford: 135–58.

Lesky. A. 1961. *Gottliche undmenschliche Motivation im homerischen Epos, Sitzungsberichte der Heidelberger Akademie der Wissenschaften*. Heidelberg.

Lesky, A. 2001. "Divine and Human Causation in Homeric Epic." *Oxford Readings in Homer's* Iliad. Ed. D. Cairns. Oxford: 170–202.

Lévi-Strauss, C. 1963. *Structural Anthropology*. 1963.

Lévi-Strauss, C. 1969. *The Raw and the Cooked*. Trans. J. and D. Weightman. New York.

Lincoln, B. 1994. *Authority: Construction and Corrosion*. Chicago.

Lincoln, B. 1999. *Theorizing Myth: Narrative, Ideology, Scholarship*. Chicago.

Lohmann, D. 1970. *Die Komposition der Reden in der Ilias*. Berlin.

Lohmann, D. 1992. "Homer als Erzähler: Die Athla im 23. Buch der *Ilias*." *Gymnasium* 99: 289–319.

Lohse, G. 1997. "Geistesgeschichte und Politik: Bruno Snell als Mittler zwischen Wissenschaft und Gesellschaft." *Antike und Abendland* 43: 1–20.

Long, A. H. 2016. *Greek Models of Mind and Self*. Cambridge, MA.

Loraux, N. 1978. "Sur la race des femmes et quelques-unes de ses tribus." *Arethusa* 11: 43–87.

Loraux, N., G. Nagy, and L. Slatkin. 2001. *Antiquities: Post-War French Thought*, Vol. 3. New York.

Lowenstam, S. 1981. *The Death of Patroklos: A Study in Typology*. Königstein.

Lowenstam, S. 1993. *The Scepter and the Spear: Studies on Forms of Repetition in the Homeric Poems*. Lanham, MD.

Lloyd-Jones, H. 1971. *The Justice of Zeus*. Sather Classical Lectures 41. Berkeley.

Lukes, S. 1971. "The Meanings of Individualism." *Journal of the History of Ideas* 1: 45–66.

Lukes, S. 1973. *Individualism*. Oxford.

Lynn-George, M. 1996. "Structures of Care in the *Iliad*." *Classical Quarterly* 90: 1–26.

Maat, H. P. 2006. "Subjectification in Gradable Adjectives." *Subjectification*, ed. A. Athanasiadou et al. Berlin: 279–320.

MacCary, W. Thomas. 1982. *Childlike Achilles: Ontogeny and Phylogeny in the Iliad*. New York.

262   References

Machacek, G. 2002. "Royalist Homer." *Transactions of the Cambridge Bibliographical Society* 12: 331–3.

Mackie, H. 1996. *Talking Trojan: Speech and Community in the Iliad.* Lanham, MD.

Macleod, C. W. 1982. *Homer, Iliad: Book 24.* Cambridge.

Marks, J. 2005. "The Ongoing Neikos: Thersites, Odysseus, and Achilles." *American Journal of Philology* 126: 1–31.

Martin, R. P. 1989. *The Language of Heroes: Speech and Performance in the Iliad.* Ithaca, NY.

Martin, R. P. 2015. "Epic." *Oxford Handbook of Ancient Greek Religion*, ed. E. Eidinow and J. Kindt. Oxford: 151–64.

Martin, R. P. 2019. "Until It Ends: Varieties of Iliadic Anticipation." *Mythologizing Performance.* Ithaca, NY: 383–405.

Marx, K. and F. Engels. 2004. *The German Ideology.* Ed. C. J. Arthur. New York.

Massetti, L. 2013/2014. "Gr. ἀρετή, ved. ṛtá-, av. aṧa e e l'eccellenza come ordine aggiustato." *Münchener Studien zur Sprachwissenschaft* 67.2: 123–48.

Matthiessen, K. 2003. "Wilhelm von Humboldt und das Studium des Alterums." *Aktualisierung von Antike und Epochenbewusstsein: Erstes Bruno Snell-Symposion der Universität Hamburg am Europa-Kolleg*, ed. G. Lohse. Leipzig: 179–97.

Mauss, M. 1970. *The Gift: Forms and Functions of Exchange in Archaic Societies.* Trans. I. Cunnison. London.

Mauss, Marcel. 1985. "A Category of the Human Mind: The Notion of Person, the Notion of Self." *The Category of the Person: Anthropology, Philosophy, History*, ed. M. Carrithers, S. Collins, and S. Lukes. Cambridge: 1–25.

Mazon, P. 1948. *Introduction à l'Iliade.* Paris.

McGlew, J. F. 1989. "Royal Power and the Achaean Assembly at *Iliad* 2.84–393." *Classical Antiquity* 8.2: 283–95.

McGlew, J. F. 1993. *Tyranny and Political Culture in Ancient Greece.* Ithaca, NY.

Meier, C. 1972. "Macht und Herrschaft in der Antike." *Geschichtliche Grundbegriffe: Historisches Lexikon zur politisch-sozialen Sprache in Deutschland*, ed. O. Brunner and R. Koselleck. Stuttgart: 3820–30.

Meuli, K. 1968. *Der griechische Agon: Kampf und Kampfspiel im Totenbrauch, Totentanz, Totenklage und Totenlob.* Cologne.

Meyerson, I., ed. 1973. *Problèmes de la personne.* Paris.

Miller, P. A. 1998. "The Classical Roots of Poststructuralism: Lacan, Derrida, and Foucault." *International Journal of the Classical Tradition* 5.2: 204–25.

Miller, P. A. 2003. "The Trouble with Theory: A Comparatist Manifesto." *Symplokē* 11.1: 8–22.

Miller, P. A. 2007. *Postmodern Spiritual Practices: The Construction of the Subject and the Reception of Plato in Lacan, Derrida, and Foucault.* Columbus.

Miller, P. A. 2010. "The Platonic Remainder: Derrida's *Khôra* and the Corpus Platonicum." *Derrida's Antiquity*, ed. M. Leonard. Oxford: 321–41.

Miller, P. A. 2015a. "Placing the Self in the Field of Truth: Irony and Self-Fashioning in Ancient and Postmodern Rhetorical Theory." *Arethusa* 48.3: 313–37.

Miller, P. A. 2015b. "Classics: That Dangerous Supplement?" *Classical World* 108.2: 269–79.

Miller, R. L. 1968. *The Linguistic Relativity Principle and Humboldtian Ethnolinguistics: A History and Appraisal.* Paris.

References 263

Minchin, E. 2005. "Homer on Autobiographical Memory: The Case of Nestor." *Approaches to Homer*, ed. R. Rabel. Swansea: 55–72.

Minchin, E. 2007. *Homeric Voices: Discourse, Memory, Gender*. Oxford.

Mitchell, W. J. T. and A. I. Davidson. 2007. *The Late Derrida*. Chicago.

Mondi, R. 1980. "Skeptouchoi basileis: An Argument for Divine Kingship in Early Greece." *Arethusa* 13.2: 203–15.

Morgan, C. 1990. *Athletes and Oracles: The Transformation of Olympia and Delphi in the Eighth Century BC*. Cambridge.

Morris, J. 1997. "Kerostasia, the Dictates of Fate, and the Will of Zeus in the *Iliad*." *Arethusa* 30.2: 273–96.

Morrison, J. 1991. "The Function and Context of Homeric Prayers: A Narrative Perspective." *Hermes* 119.2: 145–57.

Morrison, J. 1991. "*Kerostasia*, the Dictates of Fate, and the Will of Zeus in the *Iliad*." *Arethusa* 30: 273–96.

Mueller, M. 2016. *Objects as Actors: Props and the Poetics of Performance in Greek Tragedy*. Chicago.

Muellner, L. 1976. *The Meaning of Homeric Euchomai through its Formulas*. Innsbruck.

Muellner, L. 1996. *The Anger of Achilles: Mēnis in Greek Epic*. Ithaca, NY.

Mühlestein, H. 1972. "Euphorbus und der Tod des Patroklos." *Studi miceni ed egeo-anatolici* 15: 79–90.

Mühlhäusler, P. 2000. "Humboldt, Whorf, and the Roots of Ecolinguistics." *Explorations in Linguistic Relativity*, ed. M. Pütz and M. H. Verspoor. Amsterdam: 89–101.

Müller, M. 1990. "Martin Heidegger: A Philosopher and Politics: A Conversation." *Martin Heidegger and National Socialism*, ed. G. Neske and E. Kettering. New York: 175–95.

Myers, T. 2019. *Homer's Divine Audience: The Iliad's Reception on Mount Olympus*. Oxford.

Naas, M. 1995. *Turning: From Persuasion to Philosophy*. Atlantic Highlands, NJ.

Naddaf, G. 2005. *The Greek Concept of Nature*. Albany.

Nagy, G. 1974. *Comparative Studies in Greek and Indic Meter*. Cambridge, MA.

Nagy, G. 1979. *The Best of the Achaeans: Concepts of the Hero in Archaic Greek Poetry*. Baltimore.

Nagy, G. 1981. "Another Look at *Kleos Aphthiton*." *Würzburger Jahrbücher des Alterumswissenschaft* 7: 113–16.

Nagy, G. 1990a. *Pindar's Homer: The Lyric Possession of an Epic Past*. Baltimore.

Nagy, G. 1990b. *Greek Mythology and Poetics*. Ithaca, NY.

Nagy, G. 2012. "Signs of Hero Cult in Homeric Poetry." *Homeric Contexts: Neoanalysis and the Interpretation of Homeric Poetry*, Eds. F. Montanari, A. Rengakos, and C. Tsagalis. Berlin and Boston: 27–71.

Nagy, G. 2013. *The Ancient Greek Hero in 24 Hours*. Cambridge, MA.

Naiden, F. S. 2013. *Smoke Signals for the Gods: Ancient Greek Sacrifice from the Archaic through Roman Periods*. New York.

Nancy, J.-L. 1991. *The Inoperative Community*. Minneapolis.

Nayar, P. K. 2013. *Posthumanism*. Cambridge.

Nelson, T. R. M. E. 1996/1997. "Deception, Gods and Goddesses in Homer's *Iliad*." *Acta Antiqua Academiae Scientiarum Hungaricae* 37: 181–97.

Nickel, R. 2002. "Euphorbus and the Death of Achilles." *Phoenix* 56.3–4: 215–33.

264 References

Niemeier, S. and R. Dirven, eds. 2000. *Evidence for Linguistic Relativity*. Amsterdam.

Nietzsche, F. 2005. *Prefaces to Unwritten Works*. Trans. M. W. Grenke. South Bend, IN.

Nilsson, M. 1924. "Götter und Psychologie bei Homer." *Archiv für Religionswissenschaft* 22: 363–90.

Nilsson, M. 1925. *A History of Greek Religion*. Trans. F. J. Fielden. Westport, CT.

Nilsson, M. 1933. *Homer and Mycenae*. London.

Nunlist, R. 2012. "Nestor and Speaking Silence." *Philologus* 156.1: 150–6.

Nussbaum, A. 1998. "Severe Problems." *Mír Curad: Studies in Honor of Calvert Watkins*, ed. J. Jasanoff, C. Melchert, and L. Olivier. Innsbrück: 521–39.

O'Higgins, D. M. 1989. "The Second Best of the Achaeans in Homer and Sophocles." *Hermathena* 147: 43–5.

O'Maley, J. 2018. "Diomedes as Audience and Speaker in the *Iliad*." *Homer in Performance*, ed. J. L. Ready and C. C. Tsagalis. Austin: 278–98.

Olson, D. S. 1995. *Blood and Iron: Stories and Storytelling in the Odyssey*. Leiden.

Otto, W. F. 1954. *The Homeric Gods: The Spiritual Significance of Greek Religion*. Trans. M. Hadas. New York.

Papakonstantinou, Z. 2002. "Prizes in Early Archaic Greek Sport." *Nikephoros* 15: 51–67.

Papakonstantinou, Z. 2008. *Lawmaking and Adjudication in Archaic Greece*. London.

Parker, R. 1998. "Pleasing Thighs: Reciprocity in Greek Religion." *Reciprocity in Ancient Greece*, ed. C. Gill, N. Postlethwaite, and R. Seaford. Oxford: 105–25.

Parks, W. 2014. *Verbal Dueling in Heroic Narrative: The Homeric and Old English Traditions*. Princeton, NJ.

Parry, A. 1981. *Logos and Ergon in Thucydides*. Salem, NH.

Parry, A. ed., 1971. *The Making of Homeric Verse: The Collected Papers of Milman Parry*. Oxford.

Pavel, T. G. 2001. *The Spell of Language: Poststructuralism and Speculation*. Chicago.

Pelliccia, H. 1995. *Mind, Body, and Speech in Homer and Pindar*. Göttingen.

Pelliccia, H. 2011. "Double Motivation." *Homer Encyclopedia*, Vol. 1, ed. M Finkelberg. Chichester: 218–19.

Penn, J. M. 1972. *Linguistic Relativity versus Innate Ideas: The Origins of the Sapir-Whorf Hypothesis in German Thought*. The Hague.

Pironti, G. and C. Bonnet, eds. 2017. *Les dieux d'Homère: polythéisme et poési en Grèce ancienne*. *Kernos* Supplement 31. Liège.

Poliakoff, M. 1987. *Combat Sports in the Ancient World: Competition, Violence, and Culture*. New Haven.

Pommier, G. 2010. "Existe-t-il une pulsion de donner? Une remarque sur la place de l'obligation, dans le paradigme de Marcel Mauss." *Revue du MAUSS* 36.2: 385–90.

Porter, J. 2000. *Nietzsche and the Philology of the Future*. Stanford.

Porter, J. 2004. "Nietzsche, Homer, and the Classical Tradition." *Nietzsche and Antiquity: His Reaction and Response to the Classical Tradition*, ed. P. Bishop. Rochester, NY: 7–26.

Porter, J. 2021. *Homer: The Very Idea*. Chicago.

Porter, J. and M. Buchan. 2004. "Introduction." *Before Subjectivity? Lacan and the Classics*, ed. J. Porter and M. Buchan. *Helios* 31: 1–20.

Postlethwaite, N. 1988. "Thersites in the *Iliad*." *Greece and Rome* 35: 123–36.

References 265

Postlethwaite, N. 1995. "Agamemnon, Best of Spearmen." *Phoenix* 49: 95–103.

Powell, B., trans. 2014. *The Iliad*. New York.

Pucci, P. 1987. *Odysseus Polutropos: Intertextual Readings in the Odyssey and the Iliad*. Ithaca, NY.

Pucci, P. 1998. *The Song of Sirens*. Lanham, MD.

Pucci, P. 2002. "Theology and Poetics in the *Iliad*." *Arethusa* 35: 17–34.

Pucci, P. 2018. *The Iliad: The Poem of Zeus*. Berlin.

Pulleyn, S. 2000. *Iliad Book One*. Oxford.

Purves, A. 2006. "Falling into Time in Homer's *Iliad*." *Classical Antiquity* 25.1: 179–209.

Purves, A. 2011. "Homer and the Art of Overtaking." *American Journal of Philology* 132.4: 523–51.

Purves, A. 2015. "Ajax and Other Objects: Homer's Vibrant Materialism." *New Essays on Homer: Language, Violence, and Agency*, ed. S. Lindheim and H. Morales. *Ramus* 44.1–2: 75–94.

Purves, A. 2019. *Homer and the Poetics of Gesture*. Oxford.

Pütz, M. and M. H. Verspoor, eds. 2000. *Explorations in Linguistic Relativity*. Amsterdam.

Raaflaub, K. 1993. "Homer to Solon: The Rise of the Polis." *The Ancient Greek City State*, ed. M. H. Hansen. Copenhagen: 41–105.

Ready, J. L. 2010. "Why Odysseus Strings his Bow." *Greek, Roman and Byzantine Studies* 50.2: 133–57.

Ready, J. L. 2011. *Character, Narrator, and Simile in the Iliad*. Chicago.

Rebenich, S. 2011. "The Making of a Bourgeois Antiquity." *The Western Time of Ancient History*, ed. A. Lianeiri. Cambridge: 119–37.

Redfield, J. 1983. "The Economic Man." *Approaches to Homer*, ed. C. A. Rubino and C. W. Shelmerdine. Austin: 218–47.

Redfield, J. 1994. *Nature and Culture in the Iliad: The Tragedy of Hector*. Expanded edition. Durham, NC.

Reines, M. F. and J. Prinz. 2009. "Reviving Whorf: The Return of Linguistic Relativity." *Philosophy Compass* 4.6: 1022–32.

Reinhardt, K. 1960. *Tradition und Geist: Gesammelte Essays zur Dichtung*. Göttingen.

Reinhardt, K. 1961. *Die Ilias und ihr Dichter*. Göttingen.

Renehan, R. 1979. "The Meaning of $\Sigma\Omega MA$ in Homer: A Study in Methodology." *California Studies in Classical Antiquity* 12: 269–82.

Rengakos, A. 2004. "Die Argonautika und das 'kyklische Gedicht.' Bemerkungen zur Erzähltechnik des griechischen Epos." *Antike Literatur in neuer Deutung*, eds. A. Bierl, A. Schmitt, and A. Willi. Munich and Leipzig: 277–304.

Richardson, N. J. 1974. *The Homeric Hymn to Demeter*. Oxford.

Richardson, N. J. 1993. *The Iliad: A Commentary*, Vol. VI: *Books 21–24*. Cambridge.

Ritner, S. B. 2017. "The Training of the Soul: Simone Weil's Dialectical Disciplinary Paradigm, a Reading alongside Michel Foucault." *Simone Weil and Continental Philosophy*, ed. R. Rozelle-Stone. London: 187–204.

Roisman, H. 1988. "Nestor's Advice and Antilochos' Tactics." *Phoenix* 42.2: 114–20.

Roisman, H. 1990. "*Kerdion* in the *Iliad*: Profit and Trickiness." *Transactions of the American Philological Association* 120: 23–35.

Roisman, H. 2005. "Nestor the Good Counsellor." *The Classical Quarterly* 55.1: 17–38.

266 References

Rollinger, R. 2015. "Old Battles, New Horizons.:The Ancient Near East and the Homeric Epics." *Mesopotamia in the Ancient World*, ed. R. Rollinger and E. van Dongen. Münster: 5–32.

Rose, P. 1988. "Thersites and the Plural Voices of Homer." *Arethusa* 21.1: 5–25.

Rosen, R. M. 2007. *Making Mockery: The Poetics of Ancient Satire*. Oxford.

Rousseau, P. 1992. "Fragments d'un commentaire antique du recit de la course des chars dans le XXIIIe chant de l'*Iliade*." *Philologus* 136: 158–80.

Rousseau, P. 2010. "L'oubli de la borne (*Iliade* XXIII, 262–652)." *Mélanges Bollack*, ed. C. Koenig and D. Thouard. Lille: 27–56.

Ruehl, M. 2003. "Politeia 1871: Nietzsche contra Wagner on the Greek State." *Bulletin of the Institute of Classical Studies* 46.79: 61–86.

Russo, J. 1997. "The Formula." *New Companion to Homer*, ed. I. Morris and B. Powell. Leiden: 238–60.

Ruzé, F. 1997. *Délibération et pouvoir dans la cité grecque de Nestor à Socrate*. Paris.

Sahlins, M. 1972. *Stone Age Economics*. Chicago.

Sahlins, M. 2013. *What Kinship Is—and Is Not*. Chicago.

Saïd, S., ed. 1979. *Études de litterature ancienne*. Paris.

Sammons, B. 2010. *The Art and Rhetoric of the Homeric Catalogue*. Oxford.

Satlow, M. L., ed. 2013 *The Gift in Antiquity*. Hoboken, NJ.

Saussure, F. de 1983. *Course in General Linguistics*. Ed. C. Balley and A. Sechehaye with the collaboration of A. Riedlinger, trans. R. Harris. London.

Scanlon, T. 1983. "The Vocabulary of Competition: *Agon* and *Aethlos*, Greek Terms for Contest." *Arete* 1.1: 185–216.

Scanlon, T. 2002. *Eros and Greek Athletics*. Oxford.

Scanlon, T. 2018. "Class Tensions in the Games of Homer: Epeius, Euryalus, Odysseus, and Iros." *Sport and Social Identity in Classical Antiquity: Studies in Honor of Mark Golden*, ed. S. Bell and P. Ripat. *Bulletin of the Institute of Classical Studies* 61.1: 5–20.

Schein, S. 1984. *The Mortal Hero: An Introduction to Homer's Iliad*. Berkeley.

Schein, S. 2016. *Homeric Epic and its Reception: Interpretive Essays*. Oxford.

Schironi, F. 2017. "Tautologies and Transpositions: Aristarchus' Less Known Critical Signs." *Greek, Roman, and Byzantine Studies* 57: 607–30.

Schmidt, J.-U. 2002. "Thersites und das politische Anliegen des Iliasdichters." *Rheinisches Museum* N.F. 145: 129–49.

Schmidt, M. 2012. "Snells Erben: Zur Geschichte des Lexikons des frühgriechischen Epos." *Homer, gedeutet durch ein großes Lexikon*, ed. M. Meier-Brügger. Berlin: 253–61.

Schmitt, R. 1967. *Dichtung und Dichtersprache in indogermanischer Zeit*. Wiesbaden.

Schmitt, A. 2012. "Vom Gliedergefüge zum handelnden Menschen." *Homer, gedeutet durch ein großes Lexikon*, ed. M. Meier-Brügger. Berlin: 263–318.

Schofield, M. 1986. " 'Euboulia' in the *Iliad*." *Classical Quarterly* 36.1: 6–31.

Schofield, M. 1999. *Saving the City: Philosopher-Kings and Other Classical Paradigms*. London.

Schrade, H. 1952. *Götter und Menschen Homers*. Stuttgart.

Schwyzer, E. 1931. "Drei griechische Wörter." *Rheinisches Museum* 80: 213–17.

Schwyzer, E. 1968. *Griechische Grammatik*. Munich.

References **267**

Scodel, R. 1992. "Inscriptions, Absence and Memory: Epic and Early Epitaph." *Studi Italiani di Filologia Classica* 3.10: 57–76.

Scodel, R. 2002. *Listening to Homer: Tradition, Narrative, and Audience.* Ann Arbor, MI.

Scodel, R. 2008. *Epic Facework: Self-Presentation and Social Interaction in Homer.* Swansea.

Scott, J. 1921. *The Unity of Homer.* Sather Classical Lectures. Berkeley.

Scott, W. C. 1997. "The Etiquette of Games in *Iliad* 23." *Greek, Roman and Byzantine Studies* 38.3: 213–27.

Scully, S. 2015. *Hesiod's Theogony: From Near Eastern Creation Myths to Paradise Lost.* Oxford.

Seaford, R. 1994. *Reciprocity and Ritual: Homer and Tragedy in the Developing City-State.* Oxford.

Seaford, R. 2004. *Money and the Early Greek Mind: Homer, Philosophy, Tragedy.* Cambridge.

Segal, C. 1962. "The Phaeacians and the Symbolism of Odysseus' Return." *Arion* 1.4: 17–64.

Segal, C. 1971a. "Nestor and the Honor of Achilles (*Iliad* 1.247–84)." *SMEA* 13: 90–105.

Segal, C. 1971b. *The Theme of the Mutilation of the Corpse in the Iliad.* Leiden.

Sfyroeras, P. 2009. "The Scepter and Achilles' Oath in *Iliad* 1.233–246." *Antiphilēsis: Studies on Classical, Byzantine, and Modern Greek Literature and Culture in Honour of John-Theophanes A. Papademtriou,* ed. E. Karamalengou and E. Makrygianni. Stuttgart: 48–56.

Simon, E. 1986. "Bia et Kratos." *Lexicon Iconographicum Mythologiae I.* Zürich: 114–15.

Slatkin, L. M. 1991. *The Power of Thetis: Allusion and Interpretation in the Iliad.* Berkeley.

Sloterdijk, P. 2010. *Rage and Time: A Psycho-Political Investigation.* Trans. M. Wenning. New York.

Snell, B. 1930. "Das Bewusstsein von eigenen Entscheidungen im fruhen Griechentum." *Gesammelte Schriften.* Göttingen: 18–31.

Snell, B. 1939a. "Die Sprache Homers als Ausdruk siener Gedankenwelt." *Neue Jahrbuche für Antike und deutsche Bildung* 2: 393–418.

Snell, B. 1939b. "Vom Übersetzen aus den alten Sprache." *Neue Jahrbuche für Antike und deutsche Bildung* 2: 315–31.

Snell, B. 1953. *The Discovery of the Mind: The Greek Origins of European Thought.* Trans. T. G. Rosenmeyer. Oxford.

Snell, B. 1961. *Poetry and Society.* Bloomington, IN.

Snell, B. 2009. *Die Entdeckung des Geistes: Studien zur Entstehung des europäischen Denkens bei den Griechen.* Göttingen.

Solmsen, F. 1949. *Hesiod and Aeschylus.* Ithaca, NY.

Sourvinou-Inwood, C. 1987. "A Series of Erotic Pursuits: Images and Meanings." *Journal of Hellenic Studies* 107: 131–53.

Sowa, C. A. 1984. *Traditional Themes and the Homeric Hymns.* Chicago.

Stein, C. 2016. "The Life and Death of Agamemnon's Scepter: The Imagery of Achilles (*Iliad* 1.234–239)." *Classical World* 109.4: 447–63.

268 References

Steiner, D. 2009. "Diverting Demons: Ritual, Poetic Mockery and the Odysseus-Iros Encounter." *Classical Antiquity* 28.1: 71–100.

Stocking, C. H. 2017a. *The Politics of Sacrifice in Early Greek Myth and Poetry.* Cambridge.

Stocking, C. H. 2017b. "Hesiod in Paris: Justice, Truth, and Power between Past and Present." *Arethusa* 50.3: 385–427.

Stocking, C. H. 2020. "The 'Paris School' and the 'Structuralist Invasion' in North America." *Qu'est-ce que faire école? Regards sur "l'école de Paris"*. Ed. F. de Polignac. *Cahiers mondes anciens.* 13. <https://journals.openedition.org/mondesanciens/2739>

Stocking, D. 2007. "Res Agens: Towards an Ontology of the Homeric Self." *Reading Homer in the 21st Century. College Literature* 34.2: 56–84.

Strathern, M. 1988. The Gender of the Gift: Problems with Women and Problems with Society in Melanesia. Berkeley.

Summers, J. H. 1981. "Notes on Simone Weil's *Iliad*." *Simone Weil: Interpretation of a Life*, ed. G. A. White. Amherst: 87–93.

Taplin, O. 1980. "The Shield of Achilles within the *Iliad*." *Greece and Rome* 27: 1–21.

Taplin, O. 1990. "Agamemnon's Role in the *Iliad*." *Characterization and Individuality in Greek Literature*, ed. C. Pelling. Oxford: 60–82.

Taplin, O. 1992. *Homeric Soundings.* Oxford.

Thalmann, W. G. 1988. "Thersites: Comedy, Scapegoats, and Heroic Ideology in the *Iliad*." *Transactions of the American Philological Association* 118: 1–28.

Thalmann, W. G. 2015. "'Anger Sweeter than Dripping Honey': Violence as a Problem in the *Iliad*." *New Essays on Homer: Language, Violence, and Agency*, ed. S. Lindheim and H. Morales. *Ramus* 44.1–2: 95–114.

Thür, G. 1996. "Oaths and Dispute Settlement in Ancient Greek Law." *Greek Law in its Political Setting: Justifications not Justice*, ed. L. Foxhall and A. D. E. Lewis. Oxford: 57–72.

Toohey, P. 1994. "Epic and Rhetoric." *Persuasion: Greek Rhetoric in Action*, ed. I. Worthington. London: 153–75.

Trabant, J. 2000. "How Relativistic Are Humboldt's 'Weltansichten'?" *Explorations in Linguistic Relativity*, ed. M. Pütz and M. H. Verspoor. Amsterdam: 25–45.

Tsagarakis, O. 1980. "Die Epiphanie Athenes im A der *Ilias*: Psychologie oder Religion?" *Gymnasium* 87: 57–80.

Tuncel, Y. 2013. *Agon in Nietzsche.* Milwaukee, WI.

Turkeltaub, D. 2007. "Perceiving Iliadic Gods." *Harvard Studies in Classical Philology* 103: 51–82.

Ulf, C. 2006. "Elemente des Utilitarismus im Konstruk des 'Agonalen'." *Nikephoros* 19: 67–79.

Ulf, C. 2008. "Antiker Sport und Wettbewerb- ein soziokulturelles Phänomen." *Antike Lebenswelten: Konstanz, Wandel, Wirkungsmacht: Festschrift für Ingomar Weiler zum 70. Geburtstag*, ed. P. Mauritsch, C. Ulf, and R. Rollingers et al. Wiesbaden: 5–23.

Ulf, C. 2011. "Ancient Greek Competition: A Modern Construct?" *Competition in the Ancient Word*, ed. N. Fisher and H. van Wees. Swansea: 85–111.

Ungar, S. 2004. "Saussure, Barthes, and Structuralism." *The Cambridge Companion to Saussure*, ed. C. Sanders. Cambridge: 157–73.

Unruh, D. 2011. "Skeptouchoi: A New Look at the Homeric Scepter." *Classical World* 104.3: 279–94.

van der Ben, N. 1980. "De Homerische Aphrodite-hymne I—De Aeneas—passages in de *Ilias*." *Lampas* 13: 40–77.

van der Mije, S. R. 1987. "Achilles' God-Given Strength: *Iliad* A 178 and Gifts from the Gods in Homer." *Mnemosyne* 40: 241–67.

van der Valk, M. 1952. "Ajax and Diomede in the *Iliad* 1." *Mnemosyne* 5.1: 269–86.

van Wees, H. 1992. *Status Warriors: War, Violence and Society in Homer and History*. Amsterdam.

van Wees, H. and N. Fisher. 2015. "The Trouble with 'Aristocracy'." *'Aristocracy' in Antiquity*, ed. N. Fisher and H. van Wees. Swansea: 1–58.

Vergados, A. 2013. "The Cyclopes and Hundred-Handers in Hesiod *Theogony* 139–153." *Hermes* 141.1: 1–7.

Verity, A., trans. 2011. *The Iliad*, introduction and notes B. Graziosi. Oxford.

Vermeule, E. 1979. *Aspects of Death in Early Greek Art and Poetry*. Berkeley.

Vernant, J.-P. 1965. "Genèse et structure dans le mythe Hésiodique des races." *Entretiens sur les notions de genèse et de structure*, ed. M. de Gandillac, L. Goldmann, and J. Piaget. Paris: 95–124.

Vernant J.-P., 1973. "Aspects de la personne dans la religion grecque." *Problèmes de la Personne*, ed. I. Meyerson. Paris: 23–37.

Vernant, J.-P. 1988. *Myth and Society in Ancient Greece*. New York.

Vernant, J.-P. 1989. *L'individu, la mort, l'amour: soi-même et l'autre en Grèce ancienne*. Paris.

Vernant, J.-P. 1991. *Mortals and Immortals*. Ed. F. Zeitlin. Princeton, NJ.

Versnel, H. S. 2011. *Coping with the Gods: Wayward Readings in Greek Theology*. Leiden.

Vine, B. 1998. *Aeolic ὄρπετον and Deverbative *-etó- in Greek and Indo-European*. Innsbruck.

Viveiros de Castro, E. 2014. *Cannibal Metaphysics*. Trans. P. Skafish. Minneapolis.

Volk, K. 2002. "Kleos Aphthiton Revisted." *Classical Philology* 97.1: 61–8.

Wacker, C. 2006. "Antike Sportgeschichte versus Geschichte des Agon." *Jahrbuch 2005 der Deutschen Gesellschaft für Geschichte der Sportwissenschaft*, ed. J. Court. Berlin: 39–43.

Walsh, T. 2005. *Fighting Words and Feuding Words: Anger and the Homeric Poems*. Lanham, MD.

Watkins, C. 1977. "A propos de *mênis*." *Bulletin de la société de linguistique de Paris* 72: 187–209.

Watkins, C. 1995. *How to Kill a Dragon: Aspects of Indo-European Poetics*. New York.

Weil, S. 1955. *Oppression et liberté*. Paris.

Weil, S. 1960. *Ecrits historiques et politiques*, Deuxième partie: *Politique*. Paris.

Weil, S. 1965. *Seventy Letters*. Ed. and trans. R. Reese. London.

Weil, S. 2003. *The Iliad or the Poem of Force*. Ed. and trans. J. P. Holoka. New York.

Weiler, I. 2010. "Athletik und Agonistik in der griechischen Antike." *Handbuch Sportgeschichte*, ed. M. Krüger and H. Langenfeld. Schorndorf: 128–42.

West, M. L. 1966. *Hesiod, Theogony*. Oxford.

West, M. L. 1997. *The East Face of Helicon: West Asiatic Elements in Greek Poetry and Myth*. Oxford.

270 References

West, M. L. 1998. *Homeri Ilias*. Stuttgart.

West, M. L. 2001. *Studies in the Text and Transmission of the Iliad*. Munich.

West, M. L. 2003a. *Homeric Hymns, Homeric Apocrypha, Lives of Homer*. Cambridge, MA.

West, M. L. 2003b. "'Iliad' and 'Aethiopis'." *The Classical Quarterly* 53.1: 1–14.

West, M. L. 2012. "Towards a Chronology of Greek Epic." *Relative Chronology in Early Greek Epic Poetry*, ed. Ø. Andersen and D. Haug. Cambridge: 210–41.

Whitley, J. 2013. "Homer's Entangled Objects: Narrative, Agency and Personhood in and out of Iron Age Texts." *Cambridge Archaeological Journal* 23.3: 395–416.

Whitman, C. 1958. *Homer and the Heroic Tradition*. Cambridge, MA.

Whitman, C. 1982. *The Heroic Paradox: Essays on Homer, Sophocles, and Aristophanes*. Ithaca, NY.

Widzisz, M. 2012. "Timing Reciprocity in the *Iliad*." *Arethusa* 45.2: 153–75.

Wilamowitz-Moellendorf, U. von. 2000. "Futurephilology! A Reply to Friedrich Nietzsche's *Birth of Tragedy*." Trans. G. Postl, B. Babich, and H. Schmid. *New Nietzsche Studies* 4.1: 1–33.

Willcock, M. M. 1973. "The Funeral Games of Patroclus." *Bulletin of the Institute of Classical Studies* 20: 1–11.

Williams, B. 1993. *Shame and Necessity*. Berkeley.

Willis, W. H. 1941. "Athletic Contests in Epic." *Transactions and Proceedings of the American Philological Association* 72: 392–417.

Wilson, D. F. 2002, *Ransom, Revenge, and Heroic Identity in the Iliad*. New York.

Wolfe, C. 2010. *What Is Posthumanism?* Minneapolis.

Wolfe, J. 2015. *Homer and the Question of Strife from Erasmus to Hobbes*. Toronto.

Wolff, H. J. 1946. "The Origin of Judicial Litigation among the Greeks." *Traditio* 4: 31–87.

Wyatt, W. 1994–5. "Homeric and Mycenaean *laos*." *Minos* n.s. 29–30: 159–70.

Yasumura, N. 2011. *Challenges to the Power of Zeus*. London.

Zeitlin, F. 1996. *Playing the Other: Gender and Society in Classical Greek Literature*. Chicago.

Index Locorum

For the benefit of digital users, indexed terms that span two pages (e.g., 52–53) may, on occasion, appear on only one of those pages.

Iliad 1.173–6 45
Iliad 1.184–6 67
Iliad 1.188–92 23
Iliad 1.207 23
Iliad 1.210–14 24–5
Iliad 1.237–9 28
Iliad 1.245 29–30
Iliad 1. 247–84 33–4
Iliad 1. 259 34
Iliad 1. 260–1 39
Iliad 1.266–8 34
Iliad 1.268 39
Iliad 1.271–3 38
Iliad 1.271 39, 41–2
Iliad 1. 277–9 43
Iliad 1.178 46–7
Iliad 1.279 47
Iliad 1.280–1 35, 46–7, 68
Iliad 1.287–9 50
Iliad 1.287–8 224
Iliad 1.509–10 86–7

Iliad 2.37–8 96
Iliad 2.101–8 30
Iliad 2.118 102
Iliad 2.176–8 171
Iliad 2.196–7 45
Iliad 2.197 102–3
Iliad 2.203–6 73
Iliad 2.204 79
Iliad 2.205–6 79
Iliad 2.213–16 43
Iliad 2.247–8 44
Iliad 2.248–9 75
Iliad 2.412–18 94
Iliad 2.419–20 95
Iliad 2.760–2 143
Iliad 2.763–7 144
Iliad 2.768–9 144
Iliad 2.770 145

Iliad 3.298–301 181

Iliad 6.407–9 199

Iliad 7.197–9 149
Iliad 7.202–5 150
Iliad 7.288–92 150

Iliad 8.12 81–2
Iliad 8.17 82, 92–3
Iliad 8.27 82
Iliad 8.39–40 91
Iliad 8.139–44 106

Iliad 9.25 102
Iliad 9.32–3 103–4
Iliad 9.35 104–5
Iliad 9.37–9 105
Iliad 9.39 107
Iliad 9.96–9 51
Iliad 9.103–5 51
Iliad 9.98–102 99
Iliad 9.108–11 52

Iliad 10.402–4 179

Iliad 15.64–8 189
Iliad 15.158–67 66
Iliad 15.164–5 67
Iliad 15.183–7 67
Iliad 15.187–9 69
Iliad 15.195–6 68

Iliad 16.419–25 188
Iliad 16.420 190
Iliad 16.434 190
Iliad 16.438 190
Iliad 16.433–8 189
Iliad 16.543 191–2
Iliad 16.703–4 192
Iliad 16.698–701 192
Iliad 16.791–2 193
Iliad 16.834–6 204
Iliad 16.844–54 194

Iliad 17.76–8 179

Iliad 18.429–34 180

272 Index Locorum

Iliad 19.409–10 196
Iliad 19.416–17 197

Iliad 20.104–9 54
Iliad 20.200–9 55
Iliad 20.241–3 56
Iliad 20.293–6 57
Iliad 20.332–4 58

Iliad 21.184–91 59

Iliad 22.18–20 222
Iliad 22.96–7 198
Iliad 22.106 198
Iliad 22.108–10 201
Iliad 22.174–6 201
Iliad 22.202–4 203
Iliad 22.213–14 202
Iliad 22.216–18 205
Iliad 22.270–1 205
Iliad 22.299–303 203
Iliad 22.445–6 206
Iliad 22.454–9 199

Iliad 23.274–5 114
Iliad 23.275–8 145
Iliad 23.288–9 143
Iliad 23.309 122–3
Iliad 23.311–18 118
Iliad 23.313–14 139
Iliad 23.352–7 147
Iliad 23.571–2 124

Iliad 23.573–8 129
Iliad 23.579–85 130
Iliad 23.587–8 132
Iliad 23.588 132
Iliad 23.591–5 136–7
Iliad 23.711–13 153
Iliad 23.719–20 153
Iliad 23.723–4 154
Iliad 23.735–7 155
Iliad 23.787–92 133
Iliad 23.822–5 157
Iliad 23.842–3 158
Iliad 23.847 159
Iliad 23.890–4 163

Odyssey 2.80–1 29–30
Odyssey 8.197–8 159
Odyssey 11.548–51 160
Odyssey 14.468 223–4
Odyssey 14.503 223–4
Odyssey 21.426 223–4

Hesiod, *Theogony* 383–8 80, 87
Hesiod, Theogony 389–94 90
Hesiod, Theogony 435–8 88
Hesiod, Works and Days 35–9 140

Homeric Hymn to Demeter 146–7 98

Pindar *Isthmian* 8.31–5 49

Aristotle, Metaphysics 1076a 79

Index

For the benefit of digital users, indexed terms that span two pages (e.g., 52–53) may, on occasion, appear on only one of those pages.

Achilles 6–8, 12, 17–18, 20–31, 33–8, 42–56, 58–72, 96–7, 103–4, 113–15, 123–4, 135–8, 144–9, 151–2, 155–8, 160–6, 171, 179–81, 189–90, 193–215, 221–4
Aeneas 54–8, 61–2
Agamemnon 16–17, 23–5, 28–38, 42–8, 50–3, 66–8, 71, 73, 75, 85, 93–109, 114–15, 130, 144, 163–5, 184–6, 209–11, 224
Agency 8–10, 88–9, 91, 107, 109–10, 117–18, 124–5, 146–7, 168–9, 175–9, 183–7, 190–208
Agōn 13, 86–9, 111–17, 128, 131, 138, 142, 163–6, 223–4
Ajax, son of Telamōn 133–4, 144–5, 149–63, 212–13
Alkē 2–5, 15–16, 105–8, 210–11, 231–3
Andromache 16–17, 182, 198–201, 207–8, 221
Antilochus 117–42, 145, 147–8, 164–5
Apollo 54–5, 57–9, 72, 96–7, 144, 146–7, 192–6, 202–3, 208, 213–14, 221–2
Aretē 28–9, 124, 129–30, 145–6, 165–6, 212–13
Aristos/Aristeia 16–17, 143–5, 148, 163–6, 212–13
Asteropaeus 17–18, 59–65, 157–8
Athena 16–17, 20–1, 23–7, 62, 91–2, 123–4, 146–7, 158–9, 170, 193–4, 197–8, 202–7, 209–10, 212–16, 221, 223–4
Athla 114–15
Austin, J. L. 26–7, 31, 39–41, 126–7
Avowal 126–9, 132–4

Benveniste, Émile 3–5, 15, 28–9, 34–5, 39–42, 82–3, 86–7, 89–90, 98–100, 103–4, 106–7, 126–7
Biē 2, 18–19, 66, 68–9, 80–1, 87–90, 118–25, 128–30, 145, 149–54, 156, 159–61, 198, 220–4, 233–7
Bourdieu, Pierre 9–11, 31, 52–3, 214–15

Briseis 51–2, 67
Burckhardt, Jacob 111–12

Chariot Race 16–17, 116–49

Damazō/damnēmi 20–1, 167–8, 179–208, 213–16, 246–9
Demeter 97–8, 102
Democracy 73–4, 76–9, 84–5, 170
Dēmos 73–4
Derrida, Jacques 9–13, 76–87, 91, 102–4, 109–10, 214–15
Detienne, M. 80–1, 86, 115–16, 118–20
Différance 76–9, 84, 86–7, 91, 93–4, 100, 102–4, 108–9
Dikē 131, 137, 139–40
Diomedes 16–17, 32–3, 50–1, 62, 100–9, 117–18, 127–8, 146–8, 156–60, 165–6, 210–11
Dream 93–6, 101–2, 109, 210
Dumézil, George 135–6
Dumont, Louis 218
Dynamis/ dynamai 2, 8–9, 19–20, 153–4, 221–2, 244–6

Empedos/empedon ("firm," "fixed") 120–1, 124–5, 161, 222–4
Énonciation ("utterance") 39–42, 126–7
Epiphany 25–6, 193–4
Eumelus 117–18, 123–5, 127–8, 137, 142–9, 160–1, 165–6, 212–13
Euphorbus 194–6, 213–14

Fate – see *moira*
Foucault, Michel 9–13, 115–17, 125–42, 160, 214–15

Genealogy 17–18, 27–8, 30–3, 49–50, 53–65, 72, 89–90, 117–18, 146, 179–80, 209–10
Geras 51–2, 67

274 Index

Gift 8–9, 24–5, 48, 96–8, 102, 105–6, 108, 114–15, 117–18, 140, 146–8, 151–2, 161, 179–80, 221–2

Haraway, Donna 61–2, 145, 212–13, 219–22
Hector 16–17, 20–1, 149–52, 182, 185–6, 189–90, 194–208
Hecate 88–9, 91
Hegel 216–17
Hephaestus 64–5, 180
Heracles 18–19, 39, 153–4
Hermes 30, 32–3
Horses 106–7, 143–9, 160–1, 179–80, 196–7, 208, 212–13
Hubris 24–5

Identity 6–8, 18–19, 82–3, 120–7, 145, 184, 220–1, 223–4
Individual, idea of 2–6, 8–9, 13, 21–2, 127, 145, 168–9, 175–6, 216–24
Interformularity 13–14, 47, 67, 71, 101–2, 104–6, 158–60, 223–4

Kinship 17–18, 27, 53–5, 62
Kleos 18–19, 200–1
Krainein 98–100
Kratos 2–5, 11, 15–17, 34–7, 46–50, 52, 56–7, 62–3, 66–9, 72, 76–82, 84–94, 100–5, 107–10, 120–1, 188, 209–11, 214–15, 224–31
Kudos 43–5, 71, 88, 94, 107, 150, 197, 205, 222

Lapiths 36–9, 209–10

Marx/ Marxism 173–9
Moira (fate) 171, 184–5, 189–91, 195–6
Memory 41, 106–7, 134–5, 190–1, 212–13
Menelaus 117–18, 122–4, 127–39, 145, 147–8, 161–3, 181, 185–6, 212–13
Mēnis 24, 144–5
Mētis 45–6, 79–80, 86, 102–3, 118–25, 128, 139, 150, 152–4
Menos 2, 5, 16–19, 23–4, 62–3, 106, 193–4, 198–201, 203–5, 209–10, 212–13, 221, 223–4, 237–41
Muse/ Muses 116–17, 134–5, 143–7
Muthos 26–7, 38–9, 42–3, 91–3, 140–2, 161–3

Nēpie ("fool") 207–8
Nestor 27–8, 33–53, 67–8, 71–2, 98–9, 106–7, 109, 117–25, 130, 138–9, 209–12, 222–4
Nietzsche, Friedrich 75, 111–12, 114–15
Nostos 37, 200

Obey/Obedience 11, 23, 25, 34, 39, 42, 50, 52–3, 66, 68, 156, 198, 224
Odysseus 32–3, 44–6, 69, 71, 73–6, 79–82, 84–5, 93–4, 100, 102–6, 108–9, 133–4, 152–5, 158–60, 170–1, 179, 210–24

Patroclus 16–17, 37, 187–98, 202, 204, 207–8, 212–16
Performative 26–8, 31, 33–4, 38–43, 48, 52–3, 56–7, 72, 91–2, 126–7, 140, 211–12
Pherteros 18–19, 35–6, 48–50, 52, 67–9, 72, 209–12
Pindar 49–50, 54–5, 57–8, 181
Poseidon 27–8, 49, 57–8, 66–72, 145–7, 179–80, 211–12, 214–15
Posthumanism 218–20
Power 9–11, 31, 46–8, 50–3, 58–9, 82–3, 126–7, 169–74, 176–7, 181, 209–12, 214–16

Reciprocity 90, 96–8, 102, 114–15, 139

Sacrifice 94–7, 101–2, 109, 181, 186, 210
Sahlins, Marshall 53–4, 62
Sarpedon 20–1, 157–8, 187–93, 195–6, 202, 205, 213–14
Scamander/Xanthus (river) 61–5
Scales of Zeus 202–3
Scepter 28–33, 43–5, 51, 55, 65–6, 71–6, 79, 99–100, 105–6, 108, 210, 214–15
Slave 20–1, 167–8, 176, 178–9, 182
Snell, Bruno 2–3, 8–9, 21–2, 184, 216–17, 221–2
Sovereign/Sovereignty 11, 15, 71, 74, 78–9, 81–5, 87, 91, 214–15
Sthenos 2–4, 17–18, 62–4, 241–3
Strathern, Marilyn 218–19
Structuralism/Poststructuralism 9–14, 61–2, 77–9, 214–15
Styx 80, 87–91
Status 25, 27–8, 31, 34, 38–9, 41–2, 44, 49–50, 52–5, 59–61, 69, 71, 89–90, 103–4, 111–18, 121–2, 124–5, 132–3, 145, 149, 165–6, 209–10, 221–2

Index   275

Subject/ Subjectivity 1, 3, 5–6, 8–18, 20–3, 41–2, 51–2, 62, 86–7, 107, 120–2, 126–7, 168–9, 172, 177–87, 191–2, 199–200, 205–8

Timē 43, 45–6, 52, 69, 71, 90–1, 113–15
Thersites 43–4, 74–6, 81–2, 210
Thetis 49–50, 54–5, 58–61, 86–7, 96–7, 179–81, 197, 209–10
Thumos 45–6, 52, 66, 91, 99, 118, 138–9, 163–5
Truth 9–11, 13, 59, 101–2, 115–17, 125–36, 139–42, 165–6

Vernant, Jean-Pierre 80–1, 86, 115–16, 118–19
Victory 80, 88–9, 117–19, 130, 150–2, 155–6, 159–60, 170, 194–5, 212–13

Weil, Simone 1, 3, 8–9, 23, 167–79, 182–4, 186–7, 190–1, 206–8
(w)is/ iphi 2, 8–9, 19, 153–4, 243–4

Zeus 15–18, 20–1, 28–30, 32–3, 43–50, 52, 54–61, 63–72, 76, 79–110, 140, 150–2, 154–5, 180–2, 185–6, 189–92, 194–6, 201–5, 209–16, 221, 224